Teaching Reading to High-Risk Learners

Related Titles of Interest

Teaching Reading to High-Risk Learners

A Unified Perspective

Karen D. Wood
Bob Algozzine
University of North Carolina, Charlotte

EDITORS

Allyn and Bacon
Boston • London • Toronto • Sydney • Tokyo • Singapore

Copyright © 1994 by Allyn and Bacon
A Division of Simon & Schuster, Inc.
160 Gould Street
Needham Heights, Massachusetts 02194

Library of Congress Cataloging-in-Publication Data

Teaching reading to high-risk learners : a unified perspective /
    edited by Karen D. Wood, Bob Algozzine.
        p.   cm.
    Includes bibliographical references and index.
    ISBN 0-205-14582-5
    1. Reading—United States—Remedial teaching. I. Wood, Karen D.
II. Algozzine, Robert. III. Title: High-risk learners.
LB1050.5.T43 1994
372.4′3—dc20   93-27345
                                                                  CIP

Printed in the United States of America

10 9 8 7 6 5 4 3 2 1   97 96 95 94 93

To David, Eric, Ryan, Kevin, and Lauren
K. D. W.

To Kate, Kathryn, and Mike
B. A.

Contents

Preface

Throughout the United States, there is an increasing effort to approach educational issues from a global perspective. Among the many changes resulting from this effort are the tendencies to view instruction holistically rather than atomistically, to remediate high-risk readers within the general classroom as well as the resource room, and to encourage collaboration among peer groups (students and teachers alike) rather than perpetuating an individualistic model of learning and teaching.

In *Teaching Reading to High-Risk Learners: A Unified Perspective,* we have extended this notion of unification and collaboration a step further and have developed a text to merge the thinking of two closely related but typically distant fields: reading education and special education. Our authors have contributed the current research, theories, and practices from their respective fields to give readers a balanced view of who are the students at risk in reading and how we can best teach them.

These experts from reading and special education have presented their perspectives in four major areas. Part I introduces the reader to an overview of the current research. Part II identifies the high-risk reader and offers suggestions for teachers. Part III examines the issue of assessment. Finally, Part IV, the largest portion of the book, deals with effective instructional practices.

High-risk readers can be found in general classrooms, Chapter 1 classrooms, or special education classrooms; they can be gifted and talented and they can go unnoticed, unidentified, and unserved. We designed this book to meet the needs of those who teach these students. Therefore, *Teaching Reading to High-Risk Learners: A Unified Perspective* is for teachers, teacher educators, and administrators at all grade levels and in all subject areas who want to know what the fields of reading and special education say about teaching and reaching today's high-risk learners.

Karen D. Wood
Bob Algozzine

Acknowledgments

In addition to the many outstanding chapter authors, a number of other noteworthy individuals deserve credit for this publication. We would like to thank the reviewers for their insightful comments leading to the revisions made in this text. Their hard work and perceptive editing are most appreciated. They are: Judith L. Irvin, Florida State University; Joyce S. Choate, Northeast Louisiana University; and Marcia L. Modlo, Vestal School District in New York. A special note of thanks goes to Saundra Deltac, our graduate assistant, whose conscientious efforts and precision made this book a reality.

K. D. W.
B. A.

About the Authors

Bob Algozzine has taught students labeled educable mentally retarded, disabled readers, and emotionally handicapped. He has been a teacher in a vocational institution and center for disturbed students as well as an educational diagnostician in a large school system. He received his doctorate from the Pennsylvania State University in 1975. He taught at the University of Florida for twelve years and has been a faculty member at the University of North Carolina–Charlotte since 1987. For five years, he was a research associate at the University of Minnesota's Institute for Research on Learning Disabilities. He is co-author with James Ysseldyke of *Critical Issues in Special and Remedial Education, Introduction to Special Education* (second edition), and *Strategies and Tactics for Effective Instruction*. Additionally, he is co-author of *Childhood Behavior Disorders: Applied Research and Educational Practice* and author of *Problem Behavior Management: Educator's Resource Service* as well as author or co-author of more than two hundred journal articles dealing with a variety of topics in special education. Dr. Algozzine has been on the editorial review board of more than fifteen professional journals dealing with special education and educational research. During his years of university experience, he has directed numerous research, personnel preparation, and demonstration projects at the local, state, and federal levels. He has conducted large-scale survey research projects for federal, state, and local education agencies; he is fluent in computer programming languages essential for large-scale research projects.

Richard L. Allington is Professor of Education in the Department of Reading at the State University of New York at Albany. He was an elementary school classroom teacher and a Title I director prior to beginning his career as a university teacher trainer and researcher. His research interests include reading and learning disabilities and effective instructional environments for children who find learning to read difficult. His work includes over one hundred articles, chapters, monographs, and books. Dr. Allington was co-recipient of the Albert J. Harris Award from the International Reading Association for his "contributions to the understanding of reading and learning disabilities." He serves on the editorial advisory boards of *Reading Research Quarterly, Reading Teacher, Elementary School Journal, Review of Educational Research,* and *Remedial and Special Education.*

James F. Baumann is a Professor of Reading Education and associate director of the National Reading Research Center at The University of Georgia. His research and writing interests include reading vocabulary, comprehension, and assessment; and he is author of the book *Reading Assessment: An Instructional Decision-Making Perspective.* He also served as editor of the International Reading Association's preschool/elementary level journal *The Reading Teacher* from 1989 to 1993.

John Beattie is a faculty member at the University of North Carolina at Charlotte. He has been fortunate to have served as a teacher, a speech pathologist, and a university faculty member. His work includes instructional methods and interventions with students with mild disabilities. His research continues to focus on techniques that are effective for all students, including those with disabilities. Currently, he is working on several projects that involve meeting the needs of students with disabilities in the general education classroom. He is the author of numerous journal articles and has a text, *Introduction to Learning Disabilities,* in press.

Linda P. Blanton is a faculty member at Appalachian State University. She has been a classroom teacher, demonstration teacher, and college professor, and has served in numerous leadership and administrative roles. Her leadership roles have included chairing the consortium of special education programs in North Carolina, chairing a large special education department, being an assistant dean of a college of education, and serving as director of the Center on Excellence in Teacher Education at Appalachian State University. In addition, Dr. Blanton has served as president of the Teacher Education Division (TED) of the Council for Exceptional Children. Dr. Blanton has been the director of numerous federal grants; has published articles/research on a variety of topics in special education; has been an associate editor of *Exceptional Children* and a guest reviewer for other journals; and has presented extensively at national, state, and local conferences and meetings. Her extensive activities in program development/review have included the development of a variety of undergraduate and graduate programs in special education teacher training; the development and coordination of inter-disciplinary programs in two university-affiliated programs; and involvement in numerous site visit teams and panels at the local, state, and national levels. Dr. Blanton completed a post-doctoral program where she studied microcomputer applications for special needs learners.

William E. Blanton is a faculty member at Appalachian State University. Dr. Blanton has published articles on reading in *The Reading Teacher, Journal of Reading, Reading Research and Instruction,* and *Reading Psychology,* along with making contributions to a number of textbooks on reading. He is a past president of the College Reading Association and is currently co-editor of *Reading Research and Instruction.*

Robert B. Cooter, Jr., is Associate Professor and Chair of the Department of Curriculum and Instruction at Texas Christian University in Fort Worth. Cooter has taught in most elementary grades, as a Chapter 1 reading teacher, and in high school history classes. He is co-author of *Teaching Children to Read; From Basals to Books* (with D. Ray Reutzel, 1992), which helps teachers make transitions toward whole language teaching, and *The Flynt-Cooter Reading Inventory for the Classroom* (with E. Sutton Flynt, 1993), a reading assessment instrument for holistic classrooms. His main research interests at this time concern holistic/naturalistic assessment and whole language applications for content area classes. Cooter is also editor of *Reading Research and Instruction,* the journal of the College Reading Association.

Susan S. Evans is an Associate Professor of Special Education at the University of West Florida in Pensacola. She holds the master's degree and doctorate from the University of Florida, where she majored in the area of learning disabilities. She has had experience as an elementary classroom teacher, a special education teacher at the elementary and middle school levels, and director of a federally funded paraprofessional training program. She has authored articles and chapters on assessment and instructional and behavior management and has co-authored three books—*Assessment for Instruction, Behavior and Instructional Management: An Ecological Approach,* and *Instructional Management for Detecting and Correcting Special Needs.* In addition, Dr. Evans serves as an executive editor for *Preventing School Failure.*

William H. Evans is a Professor and Chairman of the Department of Special Education at the University of West Florida in Pensacola. He holds the master's degree and doctorate the University of Florida, where he majored in the area of emotional handicaps. He has had experience as a social studies teacher at the secondary level and as a special education teacher at the elementary and middle school levels. He has authored articles and chapters on assessment and instructional/behavior management and has co-authored three books—*Assessment for Instruction, Behavior and Instructional Management: An Ecological Approach,* and *Instructional Management for Detecting and Correcting Special Needs.* In addition, Dr. Evans is active with the Council for Children with Behavior Disorders.

Nancy Farnan is an Associate Professor of Reading, Language Development, and English/Language Arts Education at San Diego State University, where she teaches postgraduate courses in children's literature, English education, reading/language arts, and middle school education. Before teaching at the university, she worked in both Ohio and California with elementary, middle, and secondary school students. Her numerous publications include *Content Area Reading and Learning* and articles in such journals as *Journal of Reading, Writing Teacher, Reading and Writing Quarterly, Middle School Journal,* and *The Reading Teacher.* She serves on editorial review boards for *The Reading Teacher* and *Reading and Writing Quarterly.* In addition, she is a frequent presenter on the subjects of writing, response-based instruction, and middle school instruction at both local and national conferences.

James Flood is Professor of Reading and Language Development at San Diego State University, where he teaches courses in literacy development, reading-writing strategies, literature, and language development. He received his Ph.D. from Stanford University and has been a faculty member of Boston University and San Diego State University, and a Fulbright Research Scholar at the University of Lisbon, Portugal. He is currently serving as president-elect of the National Reading Conference. Some of his publications include *Handbook of Research on Teaching the English Language Arts, Teaching Reading to Every Child* (3rd edition), Content Area Reading and Learning, and *Understanding Reading Comprehension.* He serves on several editorial boards for literacy journals, and he is a frequent contributor to reading/writing/literature journals.

Robert A. Gable is a faculty member in Child Study and Special Education at Old Dominion University, Norfolk, Virginia. Dr. Gable is a former special classroom teacher and special education principal and has been involved in preservice and inservice regular and special education teacher preparation for nearly twenty years. His research has been in the area of assessment for instruction, database instructional decision making, accommodating special needs students in regular classrooms and teacher collaboration in the schools. Among his many publications are *Assessing Students with Special Needs* (with Jo M. Hendrickson), and *Instructional Materials for Exceptional Children* (with Jo M. Hendrickson and Joseph J. Stowitschek). Finally, Dr. Gable serves as executive editor for *Preventing School Failure* and as consulting editor for *Behavioral Disorders, Education and Treatment of Children,* and the *Journal of Emotional and Behavioral Disorders.*

Janet S. Gaffney is an Assistant Professor of Special Education at the University of Illinois at Urbana-Champaign, where she works at the Center for the Study of Reading as the director of the Illinois Reading Recovery Project. Her research is focused on the effects of inservice education, in the area of literacy, on teachers and their students and on the contextual factors that support systemic change.

Gregory F. Harper is Professor of Education at the State University of New York, College at Fredonia. A former school psychologist, he has focused his research on practical, easily implemented classroom strategies to improve student achievement and social acceptance. He has published widely in the area of peer-mediated instruction in both regular and special education settings. He recently collaborated on production of a videotape and instructor's manual for Classwide Student Tutoring Teams.

Diane Lapp is a Professor of Reading and Language Education at San Diego State University. Prior to her university teaching of undergraduate, master's, and doctoral candidates, she was a primary and middle school teacher. Her research interests include issues in teacher preparation, language arts, first and second language acquisition and development, content area reading, and integrated curricula. Among her many publications for children, parents, and educators are *Language Skills in Elementary Education* (4th edition), *Teaching Reading to Every Child* (3rd edition), both published by Macmillan McGraw-Hill Publishing Company, and *The Handbook of Research in* *the Teaching of English Language Arts,* which was published by Macmillan Publishing Company, National Council of Teachers of English, and International Reading Association. In addition, she currently serves on the editorial boards of *The Reading Teacher* and *Reading Research and Instruction.*

Larry Maheady is an Associate Professor in the Department of Education, State University of New York, College at Fredonia. For the past twelve years, he has been involved in the identification and validation of classroom-based instructional strategies that enhance the academic and social performance of mainstreamed learners. Dr. Maheady's current interests include peer-mediated instruction, student-managed instructional options, and developing support systems to assist teachers in carrying out these instructional strategies.

Barbara Mallette is an Associate Professor in the Department of Education, State University of New York, College at Fredonia. She is a former special education teacher, and her current focus is on both peer-mediated instruction and the development of communicative competence among children with disabilities. Dr. Mallette has also been active in the New York State Council for Exceptional Children.

Mary Beth Marr is currently a Clinical Assistant Professor in the Department of Teaching Specialties at the University of North Carolina at Charlotte. Her professional experience includes teaching at the elementary level; teaching reading (K–4); and teaching undergraduate, master's, and doctoral level courses at SUNY-Albany and UNCC. She has written several articles examining the comprehension problems of disabled readers. At present her research interests include examining effective intervention programs for at-risk readers.

Bruce A. Murray is a doctoral student in Reading Education at The University of Georgia. Between classes, he works as a research assistant on a project at the National Reading Research Center and as an editorial assistant for *The Reading Teacher.* Bruce has sixteen years' teaching experience in elementary schools. He is conducting research on how phonemic awareness and alphabet knowledge play into reading acquisition.

Dorothy J. O'Shea is a faculty member at Florida Atlantic University. She has been a teacher, school supervisor, and teacher trainer in special education. Her research interests entail methods of instruction for students with mild and moderate disabilities and for families of students with special needs. Among her publications are books, articles, and monographs on teacher effectiveness and transition needs of beginning teachers in special education.

Lawrence J. O'Shea is an Associate Professor of Exceptional Student Education at Florida Atlantic University. His research interests have been in the area of reading, teacher preparation, and the evolution of theories and instructional practices. Prior to joining the faculty at FAU, he was a lecturer at the University of Queensland and an assistant and associate professor at the University of Florida. He completed his graduate work at the Pennsylvania State University, which included work in the area of mildly handicapping conditions and public policy and administration of special education programs. His classroom teaching experience includes two years as a secondary teacher of educably mentally handicapped adolescents at the Western Hills School in Pittsburgh, Pennsylvania. He spent the first three years of his professional career as an elementary and special education teacher at the Goodooga Central School in Goodooga, New South Wales, Australia.

David Pomerantz is on the Exceptional Education faculty at the State University College of New York–College at Buffalo. He has a long-standing interest in instructional applications that increase participation of individuals with disabilities in normative school, community, and employment endeavors. Dr. Pomerantz's current research focuses on the enhancement of teacher preparation models in relation to the demands of inclusive schooling practices. He also directs the Collaborative Teacher Preparation Project, a combined university–school approach to field-based teacher education. Dr. Pomerantz also works with numerous school districts in support of their efforts to provide well-designed instruction to widely diverse student populations.

D. Ray Reutzel is Professor and Chair of the Department of Elementary Education at Brigham Young University in Provo, Utah. He teaches courses in research design, reading, and language arts for preservice and inservice teachers at BYU. Reutzel has taught at the kindergarten, first-, third-, fifth-, and sixth-grade levels as a classroom teacher. He is the recipient of the prestigious Karl G. Maeser Award for Outstanding Research at BYU and the Distinguished Research Paper Award (AERA). He has authored or coauthored over fifty articles in such journals as *Reading Research Quarterly, The Reading Teacher,* and the *Journal of Educational Research.* Reutzel is also coauthor of *Teaching Children to Read: From Basals to Books* (with Robert B. Cooter, Jr., 1992), which helps teachers make transitions toward whole language teaching.

Katherine C. Sacca coordinates the Collaborative Teacher Preparation Project for the Research Foundation of the State University of New York–College at Buffalo. This five-year federal project provides preservice and inservice teachers with training in peer-mediated approaches to improve the success rates of at-risk and disabled children. Through collaboration with the Exceptional Education and Elementary Education and Reading Departments, preservice methods and practicum courses are taught cooperatively with classroom teachers in a professional development school setting at a local school district. She continues to present staff development workshops nationally, most recently emphasizing adaptations for inclusion of severely disabled students.

Karen D. Wood is a Professor in the Department of Teaching Specialists at the University of North Carolina at Charlotte. A graduate of the University of Georgia with a Ph.D. in Reading Education, she is a former middle school teacher and K–12 instructional coordinator in the public schools. Dr. Wood is the author of over eighty-five articles and chapters relating research and theory to classroom practices, which have appeared in publications such as *The Reading Teacher, Journal of Reading,* and *Middle School Journal* and is the current coeditor of *Reading Research and Instruction.* She is the editor of *Exploring Literature in the Classroom: Content and Methods,* a book published by Christopher-Gordon Publishers in 1992, and is coauthor with Diane Lapp and Jim Flood of *Study Guides for Effective Instruction,* just published by the International Reading Association. Dr. Wood is a member of the authorship team for the 1993 Macmillan–McGraw-Hill basal reading program, *A New View.*

Reading and Special Education in the Twenty-first Century: Time to Unify Perspectives

BOB ALGOZZINE   *KAREN D. WOOD*
University of North Carolina at Charlotte

Key Concepts

- Identification of high-risk students
- Regular education initiative
- Engaged time
- Reading instruction methodologies

Focusing Questions

- How is the U.S. public school system currently organized to deal with high-risk students?
- What are some effective basic approaches to deal with high-risk learners?
- To whom does the responsibility for students with special learning needs fall? Why?

Discussion Questions

- Discuss the possible advantages and disadvantages of both the separation of regular and special education students and programs and their unification, respectively. Give possible examples.
- Define *engaged time* and explain its importance to a high-risk student?
- Discuss some effective principles of teaching high-risk readers. Why do you think they are effective?

At the turn of the century, J. L. Horn observed that "of all the children who enter first grade of the U.S. public schools every year at the approximate age of six, from one third to one fourth find it impossible to master the curriculum content of that grade. Many children nine, ten, and even eleven years of age are to be found in the schools of every American city who have not yet attained a degree of mastery over the rudiments to entitle them to rank as second graders" (1924, p. 4). The more things change, the more they stay the same: "The fact is that at least one-third of the nation's children are at risk of school failure even before the enter kindergarten" (Hodgkinson, 1991, p. 10).

Who Are High-Risk Students?

High-risk students are those who are likely to experience school failure; students at risk in reading are likely to experience significant problems with achieving even the most basic skills of literacy. Although this appears to be defining the obvious, the litany of reasons children can be at risk in school and reading is long and complex: single-parent homes, low family income, grade retention, being home alone, limited English proficiency, limited parental education, fetal alcohol syndrome, drug-addicted mothers, poor maternal nutrition and smoking during pregnancy, lead exposure, premature birth, teenage mothers, child abuse, criminal activity, suicide attempts, drug or alcohol abuse, and poor teaching (Hodgkinson, 1991). Factors putting students at risk have created the most diverse student population in modern educational history. Naturally occurring student diversity is heightened by a typical by-product of the press for reform that periodically surfaces in American education. As the push for excellence and reform increases, more students will be at risk for school failure, and making progress will require collaboration and "nothing less than a wholly reorganized system operating on a different set of expectations and incentives" (Hodgkinson, 1991, p. 21). Professionals will need to embrace a unified system for meeting special needs, not one of separate but equal or segregated educational experiences. Fractionated programs will need to be replaced by coherent educational objectives, approaches, tools, and structures (Hodgkinson, 1991).

In the years following the passage of Public Law 94-142, the demand for special educational personnel grew at unprecedented rates as school districts delivered more and varied services to broader numbers and wider age ranges of students with disabilities and handicaps (U.S. Department of Education, 1990). The need for qualified personnel to work with people with special learning needs will probably continue into the next century. Special education populations continue to grow, and there is no reason to believe that this growth will subside; in fact, new groups of people with special learning needs (e.g., children with acquired immune deficiency syndrome [AIDS], so-called crack babies, minority students with learning problems) are increasingly appearing as "hot topics" in professional journals (Barnes, 1986; Cantwell & Baker, 1991; Centers for Disease Control, 1987a, 1987b; Fradd & Correa, 1989; Jason et al., 1990; Shaywitz & Shaywitz, 1991). At the same time, teacher attrition rates in special education are increasing, and enrollments in and graduations from personnel preparation programs are declining (U.S. Department of Education, 1990). It is extremely likely that many of these students will be at risk in reading. Failure in reading will be a constant reminder that something about schooling has failed them. If they can avoid reading, they probably will; this, of course, further exacerbates their reading failure (Vacca & Padak, 1990). Being at risk in reading means being at risk for assignment to special education because characteristics of students at risk in reading mirror those of large numbers of students in special education classrooms today (see Table 1.1).

What Can Be Done for High-Risk Students?

Who is responsible for teaching basic literacy skills to students? Who should teach students to read? Who is responsible for students in special education? Where should remedial services be delivered? Who should provide special education's services? Answers to these questions depend on views about whether students needing special education are a regular or a special responsibility.

Current educational structures promote the separation of regular and special education students and programs. An elaborate system of assessment and classification has evolved to support these separate educational systems. Although the education provided in separate structures is not inferior, some professionals have questioned the appropriateness of creating two separate but equal educational systems.

In a report to the Secretary of the U.S. Department of Education, then Assistant Secretary Madeleine Will (1986) presented arguments to support her belief that although much has been accomplished in special education programs, "problems have emerged which create obstacles to effective education of students with learning problems" (p. 4). She did not use the term *obstacles* to imply that special programs have failed dismally in their mission to educate children with learning problems," or to suggest that the "existing general system of education for these children warrants radical reform and redesign" (Will, 1986, p. 4). She did use the term to "convey the idea that the creation of special programs has produced unintended effects, some of which make it unnecessarily cumbersome for educators to teach — as effectively as they desire — and children to learn — as much and as well as they can" (p. 4).

Will (1986) identified problems created by dual (perhaps dueling) administrative systems for special programs that "contribute to a lack of coordination, raise questions

TABLE 1-1   Comparison of Students at Risk in Different Areas of Competence

Area of Competence	Student Group	
	At Risk in Reading	Assigned to Special Education
Knowledge of reading process	Develop limited cognitive skills in handling demands inherent in learning from texts	Demonstrate limited cognitive skills in handling demands inherent in learning from texts
	Develop limited knowledge of their own reading processes, what reading is for, and what their roles should be as readers	Demonstrate limited knowledge of their own reading processes, what reading is for, and what their roles should be as readers
Self-image	Often don't see themselves as competent readers	Often are not competent readers
	Often don't read because they believe they can't read successfully	Often don't read because they can't read successfully
	Often avoid reading, procrastinate, approach assignments without a sense of purpose, display little confidence in ability to comprehend text	Often avoid reading, procrastinate, approach assignments without a sense of purpose, display little competence in ability to comprehend text
Strategy repertoire	Often have limited set of strategies for reader	Often have limited set of strategies for reading
	Wage a continual struggle with text	Wage a continual struggle with text
	Need specific instruction in analyzing reading tasks, devising plans for reading, constructing meaning from reading, and overcoming obstacles encountered when reading	Need specific instruction in analyzing reading tasks, devising plans for reading, constructing meaning from reading, and overcoming obstacles encountered when reading
Reading attitude and interest	Fail to value reading as a source of information and enjoyment	Fail to value reading as a source of information and enjoyment
	Alienate themselves from the world of print	Alienate themselves from the world of print
	Do not believe reading can help in school or life and often do not use reading to solve problems	Do not believe reading can help in school or life and often do not use reading to solve problems

Source: Data from R. T. Vacca & N. D. Padak, "Who's at Risk in Reading," *Journal of Reading,* April 1990, pp. 486–488.

about leadership, cloud areas of responsibility, and obscure lines of accountability within schools" (p. 6). She identified problems created by segregating students from their peers and attaching labels to them that sometimes result in lowered expectations for success, which "have been fully described in the literature" (p. 7). She identified problems created by a decision-making process that sometimes turns a valuable partnership between parents and teachers into a series of "adversarial, hit-and-run encounters" (p. 7) that leave everybody tallying points instead of considering unique learning needs and most appropriate educational services to the greatest extent possible.

In describing "a solution to the problem," Will provided an important qualification for her argument: "Although for some students the 'pullout approach' may be appropriate, it is driven by a conceptual fallacy: that poor performance in learning can be understood solely in terms of deficiencies in the student rather than deficiencies in the learning environment" (p. 9). She believes that the premise that creating new educational environments as the primary way to improve student performance is flawed; the alternative she advocates would "adapt the regular classroom to make it possible for the student to learn in that environment" (p. 9). In closing, she challenged states "to renew their commitment to serve [children with learning problems] effectively" and points to the heart of the commitment being a "search for ways to serve as many of these children as possible in the regular classroom by encouraging special education and other special programs to form a partnership with regular education" (p. 19).

The principles embodied in Will's call for a partnership between regular education and special education in meeting the special learning needs of students have become known as the "regular education initiative." Called the "hottest debate in special education" (Viadero, 1988, p. 1), deciding whether and how to improve services provided to students with disabilities has sparked controversy throughout the field (Lipsky & Gartner, 1989; Stainback, Stainback, & Forest, 1989). Conferences, professional presentations, and numerous articles and special journal issues have been devoted to praising or maligning professionals who believe that regular education should assume more responsibility for students with special learning needs (cf. Kauffman, Gerber, & Semmel, 1988; Kauffman, Lloyd, & McKinney, 1988; Keogh, 1988; Lloyd, Crowley, Kohler, & Strain, 1988; Wang & Walberg, 1988; Wang, Reynolds, & Walberg, 1987). Kauffman (1989) characterized the regular education initiative as a flawed policy that did not have support of critical constituencies. He called the movement a "trickle-down theory of education for the hard-to-teach" and suggested that "it rests on illogical premises, ignores the issue of specificity in proposed reforms, and reflects a cavalier attitude toward experimentation and research" (p. 256). His position was reaffirmed and critically reviewed by other professionals (cf. Goetz & Sailor, 1990; Kauffman & Hallahan, 1990; McLeskey, Skiba, & Wilcox, 1990; Pugach, 1990). After all the dialogue, questions of where best to educate special education students and how best to teach them remain.

Children born with disabilities are at risk for serious reading problems. Students who develop reading problems are at risk of placement in special education. Many students currently in special education have serious reading problems, and many students with reading problems will end up in special education. Depending on when the problem is addressed, it is difficult to separate cause and effect, and perspectives on research and interventions illustrate that it may not be important to do so.

Importance of Engaged Time

Recent research has consistently demonstrated that active academic responding (e.g., reading, writing, computing) is highly related to achievement, especially for at-risk, low-achieving students (Cooley & Leinhardt, 1980; Brophy & Good, 1986; Ysseldyke, Algozzine, & Thurlow, 1992). The Reverend Jesse Jackson put it this way:

> *We keep saying Johnny can't read because he's deprived, because he's hungry, because he's discriminated against. We say Johnny can't read because his daddy is not in the home. Well, Johnny learns to play basketball without daddy.*
> *We do best what we do most, and for many of our children that is playing ball. One of the reasons Johnny does not read well is that Johnny doesn't practice reading. (Raspberry, 1976, p. A19)*

Although the relationship between doing something and doing something well seems obvious, the time spent reading by many students is very low (Allington, 1977, 1983; Allington & McGill-Franzen, 1989; Ysseldyke, Thurlow, Mecklenburg, & Graden, 1984).

Importance of Multiple Methodologies

There is no one right way to teach reading. What works for one student or for one teacher may not work for another. What works at one grade level or for one type of content may not work in another situation. Again, although this may appear to be stating the obvious, the histories of special education and reading are full of professional arguments about the best way to teach students at risk for school failure.

The complexity of possible interactions of student characteristics, teacher characteristics, and instructional methods is enormous, but some general principles have been posited (Knapp & Needels, 1991):

- Reading instruction that is active and focused on comprehension of meaning from the earliest stages is likely to be more effective with high-risk students.
- Reading instruction that uses a wide variety of text (and little or no phonetically controlled or vocabulary-controlled readers) is likely to be more effective with high-risk students.
- Reading instruction in which students are a resource for one another's learning is likely to be more effective with high-risk students.
- Reading instruction in which teachers are active, especially in teaching comprehension strategies, is likely to be more effective with high-risk students.
- Reading instruction in which activities place reading in a real-life context is likely to be more effective with high-risk students.

Teaching Reading to High-Risk Learners

Professionals in reading and special education have much to say about teaching reading to high-risk learners. Their views about what works and why are not always consistent, and what works in one setting may not work in another. The context of deciding what works should not be ignored. Views of different professionals on characteristics of high-risk readers and assessment methods are important in efforts to improve literacy skills. Sometimes what one group says does not blend well with what another group says. This is a reality that survives in an educational system that is fractionated by categories of special students and separated by perceived differences in who is responsible for them. Regardless, competing views must be aired if progress is to be made in providing literacy instruction to students at risk for failure in U.S. schools.

Effective instruction of high-risk learners begins and ends with teachers. Teachers have an neverending need for knowledge of effective practices for teaching high-risk learners to read. Professionals in special education and reading have much to say about effective practices. Often what they say illustrates a simple fact: Good teaching is good teaching, and names assigned to people who do it and people who receive it have little to do with the extent to which it occurs.

References

Allington, R. L. (1977). If they don't read much, how they ever gonna get good? *Journal of Reading, 21,* 57–61.

Allington, R. L. (1983). The reading instruction provide readers of different abilities. *Elementary School Journal, 83,* 549–559.

Allington, R. L., & McGill-Franzen, A. (1989). Different programs, indifferent instruction. In D. Lipsky & A. Gartner (Eds.), *Beyond separate education.* Baltimore, MD: Brookes.

Barnes, D. M. (1986). Brain function decline in children with AIDS. *Science, 232,* 1196.

Brophy, J. E., & Good, T. L. (1986). Teacher behavior and student achievement. In M. C. Wittrock (Ed.), *Handbook, of research on teaching,* 3rd ed. New York: Macmillan.

Cantwell, D. P., & Baker, L. (1991). Association between attention deficit-hyperactivity disorder and learning disorders. *Journal of Learning Disabilities, 24,* 88–95.

Centers for Disease Control. (1987a). Classification system for human immunodeficiency virus (HIV) infection in children under 13 years of age. *Morbidity and Mortality Weekly Report, 36,* 225–230.

Centers for Disease Control. (1987b). Human immunodeficiency virus infection in the United States: A review of current knowledge. *Morbidity and Mortality Weekly Report, 36* (Suppl. 5–6), 1–9.

Cooley, W. W., & Leinhardt, G. (1980). The instructional dimensions study. *Educational Evaluation and Policy Analysis, 2*(1), 7–25.

Fradd, S. H., & Correa, V. 1. (1989). Hispanic students at-risk: Do we abdicate or advocate. *Exceptional Children, 56,* 105–110.

Goetz, L., & Sailor, W. (1990). Much ado about babies, murky bathwater, and trickle down politics: A reply to Kauffman. *Journal of Special Education, 24,* 334–339.

Hodgkinson, H. (1991). Reform versus reality. *Phi Delta Kappan, 73*(1), 9–27.

Horn, J. L. (1924). *The education of exceptional children: A consideration of public school problems and policies in the field of differentiated education.* New York: Century.

Jason, L. A., Betts, D., Johnson, J. H., Weine, A. W., Warre-Sohlberg, M. L., Shinarer, C. S. I., Neuson, L., Filipelli, L., & Lardon, C. (1990). Prompting competencies in high-risk transfer children. *Special Services in the Schools, 1–2,* 21–36.

Kauffman, J. M., Gerber, M. M., & Semmel, M. I. (1988). Arguable assumptions underlying the regular education initiative. *Journal of Learning Disabilities, 21,* 6–12.

Kauffman, J. M., & Hallahan, D. P. (1990). What we want for children: A rejoinder to REI proponents. *Journal of Special Education, 24,* 340–345.

Kauffman, J. M., Gerber, M. M., & Semmel, M. I. (1988). Arguable assumptions underlying the regular education initiative. *Journal of Learning Disabilities, 21,* 6–12.

Kauffman, J. M., & Hallahan, D. P. (1990). What we want for children: A rejoinder to REI proponents. *Journal of Special Education, 24,* 340–345.

Kauffman, J. M., Lloyd, J. W., & McKinney, J. D. (1988). [Special issue]. *Journal of Learning Disabilities, 21*(1).

Kauffman, M. J., Kameenui, E. J., Birman, B., & Danielson, L. (1990). Special education and the process of change: Victim or master of educational reform? *Exceptional children, 57,* 109–115.

Keogh, B. K. (1988). Improving services for problem learners; Rethinking and restructuring. *Journal of Learning Disabilities, 21,* 19–22.

Knapp, M. S., & Needels, M. (1991). Review of research on curriculum and instruction in literacy. In M. S. Knapp & P. M. Shields (Eds.), *Better schooling for the children of poverty: Alternatives to conventional wisdom* (pp. 85–121). Berkeley, CA: McCutchan.

Lipsky, D. K., & Gartner, A. (1989). *Beyond separate education: Quality education for all.* Baltimore, MD: Brookes.

Lloyd, J. W., Crowley, E. P., Kohler, F. W., & Strain, P. S. (1988). Redefining the applied research agenda: Cooperative learning, prereferral, teacher consultation, and peer-mediated interventions. *Journal of Learning Disabilities, 21,* 43–52.

McLeskey, J., Skiba, R., & Wilcox, B. (1990). Reform and special education: A mainstream perspective. *Journal of Special Education, 24,* 319–325.

Pugach, M. (1990). The moral cost of retrenchment in special education. *Journal of Special Education, 24,* 326–333.

Raspberry, W. (1976). Racism and victims. *Washington Post, March 8,* p. A19.

Shaywitz, S. E., & Shaywitz, B. A. (1991). Introduction to the special series on attention deficit disorder. *Journal of Learning Disabilities, 24,* 68–71.

Stainback, S., Stainback, W., & Forest, M. (1989). *Educating all students in the mainstream of education.* Baltimore, MD: Brookes.

U.S. Department of Education. (1990). *Twelfth annual report to Congress on the implementation of the Education of the Handicapped Act.* Washington, DC: Author.

Vacca, R. T., & Padak, N. D. (1990). Who's at risk in reading? *Journal of Reading* (April), 486–488.

Wang, M. C., Reynolds, M. C., (Walberg, H. J. (1987). *Repairing the second system for students with special needs.* Paper presented at the Wingspread Conference on the Education of Children with Special Needs.

Wang, M. C., & Walberg, H. J. (1988). Four fallacies of segregationism. *Exceptional Children, 55,* 128–137.

Will, M. (1986). *Educating children with learning problems: A shared responsibility.* Washington, DC: U.S. Department of Education, Office of Special Education.

Ysseldyke, J. E., Algozzine, B., & Thurlow, M. (1992). *Critical issues in special education,* 2nd ed. Boston: Houghton Mifflin.

Ysseldyke, J. E., Thurlow, M. L., Mecklenburg, C., & Graden, J. (1984). Opportunity to learn for regular and special education students during reading instruction. *Remedial and Special Education, 5,* 29–37.

Providing Reading Instruction to Mildly Disabled Students: Research into Practice

LINDA P. BLANTON

WILLIAM E. BLANTON
Appalachian State University

Key Concepts

- Interactive strategies
- Mildly disabled
- Mentally retarded
- Learning disabilities
- Factors contributing to reading achievement
- Automaticity, organization
- Metacognition
- Cognitive strategies

- Text pattern guides
- Reading guides
- Decoding strategies
- Text structure understanding
- Reading recovery
- Reciprocal teaching
- Success for all program
- Visual displays
- Predictive strategies

Focusing Questions

- Why has there historically been a low level of success in teaching mildly disabled students to read?

- Why is reading considered a dynamic process?
- What roles do motivation and expectation play in a successful reader?
- How is the concept of *organization* applied to reading?
- What are some available instructional programs to provide appropriate instruction?
- What are the benefits of a clearly defined role of purpose in terms of facilitating reading comprehension?

Discussion Questions

- Discuss the function of reading in our society.
- Out of the dozen or so factors listed as contributing to reading achievement, which do you think are most important and why?
- Discuss why organization is a critical factor for a high-risk learner, and how can that process be improved?
- Discuss possible forms of teacher feedback and reinforcement.

A major goal of public education is the successful academic performance of students during the years they are in school. A second goal is to prepare students, both academically and socially, to meet the challenges of employment, higher education, marriage, and family and community life. Although a majority of students exiting schools are prepared to function adequately as adults, some are less fortunate and face the prospects of unemployment and community isolation. These students are the ones who have experienced learning problems during school and who may have been identified for special education services. Clearly, they are the students who most often fail to reach the desired goals of public education.

Without question, the acquisition of reading skill promotes better overall school performance. Reading is the essential skill that enables learners to acquire content knowledge needed to succeed in every academic subject area. For example, over 90 percent of all subject matter instruction is achieved with textbooks (Armbruster, 1985; Cole & Sticht, 1981; Goodlad, 1976). Thus, if students fail to succeed in reading, they also fail to succeed in most other subject areas. As students move from grade to grade in their schooling, they must build progressively upon their repertoire of knowledge in each subject area to continue to be successful learners. For students with learning problems, early reading failure often leads to poor school performance in general. Even worse, these students experience cumulative deficits. Upon entering ninth grade, many are three to five years behind their peers in reading performance (Zigmond, 1990).

Reading ability also underpins the accomplishment of everyday activity. The idea that reading skill is necessary for participation in a democratic society is commonplace. Reading ability is also essential to work performance. As an illustration, workers on the job read more often than students in school (Mikulecky, 1982). In addition, the ability to read is requisite for activities such as shopping, completing job applications, reading labels on food packages, and reading and understanding information about health. Just as important, reading provides an alternative to everyday, humdrum life. In other words, the ability to read is intrinsically linked to the quality of a person's life.

In this chapter we review current research on learning, instructional effectiveness, reading education, and students at risk for reading problems who are labeled for special education services and discuss the implications of this literature for teaching reading to these high-risk students in general education classrooms. The students we target for discussion are those who are referred to in special education as mildly disabled learners. In recent years, it has become common in special education to use the term *mild disabilities* or *mildly disabled learners* to describe the mild expressions of the three traditional categories of learning disabilities, mental retardation, and behavoral/emotional disorders. This use of broader terminology has been the outgrowth of practical experience and research demonstrating that these students, regardless of their label, display similar reading problems (Stanovich, 1985) and benefit from similar instructional arrangements and methodologies (Brophy, 1988; Larrivee, 1989; Reschly, 1987). We emphasize mildly disabled learners in this chapter because large numbers of these students receive a majority of their instruction in general education classrooms (U.S. Department of Education, 1991). In addition, there is an expanding knowledge base on which to ground reading instruction for this group of students.

In the sections that follow, three major areas are addressed. The first, "Reading Achievement of Mildly Disabled Learners," provides an overview of the status of mildly disabled students' performance in reading and a discussion of the learning and instructional variables shown to be critical to students' performance in reading. In addition, this section provides a discussion of the implications of learning and instructional variables for instructing mildly disabled students. The next section, "The Quality of Classroom Reading Instruction," provides a review of the findings of observations of reading instruction in general and special education classrooms. The third section, "Providing Reading Instruction," presents a discussion of curricula, instructional programs, and instructional strategies that have been shown to be successful with mildly disabled students in mainstream settings.

Reading Achievement of Mildly Disabled Learners

Teachers in general education classrooms face the challenge of working with students exhibiting a wide range of individual differences. Included within this range are those students labeled as having mild disabilities. Because the labels assigned to these students often elicit strong negative attributions, it is not unusual for teachers to assume that there are far greater differences between mildly disabled students and nonlabeled regular students than actually exist. In addition, teachers may not have had opportunities to sort out and gain understanding of the numerous individual, contextual, teacher, and instructional factors that contribute to disabled students' academic achievement in school. As a beginning point, the following sections explore a number of dimensions of reading achievement with students exhibiting mild disabilities and illustrate the need to consider instructional alternatives in teaching reading to these students.

Current and Potential Reading Performance Levels

Research in special education reveals that by early high school, both learning-disabled and mildly mentally retarded students reach a plateau in their reading achievement. Learning-disabled students, for example, seem to plateau at a fourth- or fifth-grade level of reading performance (Snider & Tarver, 1987). Similarly, research examining the reading achievement of mildly retarded students shows that reading performance levels attained by this group rarely exceed grade four (Semmel, Gottlieb, & Robinson, 1979). Given these data, it is not surprising that teachers view the acquisition and application of reading skill by students with mild disabilities as difficult or even hopeless.

A brief examination of the history of special education, and the research in the field, however, might provide insight into the reasons that our schools have not achieved greater success in teaching mildly disabled students to read. First, the history of special education within public school contexts is not a lengthy one. Although special students have received services in public schools for over a century, these services have been sporadic, with a history of segregation within schools. Only since 1975, with the passage and subsequent implementation of P.L. 94-142, have teachers in general education been expected to provide systematic instruction for students with disabilities in their classrooms.

Second, until the mid-1960s the term *learning disabilities* did not exist in the special education literature, and no concentrated work or research with this group had begun. Third, in much of the early reading research with mildly disabled groups, the focus was not on how to change instruction as the way to ameliorate the learning problems displayed by these students. Rather, research was aimed at the disability itself as a way of explaining the specific reading problems demonstrated by disabled students. Researchers sought learner characteristic variables that might explain their poor acquisition of reading skill. For example, attempts have been made to relate reading disabilities to variables such as perceptual motor skills, modality, and attention disorders. Most of these efforts have not met with a great deal of success, and exploration of some of these variables has all but ceased. Exploration of others, however, has only recently begun, while still others linger as long-term, debatable issues (Blanton, 1988; Blanton & Semmel, 1987; Blanton, Sitko, & Gillespie, 1976).

Since 1975, the professional literature from several fields (reading education, cognitive psychology, linguistics, and special education) has begun to merge and to produce knowledge leading to a greater understanding of the instructional needs of mildly disabled students. We know now, for example, that mildly disabled students' potential reading performance may be far greater than we thought earlier. In the following section, we discuss major factors that we believe contribute strongly to reading achievement of all students, with particular emphasis on students with mild disabilities.

Factors Contributing to Reading Achievement

Current View of Reading

In the past, reading was considered to be a set of sequential and hierarchical skills. It was assumed that mastery of word meaning, word attack skills, contextual analysis skills, dictionary skills, comprehension skills, and study skills enabled successful reading comprehensions. The main concerns of reading instruction were with issues such as the best method to teach reading, whether to teach the alphabet first, and when reading instruction should begin. With the knowledge that has been produced during the last fifteen years, however, this orientation to reading has changed.

The current orientation is that reading is the dynamic process of constructing meaning though the interaction among the prior knowledge of the reader, the text written by the author, and the reading setting. The interactive process of reading implies that the reader's knowledge and skill are just as important as those of the author. The idea of reading as the construction of meaning suggests that the meaning of text does not simply exist on the printed page but meaning must be created by the reader, who actively constructs a link between his prior knowledge and the information provided by the author. The dynamic nature of reading implies that readers must utilize reading strategies appropriate for the purpose of reading and the kind of text to be read. As might be guessed, a number of factors related to learning and instruction interact with the kind of reading described here.

The research literature on student learning and instructional effectiveness has grown extensively in the last decade. Much of this growth can be attributed to the influence of cognitive psychology and to the press by school reform groups to improve classroom instruction. Close examination of these large bodies of research reveals that there are a number of learning and instructional variables that are shown consistently to be critical to students' performance in academic areas. Others, however, relate more directly to reading behavior and the presentation of reading lessons. If teachers are to enhance the reading performance of both those who are labeled for special education and those who are not, they need a basic understanding of these variables and how they affect the acquisition of reading. In this review, we chose only those variables that appear frequently in the literature and have been shown to have a positive effect on the outcomes of reading instruction for students of various ages and levels of ability. Table 2-1 lists these variables, including summary statements highlighting critical research findings and, for each variable, implications for the teaching of reading.

Active Participation

Conceptions of how students learn have changed dramatically over the last decade. These changes have emanated from research in cognitive psychology which explores how individuals process information. At the forefront is the view that learning is an active, constructive process (Harris & Pressley, 1991; Shuell, 1986). This means that the learner actively processes and manipulates information to acquire new knowledge. Thus, the learner must make use of various learning strategies, select and organize incoming information, and understand his role in his own learning.

During reading instruction, it is important for students to learn that meaning is not found in the text. They must learn that they are responsible for actively constructing meaning by building bridges between what they already know and the new information presented in the text. The role of the teacher is to teach the strategic use of reading strategies and to select instructional activities that ensure students' active involvement in learning. In addition, it is important for teachers to work with students in understanding that they are responsible for their own learning. Thus, teachers should expect that

TABLE 2-1   Instructional Implications of Learning and Instructional Features

Critical Learning and Instructional Features	Implications for Classroom Reading Instruction
Active Participation • Learning is an active, dynamic process (Harris & Pressley, 1991; Shuell, 1986; Weinstein & Mayer, 1986). • Mildly disabled learners approach learning passively and often fail to understand the link between their own effort and their academic performance (Pressley, 1990; Thomas & Pashley, 1982; Wong, 1986).	• Help students, especially students with learning problems, to understand that they are active learners and will gradually accept responsibility for their own reading performance. • Emphasize how a student's effort will affect his performance in reading.
Motivation • Students must be motivated if instruction is to be effective (Brophy, 1988); Leinhardt & Bickel, 1987). • Mildly disabled learners often exhibit low levels of motivation (Ellis, Deshler, Lenz, Schumaker, & Clark, 1991; Scruggs & Brigham, 1990; Whitman, 1990).	• Help students establish realistic goals for their reading performance and achievement. • Expect students, including students with learning problems, to become independent readers by using instructional strategies that are matched to particular reading goals. • Teach students to employ self-reinforcement techniques during reading.
Success • Higher achieving students are likely to accept responsibility for their academic successes and failures (Wang & Peverly, 1987). • Mildly disabled learners hold low expectations for their success in academic performance (Paris & Oka, 1986; Scruggs & Brigham, 1990; Whitman, 1990).	• Ensure that students achieve success in reading performance on a regular basis. • Teach students to explain their reading performance in positive terms; remind them to practice positive affirmations about their reading performance.
Expectations • The expectations that teachers hold about students' performance will often influence how students view themselves and their performance (Wineburg, 1987). • Higher performance expectations by teachers stimulates effort and increased student performance (Gersten, Walker, & Darch, 1988). • Teachers may view students labeled for special education more negatively than nonlabeled pupils (Christenson, Ysseldyke, & Thurlow, 1989; Mac-Millan, Keogh, & Jones, 1986).	• Communicate high (and positive) expectations for students' reading performance, including students who may be labeled as learning disabled or mildly mentally retarded. • Require students, including mildly disabled students, to respond to higher level comprehension questions to improve critical thinking and problem-solving skills.

Time
- Learning requires that sufficient time be allocated to academic tasks and that students be academically engaged during that time (Goodman, 1990; Leinhardt & Bickel, 1987).
- Mildly disabled students may require longer periods of time to complete tasks and may require additional help from the teacher during completion of tasks (Gerber, 1986; Goodman, 1990).

- During the time allocated for reading instruction, ensure that all students remain actively involved in instructional tasks.
- Provide additional instructional time in reading, if necessary, for students experiencing learning problems; ensure consistent teacher, or peer tutor, monitoring and support.
- Provide opportunities for free reading.

Attention
- Learning requires that students' attention be focused and maintained (Miller, 1985).
- Mildly disabled learners may exhibit problems in focusing on important information (selective attention) and in sustaining attention (Derry, 1990; Wong, 1985).

- Monitor students' attention and remind them to stay focused on their reading task.
- Teach students, especially mildly disabled students, to monitor their own attention behaviors; students should understand what is meant by being on and off task.
- Help students focus on relevant information in text by highlighting or underlining key points and/or main ideas.

Automaticity
- Students must develop the automatic use of basic skills underlying accomplished performance (LaBerge & Samuels, 1974).
- Mildly disabled students fail to develop automaticity of many basic skills; thus, their attention is diverted from higher order processing (Sternberg & Wagner, 1982).

- Teach decoding skills to a level of automaticity so that attention can be devoted to text comprehension.

Organization
- Recall of information and learning in general are enhanced when a student's knowledge and ideas are well organized (Derry, 1990; Weinstein & Mayer, 1986).
- Mildly disabled learners are less efficient than other learners at organizing information presented to them (MacMillan, Keogh, & Jones, 1986).

- Present new information in organized formats such as visual displays; also, instruct students in the independent use of instructional strategies (e.g., graphic organizers) that organize new and existing knowledge.
- Have students review aloud with the teacher how they might organize (in their minds) the new information that they learn.

Cognitive Strategies and Metacognition
- Learning is improved by the student's use of cognitive (or learning) strategies (Harris & Pressley, 1991; Weinstein & Mayer, 1986).

- Work with students to ensure that they understand how using learning strategies will improve their performance in reading; also, make sure that students

(Continued)

TABLE 2-1 *Continued*

Critical Learning and Instructional Features	Implications for Classroom Reading Instruction
Cognitive Strategies and Metacognition (Continued)	realize that their effort is crucial to the effective use of learning strategies.
• Students must understand that strategies are important and must know the reasons that particular strategies should be used (Paris, 1988).	• Provide explicit, detailed information about how to carry out a learning strategy and about when and where to use the strategy during reading. Such direct instruction should include concrete examples, modeling (including talking out loud while modeling), and practice. Instruction should be intense and students should be expected to use the strategy consistently.
• Direct instruction and explanation must be used to teach cognitive (or learning) strategies (Pressley, Goodchild, Fleet, Zajchowski, & Evans, 1989).	
• Effective strategy instruction requires that students possess adequate knowledge in the content areas where strategies are being used/applied (Alexander & Judy, 1988).	
• The responsibility for using strategies must be transferred from teacher to student (Harris & Pressley, 1991; Paris, 1988).	• Prior to teaching a learning strategy, ensure that students master any skills required to use the strategy.
• Long-term use of cognitive strategies requires that students use metacognitive knowledge to understand what, how, when, and why to use strategies (Pressley, Goodchild, Fleet, Zajchowski, & Evans, 1989; Wong, 1985, 1986).	• Ensure that students possess knowledge about the subjects in their reading texts prior to teaching learning strategies.
	• Assure that strategies selected for instruction are matched to the tasks where the strategies will be used (e.g., strategies to promote text comprehension must be used when text comprehension is expected).
• There must be an emphasis on the development of students' control of their own learning (i.e., using metacognition to become thoughtful and self-regulate learning) (Alexander & Judy, 1988; Paris & Winograd, 1990b; Pressley, Goodchild, Fleet, Zajchowski, & Evans, 1989).	• Cue or remind students to use strategies they have been taught; help students find ways to remind themselves to use strategies during reading.
• Mildly disabled learners demonstrate inefficient problem-solving performance (Short, Cuddy, Friebert, & Schatschneider, 1990).	• Teach students, especially mildly disabled students, how important it is to monitor, check, and evaluate the use of learning strategies during reading.
• Mildly disabled learners fail to generate cognitive strategies spontaneously and may often engage in the use of less efficient strategies (Scruggs & Mastropieri, 1990; Wong, 1985).	• Teach students to think aloud during reading as a way of monitoring, checking, and evaluating their use of learning strategies.
• Mildly disabled learners do not possess the confidence to attempt tasks (such as using strategies) and may not even try (Paris, 1988; Whitman, 1990).	• Teachers should see to it that students gradually assume responsibility for when and how to use learning strategies.

Background Knowledge
- Students learn, understand, and remember more when their background knowledge is activated and organized prior to engaging in a learning task (Shuell, 1986).
- The amount of prior knowledge possessed by a student predicts more about the acquisition of reading strategies and comprehending written material than intelligence or reading achievement (Johnston, 1984; Johnston & Pearson, 1982).
- Mildly disabled learners possess limited background knowledge (Bos & Anders, 1990b; Wang & Peverly, 1987).
- Reading comprehension can be improved by teaching background knowledge (Stevens, 1982).

- Assess students' background knowledge about the topic to be studied through activities such as brainstorming.
- Activate students' background knowledge by using predictive strategies.
- Build students' background knowledge through direct instruction, demonstrations, audiovisual presentations, field experiences, hands-on activities, discussions, and conceptual mapping.

Purpose
- The purpose or perspective by a learner determines how academic tasks are interpreted, along with what is identified as important and what is remembered (Anderson, Pichert, & Shirley, 1983; Pitchert & Anderson, 1977; Goetz, Schallert, Rynolds, & Radin, 1983; Kintsch & van Dijk, 1978).
- Poor readers fail to understand the purpose of reading and generally view the purpose as decoding rather than understanding meaning (Wong, 1986).

- Set purposes for reading such as to update knowledge, confirm or disconfirm predictions, learn about the structure of text, apply a strategy and understand how it works, apply information obtained from text, and pleasure.
- Guide students toward developing the ability to set personally relevant purposes when reading independently.
- Match the purpose for reading with appropriate instructional strategies to accomplish the purpose.

Direct Instruction and Teacher Explanation
- Providing skill instruction with a model that begins with teacher responsibility and gradually gives the student responsibility for learning is desirable (Duffy & Roehler, 1987; Pearson & Gallagher, 1983; Pearson & Dole, 1988).
- The goal of instruction is to assist students in learning *what* (declarative knowledge), *how* (procedural knowledge), and *when* and *why* (conditional knowledge) (Gerber, 1986; Paris, Lipson, & Wixon, 1983).
- Direct instruction has been shown to be effective with mildly disabled students (Frudden & Healy, 1987; Larrivee, 1989).

- Explain what a skill is.
- Show, model, think aloud how to perform skill.
- Explain why skill is important and it should be used.
- Provide independent and guided practice.
- Provide for application.
- Remind students to apply skill.

(Continued)

TABLE 2-1 *Continued*

Critical Learning and Instructional Features	Implications for Classroom Reading Instruction
Feedback and Reinforcement • Students' academic performance is improved when feedback is explicit, systematic, and corrective (Ysseldyke & Christenson, 1987). • Praise is an important reinforcer but must be used cautiously if it is not to lose its power as a modifier of behavior (Zigmond, Sansone, Miller, Donahoe, & Kohnke, 1986).	• Provide instructional feedback that relates directly to student responses. Assure that the feedback is explicit, systematic and corrective. • Reinforce students' reading performance with positive statements.

students will learn the strategies taught, actively use them in reading, and gradually adopt them for their own use.

Not all students may be quick to learn and use the reading strategies introduced by teachers. In fact, a number of students may appear to approach learning passively. Most notably, the research with mildly disabled students reveals that they respond to learning in a passive manner (Pressley, 1990; Thomas & Pashley, 1982; Wong, 1986). Moreover, these students generally fail to see a link between their own effort and their subsequent performance in areas such as reading (Pressley, 1990; Thomas & Pashley, 1982; Wong, 1986). In addition, when students view learning to read as being competitive, they become reluctant to participate. When they believe their reading performance is being evaluated in relation to that of others, they protect themselves during reading instruction with defensive strategies (Johnston & Winograd, 1985). Contributing to a passive profile in reading for these students are their responses to failure and success and their motivation and feelings of helplessness, along with teacher and student expectations. These areas are discussed in upcoming sections. In addition, the idea of learning and reading as active, dynamic processes is highlighted in the discussions of background knowledge, purpose, organization, and cognitive strategies and metacognition.

Motivation, Success, Expectations

A large body of research speaks to the need for students to be positively motivated when engaging in academic learning tasks (Brophy, 1988; Leinhardt & Bickel, 1987). As might be expected, mildly disabled learners often exhibit poor motivation (Ellis, Deshler, Lenz, Schumaker, & Clark, 1991; Scruggs & Brigham, 1990; Whitman, 1990). Moreover, we know that most of these students are passive in their approach to learning. Although the reasons for their passivity and lack of motivation are complex, this approach seems to stem from a history of repeated failure. These students exhibit helplessness, meaning that they do not believe in their own abilities (Paris & Oka, 1986). In addition, mildly disabled learners may begin to have low expectations for any academic successes. If they do experience success, often their tendency is to attribute it to external or uncontrollable factors, such as luck (Borkowski, Weyhing, & Turner, 1986; Scruggs & Brigham, 1990). In contrast, they often attribute their failure to their own lack of ability (Wong, 1986).

Higher achieving students, unlike their peers with learning problems, are more likely to accept responsibility for *both* their academic successes and their failures. In addition, higher achieving students may have perceived that teachers responded to them favorably when they demonstrated successful academic performance. Extensive research demonstrates that the expectations that teachers hold about students' performance will often influence how students view themselves and their performance (Wineburg, 1987). There is also evidence showing that teachers tend to view students labeled for special education more negatively than students who are not labeled (Christenson, Ysseldyke, & Thurlow, 1989; MacMillan, Keogh, & Jones, 1986). During reading instruction, these negative views take the form of briefer and less informative feedback, less praise for success, less attention and interaction, and more criticism for failure (Johnston & Winograd, 1985). Similarly, during reading instruction, teachers interrupt low-achieving students more often and ask them more literal questions than their high-achieving peers.

Teachers can play a significant role in how students with mild disabilities view themselves in relation to academic tasks such as reading. First and foremost, teachers should examine their own beliefs about low-achieving students and reflect on their interactions with them. For low-achieving students to become motivated and actively involved in their own learning, teachers need to accept an active role in changing students' attributions toward their success and failure in reading. Most important, teachers must understand that low-achieving students' helplessness, low expectations, resignation, and generally negative approach to themselves in relation to learning to read *can* be changed. To ensure changes in learning to read, students with mild disabilities require (1) learning situations that produce success; (2) retraining of attributions so that they understand their own role in successful reading, and not just in failure; and (3) retraining of attributions so that the explanations they give for their own performance are less negative and more positive.

Time

Consistently, the research on instructional time demonstrates two factors that ensure learning will take place. First, sufficient time must be allocated to an academic task (Leinhardt & Bickel, 1987). If time is not made available for a task, the task cannot be learned by students. Second, it is essential that students are academically engaged during allocated time. Little can be learned by students if they are not attending to the task or if they are involved in irrelevant aspects of the task.

The importance of instructional time and reading achievement is well documented in the literature. As early as 1966, Harris and Serwer reported that instructional time correlated higher with student performance on measures of word recognition and comprehension than either ability of teacher or instructional method. Similarly, Guthrie, Martuza, and Seifert (1979) found that instructional time had greater impact on reading achievement than instructional programs. In short, there is almost universal agreement among studies demonstrating that instructional time is a major variable affecting reading achievement (e.g., Lahaderne, 1968; Rosenshine & Berliner, 1978; Samuels & Turnure, 1974).

Evidence offered by Leinhardt, Zignance, and Cooley (1981) provides a dramatic illustration of the relationship between instructional time and reading achievement of mildly disabled students. The results of their study suggest that a moderate increase of five minutes per day in silent reading may result in a one-month gain in end-of-year reading achievement.

It is not enough, however, to know that time must be allocated and used wisely if students are to learn. It is also critical to know that learners exhibit characteristics that influence how teachers should manipulate time to the best advantage of all students. For example, it is generally accepted that mildly disabled students learn at a slower rate than their peers of the same age (Gerber, 1986). Thus, teachers should be prepared to provide longer instructional time periods for these students during reading instruction. For example, if students with mild disabilities possess limited background knowledge about a topic, the teacher may need to allocate more prereading instruction time to provide it. In contrast, less prereading time may be needed for regular students having high background knowledge. In addition, reading instruction during the allocated time may require more teacher involvement in terms of elaborating on explanations and providing help during practice.

Attention

Learning requires that students' attention be focused on a task and, in addition, that students' attention be maintained during the completion of the task (Miller, 1985). For many students, the ability to focus and sustain attention seems to present few problems. For younger students and for students experiencing learning problems, however, difficulties in maintaining attention seem to occur with greater frequency (Derry, 1990; Wong, 1985). Research with mildly disabled groups, for example, has demonstrated that these students may fail in directing their attention to a task, may show difficulty in identifying the critical features of a task (selective attention), and may also fail to sustain attention throughout the completion of academic tasks (Derry, 1990; Wong, 1985). It is crucial to note, however, that these research findings are equivocal. Results of other research reveal that the attention of mildly disabled students varies, depending on the topic. Further, some studies have shown that mildly disabled students demonstrate sustained attention to nonacademic tasks, while failing to attend to their academic tasks (Samuels, 1987). In other words, the nature of the task, rather than poor attention, may be the cause of the problem.

For teachers, the poor attention of students during reading instruction may present the greatest controversy. Controversy stems from misunderstandings associated with attention problems and students with mild disabilities. These students may have attention problems and may, in fact, demonstrate these problems more frequently than their regular peers. We cannot assume, however, that all mildly disabled students will experience attention problems or that the problems will be as serious as those of other students. Moreover, as noted earlier, mildly disabled students are often unmotivated, have failed to achieve academic success, and may often be the victims of negative teacher expectations. These factors require careful deliberation when deciding whether poor attention is the real cause of mildly disabled learners' response to reading instruction.

Regardless of the many complex reasons that may contribute to attention problems exhibited by mildly disabled students, the teacher's role is to intervene with instructional strategies that have the potential to improve their ability to focus and sustain attention.

Strategies that may be used include (1) showing the student where to focus his attention when reading in a text, (2) highlighting main ideas and key points in text and other written materials, and (3) closely monitoring the child's attention to the task.

Automaticity
The development of higher level skills and processes requires mastery of component sub-skills or subprocesses (LaBerge & Samuels, 1974). For example, in reading, students must develop decoding skills to a level of automaticity if they are to be proficient at comprehending text material. If students do not possess the automatic use of decoding skills, their attention will be diverted to accomplishing these skills rather than to comprehending what is being read. Similarly, if students do not automatically access word meanings, the comprehension process is disrupted (Lesgold & Perfetti, 1978).

It has been argued that the reading achievement problems of mildly disabled students may be due to the lack of automaticity of subskills (Sternberg & Wagner, 1982). Because these students often fail to develop basic skills, especially decoding skills in reading, teachers must emphasize these skills in early reading instruction (Wong, 1986).

Organization
At the heart of learning is the ability of learners to organize and reorganize their current and new knowledge. Because the capacity of human working memory is small, learners are limited in the amount of information they can process at a given time. Consequently, during tasks such as reading, learners generate frameworks for organizing incoming information so that it is manageable. For example, foods are organized under the categories of vegetables, fruits, meats, and grains. These organizational arrangements represent the knowledge structure for foods that students may store in their memories. The knowledge structures, or schemata, that students bring to a learning situation such as reading determine how information is interpreted and what will be understood and later recalled. If this structure is poorly organized, students will experience difficulty in constructing meaning and recalling information (Derry, 1990; Weinstein & Mayer, 1986).

Research has shown that mildly disabled students are less efficient than other learners at organizing new information (MacMillan et al., 1986). In the presentation of new knowledge to mildly disabled students, it is necessary for teachers to utilize instructional strategies that facilitate the organization of information. In addition, there must be public discussions between teachers and students about the ways that knowledge can be organized and reorganized. Further, students should be instructed in the use of strategies (e.g., graphic organizers and compare/contrast matrices) that facilitate the organization of information (Derry, 1990; Jones, Amiran, & Katims, 1985).

Cognitive Strategies and Metacognition
In recent years, research has shown that learning is improved when students employ learning strategies to complete academic tasks (Weinstein & Mayer, 1986). These strategies, broadly defined as any processes or procedures used intentionally to facilitate academic performance, include activities such as rehearsal and rereading. An example of a strategy used specifically in reading is prediction, a strategy to help students read with anticipation

and active purpose and to link their prior knowledge to the new information obtained by reading.

In order for students to be able to learn and use strategies effectively, they must possess an adequate knowledge base in the content area where strategies are to be applied (Alexander & Judy, 1988). In reading, for example, the number and quality of predictions made by students are determined by their knowledge about the content of a story or topic to be read. Equally important in students' use of learning strategies is the understanding that strategies are useful for learning (Paris, 1988). Further, students need to develop such executive or metacognitive skills as knowing when and why to use particular strategies (Pressley, Goodchild, Fleet, Zajchowski, & Evans, 1989).

Teachers should assume responsibility for directly teaching students learning strategies. Instruction should include teacher explanation and monitoring, along with discussion of the importance and value of the strategy (Pressley et al., 1989). For students to continue using the strategies they learn, teachers must not overlook including metacognitive elements in strategy instruction (Pressley et al., 1989; Wong, 1985, 1986). The inclusion of these elements increases the probability that learners will know how to select, monitor, and evaluate learning strategies when working on an academic task.

The goal of learning strategy instruction in reading is the development of students' control of their own learning (Alexander & Judy, 1988; Paris & Winograd, 1990b; Pressley et al., 1989). Although teachers assume a great deal of responsibility during the early stages of students' acquisition of learning strategies, the responsibility for using strategies is gradually transferred to students (Harris & Pressley, 1991; Paris, 1988).

Mildly disabled students have been shown to be comparatively inferior to their non-disabled peers in the use of cognitive strategies (Borkowski et al., 1986). As a rule, mildly disabled learners are shown to be inefficient problem solvers, to fail to employ cognitive strategies spontaneously, and to engage often in the use of less efficient strategies (Scruggs & Mastropieri, 1990; Short, Cuddy, Friebert, & Schatschneider, 1990). It is important to point out, however, that, when trained in their use, students with mild disabilities use cognitive learning strategies effectively to perform academic tasks (Scruggs & Mastropieri, 1990).

The failure of mildly disabled students to transfer and generalize strategies has increased research emphasis on metacognition (Gerber, 1986). Recent investigations have demonstrated the effectiveness of metacognitive skill instruction with mildly disabled learners, especially in the improvement of their ability to transfer and generalize learning strategies to academic tasks such as reading (Reeve & Brown, 1985). Additional research has demonstrated the effectiveness of combining self-attribution training with metacognitive instruction to change the attitudes and levels of motivation of mildly disabled learners (Borkowski et al., 1986; Paris & Oka, 1986). As noted previously, teachers can play a vital role in helping students with mild disabilities explain their performance in positive rather than negative terms.

Background Knowledge
Research on background knowledge has firmly established that students learn, understand, and remember more when their background knowledge is activated and organized prior to engaging in a learning activity. In other words, learning is cumulative, and new

knowledge must be linked to and related to the individual's existing knowledge (Shuell, 1986). Moreover, research shows that the amount of prior knowledge possessed by a student is one of the strongest predictors of how well the student will comprehend written material (Adams & Bruce, 1980; Johnston, 1984; Johnston & Pearson, 1982; Rumelhart, 1980). The implication for instruction is that teachers need to help students focus on and relate their background knowledge to the topic of the reading material. In addition, teachers need to be alert to the differences among students in the amount of background knowledge each possesses. For example, it is not uncommon for mildly disabled learners to possess limited background knowledge about most reading topics (Bos & Anders, 1990b; Wang & Peverly, 1987). Despite this fact, these students benefit from instruction to expand their knowledge on a variety of topics (Graham & Johnson, 1989).

To summarize, teaching background knowledge is not limited to students experiencing success. Research shows that the comprehension of text can be improved for all students by manipulating background knowledge. Teachers, then, should make it a regular practice to activate and organize all students' background knowledge and/or provide it when engaging them in reading selections or providing strategy instruction. In fact, activating and organizing students' prior knowledge may be the most crucial role the teacher plays in the instructional sequence.

Purpose
The role of purpose in facilitating comprehension during reading has been affirmed with a great deal of research evidence (Blanton, Wood, & Moorman, 1990; Lindsey, 1980). When students are expected to read any type of material, their first problem is to determine the purpose for reading. If readers understands the purpose for reading, their comprehension will be facilitated in a number of ways. Purpose setting evokes the interrelated associations students have about a topic, activates their background knowledge, generates a plan for reading, and sets them up for postreading discussion. Purpose also helps readers know what to focus their attention on while reading by providing the criteria for selecting relevant information and eliminating irrelevant information.

It is important that teachers understand their role in helping students develop purpose. When students are in the early stages of reading, for example, teachers are responsible for setting the purpose for reading. Gradually, responsibility for setting purpose is released to students. Mildly disabled learners and other students at risk for reading problems, however, will be less likely to understand purposes and to assume responsibility for setting their own purposes for reading. As a result, teachers should be prepared to provide direct instruction and explanation on how purpose works in reading.

Of equal importance in setting purpose is that the purpose for reading should be carefully matched with appropriate instructional strategies. Space does not permit a discussion of the different purposes for reading and the different instructional strategies that can be used to accomplish these purposes. The reader is referred to Blanton, Wood, and Moorman (1990) for a detailed discussion.

Direct Instruction and Teacher Explanation
Traditionally, reading instruction in the public schools has emphasized mastery of discrete reading skills. This tradition has been supported by the scope and sequence of skills

outlined in commercial reading programs and by the emphasis measurement has placed on skill acquisition. Unfortunately, students have been expected to master reading skills by performing repeated practice on worksheets. This kind of instruction has produced readers who do not understand how, when, or why to use the skills they have learned.

The goal of reading skill instruction should be to help all students, including students with learning problems, learn *what* the reading skill is, *how* to perform the reading skill, and *when* and why to use it (Gerber, 1986; Paris, Lipson, & Wixon, 1983). The model of reading skill instruction most often proposed in the literature begins with teacher responsibility for explaining the skill. The student gradually assumes responsibility for the skill during guided and independent practice (Pearson & Dole, 1988; Pearson & Gallagher, 1983; Duffy & Roehler, 1987).

Although direct instruction and teacher explanation are recent innovations, the research literature indicates that they facilitate the acquisition of reading skills. This kind of instruction has been very successful with regular students (Winograd & Hare, 1988). Similarly, it has been applied successfully in teaching students with mild disabilities (Frudden & Healy, 1987; Larrivee, 1989).

Feedback and Reinforcement

Research has consistently shown that academic performance is improved when teachers provide instructional feedback that relates directly to student responses during instruction. Moreover, feedback for mildly disabled students is most effective when it is explicit, systematic, and corrective (Ysseldyke & Christenson, 1987). One factor that has been demonstrated to affect how teachers provide feedback is the expectations they hold for different students. For example, teachers have been shown to hold negative expectations of students who are labeled for special education. As a result of these negative views, teachers often provide briefer and less informative feedback to labeled students during reading instruction (Johnston & Winograd, 1985). To overcome the likelihood that negative expectations may result in diminished instructional feedback to mildly disabled students, teachers should plan how they will provide instructional feedback and should reflect on whether feedback was provided equitably (Billingsley & Wildman, 1990).

The quality of teachers' feedback should be coupled with consistent positive reinforcement of both instructional and noninstructional student behaviors. Although praise can be used regularly, teachers should consider carefully how students' reading behaviors are being reinforced and/or modified by its use. If used too frequently with mildly disabled students, praise may lose its power as a modifier of behavior (Zigmond, Sansone, Miller, Donahoe, & Kohnke, 1986).

In summary, a review of literature on factors that have a significant effect on the reading achievement of mildly disabled and general education students provides insight into what would be expected if observations were made of ideal reading instruction for mildly disabled students in mainstreamed settings. First, it seems reasonable to expect that students would be doing most of the talking as they actively work in small groups. A great deal of the talk would probably be related to what they know about what they are reading and their purpose for reading. Most important, observations would show students who are motivated about what they are learning because they are successful and receive positive feedback and encouragement from the teacher.

Next, during the presentation of well-organized reading lessons, observation would show teachers explaining and demonstrating how to perform reading skills and why the skills are important. Rather than telling students what they don't know, teachers would be helping students learn whatever they don't know. In other words, teachers would be providing instruction such that students are led to accept responsibility for their own learning.

Ideally, teachers would move around classrooms giving students assistance as it is needed. As teachers move around, they would ask students questions such as, "What do you already know about this?" "What do you predict will happen?" "What does this mean?" "What are you thinking?" "Have you already learned something you can use here?" "How can you do this better next time?"

Teachers would also be providing instruction with a wide range of teacher-made and authentic reading materials. Before, during, and after reading, students would be observed engaged in writing and using charts, graphs, diagrams, and other visual displays to represent and discuss the parts of text and the interrelationship among the information and ideas they were learning. There would also be discussions of how what students knew before they read changed as a result of reading.

Last, students would be observed having time each day to read and enjoy authentic material of their choice. Also, students would have a great deal of opportunity to reflect on what they are reading and to discuss it with their peers in a nonthreatening atmosphere.

The Quality of Classroom Reading Instruction

In the preceding section we reviewed a set of variables that affect mildly disabled students' acquisition of reading ability, and we discussed the implications of these variables for instruction. We also presented a scenario of the kind of instruction we would expect mildly disabled learners to be exposed to in regular classrooms. Now, we turn to the question of *whether* students with mild disabilities really do receive this kind of reading instruction. To address this question, we review the classroom research on reading instruction in general and special education provided for mildly disabled and general education students.

Given the research evidence related to time and reading, one might expect to find that all students, including students with mild disabilities, spend a reasonable amount of time engaged in reading lessons and actually reading. Likewise, one might expect to find mildly disabled students receiving more instructional time in reading than their peers in general education. Unfortunately, this is not the case. The evidence indicates that students in general education spend about 6 percent of directed reading lesson time (Blanton & Moorman, 1990; Mason, 1984) and 15 percent of total school time (Goodlad, 1984) actually reading. Similar findings have been obtained for mildly disabled students (Haynes & Jenkins, 1986; Thurlow, Graden, Ysseldyke, & Algozzine, 1984). The results are surprising, given the contention that the best way to improve reading ability is to provide opportunities for students actually to spend time reading (Allington, 1977, 1980, 1983; Barr, 1982; Leinhardt, Zignance, & Cooley, 1981).

There seems to be very little difference in the time allocated to reading instruction for mildly disabled and regular students (Allington & McGill-Franzen, 1989; Haynes & Jenmkins, 1986; Thurlow et al., 1984). Both groups seem to spend similar amounts of engaged time on the same kinds of reading tasks, such as reading basal readers and working in workbooks (Gelzheiser & Meyers, 1991; Thurlow, Graden, Greener, & Ysseldyke, Thurlow, Mecklenburg, & Graden, 1984).

Classroom observations reveal that most of the time both regular and mildly disabled students spend engaged in reading instruction is passive (Ysseldyke et al., 1984). Both groups spend at least 50 percent of their instructional time engaged in management and/or waiting and as little as 12 percent of time actively responding to instruction (Haynes & Jenkins, 1986; Thurlow, Ysseldyke, Graden, & Algozzine, 1984). In particular, mildly disabled students have been observed spending over 50 percent of their reading instruction time waiting for interaction with the teacher (Haynes & Jenkins, 1986; Miramontes, Cheng, & Trueba, 1984; Thurlow, Graden, Ysseldyke, & Algozzine, 1984).

The results of classroom observation research do not portray a positive picture of reading lessons presented to either regular or special students. Durkin (1974a, 1974b, 1974c, 1975a, 1975b), for example, found that general education teachers: (1) did not use diagnosis to determine student needs, (2) asked endless questions about material read, and (3) assigned more and longer written work as a reward for being good readers. These conclusions were sustained in a later study by Durkin (1978–1979). She reported that teachers devoted less than 1 percent of time to actually teaching students how to comprehend. In contrast, most time was used to ask students questions about what they had read. Similarly, Mason (1984) reported that most elementary reading instruction procedures were either question–answer, lecture, or round-robin reading. In addition, Baker and Zigmond (1990) have presented evidence revealing that reading instruction in classrooms containing mainstreamed mildly disabled students may mirror these findings. As a result, the extent to which regular classrooms provide appropriate reading instruction for mildly disabled students may be seriously questioned.

The results of three case studies of classroom reading instruction for mildly disabled students have also revealed discouraging results. First, Stephens and Clyde (1985) found that reading was not presented to students as an enjoyable activity and that students were encouraged to depend on the teacher. Second, Rowe (1985) reported that teachers of mildly disabled students did not present reading as a tool for lifelong learning, asked questions from commercial manuals, failed to set purpose for reading, and used workbooks for postreading instruction. Of greatest interest, however, was the finding that students were asked to work without talking to each other. Finally, Crissmore's (1985) finding revealed that students with mild disabilities did not use materials requiring generative activities during reading instruction.

Research findings also indicate that both mildly disabled students and their peers in general education spend 30 to 60 percent of allocated reading instruction time in seatwork activities (Anderson, 1984; Blanton & Moorman, 1990; Haynes & Jenkins, 1986; Rowe, 1985; Rupley & Blair, 1987; Stephens & Clyde, 1985), usually presented with commercially prepared workbooks and dittos. More important, rather than these students receiving instruction on the relevance and "how" of the strategic use of reading skills, instruction seems to be limited to verbal instructions on how to complete assignments.

In short, it appears that regular students (Blanton & Moorman, 1990) and special students (Gelzheiser & Meyers, 1991; Haynes & Jenkins, 1986) are engaged in instruction where teachers use as little as 5 to 7 percent of teaching time to demonstrate, model, and think aloud *how, when,* and *why* to use a reading strategy.

Classroom reading instruction also seems to be driven by the use of commercial materials. Research underlines the wide use of basal readers and other commercial materials (Blanton & Moorman, 1990; Mason, 1984; Shannon, 1983; Woodward, 1986). Interviews with teachers (Duffy & McIntyre, 1982) indicate that they perceive their role in reading instruction as that of a pilot who guides students through commercial materials.

Baker and Zigmond (1990) observed regular reading instruction to determine changes needing to be made to accommodate mainstreamed students. They reported that reading instruction was derived directly from the teacher's manual. For prereading activities, teachers used skill and vocabulary activities suggested in the manual. During reading activities involved having students read page by page and answer questions. Postreading instruction involved practice in workbooks. Most often, reading skills lessons involved whole group activities and the completion of workbook pages.

Given the finding tht teachers use commercial reading materials to the exclusion of other types of instruction, one might expect reading lessons to be well organized. This does not appear to be the case. Teachers often omit instructional components such as introduction to material to be read and postreading discussion. Likewise, when following the teacher's manual, teachers seem to ignore most prereading activities, such as activating background knowledge, vocabulary development, and purpose-setting questions. However, teachers consistently use questions provided for postreading discussion and worksheets (Durkin, 1984).

Classroom observations in content area classrooms follow similar patterns of reading instruction (Neilsen, Rennie, & Connell, 1982; Ratekin, Simpson, Alvermann, & Dishner, 1985; Smith & Feathers, 1983). Worksheets are widely used, introductions to reading material and purposes for reading are short and general, interactions are dominated by question-asking and telling students what to know, visual displays are seldom used, and single textbooks are used for virtually all reading assignments.

In summary, observations of reading instruction in general and special education classrooms suggest that there is very little difference in reading instruction provided for mildly disabled students and for students in general education. Time allocated for reading instruction is about the same, and students seem to be engaged in similar reading tasks and activities. Both groups of students spend the majority of their time in reading skills instruction rather than actually reading.

Reading lessons appear to be driven by manuals. Teachers provide instruction by the manual and following the lesson sequence. Rather than modifying the instruction presented in manuals, teachers are more likely to delete important parts of prereading instruction, such as developing background knowledge and purpose setting or asking the suggested postreading questions.

The dominant instructional strategy in reading lessons tends to be assigning students a selection to read, followed by the teacher asking a series of questions presented in the manual or developed by the teacher. In more cases than not, teachers do not use research-based strategies such as generative activities requiring active involvement and deep processing of material to engage students in reading.

In general, teachers miss the opportunity to provide students with instruction on the strategic use of reading skills. Instead of providing instruction that explains a reading skill, along with *when, how,* and *why* it should be used, reading skills instruction is used to manage students. Workbooks and skills sheets are the dominant management devices. In short, instruction on reading skills is probably not very meaningful for either mildly disabled or general education students.

In most cases, students are passive during reading instruction, and reading is not presented as an enjoyable activity. Teachers ask students questions and tell them information when the students do not have the answers. Most important, students seem to spend a great deal of instructional time simply waiting on directions, questions, and other interactions with teachers.

The overall impression gained from the literature reviewed in this section is that fundamental changes must occur in both general and special education classrooms if mildly disabled students are to receive the best possible reading education. Teachers need to reconsider the time allocated to reading tasks and the kinds of tasks presented to students. The organization and presentation of reading lessons should also include application of the current knowledge base on reading instruction. It is also timely to expect that teachers begin to use research-based instructional strategies and approaches to engage students in reading instruction.

Providing Reading Instruction

In this section, we present a discussion of reading curriculum for mildly disabled students, selected instructional programs, and research-based instructional strategies. We begin by emphasizing three points. First, underlying all decisions about curriculum and instruction for students with mild disabilities is the requisite knowledge about learning and instructional features, such as the review presented in the first section of this chapter. Similarly, curriculum and instruction decisions are influenced by one's understanding of the status of current reading practices, such as the overview presented in the second section. Third, it is apparent that many of the reading instruction strategies found to be successful for students with mild disabilities are the same strategies researched and developed for students in general education (Graham & Johnson, 1989). Consequently, it is reasonable to suggest that teachers begin to apply research-based general education reading instruction for mildly disabled students. As this knowledge is applied, teachers will begin to develop wisdom of practice about how each strategy should be modified and shaped to meet the reading instruction needs of both mildly disabled and general education students.

Reading Curriculum

There is evidence to suggest that the predominant reading curriculum for mildly disabled students is made up of skills. Resource room teachers, for example, seem to view reading as learning a series of skills (Stephens & Clyde, 1985). The skills are usually identified on an Individualized Education Program (IEP), along with criteria for mastery. In addition, Bos and Anders (1990a) argue that the reading instruction focus for mildly disabled students is on basic decoding skills and literal comprehension. The ubiquitous use of skill sheets, workbooks, and ditto sheets also attests to an emphasis on discrete reading skills (e.g., Haynes & Jenkins, 1986). The unfortunate product of this emphasis may be that students with mild disabilities are not exposed to a balanced reading program.

As noted previously, the traditional view of reading instruction has been as an activity designed to assist students in acquiring discrete reading skills. In turn, successful reading performance has been viewed as satisfactory performance on measures of reading achievement. This view of reading has dominated the scope and sequence of most reading instruction, particularly basal reading programs and the curriculum guidelines of state departments of public instruction. The focus on skill instruction has led teachers to depend more on manuals, to feel compelled to cover all the skills outlined in scope and sequence charts, and to make and check seatwork assignments in a mechanical manner. Wong (1986), for example, has described students as believing that reading was simply decoding words because they had practiced large numbers of decoding skills on isolated worksheets. In other words, students learned that the purpose of reading was just to get their work done, not to construct meaning from the printed page.

As also noted previously, views of reading have changed. The current orientation is that reading involves the construction of meaning. In constructing meaning, readers must select strategies appropriate for the purpose of reading and the kind of text to be read. With this new emphasis on strategies, it is important to understand the differences between reading skills and reading strategies. According to Pearson, Roehler, Dole, and Duffy (1990), reading skills are often viewed as being taught by the teacher. Later, they emerge automatically and effortlessly as needed by students. Reading strategies, on the other hand, are seen as being controlled by the reader. The reader intentionally plans and decides which strategy to use as the purpose for reading changes or the kind of text to be read changes. As can be seen, the idea of reading strategies is more reflective of reading as the active construction of meaning.

The new view is that reading is the implementation of flexible plans designed by the reader to construct meaning. For example, a reader may use one set of strategies to generate the main idea of a short story and another set to generate the main idea of a chapter in a science text. Curriculum and instruction emphasizes "how" reading works. The goal is to produce students who are intentional, skillful, willful readers. To attain this goal requires that the following components be included in curriculum and instruction for all learners, especially those who are at risk for reading problems.

Decoding Strategies

The curriculum should present an intensive decoding program for students with mild disabilities. There is ample evidence demonstrating that instruction on decoding skills facilitates word recognition and comprehension (Adams, 1990). In addition, the literature supports the idea that students should acquire decoding skills to a level of automaticity (LaBerge & Samuels, 1974). Automatic decoding ability leads to instant word recognition and instant access to word meanings for the processing of text and comprehension.

Vocabulary Development

Traditionally, vocabulary has been emphasized in reading instruction because of its correlation with performance on measures of comprehension. However, this relationship does not seem to be causal. Teaching students word meaning to increase their comprehension has not been successful (e.g., Pany & Jenkins, 1978). The focus of vocabulary instruction should be on preteaching vocabulary prior to engaging students in reading. the conventional wisdom is to teach one or two word meanings critical to understanding the material. This is true for regular students (Beck, Perfetti, & McKeown, 1982; Kameenui, Carnine, & Freschi, 1982; Stallman et al., 1990) and for students with mild disabilities (Kameenui, Carnine, & Freschi, 1982; Sacks, 1983, 1984).

The importance of vocabulary development is easy to understand when we consider that learning word meaning improves students' background knowledge for later comprehension (Beck, McKeown, McCaslin, & Burkes, 1979). Similarly, Johnson and Pearson (1984a) propose that the acquisition of new word meanings provides students with an anchor on which to hook new information. As noted earlier, students with mild disabilities may lack relevant prior knowledge needed for the successful performance of reading activity. For both regular and mildly disabled students, vocabulary should be taught in semantically and topically related groups (Anders, Bos, & Filip, 1984; Beck et al., 1982; Bos & Anders, 1990a; Bos, Anders, Filip, & Jaffee, 1985; Johnson & Pearson, 1984a; Stevens, 1982).

Comprehension Strategies

Next, with regard to comprehension skills, we agree with Pearson and his colleagues (Pearson et al., 1990) that the reading comprehension curriculum should provide an opportunity for students to learn a few well-taught, well-learned strategies. As noted in the review of classroom observation studies, most skill instruction is accomplished by teachers mentioning skills and assigning practice. Rarely do students receive explanations relevant to the strategic application of skills. However, a curriculum made up of a reasonable set of comprehension skills may result in a qualitative improvement in instruction and the willful application of skills to the actual reading of real material.

Metacognitive Reading Strategies

The reading curriculum should focus on metacognitive reading instruction: developing independent, self-regulated readers who are planful, skillful, and willful (Paris & Newman, 1990). In the past, a curriculum of this kind has been difficult to conceptualize for a number of reasons. First, "thinking" about reading is an abstract process. It is not easy for teachers to help students "see" what we do when we read. Second, students have not had an opportunity to discuss and think about *how* reading works before, during, and after reading. Last, accountability has emphasized performance on achievement tests, which have seldom measured the strategic use of reading skills.

Fortunately, reading research has produced evidence that students can learn to become active, independent, thoughtful readers (e.g., Paris, Cross, & Lipson, 1984; Paris, Lipson, & Wixon, 1983; Paris & Winograd, 1990a; Winograd & Hare, 1988). As a result, a reading curriculum for general and mildly disabled students should target the development of flexible readers who are in charge of their own reading and understand that one uses reading strategies selectively, depending on the purpose for reading and kind of text to be read. As illustrated in Table 2-2, curriculum outcomes based on metacognition help students to think about reading skills in terms of strategies used to plan, monitor, and evaluate their reading: *what* strategies can be used for different purposes, *how* they are used, *when* they should be used, and how they can be used better next time.

Text Structure Understanding

The majority of what students are expected to learn in school is presented in textbooks. As a result, most early reading instruction is accomplished with basal reading programs (e.g., Shannon, 1983; Wiesendanger & Birlem, 1981; Woodward, 1986). Similarly, the majority of content area instruction is based on textbooks (Armbruster, 1985; Cole & Sticht, 1981; EPIE Institute, 1977). This kind of prepackaged learning creates numerous problems for students with mild disabilities and their peers in general education. For example, textbooks have been found to be poorly organized and incoherent (Anderson, Armbruster, & Kanton, 1980). In addition, they often create settings where learning is accomplished by repeated practice rather than by teacher explanation and direct instruction, (Armbruster & Gubrandsen, 1984) and where subject matter is presented without providing learners with assistance (Elliot, Nagel, & Woodward, 1986).

Given the wide use of texts, the curriculum should expose students to a wide variety of text structures. Research indicates that readers benefit from knowledge about the organization of text (Bartlett, 1978). This includes an understanding of how authors organize narrative text and how authors use patterns such as simple listing, cause–effect, compare and contrast, time order, and problem–solution to present information in expository text.

The structure of text specifies how information is organized and connected (Meyer & Freedle, 1984). Thus, knowledge about text patterns facilitates the reader's organization and recall of material read (Taylor & Beach, 1984; Taylor & Samuels, 1983). In

TABLE 2-2   Metacognitive Reading

Plan Before Reading	Monitor During Reading	Reflect After Reading
• What is this text about? • What do I know about this? • How is this organized? • What am I suppose to learn? • What are some key words about this? • What reading strategy should I use? • How much time should I spend on this?	• Am I attaining my purpose? • How do I know I'm learning what I'm suppose to learn? • What are the important ideas? • How is this related to what I already know? • If I'm not learning, what should I do?	• Did I learn what I was supposed to learn? • Has what I knew about this before I started changed? • How has what I knew about this changed? • Can I put what I've learned in my own words? • How can I use what I've learned? • Do I need to learn something else about this? • How can I do this better next time?

In particular, there seems to be a difference between mildly disabled and general education students' sensitivity to text structure, favoring general students (Englert, Raphael, Anderson, Gregg, & Anthony, 1989; Englert & Thomas, 1987; Laughton & Morris, 1989). Research with regular students (Armbruster & Anderson, 1980; Geva, 1983; Taylor, 1982) and mildly disabled students (Carnine & Kinder, 1985; Dimino, Gersten, Carnine, & Blake, 1990; Idol-Maestas, 1985; Varnhagen & Goldman, 1986; Williams, 1986) indicates that both groups profit from direct instruction on text structure.

Time for Free Reading

Next, the curriculum should provide an opportunity for students actually to read. As noted earlier, students in both general and special education spend as little as 7 percent of allocated time reading. Research has demonstrated that time spent on free reading is one of the best predictors of vocabulary and reading achievement gains of mildly disabled and general education students (Fielding, Wilson, & Anderson, 1986; Leinhardt, Zignance, & Cooley, 1981). The reminder of Allington (1977) that students are not going to learn to read well if schools fail to provide time for them to practice reading is also noteworthy. In addition, as Rosenblatt (1978) points out, time for joyful, pleasurable reading is active reading and a legitimate goal of reading instruction. The setting it creates is nonthreatening (Nicholls, 1983). Consequently, allocating time for free reading should help both general education and mildly disabled students to become active readers (Bristow, 1985; Fitzgerald, 1983; Holdaway, 1980).

Understanding the Social Nature of Reading

Last, the reading curriculum should emphasize the social nature of reading. In the real world, reading is a content-dependent, technical skill. People who read at work must interact with others about information they obtain as they read for the purposes of identifying and solving problems and making decisions. Current data on employment reveal that most adults who are released from work, regardless of whether they were labeled in public schools, are let go because they lack social skills necessary for performing on the job (e.g., Edgar, 1990; Fourgurean & LaCourt, 1990). This serious problem can be addressed by ensuring that the reading curriculum provides opportunities for cooperative learning and group interaction during reading instruction.

Selected Instructional Programs

A number of reading instruction programs provide instruction appropriate for the curriculum we have discussed. In the following section, we present programs that we believe to be particularly suitable for students with mild disabilities.

Reading Recovery

Reading Recovery is a highly successful program that has great potential for students who are at risk, including students with mild disabilities (Slavin & Madden, 1989). The goal of the program is to help the poorest readers in a class make progress until they read as well as the average readers in class. To qualify for this program, students must fall in a group described as the lowest 20 percent in reading ability in their class.

Students are provided with thirty-minute one-on-one lessons each day by specially trained teachers. Lessons include reading stories, composition, and word analysis. Instructors teach students how to use the same strategies successful readers use. Available research indicates a success rate of 85 to 90 percent for students in this program (Clay, 1985; DeFord, Pinnell, Lyons, & Young, 1987; Pinnell, DeFord, & Lyons, 1988). More important, student gains do not appear to "wash out" after students exit the program. The success of this program is produced by the active instruction of tutors and the active participation of students, each a desirable instructional element for students with mild disabilities.

DISTAR

The DISTAR reading program (Becker & Carnine, 1980) is a K–6 reading program with a great deal of promise for students who are at risk (Slavin & Madden, 1989). In this program, teachers instruct small groups of students with structured, scripted lessons. Instruction is highly interactive, with active student participation, meeting specific needs of students with mild disabilities.

Kamehameha Early Education Program

The Kamehameha Early Education Program (KEEP) (Tharp et al., 1984) provides the kind of instruction potentially useful for students with mild disabilities. Instruction is organized around centers where students receive practice and feedback on reading skills before they are applied independently. Lessons are organized around E-T-R (Experience, Text, Relationship). As described by Au (1979), instruction begins by discussion of students' prior knowledge, followed by text-based discussion, and ending with the construction of relationships between readers' prior knowledge and the text. Usually, the questions posed by the teacher are group questions. Consequently, students must work cooperatively to answer questions. As can be seen, the activities in this program emphasize prior knowledge activation, support during critical points in learning, active participation, and interaction with other students—all areas of great need for students with mild disabilities.

Reciprocal Teaching

Reciprocal Teaching is a program emphasizing teachers' modeling of reading strategies and cooperative learning. Students are taught to focus on content and process questions after reading parts of text. Instruction deals with four components:

1. Summarizing sentences, paragraphs or complete selections read
2. Generating a question about the material read to ask a peer
3. Requesting clarity about what was not clear or did not make sense
4. Predicting or generating a question for the next part of text to be read

At first, teachers are responsible for modeling each component for students. Gradually, responsibility is released to students by teacher and student taking turns until students assume total responsibility. Teacher modeling, cooperative learning, and gradual release of responsibility to students are important instructional elements meeting the needs of mildly disabled students. Studies by Moore (1988) and Palincsar and Brown (1984,

1988) have demonstrated the success of reciprocal teaching with high-risk learners and students with mild disabilities.

Informed Strategies for Learning

Informed Strategies for Learning (Paris, 1987) is an instructional program designed to teach students metacognitive reading strategies. The progrm comprises twenty lessons. Each lesson requires one week to teach. Instruction begins with teaching from a bulletin board to introduce a target reading strategy such as the importance of prior knowledge in reading. Questions, dialogues, and modeling are used to show students how to integrate information while reading. Worksheets are used for practice, along with high-interest material for application. The bulletin board reminds students to apply the strategy in other areas over the week of instruction. For mildly disabled students, this program is strong because it provides teacher modeling and explanation, along with cues to apply strategies as they are being learned.

Success for All Program

Last, the Success for All Program (Madden, Slavin, Livermon, Karweit, & Stevens, 1987) is a K–3 program that uses reading tutors to provide ninety minutes of direct instruction in decoding, language skills, story structure, and comprehension skills. When students reach level 2 reading ability, they engage in cooperative learning activities for instruction on decoding, vocabulary development, story structure, and comprehension skills. It is also interesting to note that within the ninety-minute reading period, students receive one-on-one tutoring by certified teachers. The tutor's instruction overlaps with instruction in the classroom. Students receive additional instruction on what the classroom teacher is teaching. Evaluation results indicate that the Success for All Program has a significant effect on increasing students' reading performance (Stevens, Madden, Slavin, & Farnish, 1987). Along with direct instruction, the strength of this program is that it overlaps with classroom reading instruction, providing mildly disabled students with additional support.

Organization of Reading Lessons

In order to provide a framework for the discussion of instructional strategies, we offer an overview of how reading lessons should be organized. We begin by discussing the lesson structure for engaging students in reading text, followed by a structure for skills instruction.

Engaging Students in Reading Text

There seems to be a consensus in the field of reading that lessons should be viewed as an activity occurring in three phases (Herber & Nelson-Herber, 1987): before reading, during reading, and after reading. Tierney and Cunningham (1984) point out that effective lessons contain five elements: accessing or developing background, stating a purpose, reading for the purpose, performing a task reflecting attainment of the purpose, and feedback on performance. The primary goal of instruction during each phase of the reading lesson is to help the reader attain goals reflecting these elements (Anderson, 1980). Table 2-3 presents an organizational structure for reading lessons.

TABLE 2-3 Organization of Reading Lessons

Instructional Goals		
Before-Reading Phase	During-Reading Phase	After-Reading Phase
• Activate, organize, and/or develop background knowledge. • Activate and/or provide information on text structure. • Teach critical word meanings and concepts. • Develop interest. • Set purpose (teacher-directed or student-directed).	• Assist students in maintaining purpose. • Assist students in organizing information. • Assist students in building relationships among concepts and ideas.	• Discuss purpose for reading. • Assist students with integration of new informtion with old information. • Assist students with application. • Assist students with evaluation of performance. • Assist students with reflection on their performance.

Before-Reading Phase.   As can be seen in Table 2-3, instruction during the before-reading phase comprises activities that do the following: (1) activate and/or develop background knowledge, (2) discuss text structure, (3) introduce critical vocabulary, and (4) establish purpose for reading. For students with mild disabilities, accomplishing these activities is important for a number of reasons. First, students are "set up" to read material. Second, the prior knowledge needs of mildly disabled learners are addressed. Next, purpose for reading focuses mildly disabled students' attention on the relevant aspects of the reading task. Attention to text structure helps students with the organizational demands placed on readers when they encounter different kinds of text. As can be seen, these instructional activities have a high probability of helping mildly disabled students overcome many of their problems with learning.

During-Reading Phase.   The during-reading phase is usually limited to the actual reading of text. At times, however, students with mild disabilities need assistance during this phase, particularly when reading content material. When this is the case, instructional activities should be targeted to: (1) helping students maintain purpose for reading, (2) providing assistance in organizing information, and (3) helping students generate relationships among the information presented in the reading material. These activities focus on the problems mildly disabled students have with attention and organization.

After-Reading Phase.   The role of instruction during the after-reading phase is to help readers integrate information gained by reading "with what they knew" prior to reading the text. Among the instructional goals of this phase are: (1) discussing the purpose for reading and how well it was attained, (2) helping students evaluate and reflect on what was learned, (3) assisting students in integrating information obtained from the text with what they already knew, and providing opportunities for students to apply their new knowledge to real world tasks. Instruction during this phase requires students to engage in meaningful discussions, to be active, and to be reflective, all of which have been found to be needed by students with mild disabilities.

Reading Skills Instruction

As noted earlier, the predominant pattern for reading skills instruction has been to assign students repeated practice in the form of worksheets and seatwork. This view of reading skills instruction has changed to the idea of direct instruction and teacher explanation. According to Gersten and Carnine (1986), it is doubtful whether students with mild disabilities will learn skills we do not teach them actively and directly. They argue that students should be taught skills with the use of instructional materials designed specifically for this purpose.

There is a great deal of evidence demonstrating that general education students learn skills better when they receive active instruction from teachers (Brophy & Evertson, 1976; Good, 1979). The dominant model for teaching reading skills begins with teacher responsibility for explaining *what* the skill is that is to be learned. As can be seen in Table 2-4, this explanation includes demonstrating; thinking aloud; and modeling *how, when,* and *why* students should perform the skill (Duffy et al., 1987; Pearson & Dole, 1988; Pearson & Gallagher, 1983). Students gradually assume responsibility for the skill during practice and the eventual strategic application of the skill to the reading of authentic material.

A great deal of research has been conducted on this model of skill instruction. The unitary finding among studies on teaching comprehension skills (Adams, Carnine, & Gersten, 1982; Baumann, 1984; Carnine, Kameenui, & Woolfson, 1982; Garner, Hare, Alexander, Haynes, & Winograd, 1984; Hare & Borchardt, 1984; Patching, Kameenui, Carnine, Gersten, & Colvin, 1983), teaching question-answering skills (Raphael & Pearson, 1985; Raphael & Wonnacott, 1985), and teacher explanation and elaboration (Duffy et al., 1987) is that direct instruction and teacher explanation enhance the acquisition

TABLE 2-4 Framework for Direct Instruction

Teacher Explanation	Guided Practice	Independent Practice and Application
• Explain and define the reading skill and provide an example. • Explain why the reading skill is important. • Tell, show, model, demonstrate, and think aloud how to perform the reading skill. • Explain when to use the reading skill (kinds of texts, purposes for reading).	• Provide as much practice as students need. • Practice in material on instructional learning level (80% success rate). • Provide help when needed. • Provide feedback on why performance is correct or incorrect. • Discuss how to perform skill better next time.	• Practice in material on independent learning level (90% success rate). • Provide practice in authentic material. • Hold debriefing sessions for students to discuss what was learned about skill during independent practice and how it works in reading. • Discuss how to apply skill better next time. • Remind students to apply the reading skill.

of reading skills by both general and special education students. At present, a number of prototype lessons for teaching reading skills are available in the literature (e.g., Baumann, 1983; Baumann & Schmitt, 1986; Blanton, Moorman, & Wood, 1986; Duffy & Roehler, 1986, 1987; Schmitt & Baumann, 1986).

Research-Based Instructional Strategies

This section presents research-based instructional strategies that are useful for teaching both general and mildly disabled students. We have organized these strategies into five categories: visual displays, text pattern guides, predictive strategies, interactive guides, and strategies for free reading.

Visual Displays

This category includes instructional strategies such as *Matrix Organizational Analysis* (Jones, Amiran, & Katims, 1985), structured overviews (Barron & Earle, 1973), graphic organizers (Barron, 1969), semantic maps (Heimlich & Pittelman, 1986; Johnson & Pearson, 1984b), semantic feature analysis (Johnson & Pearson, 1984b), list-group-label (Taba, 1967), and inductive towers (Clarke, Raths, & Gilbert, 1989). Visual displays organize key vocabulary words into schematic diagrams that represent the semasntic relationships among concepts. The use of visual displays activates and organizes students' prior knowledge and enables the teacher to identify important information and how it relates to other information. In a reading lesson, displays are usually introduced or developed in the before-reading phase. After students' background knowledge has been activated, the purpose for reading becomes to update knowledge by modifying what they know, as shown in the visual display. During the after-reading phase, teacher and students return to the original display and discuss how reading changed what was known about the topic before reading, as illustrated by the changes in their displays. The use of instructional strategies such as semantic mapping (Idol, 1987a; Idol & Croll, 1987; Sinatra, Berg, & Dunn, 1985) and advance organizers (Billingsley & Wildman, 1988; Darch & Carnine, 1986; Darch & Gersten, 1986; Lenz, Alley, & Schumaker, 1987; Peleg & Moore, 1982) have been shown to be effective with students with mild disabilities.

Text Pattern Guides

Similar to visual displays, this category includes activities designed to teach students how authors organize text. The story map (Pearson, 1982) is designed to teach students how narratives similar to basal reader stories are organized. Students are presented with a visual display depicting elements of a narrative: setting (character, time place), problem, goal, events, and outcome. Students discuss the story map and write appropriate information in the map as they read. Teachers also generate discussion questions based on each part of the story map. This strategy has been shown to be effective in improving story comprehension of mildly disabled students (Idol, 1987b; Idol & Croll, 1987).

Other guides have been developed to assist students with the structure of content area reading material. These strategies include maps (Jones, Pierce, & Hunter, 1988–1989), pattern guide (Vacca, 1981), and text pattern and organization guide (Raphael & Englert, 1988). These guides are used to provide students with visual displays of how writers present information, along with the relationship among ideas presented in text. Research (Carnine & Kinder, 1985; Dimino et al., 1990; Englert et al., 1989; Englert & Thomas, 1987; Luftig & Johnson, 1982; Varnhagen & Goldman, 1986; Williams, 1986) has demonstrated that instruction using text pattern guides facilitates mildly disabled students' comprehension of text.

Predictive Strategies

K-W-L (Ogle, 1986), DR-TA (Stauffer, 1969), C-T-A (Wong & Au, 1985), Point of View Reading Guide (Wood, 1988), Previewing (Graves, Prenn, & Cooke, 1985), and What If (Pearson, 1982) are examples of strategies that activate background knowledge. During the before-reading phase, predictions activate students' prior knowledge about a topic and serve as a guide for processing information as it is encountered during reading. Discussion of predictions after reading helps students see how new information affects what they knew prior to reading. As can be seen, the strength of predictive strategies is in their activation of students' background knowledge, a need of students with mild disabilities. Although predictive strategies have not been researched with mildly disabled students, their instructional potential is evident.

Reading Guides

This category includes strategies such as Guide-o-rama (Cunningham & Shablak, 1975), Process Reading Guide (Singer & Donlan, 1980), Content Guide (Karlin, 1964), Three Level Study Guide (Herber, 1978), and Learning from Text Guide (Singer & Donlan, 1980). These strategies are particularly appropriate for focusing mildly disabled students' attention on specific content, text structure, and reading skills. A number of researchers have found guides useful with mildly disabled students in content area reading (Horton & Lovitt, 1989; Lovitt, Rudsit, Jenkins, Pious, & Benedetti, 1986; bergerud, Lovitt, & Horton, 1988; Lovitt & Horton, 1988).

Study Strategies

Many research-based study strategies are reported in the literature, including Question Answer Relationships (QAR) (Raphael, 1986), Two Column Notes (Santa, 1988), and SPARCS (Survey/Predict/Read/Construct/Summarize) (Jones, 1986). These strategies should be viewed as tools that students can acquire to help them become independent learners. They are best taught separately, with direct instruction and teacher explanation lesson formats (e.g., Blanton, Moorman, & Wood, 1986; Duffy & Roehler, 1987). This instruction should take place during the before-reading phase, with the purpose for reading being to apply the study strategy. The apparent strength of study strategies for mildly disabled students is in the potential they have for assisting independent training.

Interactive Strategies

Among the many strategies generally included in this category are Multiple Response Technique (Davey, 1989), Interactive Reading Guide (Wood, 1988), Textbook Activity Guide (Davey, 1986), and Collaborative Listening-Viewing Guide (Wood, 1990). These strategies are designed to increase the amount of interaction between and among students, teacher, and text. With each strategy, students are actively engaged in processing information presented either in the text, by the teacher, or by other students. This active involvement meets the need of mildly disabled learners to become more active learners. In addition, these strategies may assist mildly disabled learners in acquiring social skills.

Strategies for Free Reading

As we have pointed out, regular and mildly disabled students do not seem to have many opportunities simply to read in school, although it is clear that opportunities to read will increase their reading ability. Free reading creates motivated, active readers. Among the strategies that provide opportunities for reading are USSR (Hunt, 1970) and DEAR (Picarello, 1986). These strategies call for a designated time when students can read material of their choice without interruption. Teachers and students discuss how and why one reads for pleasure, along with opportunities to share what they have read and discuss how they reflect on what they have read.

Summary

We noted at the beginning of this chapter that there is an expanding knowledge base on which to ground reading instruction for students with mild disabilities. This knowledge base comprises a number of sources, many of which we have discussed in this chapter. The first source discussed comes from research on teaching and learning. An examination of this research provides an understanding of the effects of learning and instructional features on the outcomes of reading instruction for students in both general and special education. A second source of knowledge that we reviewed and that we view as crucial to the effective delivery of reading instruction to all students is derived from classroom research. This research provides rich descriptions of how reading instructional practice is actually carried out in general and special education settings. Further, the findings of this research reveal the extent to which teachers implement what is known currently about teaching and learning. Third, we reviewed research on the instructional delivery of reading, including such key areas as text structure, the organization of lessons, and strategies.

We believe that these sources of information come together to create a knowledge base that forms the basis for the delivery of effective reading instruction for students labeled in special education as mildly disabled. The challenge to the reader is to study and understand the sources of knowledge contributing to effective reading instruction. By doing so, the reader should understand that there is not a simple solution to the delivery of reading instruction. Rather, the solutions to effective reading instruction are grounded in teachers' development of broad understandings of the various factors that affect classroom reading instruction.

References

Adams, A., Carnine, D., & Gersten, R. (1982). Instructional strategies for studying content area texts in the intermediate grades. *Reading Research Quarterly, 18,* 27–55.

Adams, M. (1990). *Beginning to read: Thinking and learning about print.* Cambridge, MA: MIT Press.

Adams, M., & Bruce, b. (1980). *Background knowledge and reading comprehension* (Technical Report No. 13). Urbana: University of Illinois, Center for the Study of Reading.

Alexander, P. A., & Judy, J. E. (1988). The interaction of domain-specific and strategic knowledge in academic performance. *Review of Educational Research, 58*(4), 375–404.

Allington, R. L. (1977). If they don't read much, how they ever gonna get good? *Journal of Reading, 21,* 57–61.

Allington, R. L. (1980). Poor readers don't get to read much in reading group. *Language Arts, 57,* 872–876.

Allington, R. L. (1983). The reading instruction provided readers of differing abilities. *Elementary School Journal, 83,* 548–559.

Allington, R. L., & McGill-Franzen, A. (1989). Different programs, indifferent instruction. In D. Lipsky & A. Gartner (Eds.), *Beyond separate education* (pp. 73–97). New York: Brooks.

Anders, P. L., Bos, C. S., & Filip, D. (1984). The effect of semantic feature analysis on reading comprehension of learning disabled students. In J. Niles (Ed.), *Changing perspectives on research in reading/language processing and instruction,* Thirty-third yearbook of the National Reading Conference (pp. 162–166). Rochester, NY: National Reading Conference.

Anderson, L. (1984). The environment of instruction: The function of seatwork in a commercially developed curriculum. In G. G. Duffy, L. R. Roehler, & J. Mason (Eds.), *Comprehension Instruction.* New York: Longman.

Anderson, T. H. (1980). Studies and adjunct aids. In R. J. Spiro, B. C. Bruce, & W. F. Brewer (Eds.), *Theoretical issues in reading comprehension* (pp. 483–502). Hillsdale, NJ: Erlbaum.

Anderson, T. H., Armbruster, B. B., & Kanton, R. N. (1980). *How clearly written are childrens' textbooks? Or, of bladderworts and alpha* (Technical Report No. 16). Urbana: University of Illinois, Center for the Study of Reading.

Armbruster, B. (May 1985). *Of living stuff and golden spikes, or why Johnny can't read science and social studies textbooks.* Paper presented at the Sixth Conference on Reading Research, Center for the Study of Reading, New Orleans, LA, May.

Armbruster, B. B., & Anderson, T. H. (1980). *The effect of mapping on the free recall of expository text* (Technical Report No. 160). Urbana: University of Illinois, Center for the Study of Reading.

Armbruster, B. B., & Gubrandsen, B. (1984). *Reading comprehension instruction in social studies programs, or on making mobiles out of soapsuds.* (Technical Report No. 309). Urbana: University of Illinois, Center for the Study of Reading.

Au, K. H. (1979). Using the experience–text relationship method with minority children. *The Reading Teacher, 32,* 677–679.

Baker, J. M., & Zigmond, N. (1990). Are regular education classes equipped to accommodate students with learning disabilities? *Exceptional Children, 56,* 515–526.

Barr, R. (1982). Classroom reading instruction from a sociological perspective. *Journal of Reading Behavior, 14,* 375–389.

Barron, R. (1969). The use of vocabulary as an advance organizer. In H. Herber & P. Sanders (Eds.), *Research in reading in the content areas: First year report.* Syracuse, NY: Syracuse University, Reading and Language Arts Center.

Barron, R., & Earle, R. (1973). An approach for vocabulary instruction. In H. Herber & R. Barron (Eds.), *Research in reading in the content areas; Second year report* (pp. 84–100). Syracuse, NY: Syracuse University Reading and Language Arts Center.

Bartlett, B. J. (1978). *Top-level structure as an organizational strategy for recall of classroom text.* Unpublished doctoral dissertation, Arizona State University, Tempe.

Baumann, J. F. (1983). A generic comprehension instructional strategy. *Reading World, 22,* 234–294.

Baumann, J. F. (1984). The effectiveness of a direct instruction paradigm for teaching main idea comprehension. *Reading Research Quarterly, 20,* 93–115.

Baumann, J. F., & Schmitt, M. C. (1986). The what, why, how and when of comprehension instruction. *The Reading Teacher, 39,* 640–645.

Beck, I. L., McKeown, M. G., McCaslin, E. S., & Burkes, A. M. (1979). *Instructional dimensions that may affect reading comprehension: Examples from two commercial reading programs.* Pittsburgh: University of Pittsburgh Learning Research and Development Center.

Beck, I. L., Perfetti, C. A., & McKeown, M. G. (1982). Effects of long-term vocabulary instruction on lexical access and reading comprehension. *Journal of Educational Psychology, 74,* 506–521.

Becker, W. C., & Carnine, D. (1980). Direct instruction: An effective approach for education intervention with the disadvantaged and low performers. In B. J. Lahey & A. F. Kazdin (Eds.), *Advances in Child Psychology* (PP. 429–473). New York: Plenum Press.

Bergerud, D., Lovitt, T. C., & Horton, S. V. (1988). The effectiveness of textbook adaptations in life science for high school students with learning disabilities. *Journal of Reading, Writing, and Learning Disabilities, 21,* 70–76.

Billingsley, B. S., & Wildman, T. M. (1988). The effects of prereading activities on the comprehension monitoring of learning disabled adolescents. *Learning Disabilities Quarterly, 4,* 36–44.

Billingsley, B. C., & Wildman, T. M. (1990). Facilitating reading comprehension in learning disabled students: Metacognitive goals and instructional strategies. *Remedial and Special Education, 11*(2), 18–31.

Blanton, L. P. (1988). Special education: Reading curriculum and instruction. In T. Husen & N. Postlethwaite (Eds.), *International encyclopedia of education: Research and studies supplement* (vol. 1, pp. 625–629). New York: Pergamon Press.

Blanton, L. P., & Semmel, M. I. (1987). Research on the reading of mildly mentally retarded learners: A synthesis of the empirical literature. In S. Rosenberg (Ed.), *Advances in applied psycholinguistics: Vol. 2. Reading, writing, and language learning* (pp. 70–104). New York: Cambridge University Press.

Blanton, L. P., Sitko, M. C., & Gillespie, P. (1976). Reading and the mildly retarded: Review of research and implications. In L. Mann & D., Sabatino (Eds.), *The third review of special education* (pp. 143–162). New York: Grune and Stratton.

Blanton, W. E., & Moorman, G. B. (1990). The presentation of reading lessons. *Reading Research and Instruction, 29,* 33–55.

Blanton, W., Moorman, G., & Wood, K. (1986). A model of direct instruction applied to the basal skills lesson. *The Reading Teacher, 40,* 299–304.

Blanton, W. E., Wood, K. D., & Moorman, G. B. (1990). The role of purpose in reading. *The Reading Teacher, 43,* 436–493.

Borkowski, J. G., Weyhing, R. S., & Turner, L. A. (1986). Attributional retraining and the teaching of strategies. *Exceptional Children, 53*(2), 130–137.

Bos, C. S., & Anders, P. L. (1990a). Effects of interactive vocabulary instruction on the vocabulary learning and reading comprehension of junior-high learning disabled students. *Learning Disability Quarterly, 13,* 31–42.

Bos, C. S., & Anders, P. L. (1990b). Toward an interactive model: Teaching text-based concepts to learning disabled students. In H. L. Swanson & B. Keogh (Eds.), *Learning disabilities: Theoretical and research issues* (pp. 247–261). Hillsdale, NJ: Erlbaum.

Bos, C. S., Anders, P. L., Filip, D., & Jaffe, L. E. (1985). Semantic feature analysis and long-term learning. In J. Niles (Ed.), *Issues in literacy: A research perspective,* Thirty-fourth yearbook of the National Reading Conference (pp. 42–47). Rochester, NY: National Reading Conference.

Bristo, P. S. (1985). Are poor readers passive readers? Some evidence, possible explanations, and potential solutions. *The Reading Teacher, 39,* 318–325.

Brophy, J. (1988). Research linking teacher behavior to student achievement: Potential implications for instruction of Chapter 1 students. *Educational Psychologist, 23*(3), 235–286.

Brophy, J., & Evertson, C. (1976). *Learning from teaching: A developmental perspective.* Boston: Allyn and Bacon.

Carnine, D., Kameenui, E. J, & Woolfson, N. (1982). Training of textual dimensions related to text-based inferences. *Journal of Reading Behavior, 14,* 335–340.

Carnine, D., & Kinder, D. (1985). Teaching low-performing students to apply generative and schema strategies to narrative and expository material. *Remedial and Special Education, 6,* 20–30.

Christenson, S. L., Ysseldyke, J. E., & Thurlow, M. L. (1989). Critical instructional factors for students with mild handicaps: An integrative review. *Remedial and Special Education, 10*(5), 21–31.

Clarke, J., Raths, J., & Gilbert, G. (1989). Inductive towers: Letting students see how they think.

Journal of Reading, 33, 86–95.

Clay, M. (1985). *The early detection of reading difficulties: A diagnostic survey with recovery procedures.* Auckland, NZ: Heinemann Educational Books.

Cole, J., & Sticht, T. (Eds.). (1981). *The textbook in American Society, A volume based on a conference at the Library of Congress on May 2–3, 1979.* Washington, DC: Library of Congress.

Crissmore, A. (1985). Special education materials: Patterns, problems and potential. In J. Harste & D. Stephens (Eds.), *Toward a practical theory: A state of practice assessment of reading comprehension instruction* (7:1–64). Bloomington: Indiana University, Language Education Department.

Cunningham, D., & Shablak, S. (1975). Selective Reading Guide-o-rama. *Journal of Reading, 18,* 380–382.

Darch, C., & Carnine, D. (1986). Teaching content area material to learning disabled students. *Exceptional Children, 53,* 240–246.

Darch, C., & Gersten, R. (1986). Direction-setting activities in reading comprehension: A comparison of two approaches. *Learning Disability Quarterly, 9,* 235–243.

Davey, B. (1986). Using textbook activity guides to help students learn from textbooks. *Journal of Reading, 29,* 489–494.

Davey, B. (1989). Active responding in content classrooms. *Journal of Reading, 33,* 44–46.

DeFord, D. E., Pinell, G. S., Lyons, C. A., & Young, P. (1987). *Ohio's reading recovery program: Vol. III. Report of the follow-up studies.* Columbus: Ohio State University.

Derry, S. J. (1990). Remediating academic difficulties through strategy training: The acquisition of useful knowledge. *Remedial and Special Education, 11*(6), 19–31.

Dimino, J., Gersten, R., Carnine, D., & Blake, G. (1990). Story grammar: An approach from promoting at-risk secondary students' comprehension of literature. *Elementary School Journal, 91,* 19–32.

Duffy, G., & McIntyre, L. (1982). A naturalistic study of instructional assistance in primary grade reading. *Elementary School Journal, 83,* 15–23.

Duffy, G. G., & Roehler, L. R. (1986). Improving reading instruction through the use of responsive elaboration. *The Reading Teacher, 40,* 514–519.

Duffy, G., & Roehler, L. (1987). Teaching reading skills as strategies. *The Reading Teacher, 40,* 414–418.

Duffy, G., Roehler, L., Sivan, E., Rackliffe, G., Book C., Meloth, M. S., Varvus, L. G., Wesselman, R., Putnam, J., & Bassiri, D. (1987). Effects of explaining the reasoning associated with reading strategies. *Reading Research Quarterly, 22,* 347–366.

Durkin, D. (1974a). Some questions about questionable instructional materials. *The Reading Teacher, 28,* 13–17.

Durkin, D. (1974b). Phonics: Instruction that needs to be improved. *The Reading Teacher, 28,* 152–156.

Durkin, D. (1974c). After ten years; Where are we now in reading? *The Reading Teacher, 28,* 262–267.

Durkin, D. (1975a). The importance of goals for reading instruction. *The Reading Teacher, 28,* 380–383.

Durkin, D. (1975b). The little things make a difference. *The Reading Teacher, 28,* 473–477.

Durkin, D. (1978–1979). What classroom observations reveal about reading comprehension instruction. *Reading Research Quarterly, 14,* 481–533.

Durkin, D. (1984). Is there a match between what elementary teachers do and what basal reader manuals recommend? *The Reading Teacher, 37,* 734–744.

Edgar, E. (1990). Employment as an outcome for mildly handicapped students: Current status and future directions. *Focus on Exceptional Children, 21,* 1–8.

Elliot, D. L., Nagel, k., & Woodward, A. (1986). Scientific illiteracy in elementary school science textbook programs. *Journal of Curriculum Studies, 19,* 73–76.

Ellis, E. S., Deshler, D. D., Lenz, B. K., Schumaker, J. B., & Clark, F. L. (1991). An instructional model for teaching learning disabilities. *Focus on Exceptional Children, 23*(6), 1–23.

Englert, C. S., Raphael, T. E., Anderson, L. M., Gregg, S. L., & Anthony, H. M. (1989). Exposition: Reading, writing, and the metacognitive knowledge of learning disabled students. *Learning Disabilities Research, 5,* 5–24.

Englert, C. S., & Thomas, C. C. (1987). Sensitivity to text structure in reading between learning disabled and non–learning disabled students.

Learning Disability Quarterly, 10, 93–105.

EPIE Institute (1977). *Report on national study of the nature and the quality of instructional materials most used by teachers and learners.* (EPIE Report No. 7). Stonybrook, NY: Author.

Fielding, L. G., Wilson, P. T., & Anderson, R. C. (1986). A new focus on free reading: The role of trade books on reading instruction. In T. Raphael (Ed.), *The contexts of school-based literacy* (pp. 149–160). New York: Random House.

Fitzgerald, J. (1983). Helping readers gain self-control over reading comprehension. *The Reading Teacher, 37,* 249–253.

Fourgurean, J. M., & LaCourt, T. (1990). A follow-up of former special education students: A model for program evaluation. *Remedial and Special Education, 12,* 16–23.

Frudden, S. J., & Healy, H. A. (1987). Effective teaching research: Its application to special education teacher training. *Contemporary Education, 57*(3), 150–154.

Garner, R., Hare, V. C., Alexander, P., Haynes, J., & Winograd, P. (1984). Inducing use of a text lookback strategy among unsuccessful readers. *American Educational Research Journal, 21,* 789–798.

Gelzheiser, L. M., & Meyers, J. (1991). Reading instruction by classroom, remedial, and resource room teachers. *Journal of Special Education, 24,* 512–526.

Gerber, M. M. (1986). Cognitive behavioral training in the curriculum: Time, slow learners, and basic skills. *Focus on Exceptional Children, 18*(6), 1–12.

Gersten, R., & Carnine, D. (1986). Direct instruction in reading comprehension. *Educational Leadership, 43,* 70–78.

Gersten, R., Walker, H., & Darch, C. (1988). Relationship between teachers' effectiveness and their tolerance for handicapped students. *Exceptional Children, 54*(5), 433–438.

Geva, E. (1983). Facilitating reading comprehension through flow-charting. *Reading Research Quarterly, 18,* 384–405.

Goetz, E. T., Schallert, D. L., Reynolds, R. E., & Radin, D. J. (1983). Reading in perspective: What real cops and real burglars look for in a story. *Journal of Educational Psychology, 75,* 500–510.

Good, T. (1979). Teacher effectiveness in the elementary school. *Journal of Teacher Education, 30,* 52–64.

Goodlad, J. I. (1976). *Facing the future: Issues in education and schooling.* New York: McGraw-Hill.

Goodlad, J. (1984). *A place called school.* New York: McGraw-Hill.

Goodman, L. (1990). *Time and learning in the special education classroom.* Albany: State University of New York Press.

Graham, S., & Johnson, L. A. (1989). Teaching reading to learning disabled students: A review of research-supported procedures. *Focus on Exceptional Children, 21*(6), 1–12.

Graves, M. F., Prenn, M. C., & Cooke, C. L. (1985). The coming attraction: Previewing short stories. *Journal of Reading, 28,* 594–598.

Guthrie, J. T., Martuza, V., & Seifert, M. (1979). Impacts of instructional time in reading. In L. B. Resnick & P. A. Weaver (Eds.), *Theory and practice of early reading* (vol. 3, pp. 153–178). Hillsdale, NJ: Erlbaum.

Hare, V. C., & Borchardt, K. M. (1984). Direct instruction of summarization skills. *Reading Research Quarterly, 20,* 62–78.

Harris, A. J., & Serwer, B. L. (1966). The CRAFT Project: Instructional time in reading research. *Reading Research Quarterly, 2,* 27–57.

Harris, K. R., & Pressley, M. (1991). The nature of cognitive strategy instruction: Interactive strategy construction. *Exceptional Children, 57*(5), 392–404.

Haynes, M. C., & Jenkins, J. R. (1986). Reading instruction in special education resource rooms. *American Educational Research Journal, 23,* 161–190.

Heimlich, J. E., & Pittelman, S. D. (1986). *Semantic mapping: Classroom applications.* Newark, DE: International Reading Association.

Herber, H. L. (1978). *Teaching reading in the content areas.* Englewood Cliffs, NJ: Prentice-Hall.

Herber, H. L., & Nelson-Herber, J. (1987). Developing independent learners. *Journal of Reading, 30,* 584–588.

Holdaway, D. (1980). *Independence in reading.* Exeter, NH: Heinemann.

Horton, S. V., & Lovitt, T. C. (1989). Using guides with three classifications of secondary students. *The Journal of Special Education, 22,* 447–462.

Hunt, L. C. (1970). Effects of self selection, interest

and motivation upon independent, instructional and frustration levels. *The Reading Teacher, 24,* 146–151.

Idol, L. (1987a). A critical thinking map to improve content area comprehension of poor readers. *Remedial and Special Education, 8,* 28–40.

Idol, L. (1987b). Group story mapping: A comprehension strategy for both skilled and unskilled readers. *Journal of Learning Disabilities, 20,* 196–205.

Idol, L., & Croll, J. (1987). Story-mapping training as a means of improving reading comprehension. *Learning Disability Quarterly, 10,* 214–229.

Idol-Maestas, L. (1985). Getting ready to read: Guided probing for poor comprehenders. *Learning Disability Quarterly, 8,* 243–254.

Johnson, D. D., & Pearson, P. D. (1984a). *Teaching reading vocabulary.* New York: Holt, Rinehart, & Winston.

Johnson, D. D., & Pearson, P. D. (1984b). *Teaching reading vocabulary,* 2nd ed. New York: Holt, Rinehart, & Winston.

Johnston, P. (1984). Background knowledge, reading comprehension and test bias. *Reading Research Quarterly, 19,* 219–239.

Johnston, P., & Pearson, P. D. (1982). *Prior knowledge, connectivity, and the assessment of reading comprehension* (Technical Report No. 235). Urbana: University of Illinois, Center for the Study of Reading.

Johnston, P. H., & Winograd, P. N. (1985). Passive failure in reading. *Journal of Reading Behavior, 17*(4), 279–301.

Jones, B. F. (1986). SPaRCS procedure. In A. Palincsar, D. Ogle, B. F. Jones, & E. Carr (Eds.), *Teaching reading as thinking* (pp. 18–27). Alexandria, VA: Association for Supervision and Curriculum Development.

Jones, B. F., Amiran, M., & Katims, M. (1985). Teaching cognitive strategies and text structures. In J. S. Segal, S. F. Chipman, & R. Glaser (Eds.), *Learning and thinking skills: Vol. 1. Relating instruction to research* (pp. 259–290). Hillsdale, NJ: Erlbaum.

Jones, B. F., Pierce, J., & Hunter, B. (1988–1989). Teaching students to construct graphic representations. *Educational Leadership, 46,* 20–25.

Kameenui, E. J., Carnine, D. W., & Freschi, R. (1982). Effects of text construction and instructional procedures for teaching word meanings on compre-hension and recall. *Reading Research Quarterly, 17,* 367–388.

Karlin, R. (1964). *Teaching reading in high school.* New York: Bobbs-Merrill.

Kintsch, W., & van Dijk, T. (1978). Toward a model of text comprehension. *Psychological Review, 85,* 363–394.

LaBerge, D., & Samuels, S. J. (1974). Toward a theory of automatic information processing in reading. *Cognitive Psychology, 6,* 293–323.

Lahaderne, H. M. (1968). Attitudinal and intellectual correlates of attention: A study of sixth grade classrooms. *Journal of Educational Psychology, 59,* 320–324.

Larrivee, B. (1989). Effective strategies for academically handicapped students in the regular classroom. In R. E. Slavin, N. L. Karweit, & N. A. Madden (Eds.), *Effective programs for students at risk* (pp. 291–319). Boston: Allyn and Bacon.

Laughton, J., & Morris, N. T. (1989). Story grammar knowledge of learning disabled students. *Learning Disabilities Research, 4,* 87–95.

Leinhardt, G., & Bickel, W. (1987). Instruction's the thing wherein to catch the mind that falls behind. *Educational Psychologist, 22*(2), 177–207.

Leinhardt, G., Zignance, N., & Cooley, W. W. (1981). Reading instruction and its effects. *American Educational Research Journal, 18,* 343–361.

Lenz, B. K., Alley, G. R., & Schumaker, J. B. (1987). *Learning Disability Quarterly, 10,* 53–67.

Lesgold, A. M., & Perfetti, C. A. (1978). Interactive processes in reading comprehension. *Discourse Processes, 1,* 323–326.

Lindsey, J. (1980). Effects of direction, text organization, and age level on reading comprehension. *Reading Improvement, 17,* 219–223.

Lovitt, T. C., & Horton, S. V. (1988). How to develop study guides. *Journal of Reading, Writing, and Learning Disabilities, 2,* 213–221.

Lovitt, T. C., Rudsit, J., Jenkins, J., Pious, C., & Benedetti, D. (1986). Adapting science materials for regular and learning disabled seventh graders. *Remedial and Special Education, 7,* 31–39.

Luftig, R. L., & Johnson, R. E. (1982). Identification and recall of structurally important units in prose by mentally retarded learners. *American Journal of Mental Deficiency, 86,* 495–502.

MacMillan, D. L., Keogh, B. K., & Jones, R. L. 1986). Special educational research on mildly handicappped learners. In M. C. Wittrock (Ed.), *Handbook of research on teaching* (pp. 686–724). New York: Macmillan.

Madden, N. A., Slavin, R. E., Livermon, B. J., Karweit, N. L., & Stevens, R. J. (1987). *Success for all: Teacher's manual for reading.* Baltimore: Johns Hopkins University, Center for Research on Elementary and Middle Schools.

Mason, J. (1984). An examination of reading instruction in third and fourth grades. *The Reading Teacher, 36,* 906–913.

Meyer, B. J. F., & Freedle, R. O. (1984). Effects of discourse type on recall. *American Educational Research Journal, 2,* 121–143.

Mikulecky, L. (1982). Job literacy: The relationship between school preparation and workplace actuality. *Reading Research Quarterly, 17,* 400–419.

Miller, P. H. (1985). Metacognition and attention. In D. L. Forrest-Pressley, G. E. MacKinnon, & T. G. Waller (Eds.), *Metacognition, cognition, and human performance: Vol. 2. Instructional practices* (pp. 137–180). New York: Academic Press.

Miramontes, O., Cheng, L., & Trueba, H. (1984). Teacher perceptions and observed outcomes: An ethnographic study of classroom interactions. *Learning Disability Quarterly, 7,* 349–357.

Moore, P. J. (1988). Reciprocal teaching and reading comprehension: A review. *Journal of Research in Reading, 11,* 3–14.

Neilsen, A., Rennie, B., & Connell, A. (1982). Allocation of instructional time to reading comprehension and study skills in intermediate grade social studies classrooms. In J. Mills & L. Harris (Eds.), *New inquiries in reading research and instruction* (pp. 81–84). Rochester, New York: National Conference.

Nicholls, J. (1983). Conceptions of ability and achievement: A theory and its implications for education. In S. Paris, G. Olson, & H. Stevenson (Eds.), *Learning and motivation in the classroom* (pp. 211–237). Hillsdale, NJ: Erlbaum.

Ogle, D. (1986). K-W-L: A teaching model that develops active reading of expository text. *The Reading Teacher, 39,* 564–567.

Palincsar, A., & Brown, A. (1984). Reciprocal teaching of comprehension-fostering and comprehension-monitoring activities. *Cognition and Instruction, 1,* 117–175.

Palincsar, A. S., & Brown, A. L. (1988). Teaching and practicing thinking skills to promote comprehension in the context of group problem solving. *Remedial and Special Education, 9,* 53–59.

Pany, D., & Jenkins, J. R. (1978). Learning word meanings: A comparison of instructional procedures and effects on measures of reading comprehension with learning disabled students. *Learning Disability Quarterly, 1,* 21–32.

Paris, S. G. (1987). *Reading and thinking strategies.* Lexington, MA: Colamore Educational Publishing.

Paris, S. G. (1988). Models and metaphors of learning strategies. In C. E. Weinstein, E. T. Goetz, & P. A. Alexander (Eds.), *Learning and study strategies: Issues in assessment, instruction, and evaluation* (pp. 299–321). New York: Academic Press.

Paris, S. G., Cross, D. R., & Lipson, M. E. (1984). Informed strategies for learning: A program to improve children's reading awareness and comprehension. *Journal of Educational Psychology, 76,* 1239–1252.

Paris, S. G., Lipson, M. Y., & Wixon, K. K. (1983). *Contemporary Educational Psychology, 8,* 293–316.

Paris, S. G., & Newman, R. S. (1990). Developmental aspects of self-regulated learning. *Educational Psychologist, 25,* 87–102.

Paris, S. G., & Oka, E. R. (1986). Self-regulated learning among exceptional children. *Exceptional Children, 53*(2), 103–108.

Paris, S. G., & Winograd, P. (1990a). How metacognition can promote academic learning and instruction. In B. F. Jones & L. Idol (Eds.), *Dimensions of thinking and cognitive instruction* (pp. 15–51). Hillsdale, NJ: Erlbaum.

Paris, S. G., & Winograd, P. (1990b). Promoting metacognition and motivation of exceptional children. *Remedial and Special Education, 11*(6), 7–15.

Patching, W., Kameenui, E., Carnine, D., Gersten, R., & Colvin, G. (1983). Direct instruction in critical reading skills. *Reading Research Quarterly, 18,* 406–418.

Pearson, P.D. (1982). *Asking questions about stories* (Ginn Occasional Papers, No. 15). Lexington, MA: Ginn.

Pearson, P. D., & Dole, J. (1988). Explicit comprehension instruction: A review of research and a new conceptualization of instruction. *Elementary School Journal, 88,* 151–165.

Pearson, P. D., & Gallagher, M. C. (1983). The instruction of reading comprehension. *Contemporary Educational Psychology, 8,* 317–344.

Pearson, P. D., Roehler, L. R., Dole, J. A., & Duffy, G. G. (1990). *Developing expertise in reading comprehension: What should be taught? How should it be taught?* (Technical Report No. 512). Champaign: University of Illinois, Center for the Study of Reading.

Peleg, Z. R., & Moore, R. F. (1982). Effects of the advance organizer with oral and written presentation on recall and inference of EMR adolescents. *American Journal of Mental Deficiency, 86,* 621–626.

Picarello, K. (1986). Drop Everything and Read. *The Reading Teacher, 39,* 871–872.

Pichert, J. W., & Anderson, R. C. (1977). Taking different perspectives on a story. *Journal of Educational Psychology, 69,* 309–315.

Pinnell, G. S., DeFord, D. E., & Lyons, C. A. (1988). *Reading Recovery: An early intervention for at-risk first graders.* Arlington, VA: Educational Research Service.

Pressley, M. (1990). Four more considerations about self-regulation among mentally retarded persons. *American Journal on Mental Retardation, 94*(4), 369–371.

Pressley, M., Goodchild, F., Fleet, J., Zajchowski, R., & Evans, E. D. (1989). The challenges of classroom strategy instruction. *The Elementary School Journal, 89*(3), 301–342.

Raphael, T. (1986). Teachinbg question–answer relationships, revisited. *The Reading Teacher, 39,* 516–522.

Raphael, T. E., & Englert, C. S. (1988). *Integrating writing and reading instruction.* (Occasional Paper No. 118). East Lansing: Michigan State University, Institute for Research on Teaching.

Raphael, T. E., & Pearson, P. E. (1985). Increasing students' awareness of sources of information for answering questions. *American Educational Research Journal, 20,* 282–296.

Raphael, T. E., & Wonnacott, C. A. (1985). Heightening fourth-grade students' sensitivity to sources of information for answering comprehension questions. *Reading Research Quarterly, 21,* 282–296.

Ratekin, N., Simpson, M. L., Alvermann, D. E., &

Dishner, E. K. (1985). Why teachers resist content reading instruction. *Journal of Reading, 28,* 432–437.

Reeve, R. A., & Brown, A. L. (1985). Metacognition reconsidered: Implications for intervention research. *Journal of Abnormal Child Psychology, 13,* 343–356.

Reschly, D. J. (1987). Learning characteristics of mildly handicapped students: Implications for classification, placement, and programming. In M. C. Wang, M. C. Reynolds, & H. J. Walberg (Eds.), *Handbook of special education research and practice: Vol. 1. Learner characteristics and adaptive education* (pp. 35–58). New York: Pergamon Press.

Rosenblatt, L. M. (1978). *The reader, the text, the poem.* Carbondale: Southern Illinois University.

Rosenshine, B. V., & Berliner, D. C. (1978). Academic engaged time. *British Journal of Teacher Education, 4,* 3–16.

Rowe, D. W. (1985). Literacy: What messages are we sending? In J. Harste & D. Stephens (Eds.), *Toward practical theory: A state of practice assessment of reading comprehension instruction* (3:1–27). Bloomington: Indiana University, Language Education Department.

Rumelhart, D. E. (1980). Schemata: The building blocks of cognition. In R. J. Spiro, B. C. Bruce, & W. F. Brewer (Eds.), *Theoretical issues in reading comprehension* (pp. 33–58). Hillsdale, NJ: Erlbaum.

Rupley, W. H., & Blair, T. R. (1987). Assignment and supervision of reading seatwork: Looking at twelve primary teachers. *The Reading Teacher, 40,* 391–393.

Sacks, A. (1983). The effects of three prereading activities on learning disabled students' reading comprehension. *Learning Disability Quarterly, 6,* 248–251.

Sacks, A. (1984). Accessing scripts before reading the story. *Learning Disability Quarterly, 7,* 226–228.

Samuels, S. J. (1987). Why it is difficult to characterize the underlying cognitive deficits in special education populations. *Exceptional Children, 54*(1), 60–62.

Samuels, S. J., & Turnure, J. E. (1974). Attention and reading achievement in first grade boys and girls. *Journal of Educational Psychology, 66,* 29–32.

Santa, C. (1988). *Content reading including study*

systems. Dubuque, IA: Kendall/Hunt.

Schmitt, M. C., & Baumann, J. F. (1986). How to incorporate comprehension monitoring strategies into basal reader instruction. *The Reading Teacher, 40*, 28–31.

Scruggs, T. E., & Brigham, F. J. (1990). The challenges of metacognitive instruction. *Remedial and Special Education, 11*(6), 16–31.

Scruggs, T. E., & Mastropieri, M. A. (1990). The case for mnemonic instruction: From laboratory research to classroom applications. *Journal of Special Education, 24*(1), 7–32.

Semmel, M. I., Gottlieb, J., & Robinson, N. M. (1979). Mainstreaming: Perspectives on educating handicapped children in the public school. In D. Berliner (Ed.), *Review of research in education* (Vol. 7, pp. 223–279). Washington: American Educational Research Association.

Shannon, P. (1983). The use of commercial materials in American elementary schools. *Reading Research Quarterly, 19*, 68–85.

Short, E. J., Cuddy, C. L., Friebert, S. E., & Schatschneider, C. W. (1990). The diagnostic and educational utility of thinking aloud during problem solving. In H. L. Swanson & B. Keogh (Eds.), *Learning disabilities: Theoretical and research issues* (pp. 93–109). Hillsdale, NJ: Erlbaum.

Shuell, T. J. (1986). Cognitive conceptions of learning. *Review of Educational Research, 56*(4), 411–436.

Sinatra, R. C., Berg, D., & Dunn, R. (1985). Semantic mapping improves reading comprehension of learning disabled students. *Teaching Exceptional Children, 17*, 310–314.

Singer, H., & Donlan, D. (1980). *Reading and learning from text*. Boston: Little, Brown.

Slavin, R. E., & Madden, N. A. (1989). What works for students at risk: A research synthesis. *Educational Leadership, 46*, 4–12.

Smith, F., & Feathers, K. (1983). The role of reading in content classrooms: Assumption vs. reality. *Journal of Reading, 27*, 262–267.

Snider, V. E., & Tarver, S. G. (1987). The effect of early reading failure on acquisition of knowledge among students with learning disabilities. *Journal of Learning Disabilities, 20*(6), 351–356, 373.

Stanovich, K. E. (1985). Cognitive determinants of reading in mentally retarded individuals. In N. R. Ellis & N. W. Bray (Eds.), *International review of research in mental retardation* (pp. 181–214). New York: Academic Press.

Stauffer, R. G. (1969). *Directing the reading-thinking process*. New York: Harper & Row.

Sternberg, R. J., & Wagner, R. K. (1982). Automatization failure in learning disabilities. *Topics in Learning and Learning Disabilities, 2*, 1–11.

Stephens, D., & Clyde, J. A. (1985). Curriculum as theory driven: Insights from six classrooms. In J. C. Harste & D. Stephens (Eds.), *Toward practical theory: A state of practice assessment of reading comprehension instruction* (Vol. 2, pp. 1–41). Bloomington: Indiana University, Language Education Department.

Stevens, K. C. (1982). Can we improve reading by teaching background information? *Journal of Reading, 25*, 326–329.

Stevens, R. J., Madden, N. A., Slavin, R. E., & Farnish, A. M. (1987). Cooperative integrated reading and composition: Two field experiments. *Reading Research Quarterly, 22*, 433–454.

Taba, H. (1967). *Teacher's handbook for elementary social studies*. Reading, MA: Addison-Wesley.

Taylor, B. M. (1982). Text structure and childrens' comprehension and memory for expository material. *Journal of Educational Psychology, 74*, 323–340.

Taylor, B. M., & Beach, R. (1984). The effects of text structure instruction on middle grade students' comprehension and production of expository text. *Reading Research Quarterly, 19*, 134–146.

Taylor, B. M., & Samuels, S. J. (1983). Children's use of text structure in the recall of expository material. *American Educational Research Journal, 20*, 517–528.

Tharp, R. G., Jordan, C., Speidel, G. E., Au, K. H., Klein, T. W., Calkins, R. P., Sloat, K. C., & Gallimore, R. (1984). Product and process in applied developmental research: Education and the children of a minority. In M. E. Lamb, A. L. Brown, & B. Rogoff (Eds.), *Advances in developmental psychology* (Vol. 3, pp. 91–141). Hillsdale, NJ: Erlbaum.

Thomas, A., & Pashley, B. (1982). Effects of classroom training on LD students' task persistence and attributions. *Learning Disability Quarterly, 5*, 133–144.

Thurlow, M., Graden, J., Ysseldyke, J. E., & Algozzine, R. (1984). Student reading during reading class: The last activity during reading instruction.

Journal of Educational Research, 77, 267–272.

Thurlow, M. L., Ysseldyke, J. E., Graden, J., & Algozzine, B. (1984). Opportunity to learn for LD students receiving different levels of special education. *Learning Disability Quarterly, 7,* 55–67.

Tierney, R. J., & Cunningham, J. W. (1984). Research on teaching reading comprehension. In P. D. Pearson (Ed.), *Handbook of reading research* (pp. 609–655). New York: Longman.

U.S. Department of Education. (1991). Office of Special Education Programs, U.S. Office of Special Education and Rehabilitative Services, Thirteenth Annual Report to Congress on the Implementation of the Individuals with Disabilities Education Act. Washington, DC: U.S. Government Printing Office.

Vacca, R. T. (1981). *Content area reading.* Boston: Little, Brown.

Varnhagen, C. K., & Goldman, S. R. (1986). Improving comprehension: Causal relations instruction for learning handicapped learners. *The Reading Teacher, 39,* 896–904.

Wang, M. C., & Peverly, S. T. (1987). The role of the learner: An individual difference variable in school learning and functioning. In M. C. Wang, M. C. Reynolds, & H. J. Walberg (Eds.), *Handbook of special education research and practice: Vol. 1. Learner characteristics and adaptive education* (pp. 59–92). New York: Pergamon Press.

Weinstein, C. E., & Mayer, R. E. (1986). The teaching of learning strategies. In M. C. Wittrock (Ed.), *Handbook of research on teaching* (pp. 315–327). New York: Macmillan.

Whitman, T. L. (1990). Self-regulation and mental retardation. *American Journal on Mental Retardation, 94*(4). 347–362.

Williams, J. P. (1986). Teaching children to identify the main idea in expository texts. *Exceptional Children, 53,* 163–168.

Wineburg, S. S. (1987). The self-fulfillment of the self-fulfilling prophecy. *Educational Researcher, 16*(9), 28–37.

Winograd, P., & Hare, V. C. (1988). Direct instruction of reading comprehension strategies: The nature of teacher explanation. In E. T. Goetz, P. Alexander, & C. Weinstein (Eds.), *Learning and study strategies: assessment, instruction, and evaluation* (pp. 121–139). New York: Academic Press.

Wiesendanger, K., & Birlem, E. (1981). An initial look at the reading approaches and grouping patterns used in primary grades. *Reading Horizons, 22,* 54–58.

Wong, B. Y. L. (1985). Metacognition and learning disabilities. In D. L. Forrest-Pressley, G. E. MacKinnon, & T. G. Waller (Eds.), *Metacognition, cognition, and human performance: Vol. 2. Instructional practices* (pp. 137–180). New York: Academic Press.

Wong, B. Y. L. (1986). Metacognition and special education: A review of a view. *Journal of Special Education, 20*(1), 9–29.

Wong, J. A., & Au, K. H. (1985). The concept-text-application approach: Helping elementary students comprehend expository text. *The Reading Teacher, 38,* 612–618.

Wood, K. D. (1988). Guiding students through information text. *The Reading Teacher, 41,* 912–920.

Wood, K. D. (1990). The collaborative listening viewing guide: An aid for notetaking. *Middle School Journal, 22,* 53–56.

Woodward, A. (1986). Overprogrammed materials: Taking the teacher out of teaching. *American Educator, 10,* 26–31.

Ysseldyke, J. E., & Christenson, S. L. (1987). Evaluating students' instructional environments. *Remedial and Special Education, 8*(3), 17–24.

Ysseldyke, J. E., Christenson, S. L., Thurlow, M. L., & Blackwell, D. (1989). Are different kinds of instructional tasks used by different categories of students in different settings? *School Psychology Review, 18*(1), 98–111.

Ysseldyke, J. E., Thurlow, M. L., Mecklenburg, C., & Graden, J. (1984). Opportunity to learn for regular and special education students during reading instruction. *Remedial and Special Education, 5,* 29–37.

Zigmond, N. (1990). Rethinking secondary school programs for students with learning disabilities. *Focus on Exceptional Children, 23*(1), 1–22.

Zigmond, N., Sansone, J., Miller, S. E., Donahoe, K. A., & Kohnke, R. (1986). Teaching learning disabled students at the secondary school level: What research says to teachers. *Learning Disabled Focus, 1*(2), 108–115.

What Research in Special Education Says to Reading Teachers

LAWRENCE J. O'SHEA   *DOROTHY J. O'SHEA*
Florida Atlantic University

Key Concepts

- NAK approaches
- Gillingham Stillman method
- Hemisphere dominance
- Fernald VAKT method
- Kephart Perceptual Motor
- Frostig method
- Perceptual constancy
- Hemispheric routing
- Scotopic sensitivity
- Modified alphabet
- Modeling

- Multisensory instructional approaches
- Behavioral based instructional approaches
- Telescoping
- Precision teaching
- Generalization
- Holistic-based instructional approach
- Scaffolding
- Whole language approach
- Reciprocal teaching
- Direct instruction

Focusing Questions

- List some multisensory instructional approaches and methods for reading and explain their theoretical background.

- How can scotopic sensitivity inhibit a reader's ability? What are some symptoms?
- What are instructional aims based on and how are they helpful in instructional strategies?
- What is the primary objective of the cognitive/metacognitive-based instructional approach? Give examples of such an approach.
- List and explain the four stages of generalization.
- Define the concept of *self-defined learners* and its attachment to the holistic-based instructional approach.
- What are the stages in creating a whole language system?

Discussion Questions

- Why have earlier approaches to reading instruction focused on unitary bases for explaining problems (e.g., perceptual functioning), whereas later approaches have been broader in focus?
- To what extent is empirical research necessary for teachers to embrace an approach to teaching reading? Is there evidence that some approaches are popular despite research demonstrating they are not effective or in the absence of research demonstrating anything about their effectiveness?
- What are approaches to reading instruction likely to look like in the future? Do you think unitary theories will make a comeback? Why or why not?

Purposes

Delineating the contributions of special education researchers within the global knowledge base of the phenomenon of reading is a difficult task. Because of the crossover between the fields of reading research and reading disabilities research, many writers, theorists, and practitioners have addressed reading problems within both domains. In this chapter we have limited our review to those theories and methods that we believe exemplify some of the prominent contributions by individuals who have operated primarily, if not wholly, from the domain of special education, but whose contributions provide valuable informtion to all individuals interested in children and youth who demonstrate difficulties in mastering the complexities of reading. Our purpose is to highlight salient research initiatives emanating from special education by describing the theoretical explanations for reading problems, describing the instructional methods that have been derived from these theories, and providing an analysis of the research findings. Figure 3-1 graphically illustrates the key concepts to be discussed.

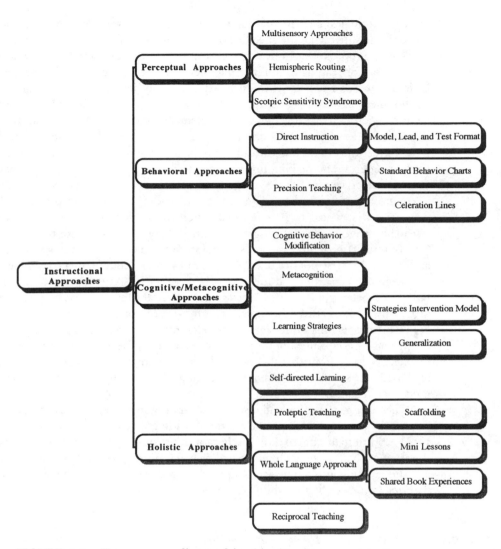

FIGURE 3-1   Key concepts discussed in this chapter

Shifts in Theory and Applications

Over the course of the past few decades, a number of views has been presented to account for learning disabilities in children and youth. Beginning with a view of learning disabilities as a psychoneurological anomaly, theorists presumed that insults to the brain cause an array of symptomatic behaviors involving perceptual problems. The presumed psychoneurological basis for reading problems has led to various theoretical and instructional models involving the specific operations of the hemispheres of the brain and the resulting perceptual functions. The shortcomings of research into a psychoneurological explanation for reading disabilities together with the emergence of behaviorism in the United States as a popular theoretical explanation of learning, subsequently led to the development of instructional approaches that focused on structuring the learning environment rather than correcting internal anomalies of individuals with reading problems. Behavioral researchers have concentrated on the instructional behaviors of teachers, the careful structuring of reading curricula, and the use of systematic techniques for monitoring student progress and making instructional decisions. However, as concerns have grown over the effectiveness of achieving generalized effects using behavioral techniques, and as cognitive psychology has gained in status, reading models and practices have been developed that focus on the role of cognition in information processing. Accordingly, researchers have been examining the cognitive characteristics of poor readers and the effects of instructional processes to assist in information encoding, storage, manipulation, and retrieval. These queries have resulted in theories about learners' awareness of their own cognitive capacities and their use of self-regulated strategies to accomplish reading tasks (i.e., metacognition). Most recently, some special educators have embraced the tenets of holism as a powerful new explanation for reading problems and their remediation. For theorists operating under a holistic model, reading is viewed as a process of constructing meaning in the context of the reader's perceptions of the world. The prominent reading practices derived from this theory are the whole language approaches to reading that are based on a sociolinguistic model of reading whereby language and its pragmatic uses guide reading instruction.

These shifts in theories and instructional applications have, at least, reduced, to some extent, the uncertainty about the nature of reading disabilities. At best, they have provided conditionally effective approaches for improving students' school performance. In the sections that follow, a more detailed overview is provided of these theoretical models and the resulting instructional techniques that have contributed to the present knowledge base regarding reading disabilities.

Perceptually Based Instructional Approaches

An early focus on reading problems involved the perceptual aspects of reading and the role of processes used to encode visual information attributed to the brain hemispheres. Researchers have attributed specific functions to each hemisphere (i.e., the left hemisphere controls linguistic, analytic, abstract sequential processing, or mediation; the right hemisphere controls nonlinguistic, spatial, and holistic processing, or manual pattern recognition) and have geared their remedial treatments toward overcoming some hypothesized physical insult to the brain by developing the neurolinguistic capacity of the left hemisphere (Blau & Loveless, 1982; van den Honert, 1977). The general process used to facilitate increased neurolinguistic capacities has been various forms of multisensory approaches involving combinations of visual, auditory, kinesthetic, and tactile sensory channels.

A more recent and equally controversial development in the treatment of reading disabilities has been the assertions by Irlen (1983) that a subgroup of individuals with reading disabilities suffers from what she refers to as scotopic sensitivity syndrome. That is, some individuals are sensitive to various light frequencies. Without some adjustments, scotopic-sensitive individuals experience perceptual difficulties that result in reading problems. Irlen's treatment entails the use of a colored lens tht reduces the intensity of frequencies of light and thus ameliorates the perceptual difficulties.

Multisensory Approaches

The *Visual, Auditory, and Kinesthetics* (VAK) approach involves combining visual and auditory associations with writing (kinesthetic) procedures. For example, students see a word, say a word, try to write it from memory, and compare the results with the original word. The *Visual, Auditory, Kinesthetic, and Tactile* (VAKT) method uses the tactile modality in addition to the visual, auditory, and kinesthetic channels by having students trace letters with salient tactile features, such as letters cut out of sandpaper or fabric or tracing letters in Jell-O or cornmeal.

Gillingham-Stillman Method

Orton (1925), credited with much of the early developments in *hemispheric dominance* theories of reading, assumed sensory impulses were received by both hemispheres simultaneously, forming memory traces in the form of mirrored images (see Figure 3-2). If dominance did not exist because of some impairment to the brain, perceptions would be confusing and inconsistent, resulting in reading difficulties. Accordingly, Gillingham and Stillman (1965) devised an instructional method to increase the contribution of the auditory channel (e.g., the phonics element) by employing a multisensory synthetic phonics approach involving a tracing (i.e., tactile-kinesthetic modality) technique for teaching single letters and their sound equivalents.

The Gillingham-Stillman method requires instruction five times a week for a minimum of two years. Six fundamental associations are taught:

1. V-A (Visual-Auditory). Written words and letters are associated with their sounds. The student does not have to vocalize these sounds.
2. A-V (Auditory-Visual). The sounds of letters and words are associated with the visual image. This is a spelling-like task.
3. A-K (Auditory-Kinesthetic). The sounds of letters and words are associated with muscle action through speech and writing.
4. K-A (Kinesthetic-Auditory). The student's hand is guided to trace or to write a letter form while associating it with the name or sound of the letter.
5. V-K (Visual-Kinesthetic). Printed letters and words are associated with the muscular actions of speech and writing.
6. K-V (Kinesthetic-Visual). The muscular act of speech or writing is associated with the visual appearance of the letters (Richek, List, & Lerner, 1983, p. 188).

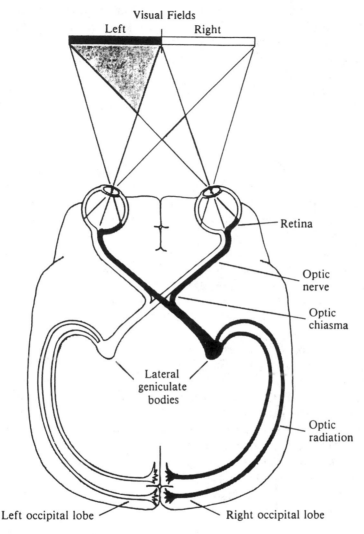

Visual Fields
Left   Right

Retina

Optic
nerve

Optic
chiasma

Lateral
geniculate
bodies

Optic
radiation

Left occipital lobe   Right occipital lobe

FIGURE 3-2   The visual pathways from the retinae of both eyes to the occipital lobes

In the *first stage* of developing letter–sound associations, a visual and auditory (V-A) association is developed between the grapheme and the letter name. The teacher presents a card with a letter on it, says the letter name, and has students repeat it. In saying the letter, an A-K association is made, which is the foundation for oral reading. Following mastery of the letter name, a V-A association between the grapheme and phoneme is developed by having the teacher show the letter card, say the sound, and then have students repeat the sound (Richek et al., 1983).

The *second stage* entails students developing the ability to relate the sound to the letter name, which is the basis for oral spelling skills. The teacher simply makes the letter sound and the pupil tells the name of the letter (Richek et al., 1983).

In the *third stage,* the teacher prints the letter and describes how it is formed. Next, students trace over the letter, copy it, and write the letter from memory without looking at the paper. Finally, the teacher says the sound, and students write the corresponding letter (Richek et al., 1983).

Once students have mastered the letter sound associations for the vowels *a* and *i* and the consonants, *b, g, h, j, k, m, p,* and *t,* word recognition skills are developed using a sound-blending technique. Word patterns such as consonant-vowel-consonant (CVC) are used to teach phonetically regular words. Eventually, other letter–sound correspondences and patterns are introduced. Ultimately, words are combined to form simple sentences and stories to develop reading in meaningful contexts (Richek et al., 1983).

Fernald VAKT Method

Fernald developed a similar technique using the tactile and kinesthetic modalities to help to remediate students' reading and spelling problems (Lovitt, 1989). She combined a whole word, language experience approach with emphasis on the visual, auditory, kinesthetic, and tactile senses, resulting in the VAKT models of learning (Fernald, 1943; Miccinati, 1979; Myers, 1978). The approach is based on the assumption that multisensory experiences with stimuli provide redundant cues about the stimuli that assist readers in accurate perception (Hallahan, Kauffman, & Lloyd, 1985).

The *four stages of the Fernald approach* are as follows:

1. Trace and write from memory individually presented words.
2. Write from memory individually presented words.
3. Write from memory words found in text.
4. Learn by sight words presented in text (Richek et al., 1983, p. 186).

In *Stage 1* students select a word that they would like to learn to read. The teacher writes the word in crayon on a large card or piece of paper and says the word. Students trace over the word using their fingers while saying each part of the word as it is traced. Students repeat the tracing until they believe they can write the word from memory. Students then attempt to write the word from memory. If they are unsuccessful, they continue the tracing procedure until they can trace the word from memory. When they are successful, the word is stored in a word bank (Mercer & Mercer, 1989).

Once several words have been learned, students are encouraged to write their own stories. As students need new words to complete stories, these words are targeted for learning.

During *Stage 2,* students no longer need to trace words in order to learn them. Students look at and say the word, then attempt to write it while saying it without looking at the original.

In *Stage 3,* students begin to read from texts. Words targeted for learning are selected from texts. When students encounter an unfamiliar word, they examine the word and attempt to write it from memory. They repeat this procedure until they can successfully write the word from memory. Newly learned words are then placed into each student's word bank.

   Stage 4 is characterized by the omission of the writing-from-memory step used in earlier stages. As students encounter unfamiliar words, they use textual cues or associate them with known words to read the word, say it, and remember it for future reading. Words that the student cannot decode using these strategies are written down for further review.

Kephart's Perceptual Motor Method

Kephart's (1960, 1971) model regarding the relationship between perception and motor development is one of the most widely recognized. The core of his model deals with the developmental match between perception and motor functioning that allows perceptual information to guide motor responses. In *Stage 1,* the hand is used to lead the eyes in generating visual perceptions as young children explore their environment. In *Stage 2,* the tactile and kinesthetic sensations from the hand are used only to confirm the visual information or to solve complex problems in perception. Finally, in *Stage 3,* the match between perception and motor activity is refined enough that children explore their environment with their eyes in the same way they once explored with their hands (Kephart, 1971).

Frostig Method

Frostig and Horne (Frostig, 1965) developed a series of activities designed to assist readers having visual perceptual difficulties. Frostig theorizes that remediation of the underlying perceptual problems will result in improved reading performance. Consequently, no alphabet-based stimuli are used in the activities. The five sets of activities are congruent with the domains of the Marianne Frostig Developmental Test of Visual Perception. In the set of *eye–hand coordination* activities, students are to draw lines within the boundaries of two parallel lines. The degree of difficulty of this task is varied by the inclusion of curved parallel lines and an increasingly narrow distance between parallel lines. A second set of activities requires students to trace figures that are overlaid on other figures and lines in order to develop *figure-ground perception.* In a third set of activities, *perceptual constancy* exercises, students are trained to recognize that a figure remains the same figure even though its form, size, color, or context may vary (see Figure 3-3). The fourth set of activities is designed to develop students recognition of figures' *position in space.* Worksheets are provided on which students are to discriminate figures in various positions. The fifth set of activities deals with the *spatial relations* between and among figures.

Hemispheric Routing

Blau and Loveless (1982) followed an *overload theory* developed by Myklebust. He believed that when two or more types of information are delivered to the brain, a breakdown occurs resulting in confusion, poor recall, or even seizures. Luchow and Shepard (1981) provided supportive evidence for the overload theory in finding that input from the

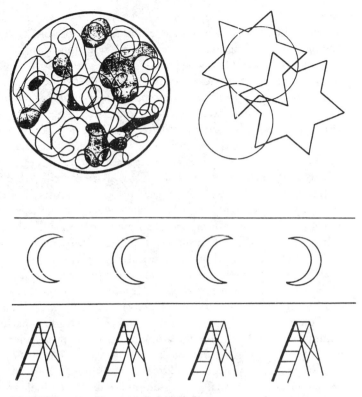

FIGURE 3-3   Example stimuli for perceptual constancy
(top) and figure ground activities (bottom)

auditory and tactile channels does not aid perception and in some cases actually interferes
with performance on matching tasks.

However, Blau and Loveless (1982) challenged the benefits of the visual modality
in assisting in multisensory programs. Their model is designed to provide for the most
direct hemispheric input, using the left hand to tap the specialization of the right
hemisphere for spatial arrangement and manual patterns (i.e., routing, stimulation) and
eliminating visual interference by the use of blackened goggles. The reading theory and
training differ from those of Orton and Gillingham (1968) in that the emphasis is on
using the right-hemisphere, holistic, manual recognition abilities rather than the analytic,
spatial, and sequential processing abilities of the left hemisphere. Blau and Loveless assume
not a hypothetical hemispheric impairment, but a lack of intervention strategies for using hemispheric specialization and interaction.

Scotopic Sensitivity

According to Irlen (1983), a subgroup of LD students may have an oversensitivity to certain frequencies of the light spectrum (Robinson & Conway, 1990). Scotopic sensitivity

syndrome is characterized by Irlen as involving print distortions caused by the contrast of black on white print (Whiting, 1985; Whiting & Robinson, 1988). Individuals suspected of having this sensitivity have been observed skipping words or lines of print unintentionally or losing their place while reading (*visual inefficiencies*). Others exhibit *eyestrain* in the form of headaches after reading, excessive fatigue after a day at school, or eye irritation. Another category of symptoms includes *photophobia,* or a preference of some readers for reading in darker areas of a room because sunlight or other bright lights are too intense. *Visual resolution* problems have been reported whereby individuals complain that print is blurred, vibrates, jiggles, shimmers, or has haloes around it. For some, this instability of the print is encountered after time if an effort is not made to retain the clarity *(difficulties with sustained focus).* A restricted *span of focus,* the amount of print that can be seen clearly when gaze is focused at a fixed point, can be as minimal as including only a single letter. The last category involves *difficulties of depth perception* that are manifest in judging distances evident in difficulties walking down stairs, catching a ball, and handwriting (Whiting & Robinson, 1988).

Irlen has hypothesized that nonoptical, tinted lenses can be used to change the light frequency and thus ameliorate these perceptual problems. Individuals are screened using the Irlen Differential Perceptual Schedule (IDPS). The procedures for the IDPS involve evaluating individuals on a series of perceptual tasks with visual stimuli presented on white paper, a questionnaire with items related to reading performance and eyestrain symptoms, and an assessment of reading performance using color tints (O'Connor, Sofo, Kendall, & Olsen, 1990; Robinson & Conway, 1990). The latter section of the screening is used to specify, by a process of elimination, a colored tint from 130 possible combinations that ameliorates visual perception problems. Individuals are fitted with the tinted lenses, which they wear when engaged in reading tasks.

Effectiveness of Perceptually Based Methods

Because of the complexities of the theory, it is difficult to access the explanatory power of psychoneurological models. There is supportive evidence of the effectiveness of the methods to improve students' reading skills, but the issue of whether they are effective because of ameliorating presumed perceptual difficulties due to hemispheric laterality is unresolved. Critics have provided evidence supporting the explanation that the benefit of multisensory reading programs is a function of the increased attention to task and not of cerebral dominance. The explanation has considerable surface validity and has not been dismissed as a competing hypothesis (Koenigsberg, 1973; Thorpe & Borden, 1985).

Additionally, multisensory reading programs are typically difficult for teachers to apply in classroom settings where one-to-one instruction for extended periods of time is impractical. For instance, reading programs such as the Orton-Gillingham method, Fernald's VAKT methods, and Blau and Loveless's hemispheric routing require extensive amounts of instructional time and effort to achieve incremental gains.

Programs such as the Frostig-Horne require students to develop visual discrimination skills ostensibly parallel to those needed in decoding, but nonalphabet stimuli are used to produce some generalized improvement in visual discrimination skills. However, there is no evidence that such programs result in a generalized improvement in perceptual skills or produce any better effect than more traditional reading programs that use letter and word stimuli.

Although researchers have reported significant benefits from the use of Irlen lenses, caution must prevail; the examination of the effectiveness of this treatment is only beginning. In a preliminary evaluation, Whiting (1985) reported that Robinson found that subjects having high, moderate, and low indicators of scotopic sensitivity syndrome who were randomly assigned to conditions that included reading using selected colored lenses or clear plastic differed significantly on measures of word-matching, word-reading, letter-reading, and number-reading tasks. In a second study, Saint-John & White (1988) reported no significant differences on a passage-reading measure and letter identification task between groups that read using plain frames, Polaroid lens (placebo), and individually selected colored transparencies.

Further studies have been conducted by Robinson and Conway (1990), O'Connor et al. (1990), and Blaskey et al. (1990). Robinson and Conway (1990) reported that after being fitted with Irlen lenses, subjects demonstrated gains in reading rate, accuracy, comprehension, and a self-perception measure. O'Connor et al. (1990) observed subjects using clear transparencies as well as scotopic and nonscotopic subjects using nonpreferred colored transparencies. On measures of reading rate, accuracy, and comprehension, O'Connor el al. reported that the scotopic subjects given the preferred colored transparencies improved significantly on all three reading measures when compared to all other groups. Blaskey et al. (1990) randomly assigned subjects who tested positive for both scotopic sensitivity and other vision problems to either an Irlen lens treatment, vision therapy treatment, or a control group and found no significant gains in reading rate, word recognition in context, or comprehension for scotopic subjects given preferred colored lenses. In seven out of eight cases in the vision therapy group, vision problems were successfully treated, but all of the scotopic group still showed significant vision anomalies following treatment.

In some ways, these results are encouraging, but each of the studies that have been reported has substantive methodological flaws (Parker, 1990). Researchers have employed relatively weak designs (e.g., Robinson & Conway, 1990) or flawed designs (e.g., treatment bias and low power due to small cell size) that leave a number of threats to the internal and external validity of these studies. Although present conclusions are tenuous at best, it is nonetheless encouraging that the debate over Irlen lenses is moving from the popular media (e.g., CBS's "60 Minutes") to the scientific community (Hoyt, 1990).

Behaviorally Based Instructional Approaches

Behaviorally based instructional programs have taken their strongest root in special education. It appears that the special educators have valued the systematic precision of behavioral programs because of the effectiveness of highly structured programs dating back to Strauss and Lehtinen (1947). The theoretical explanation for reading disabilities is that instructional interactions between teachers and students have been inadequate. Accordingly, behavioral programs are designed to control carefully the interactions between learners and various instructional antecedents and consequences external to the student in ways that optimize efficient and effective instruction.

In general, behaviorally based programs in reading usually focus on *overt behavioral responses* (not cognition) and on continuous monitoring of changes in behavioral responses. Classroom variables in the reading setting are manipulated in order to provide appropriate physical facilities, promote engagement, use functional and interesting materials and activities, pace lessons briskly, employ contingent-management techniques, structure effective transitions, provide multiple opportunities for learning (e.g., massed and distributed opportunities to read), capitalize on naturally occurring events and routines, and communicate expectations (e.g., use of rules in word formations).

A scientific-empirical approach is used to guide teachers through a set of sequential steps for diagnosing students' skills and prescribing a treatment program. Special education teachers are taught to use a *diagnostic approach* by first identifying curricular goals and then collecting baseline data to determine readers' present educational levels and distinguish the configuration of environmental variables affecting instruction. On the basis of these data, teachers then specify the reading learning objective and plan and implement intervention programs. Finally, reading progress is monitored and evaluated on a formative basis (Wolery, Bailey, & Sugai, 1988) (see Figure 3-4).

Direct Instruction

Among the more controversial developments to emerge from a behavioral framework (although other theoretical bases contribute) are the direct instruction (DI) procedures and curriculum developed by Englemann and Becker at the University of Oregon. The roots of DI date back to the mid-1970s, when Rosenshine (1976) coined the term in reference to effective teaching behaviors. During his extensive observations in classrooms, Rosenshine (1971) and others (Anderson, Evertson, & Brophy, 1979; Fisher et al., 1980) were able to identify critical teacher behaviors that correlated positively with student academic gains. Englemann and his associates (Becker, Englemann, & Thomas, 1971; Carnine, Silbert, & Kameenui, 1990; Englemann & Carnine, 1982) expanded the term *direct instruction* to include not only specific teaching procedures but also the use of highly structured curricular materials.

Englemann's development of the curriculum and its implementation in the Follow Through projects exemplifies the essence of a structured, systematic teaching approach to reading. However, the behavioral analysis component is only one of three components of DI approaches, which also include the knowledge systems analysis (e.g., structuring classes and subclasses of information on the basis of interrelationships) and communications systems analysis (e.g., faultless communications prevent the acquisition of misrules and erroneous concepts or under- and overgeneralizations) (Englemann & Carnine, 1982; Tarver, 1986).

These materials are designed to help teachers systematically direct students in making accurate responses. Scripted lesson plans are designed to ensure that precise communication occurs between teacher and student. During instruction, teachers *model* target responses, *lead* students in making the response, and periodically *test* students' skills to respond without teacher cues.

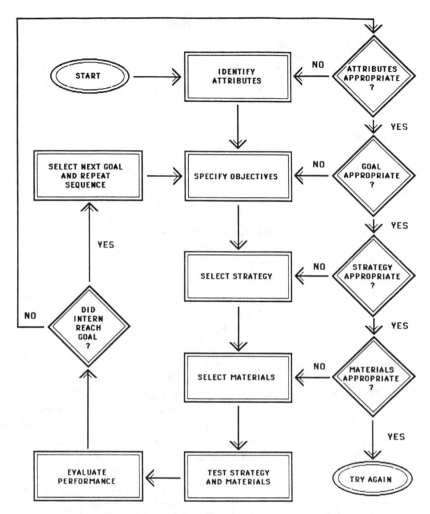

FIGURE 3-4   Flow chart of the diagnostic process used for
instructional decision making

Principal Components of Direct Instruction

The three principal components of direct instruction include the *demonstration, guided practice,* and *independent practice* stages of lesson development. The demonstration stage of lesson development entails teachers *modeling* target responses for students. The responses relate to the performance of an academic rule (i.e., sets of procedures for performing academic tasks, such as sounding out phonetically regular words) or the formation of concepts (i.e., well-defined categories of information used for classification, such as elements of story plot). For instance, if the target response for students is to see/say a set of words containing the medial short vowel sound /a/, then the teacher would point to each target word and sound out the letter sounds contained in the words (e.g., *c-a-t, m-a-t, r-a-t*).

Guided practice is supervised practice that entails teachers using cues and prompts to emit target responses. Here teachers *lead* groups of students in making the desired response; that is, the teacher and students perform the response simultaneously. As the students demonstrate accurate responses, teachers gradually fade their degree of leading. Instead of making the response with the students, the teacher presents the stimulus and has the group of students respond. In addition, teachers *test* students by calling on individual students to make responses on their own.

As students become more accurate in their responding, teachers shift the performance criterion to fast and accurate responding. Teachers concentrate on asking for as many responses as possible during a guided practice session. This increases the opportunities to respond and helps to ensure skill mastery.

Once students have performed responses accurately without cues or prompts, students practice skills independently in order to increase response accuracy and speed. Independent practice, therefore, is minimally supervised practice in which students respond with 90 percent or better response accuracy. Two important and closely related features of independent practice assist in skill development and efficient management of classroom activities. First, teachers can work with other groups of students while one group practices independently. Second, in order for the first to occur, students must be making accurate responses so they can truly work independently of the teacher.

DISTAR *and Mastery Reading Programs*
The general DI procedures that can be applied to any curriculum content have been specially adapted to reading in the DISTAR and later the Mastery Reading programs. These phonics-based approaches to reading instruction employ a modified alphabet to create a consistent set of sound–symbol relationships. Following scripted lessons, teachers integrate the steps of demonstration, guided practice, and independent practice with consideration of the stages of learning and the carefully structured phonics-based curriculum (see Table 3-1). The *modified alphabet* is faded gradually until all material appears in traditional orthography (Englemann & Bruner, 1984).

Instruction begins with teaching students letter–sound correspondence. Letter sounds are introduced with consideration to their utility; that is, the most commonly used sounds are taught first. Additionally, letter sounds that are visually or auditoraly similar are not taught initially in close proximity; to make discrimination less difficult, they are separated by several days' instruction in order to allow students time to become skilled in one letter–sound correspondence before another similar one is introduced. This occurs during the introduction phase of the acquisition stage. After days of practicing a specific letter–sound correspondence, students are taught to discriminate the visual and auditory features of the letter sounds with other letter sounds (the discrimination phase of the acquisition stage).

The overriding skill being taught in teaching letter–sound correspondences is *telescoping*. Students are taught to hold the continuous sounds (e.g., /s/, /m/, /a/) for approximately 1.5 seconds and to quickly sound the stop sounds (e.g., /b/, /t/, /p/). By teaching students to respond to cues to telescope or quickly sound out letters, teachers are

TABLE 3-1   **Example Scripted Lesson Featuring the Model-Lead-Test Instructional Sequence, Telescoping, and Modified Alphabet Used in Fast Cycle Reading Program**

As soon as you read all the words on this page without making a mistake, we'll go on to the next page.

TASK 9   Children sound out the word and say it fast

a. Touch the first ball of the arrow for mad. Sound it out. Get ready. Move quickly under each sound. *Mmmaaad.*
b. Return to the first ball. Again, sound it out. Get ready. Move quickly under each sound. *Mmmaaad.*
c. Repeat *b* until firm.
d. Return to the first ball. Say it fast. Slash. *Mad.*
   Yes, what word? *Mad.*
   Don't be (pause) **mad.**

TASK 10   Children sound out the word and say it fast

a. Touch the first ball of the arrow for **sēē.** Sound it out. Get ready. Move quickly under each sound. *Sssééé.*
b. Return to the first ball. Again, sound it out. Get ready. Move quickly under each sound. *Sssééé.*
c. Repeat *b* until firm.
d. Return to the first ball. Say it fast. Slash. *See.*
   Yes, what word? *See.*

TASK 11   Children sound out the word and say it fast

a. Touch the first ball of the arrow for ad. Sound it out. Get ready. Move quickly under each sound. *Aaad.*
b. Return to the first ball. Again, sound it out. Get ready. Move quickly under each sound. *Aaad.*
c. Repeat *b* until firm.
d. Return to the first ball. Say it fast. Slash. *Ad.*
   Yes, what word? *Ad.*

ad

TASK 12   Children sound out the word and say it fast

a. Touch the first ball of the arrow for sad. Sound it out. Get ready. Move quickly under each sound. *Sssaaad.*
b. Return to the first ball. Again, sound it out. Get ready. Move quickly under each sound. *Sssaaad.*
c. Repeat *b* until firm.
d. Return to the first ball. Say it fast. Slash. *Sad.*
   Yes, what word? *Sad.*

CRITERION

If the children read the words in tasks 9, 10, 11, and 12 without making any mistakes, present individual turns.
If the children made mistakes, say: **That was pretty good. Let's read the words again. See if you can read them without making a mistake.**

TASK 13   Individual test

Call on different children. Each child is to do task 9, 10, 11 or 12.

training students to use a sounding-out strategy as the primary mechanism for decoding words.

As students acquire skills with a set of vowels and consonants, phonetically regular words are introduced. Only words that contain letter sounds that students have practiced in isolation are introduced. Words that begin with continuous sounds, are short (e.g., fit the CVC pattern), and commonly found in reading materials are taught first. Students' skill in telescoping and are sounding stop sounds is applied to the skill of blending the sounds of words. This *sounding-out strategy* is a central part of the decoding process. Teachers signal students to telescope or sound stop sounds as words are introduced. After students sound out the target word, they are asked to say the word quickly to bridge the mediated approach of sounding out with the immediate form of responding. Once students have demonstrated they can identify a word without sounding out, the sound-blending procedure is faded and used only with unfamiliar words.

As with other phonic-based approaches, the reading material is gradually shaped to appear more like natural text as students move from mastering decoding to gaining meaning from written text.

Precision Teaching

Lindsley's work at the University of Kansas produced a set of structured procedures for academic learning termed *precision teaching* (Lovitt, 1989). The primary contributions of precision teaching are the systematic procedures for monitoring student progress through a curriculum and the tactics for making data-based instructional decisions. Guidelines for teachers to use specific teaching strategies for developing decoding or comprehension skills are not delineated as is done in direct instruction programs. Emphasis is placed on practicing skills sufficiently that readers make not only accurate responses, but fast and accurate responses to ensure mastery and maintenance of the responses (e.g., saying words from lists or in context, or stating facts recalled from a passage). Reading activities are designed to increase readers' fluency in decoding word lists organized by phonic patterns (e.g., CVC, CVCE) and words in context using graded passages. Comprehension activities involve individuals reading passages and stating as many facts as they can recall during a one-minute timing. Readers' response rates in the form of words read correctly per minute (wcpm) and the number of errors per minute (epm) in oral reading, along with the number of facts recalled per minute, are used to plot progress on standard behavior charts. Decisions based on rate data (i.e., movements per minute) are made regarding use of similarly difficult reading material, "slicing back" to less difficult stimuli, or "leaping up" to more difficult stimuli.

Like all behaviorally based instructional programs, precision teaching procedures are dictated by the observable and measurable behaviors that students demonstrate. In precision teaching, behaviors are referred to as *movements*. Movements are calibrated at levels that provide a balance between precision and ease of measurement. They may take the form of saying letter sounds or words, writing letters or words, or stating facts. Accurate movement is considered important but insufficient for mastery learning. Therefore, fast and accurate responding is emphasized through the measurement of movements per some unit of time, usually a minute. Using one-minute timings on precise behaviors allows teachers to take samples of students' performance quickly and therefore frequently.

Students' progress in mastering individual objectives is monitored through the use of performance charting. *Standard behavior charts* (see Figure 3-5) are used to represent students' progress in mastering individual instructional aims (i.e., curriculum objectives). A semilogarithmic grid contains an equal-interval scale on the horizontal axis that is used to represent either successive calendar days or instructional days. The vertical axis is a equal-ratio scale that represents students' movements per minute. The equal-ratio scale provides a representation of proportional growth or multiplicative function of students' progress over time rather than a measure of absolute or additive growth that an equal-interval scale provides. Therefore, if a student reads 35 words per minute on day 1 and then reads 45 words correctly on day 2 of an instructional program, the absolute growth is 10 words per minute, and the proportional growth is 1.29 times greater on day 2. If on day 7 the student reads 65 words correct per minute and on day 8 reads 88 wcpm,

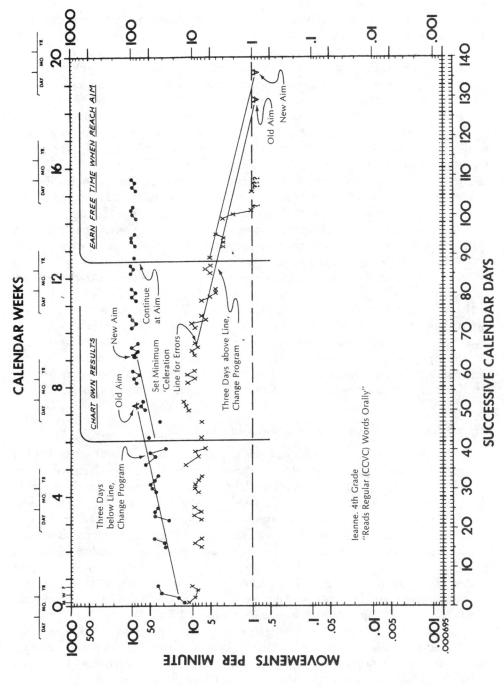

FIGURE 3-5   Example standard behavior chart with notations about instructional aims, celeration, and decision making

65

the absolute growth is 23, wcpm and the proportional growth is 1.35 times greater on day 8. In absolute terms, the gain between days 7 and 8 (23 wcpm) looks substantially greater than the difference between days 1 and 2 (10 wcpm). However, the proportional growth between these sets of instructional days is relatively similar (1.35 and 1.29, respectively). The proportional measure of growth provides a more accurate representation of the consistent and orderly way in which students develop skills (White & Haring, 1980).

Instructional aims are based on published proficiency rates or peer response rates. Published proficiency rates can be obtained for most tool skills in reading, math, and spelling but may not be available for other content areas. Peer medians are readily available regardless of content area and grade level but require sampling the rate of responding of a peer group whose members have mastered the target response. The median rate of responding (i.e., responses per minute or some other unit of time) for the peer group is used as the criterion for mastery (Rosenberg, O'Shea, & O'Shea, 1991).

Instructional decision making regarding the effectiveness of instructional strategies is based on the rate of growth demonstrated by students. A minimum *celeration line* is constructed using the students' current median level of performance and the instructional aim. The number of instructional days allocated for students to reach their aim is based on the celeration rate. Students are expected to progress at a minimum rate of 1.25 times. Therefore, if a student were reading 40 wcpm in context currently and the instructional aim were to have the student attain a rate of 120 wcpm, then the teacher would need to allocate four weeks of instruction. As long as students are progressing at or above the minimum celeration rate, the current instructional strategy is continued. When students' performance falls below the minimum celeration line for three consecutive days, then modifications to the aim or the instructional program are made.

Effectiveness of Behaviorally Based Methods

Although models based on behavioral principles have been influential in the field of learning disabilities and in their application to reading research, researchers have questioned the simplicity of the theoretical model to explain and predict developments in the reading process (Poplin, 1987, 1988). Bandura), (1977) has criticized the model for an overreliance on adult-controlled interventions. Specific concerns of teacher-directed programs such as Mastery Reading have been criticized for the strictly regimented scripted lesson format that allows for little spontaneous variation in teaching procedures. However, proponents of Mastery Reading and precision teaching point to the extensive, supportive evidence demonstrating the gains in students' academic performance when instruction is systematically directed by teachers (Abt Associates, 1977; Carnine, Silbert, & Kameenui, 1990; White & Haring, 1980; Stevens & Rosenshine, 1981).

Poplin (1988) and Heshusius (1986) have lodged their concerns on the basis of use of task-analytic techniques in curriculum development that have led to reducing academic tasks to minute and meaningless activities (e.g., using phonics instruction as the primary system for decoding). For example, when students are taught letter–sound correspondence in isolation as is done in the Mastery Reading and precision teaching curricula, they see little purpose in what they do and therefore become bored. When performance drops, then artificial reinforcement systems are used to induce higher response rates. These authors argue that students are self-directed learners who construct meaning in reading activities through their own perceptions, needs, and desires and not through fragmented curricula and teacher-controlled activities.

Nonetheless, because of its extensive application to reading instruction and to other academic areas, and the high rate of the effectiveness of practitioners employing its theoretical orientation, behaviorally based methods continue to play a significant role in reading instruction. This is evident in the adoption of the direct instruction methods by proponents of metacognitive learning strategies curricula and cognitive/developmental curricula (Reid & Hresko, 1981) and in the use of precision teaching and other data-based instructional monitoring and management systems in special education classrooms.

Cognitive/Metacognitive-Based Instructional Approaches

As behavioral scientists began to focus their efforts on antecedent events in shaping behaviors (e.g., curriculum materials and teacher behaviors), more recent behavioral approaches have been influenced by developments in cognitive psychology. The blend of behavioral principles of learning with emphasis on monitoring overt behavioral responses and verbal mediation strategies devised by cognitive psychologists has led to a hybrid of the two models in the form of *cognitive behavior modification* (CBM). CBM procedures entail students acting as their own instructors, using self-guiding verbalizations to complete a series of steps in order to demonstrate appropriate social or academic behavior (Meichenbaum, 1980).

The primary objective of CBM in reading and other academic areas has been to address the problem of students generalizing their responses over time and across settings. CBM techniques have been designed to overcome problems with generalization by using operant procedures to change inappropriate behaviors or to enhance task-appropriate and academically meaningful behaviors (Meichenbaum, 1980). By using CMB techniques, students become less dependent on others to control their behaviors (Wolery et al., 1988). For example, treatments internalized by readers (e.g., steps to self-question during silent reading) are transportable to other settings, other individuals, and over time. Individuals independently engaging in task-appropriate behaviors enhance teachers' ability to manage other groups of students simultaneously (Wolery et al., 1988).

Early CBM procedures were developed to train students to control behaviors that interfered with performing academic tasks (e.g., impulsivity) through self-verbalizations. For instance, Douglas, Parry, Marton, and Garson (1976) found significant changes in measures of listening comprehension and borderline changes in oral comprehension and spelling when students were trained to use self-guiding verbalizations to control impulsive behavior. Similarly, Wozniak and Nuechterlain (cited in Lloyd, 1980) used a mediational training program to reduce the impulsive behavior of students who displayed reading deficits. Later developments in CBM training came in the form of self-instruction procedures that focused on completion of specific academic tasks. Lloyd and Kneedler (cited in Lloyd,d 1980) trained students to verbalize a strategy used to identify words presented in flashcard drill and found consistent improvement in students' word identification accuracy. Thus, CBM work has been used to train students to self-monitor and self-instruct through the use of self-verbalization in order to improve reading and other academic task performances.

While behaviorists have continued to develop the technologies of CBM, researchers in learning disabilities with a cognitive model orientation have also continued to develop technologies to address the issue of generalization of task-appropriate behaviors. The focus, however, has been on the use of various cognitive processes by students displaying learning problems. Torgesen (1977) found that students with learning disabilities seemed to have the same cognitive capacities as peers without learning disabilities but lacked the application of various *metacognitive strategies* that aid in the use of cognitive faculties. Further research has led to the idea that these children are deficient in cognitions about cognitions or in executive planning used to carry out cognitive operations and monitor their own progress. In reading, this includes difficulties in: (1) analyzing and characterizing a reading problem at hand, (2) reflecting on what one knows or does not know that may be necessary for a solution, (3) devising a plan for attacking the reading problem, and (4) checking or monitoring one's reading progress (Brown, 1978).

Jacobs and Paris (1987) defined metacognitve strategies as those mental activities that entail *self-appraisal of cognition* and *self-management of thinking*. Appraisals of cognition include the use of declarative knowledge (i.e., what is important, schema), procedural knowledge (i.e., how to do tasks), conditional knowledge (i.e., when to do tasks), and metacognitive knowledge (i.e., knowledge of cognitive processes, and self-management). Self-management of thinking entails planning, evaluating, and regulating mental tasks (Jacob & Paris, 1987; Wong, 1988). Applied to reading, metacognition is defined as the planning, monitoring, revising, and repairing of activities used for comprehension (Brown, Day, & Jones, 1983).

Learning Strategies Approach

The most widely applied example of metacognitive-based strategies in the field of special education is the strategies intervention model (SIM) conceptualized at the University of Kansas by Alley, Deshler, Ellis, Lenz, and Schumaker. Early research by Alley and Deshler (1979) began by addressing the question: "How should adolescents with learning disabilities be instructed so as to maximize the information learned (acquired) and generalized? To answer this question, researchers drew from a line of thinking established by Bruner (1966). Like Bruner's search for some "heuristic economy" through guiding students to discover and use independently a systematic process for problem solving, developers of the SIM have sought to establish a broadly applicable curriculum that underlies the development of independent learners.

The SIM developers have either revamped earlier strategies (e.g., the SQ3R—(Survey Question, Read, Recite, Review)— method; Robinson, 1941) or developed others that provide students with a systematic set of "techniques, principles, or rules that will facilitate the acquisition, manipulation, integration, storage, and retrieval of information across situations and settings" (Deshler, Schumaker, Alley, Warner, & Clark, 1982). For example, strategies are taught that entail students pausing at invervals to paraphrase information or self-question in order to aid reading comprehension. Consequently, readers can use somewhat of a generic set of procedures to gain information from written discourse or to write well-structured sentences and paragraphs.

The SIM includes structures for *how to teach* and *what to teach*. The "what to teach" component is based on the metacognitive needs of high-risk students; that is, teachers promote awareness and regulation of the information-processing demands of the school setting (Deshler et al., 1982; Deshler, Schumaker, Lenz, & Ellis, 1984; Deshler & Schumaker, 1986). The SIM curriculum consists of learning strategies that are designed for three processes: acquisition of information, storage of information, and expression and demonstration of competencies (see Table 3-2).

The "how to teach" component is based on the behaviorally oriented DI model involving teachers modeling, leading, and testing students through the acquisition stage of learning. The strategy acquisition procedures consist of eight steps:

1. Pretest and obtain commitment to learn.
2. Describe the new strategy.
3. Model the new strategy.
4. Verbally rehearse strategy steps.
5. Students practice in controlled materials.
6. Students practice in grade-appropriate classroom materials.
7. Posttest and obtain student commitment to generalize.
8. Generalize.

During step 1, motivation to learn and use the strategies is developed by pointing out the inefficiencies or ineffectiveness of students' present strategies. In addition, the pretest step is conducted in order to ensure that the student can perform all the preskills prior to teaching the strategy. Next, the procedures for executing the strategy are described. These procedures include the major behaviors in which the student will sequentially engage to complete the strategy correctly. The teacher then models the steps through a "think out loud" process. Students are then led through a verbal rehearsal process designed to prompt the self-instruction process. Students progress from overt to covert verbal rehearsal of the steps in a way similar to CBM strategies. In order that students may focus

TABLE 3-2 Strategies Intervention Model Delineating Skill Areas by Cognitive Processing Category

Acquisition	Storage	Expression and Demonstration of Competence
Word identification	First-letter mnemonic	Sentence writing
Paraphrasing	Paired associates	Paragraph writing
Self-questioning	Listening and note-taking	Error monitoring
Visual imagery		Theme writing
Interpreting visual aids		Assignment completion
Multipass		Test-taking
SOS		

attention on learning the strategy without having to deal with new or difficult materials, initial practice is done with less demanding materials. Once students have demonstrated skill in executing the strategy in these materials, then students practice in their grade-level materials in order to further develop generalization of strategy use to regular classroom content. Students are provided a posttest to determine that mastery has been achieved, and a behavioral contract is used to gain a commitment to use the strategy in their regular classrooms (Deshler & Schumaker, 1986).

Generalization is facilitated during and after the acquisition stage. Ellis, Lenz, and Sabornie (1987a, 1987b) describe the process of teaching generalization in terms of four stages:

1. *Antecedent:* Changing negative student attitudes that might ultimately affect generalization behaviors
2. *Concurrent:* Student acquiring the skill well enough for it to become generalized
3. *Subsequent:* Applying the skill to various contexts, situations, and settings
4. *Independent:* Student using self-instruction to mediate generalization

Antecedent steps are taken to encourage generalization by changing negative student attitudes that might ultimately affect students' efforts to generalize. In addition, in planning for instruction, teachers select or are provided in the SIM materials extensive and diverse examples of the application of strategies. During strategy acquisition, concurrent steps are taken to facilitate generalization by having students learn strategies well enough for them to become generalized. Having students practice strategies in controlled materials allows the students to attend to the steps for executing the strategy without having to focus their attention on reading material that requires attention to decoding or on comprehending complex semantic relationships. After students have demonstrated mastery of strategy use in controlled materials, they are subsequently taught to apply the strategy to various contexts, situations, and settings. Less emphasis is placed on students completing the strategy steps in the regimented manner used in earlier stages. Instead, teachers vary formats, procedures, and examples as students gain mastery of a strategy in order to promote generalization. Ultimately, independence (i.e., executive functioning) is generated by teaching students to use self-monitoring procedures to mediate generalization and cue other teachers to provide reinforcement (Ellis et al., 1987a).

An example of the strategies in reading is the multipass technique. The *multipass* technique is derived from SQ3R procedures; the reader makes multiple passes through a passage in order to gain different types of information in the reading process. In the first pass (the *survey pass*) students are taught to read the title and the introductory paragraph, are taught to review the relation of the target section to other sections, are asked to read major subtitles and look at illustrations and captions, and then are asked to read a summary paragraph and paraphrase the information gained. The *size-up pass* requires students to read questions related to the section, check questions that can be answered, read the story and locate textual cues, turn cues into questions, skim through the text to answer questions, and paraphrase answers. In the *sort-out pass,* students answer questions and, if unable to do, think about the section in which information would appear. They are taught to skim for the answer until they find it.

Other learning strategies are used in word identification and reading comprehension. The *word identification strategy* is designed to enhance students' decoding of multisyllabled words (Deshler & Schumaker, 1986). *RAP* is a three-step strategy used to help students summarize what they have read by following the mnemonic: "*R*ead paragraph, *A*sk self questions, and *P*ut it in own words" (Schumaker, Denton, & Deshler, 1984). *RIDER* is an acronym for a strategy designed to have students use visual imagery to create mental pictures of text passages in order to increase reading comprehension (Deshler & Schumaker, 1986; Lovitt, 1989). The steps include: *R*ead the first sentence, *I*magine a picture in your mind, *D*escribe the image, *E*valuate your image for its completeness, and *R*epeat the process in the next passage.

Effectiveness of Cognitively Based Methods

The issue of strategy use by students with learning disabilities and other high-risk learners has generated a great deal of discussion over the past decade. When applied to reading instruction, the question is whether or not the difference between good and poor information processors is that the former have a set of strategies that they employ and the latter (students with reading disabilities) do not. Another concern is whether good readers have good executive control (i.e., awareness of purpose) to tap learning strategies, whereas poor information processors have the strategies but lack the executive control needed to call them up for use in reading. For instance, Rohwer (1980) has argued that a developmental strategy hypothesis may explain the use of memory strategies and the level of instruction needed. That is, strategy training simply triggers the use of previously learned processing capabilities that have developed over time. Pressley, Levin, and Ghatala (1984) provided support for Rohwer's hypothesis from data indicating that older children invoke and use new memory strategies following minimal levels of prompting (Derry & Murphy, 1986). Flavell (1979) proposed a production deficiency hypothesis; that is, young children fail to produce verbal mediation strategies spontaneously but are able to use such strategies to improve performance once they are made available to them. Some authors have misinterpreted Flavell's hypothesis to mean that high-risk students have these strategies but do not use them.

From a more practical point of view, learning strategies provide many in-classroom applications for a wide range of reading problems. However, the implementation of the learning strategies approach requires extensive training of teachers in the rationale, curriculum, and procedures of the model. In addition, the active support of school and district administrators and teachers in both regular and special education must be developed in order that generalization may be facilitated outside the special education classroom. Sustaining high levels of commitment can be very difficult.

In addition to teacher motivation to maintain implementation of a learning strategies curriculum, attention must be given to maintaining student interest. Students' willingness to participate in instruction and their readiness to self-verbalize, self-instruct, and self-monitor are absolutely essential to the success of learning strategy models. Yet, little is known about the effectiveness of strategies training to motivate students to fulfill the ultimate desired outcome—students using strategies as learning tools in the regular classroom in order to improve their academic performance. Beyond the initial testing of individual strategies to validate their successful acquisition of strategies by students with learning disabilities, there are few published reports to date on the efficacy of learning strategies to facilitate generalization through an *independently* conducted, comprehensive investigation of the impact of learning strategies programs.

Holistic-Based Instructional Approaches

A model for the treatment of children and youth who exhibit reading problems that is emerging in the field of special education is based on the constructs and procedures of holism. The procedural applications of holism to reading instruction in the form of "whole language" approaches have emanated primarily from work done outside the field of special education by Marie Clay, Ken and Yetta Goodman, Don Holdaway, and Frank Smith. However, proponents of the theoretical and philosophical base for holism have enjoyed strong vocal support by Lous Heshusius and Mary Poplin in special education research journals. They have argued that positivistic and empiricist traditions underlying earlier theoretical models (i.e., psychoneurological, behavioral, and cognitive) are not adequate to address the problems of understanding human behavior (Heshusius, 1986, 1989; Smith & Heshusius, 1986; Poplin, 1987, 1988). These models are based on a methodology originally designed in the natural sciences to analyze component parts of inanimate objects in isolation from the whole.

In examining the learning process, holists focus their criticisms on two key concepts: *fragmenting of meaningful tasks* like reading a story and *learning that is externally controlled by an agent other than the learner.* For instance, teachers' use of task analysis and behavioral objectives to isolate component skills in reading (e.g., letter–sound correspondences) tends to reduce the process of reading to meaningless fragments, especially when reading behaviors are reduced to extremely minute units. Teachers' efforts are placed on controlling the curriculum and manipulating teacher–student interactions, with little concern for the need to view instruction in the context of what is meaningful and functional to students both in and outside the classroom (Smith & Heshusius, 1986). Consequently, students may begin to view reading as an end in itself, rather than a self-directed process used to experience and gain an understanding of the world.

The basic tenets of the holistic view are derived from phenomonological thought, which "sets forth the importance of understanding a person's direct experience of her world, irrespective of how she conceptualizes and categorizes it" (Heshusius, 1986, p. 30). Researchers and teachers, therefore, seek to determine how children make their own reality (i.e., direct their own learning). The basic assumption is that students are self-directed, meaning-constructing, meaning-seeking individuals who act on their environments accordingly. Their knowledge base is shaped by contextual conditions and meaningfulness as well as by their individual interests and purposes. Self-directed learning is more motivating than teacher-directed learning, which imposes both the problem and the solution. Reading programs for students with learning disabilities (as well as for other students at risk) designed without consideration of the context of purpose, use, and desired social relations fail to provide motivating and meaningful environments conducive to self-directed learning.

The conceptualization of students as *self-directed learners,* central to holistic thought, emanates largely from the work of the Soviet psychologists Vygotsky and Luria. They hypothesized that socialization and motor behaviors are functions of a child internalizing the interpersonal instructions of adults or older siblings (i.e., verbal control of behaviors.) Vygotsky (1978) suggested that a child's behavior shifts from control by the language of adults and others (external) to control by the child's inner language (internal). This shift is a prerequisite to higher level cognitive functioning required in academic tasks such as reading. Luria (1961) delineated this process in a three-stage model of development:

1. The adult's speech directs and controls the child's behavior.
2. The child's overt speech directs and controls her own behavior.
3. The child's covert speech directs and controls her own behavior.

This developmental shift of control from the adult to the child is conceptualized by *proleptic teaching* (i.e., teaching in anticipation of competence.) Vygotsky believed that children first experience a set of cognitive activities in the presence of some expert and then, gradually, become able to perform tasks themselves through observation and imitation. In the instructional context of reading, this view refers to naive learners engaging in a reading task before they really have the skills to do it. In order to overcome the present skill deficit, there must be a supportive environment in which the reading teacher provides support through modeling and guiding student responses so that the learner can carry out some simple aspects of the reading task with the aid of the teacher. This supportive structure is referred to as *scaffolding.* The analogy is made to the tutelage that occurs when a parent, teacher, or master craftsperson guides the child through a particular activity and gradually relinquishes the responsibilities for completing the activity to the child as the child becomes more and more skilled in the task at hand (Palincsar & Brown, 1984).

Importantly, a teacher's decisions regarding what skills are taught and when are guided by students' interest and not by some predetermined sequence of curricular objectives. In this case, teachers are said to "lead from behind"; modeling is initiated after students attempt to engage in tasks for which they need support (Newman, 1985).

Whole Language Approach

The whole language or literacy approach exemplifies the application of the principles of holism to reading instruction. The unit of meaning is a whole story rather than some smaller part. Meaning is constructed from stories that are rich in language forms. Writing skills are encouraged through language experience activities where students dictate a story and either they or the teacher write it down. Through constant exposure to literature and writing, children begin to use different language forms that, in essence, mimic what is presented in books, so they start to speak in the expression and vocabulary that they would find in books and stories that they have heard (Holdaway, 1979).

The primary system for identifying words is the semantic relationships being expressed through meaningful stories and children's experiences (Smith, 1971). Syntax and morphology are used as a secondary system to supplement semantic elements. These two together are used to help children in decoding and appreciating language. The third and final system is the phonological system. phonic analysis is taught in mini-lessons (as are other component skills) as a mechanism to analyze words after a set of words has been learned and other contextual strategies are used (i.e., semantic and syntactic relationships among words).

Strategies essential for processing written language include self-regulating operations that involve self-monitoring of meaning construction, confirmation, and self-correction. In addition, children learn predicative strategies that enable them to use contextual cues and their knowledge of story plot and other structures to form hypotheses about words, events, and relationships in a story.

Pleasure and enjoyment of literature are developed through numerous positive experiences with books. Young children acquire an intrinsic reinforcement system that is illustrated by the amount of time they spend independently interacting with books. They enjoy being read to and enjoy pretending to read or just interacting and telling stories with the aid of a book.

Developmental Whole Language System

The initial process for developing literacy is to increase the complexity of the shared book experience in a graduated fashion. The *shared book experience* is an activity in which groups of students read from the same book, as in a traditional story time activity. During the activity, students gain familiarity with the text, become "book aware," develop motivation, and develop meaning construction strategies.

Once students possess an understanding of the relationship between oral and written language through shared book activities, they move into experiences that progress through three stages (Holdaway, 1979). In stage 1, the discovery phase, the shared book experiences are extended to encourage students' participation in making predictions, recognizing repetitive structures, and using problem-solving strategies to decode words. Stage 2 is the exploration stage, wherein students become familiar with a different text through rereadings. Innocent participation increases and is a very natural part of this whole process. Teachers provide instruction spontaneously as it is applicable to individual situations. Stage 3 involves independent experience and expression, as students begin to take books away and, individually or in small groups, imitate the teacher model. Although not necessarily recognizing individual words, they imitate the performatives of reading as if they were actually reading the book (e.g., moving the pages, asking questions, and making predictions).

As students begin to diverge because of different rates of reading development, teachers control the difficulty level of tasks. Development is a function of the number of repetitions of exposure to a book that individual students require before they are ready to read a book independently. With the use of a listening post, the teacher can again better control the tasks by increasing the number of repetitions for those students who require this while working with students who may not necessarily need that repetition. Concurrently, the emphasis is on allowing students to make predictions and accepting more open-ended types of responses or successive approximations to the actual correct response, rather than providing excessive correction. The amount of corrective feedback provided to children needs to be controlled at this early stage to avoid inhibiting students' willingness to take risks and to make predictions.

Reciprocal Teaching

A narrower application of holistic principles to reading comprehension has been developed by Palincsar and Brown (1984). The *reciprocal teaching model* is designed to assist students in what Holdaway (1979) refers to as operational factors of literacy. The model is based on students learning to use two comprehension strategies: self-directed summarization and self-directed questioning. *Self-directed summarization* entails students monitoring their progress through reading. They evaluate whether or not information is being gained and whether comprehension is progressing smoothly. If comprehension is faulty, then some remedial action is triggered. *Self-directed questioning* involves students pausing and asking questions dealing with clarifying information, interpreting information, or predicting events that are to occur later in the passage.

Teaching procedures for self-directed summarization and self-directed questioning are based generally on the concepts of proleptic teaching and expert scaffolding. The teacher provides a model of a comprehension strategy being taught and then gradually allows the child to take over the steps and procedures of applying the particular strategy. In addition, reciprocal teaching is to some extent similar to the work by Manzo (1975) in reciprocal questioning, but it is much more extensive. Teachers and students take turns not only asking questions about the text but, in the case of reciprocal teaching, also in generating summaries, making predictions about future events in reading passages, and clarifying misinterpretations of vague information that is provided in the text (see Table 3-3).

Implementation of the reciprocal teaching model involves a six-step process. First, a preview discussion is generated on the basis of information made available from reading the title and from predications about what will occur in the passage. If the reading stimulus is the continuation of a story begun during an earlier lesson, then the teacher asks questions to review several important points. Second, the students and teacher read the first segment of a passage. Third, the teacher/adult models and asks questions, makes summarization, clarifies information, and makes predictions. Fourth, the second segment of the passage is read. Fifth, students imitate asking questions, making summarizations, clarifying information, and making predictions. Sixth, the teacher then takes on the role of a facilitator, providing feedback about the quality of the questions, prompting students to ask questions, or clarifying for students what a summarization might be.

Effectiveness of Holistic Methods

The holistic model and reading instruction practices have a strong intuitive appeal. The focus on meaningful reading experiences that takes into account the terminal goal (i.e., reading to gain information and derive pleasurable vicarious experience) and the social role of reading (i.e., as a primary channel for communication of ideas) are attractive

TABLE 3-3   Self-Questioning Procedures Used to Summarize the Main Idea and Related Facts

Activate Prior Knowledge
— Tell students purpose of lesson.
— Preview discussion to call up students' relevant experiential base.
— If new passage, then read title and induce prediction through questioning.
— If continuation, ask questions to review several important points.

Model
— Read first section of passage.
— Teacher/adult models self-questioning and summarization:
    — Ask "What is the main idea?
        State, "The main idea is . . ."
    — Ask "What are two key facts?
        State, "Two key facts are . . ."
    — State, "This section is about . . ."
— Define self-questioning and summarization, show examples.
— Read next passage section.
— Teacher/adult models self-questioning and summarization:
    — Ask "What is the main idea?
        State, "The main idea is . . ."
    — Ask "What are two key facts?
        State, "Two key facts are . . ."
    — State, "This section is about . . ."

Relinquish
— Read next passage section.
— Student imitates self-questioning and summarization.
— Alternate teacher model/student imitation.
— Provide corrective feedback:
    — feedback about the quality of the self-questioning and summarizations,
    — prompting students to self-question and summarize, or
    — teaching in terms of clarifying for students what self-questioning and summarization are

to many teachers. However, the need to spend instructional time on enabling skills such as learning strategies dealing with sounding-out procedures or self-summarization need to be more openly acknowledged by whole language proponents. More descriptions need to be presented of the mini-lessons used in whole language to teach component skills. This would help explain how poor readers who characteristically do not learn well through incidental or indirect experience learn specific subskills in whole language programs.

Other criticism have been lodged regarding the lack of a workable format for evaluating student progress in reading. Ulman and Rosenberg (1986) argue that without measurable objectives to monitor incremental progress, teachers have compromised their need for accountability. Formative assessment is central to making instructional decisions that decrease the likelihood that at-risk students will flounder for extended periods of time without making progress.

Despite the concerns of proponents of a scientific approach to instruction, holists have directed teachers and researchers to consider many critical variables in reading instruction that seem to have been deemphasized in other instructional programs. The emphasis on reading as a purposeful act has sometimes been lost in an atmosphere of drilling on letter sounds and words in isolation and endless worksheet tasks. The social element of shared book experiences where students listen and read together to express written language is often overlooked in controlled vocabulary texts. The emphasis on strategies for students to construct meaning from stories instead of assuming that comprehension will improve by simply asking more comprehension questions is noteworthy. It is hoped that the debate over the merits of whole language versus more reductionistic approaches to reading instruction will continue to motivate careful reflection on theories and practices in reading instruction for at-risk learners.

Summary and Conclusion

Although no theory or method is espoused as a panacea, all have contributed in some powerful way to what we know about reading disabilities as conceptualized at the present time. Some have argued for theoretical purity and against a more eclectic accommodation of diverse perspectives. Smith and Heshusius (1986) contend, for instance, that application of holistic theory involves a foundational shift in the way theorists and practitioners view the world. This shift leads to a perspective so different that it is incompatible with earlier reductionistic views. However, Guba and Lincoln (1981) have presented a case for the parallel structures in the procedures used to study phenomena within the holistic paradigm and those used in reductionistic paradigms (i.e., psychoneurological, behavioral, and cognitive). From a more practical point of view, Kronick (1990) has argued for the need to seek to accommodate the blending of strengths from diverse paradigms and theoretical models. At the abstract level of discussing foundational principles and viewpoints, the differences among paradigms may be substantive; but at the application level, practitioners may engage in identical instructional activities yet claim allegiance to different paradigms. For instance, teachers who operate largely from a behavioral model can utilize cognitive strategies to help students gain meaning from text. Likewise, teachers who use a whole language approach can employ the structure of direct instruction methods during a mini-lesson on letter–sound correspondences. Holdaway (1979) makes the same point in acknowledging that the use of intrinsically motivating activities such as shared book experiences and writing in journals can and should be supplemented with extrinsic reinforcement.

What reading teachers can learn from special education research is that the reading problems experienced by children and youth have been studied from a range of different perspectives. There has not been any substantial breakthrough in what works derived from any one point of view. Nonetheless, there are important contributions from each that, when considered as a whole, can help teachers to construct well-balanced reading programs that provide for the total needs of their students. This includes providing sufficient structure to allow for efficient use of limited academic learning time, while still providing the opportunity for students to select preferred activities and materials and help determine their individual needs. It means helping students to develop into self-directed learners, which may entail the teacher being directive in the early stages of learning and then relinquishing control over time. It involves engaging students in functional reading and writing activities such as shared book experiences in which the social aspects of reading are encouraged and positive attitudes are shaped. This may necessarily mean decreasing the amount of instructional time dedicated to working on letter–sound correspondences or reading words in isolation. It means reading teachers making informed, data-based decisions to deviate from the structure of basal reading series by skipping stories or workbook pages in order to have students advance to more complex material or build fluency with less complex material. What reading teachers can learn from special education research is that the perspectives on reading are not necessarily incompatible; rather, they supplement each other toward unified perspectives.

References

Abt Associates. (1977). *Education as experimentation: A planned variation model.* Volume IV-B, Effects of Follow Through Models. Cambridge, MA: Abt Books.

Alley, G. R., & Deshler, D. D. (1979). *Teaching the learning disabled adolescent: Strategies and methods.* Denver: Love.

Anderson, L. M., Evertson, C. M., & Brophy, J. E. (1979). An experimental study of effective teaching in first-grade reading groups. *Elementary School Journal, 79,* 193–222.

Bandura, A. (1977). *Social learning theory.* Englewood Cliffs, NJ: Prentice-Hall.

Becker, W. C., Englemann, S., & Thomas, D. R. (1971). *Teaching: A course in applied psychology.* Chicago: Science Research Associates.

Blaskey, P., Scheiman, M., Parisi, M., Ciner, E. B., Gallaway, M., & Selznick, R. (1990). The effectiveness of Irlen filters for improving reading performance: A pilot study. *Journal of Learning Disabilities, 22,* 604–612.

Blau, H., & Loveless, E. J. (1982). Specific hemispheric-routing-TAK/v to teach spelling to dyslexics: VAK and VAKT challenged. *Journal of Learning Disabilities, 15,* 461–466.

Brown, A. (1978). Knowing when, where, and how to remember: A problem of metacognition. In R. Glaser (Ed.), *Advances in instruction psychology.* Hillsdale, NJ: Erlbaum.

Brown, A. L., Day, J. D., & Jones, R. S. (1983). The development of plans for summarizing texts. *Child Development, 54,* 968–979.

Bruner, J. S. (1966). *Toward a theory of instruction.* New York: Norton.

Carnine, D., Silbert, J., & Kameenui, E. J. (1990). *Direct instruction reading,* 2nd ed. Columbus, OH: Merrill.

Derry, S. J., & Murphy, D. A. (d1986). Designing systems that train learning ability: From theory to practice. *Review of Educational Research, 56*(1), 1–39.

Deshler, D. D., & Schumaker, J. B. (1986). Learning strategies: An instructional alternative for low-achieving adolescents. *Exceptional Children, 52,* 583–590.

Deshler, D. D., Schumaker, J. B., Alley, G. R., Warner, M. M., & Clark, F. L. (1982). Learning disabilities in adolescent and young adult populations: Research implications (Part 1). *Focus on Exceptional Children, 15*(1), 1–12.

Deshler, D. D., Schumaker, J. B., Lenz, B. K., & Ellis, E. S. (1984). Academic and cognitive interventions for LD adolescents (Part 2). *Journal of Learning Disabilities, 17*(3), 170–187.

Douglas, V. I., Parry, P., Marton, P., & Garson, C. (1976). Assessment of a cognitive training program for hyperactive children. *Journal of Abnormal Child Psychology, 4,* 389–410.

Ellis, E. E., Lenz, B. K., & Sabornie, E. J. (1987a). Generalization and adaptation of learning strategies to natural environments: Part 1. Critical agents. *Remedial and Special Education, 8,* 6–20.

Ellis, E. S., Lenz, B. K., & Sabornie, E. J. (1987b). Generalization and adaptation of learning strategies to natural environments: Part 2: Research into practice. *Remedial and Special Education, 8*(2), 6–23.

Englemann, S., & Bruner, E. (1984). *DISTAR reading I.* Chicago: Science Research Associates.

Englemann, S., & Carnine, D. (1982). *Theory of instruction: Principles and applications.* New York: Irvington.

Fernald, G. M. (1943). *Remedial techniques in basic school subjects.* New York: McGraw-Hill.

Fisher, C. W., Berliner, D. C., Filby, N. N., Marliave, R., Cahen, L. S., & Dishaw, M. M. (1980). Teaching behaviors, academic learning time, and student achievement: An overview. In C. Denham, & A. Lieberman (Eds.), *Time to learn.* Washington, DC: U.S. Government Printing Office.

Flavell, J. H. (1979). Metacognition and cognitive monitoring: A new area of psychological inquiry. *American Psychologist, 34,* 906–911.

Frostig, M. (1965). Teaching reading to children with perceptual disturbances. In R. M. Flower, F. Gorfman, & L. I. Lawson (Eds.), *Reading disorders—A multidisciplinary symposium.* Philadelphia: F. A. Davis.

Gillingham, A., & Stillman, B. (1965). *Remedial training for children with specific disability in reading, spelling, and penmanship,* 7th ed. Cambridge, MA: Educators Publishing Service.

Guba, E., & Lincoln, Y. (1981). *Effective evaluation.* San Francisco: Jossey-Bass.

Hallahan, D. P., Kauffman, J. M., & Lloyd, J. W. (1985). *Introduction to learning disabilities,* 2nd ed. Englewood Cliffs, NJ: Prentice-Hall.

Heshusius, L. (1986). Pedagogy, special education, and the lives of young children: A critical and futuristic perspective. *Journal of Education, 168*(3), 25–38.

Heshusius, L. (1989). The Newtonian mechanistic paradigm, special education, and contours of alternatives: An overview. *Journal of Learning Disabilities, 22,* 403–415.

Holdaway, D. (1979). *The foundations of literacy.* Sydney: Ashton Scholastic.

Hoyt, C. S. (1990). Irlen lenses and reading difficulties. *Journal of Learning Disabilities, 22,* 624–627.

Irlen, H. (1983, August). *Successful treatment of learning disabilities.* Paper presented at the ninety-first annual convention of the American Psychological Association, Anaheim, CA.

Jacobs, J. E., & Paris, S. G. (1987). Children's metacognition about reading: Issues in definition, measurement, and instruction. *Educational Psychologist, 22,* 255–278.

Kephart, N. C. (1960). *The slow learner in the classroom.* Columbus, OH: Merrill.

Kephart, N. C. (1971). *The slow learner in the classroom,* 2nd ed. Columbus, OH: Merrill.

Koenigsberg, R. S. (1973). An evaluation of visual versus sensorimotor methods for improving orientation discrimination of letter reversals by preschool children. *Child Development, 44,* 764–769.

Kronick, D. (1990). Holism and empiricism as complementary paradigms. *Journal of Learning Disabilities, 23,* 5–8.

Lloyd, J. (1980). Academic instruction and cognitive behavior modification: The need for attack strategy training. *Exceptional Education Quarterly, 1,* 53–63.

Lovitt, T. C. (1989). *Introduction to learning disabilities.* Boston: Allyn and Bacon.

Luchow, J. P., & Shepherd, M. J. (1981). Effects of multisensory training in perceptual learning. *Learning Disabilities Quarterly, 4,* 38–43.

Luria, A. (1961). *The role of speech in the regulation of normal and abnormal behaviors.* New York: Liveright.

Manzo, A. V. (1975). The ReQuest procedure. *Journal of Reading, 7,* 287–291.

Meichenbaum, D. (1980). Cognitive behavior modification with exceptional children: A promise yet unfulfilled. *Exceptional Education Quarterly, 1,* 83–88.

Mercer, C. D., & Mercer, A. R. (1989). *Teaching students with learning problems,* 3rd ed. Columbus, OH: Charles E. Merrill.

Miccinati, J. (1979). The Fernald technique: Modification increase the probability of success. *Journal of Learning Disabilities, 12*(3), 139–142.

Myers, C. A. (1978). Reviewing the literature on Fernald's technique of remedial reading. *The Reading Teacher, 31,* 614–617.

Newman, J. M. (1985). *Whole language: Theory in use.* Portsmouth, NH: Heinemann.

O'Connor, P. D., Sofo, F., Kendall, L., & Olsen, G. (1990). Reading disabilities and the effects of colored filters. *Journal of Learning Disabilities, 22,* 597–603.

Orton, S. T. (1925). "Word blindness" in school

children. *Archives of Neurology and Psychiatry,*
14, 581–615.

Orton, S. T., & Gillingham, A. (1968). Special disability in writing. In S. B. Childs (Ed.), *Education in specific language disability* (pp. 79–110). Pomfret, CT: Orton Society.

Palincsar, A. S., & Brown, A. L. (1984). Reciprocal teaching of comprehension-fostering and comprehension-monitoring activities. *Cognition and Instruction, 1,* 117–175.

Parker, R. M. (1990). Power, control, and validity in research. *Journal of Learning Disabilities, 22,* 613–620.

Poplin, M. (1987). Self-imposed blindness: the scientific method in education, *RASE, 8*(6), 31–37.

Poplin, M. (1988). The reductionistic fallacy in learning in learning disabilities: Replicating the past by reducing the present. *Journal of Learning Disabilities, 21,* 389–400.

Pressley, M., Levin, J. R., & Ghatala, E. S. (1984). Memory strategy monitoring in adults and children. *Journal of Verbal Learning and Verbal Behavior, 23,* 270–288.

Reid, D. K., & Hresko, W. P. (1981). *A cognitive approach to learning disabilities.* Toronto: McGraw-Hill.

Richek, M. A., List, L. K., & Lerner, J. W. (1983). *Reading problems: Diagnosis and remediation.* Englewood Cliffs, NJ: Prentice-Hall.

Robinson, L. W., & Conway, R. N. F. (1990). The effects of Irlen colored lens on students' specific reading skills and their perception ability: A twelve-month validity study. *Journal of Learning Disabilities, 22,* 588–596.

Robinson, R. P. (1941). *Effective study.* New York: Harper & Row.

Rohwer, W. D. (1980). An elaborative conception of learner differences. In R. E. Snow, P. A. Federico, & W. E. Montague (Eds.), *Aptitude, learning and instruction* (pp. 23–43). Hillsdale, NJ: Erlbaum.

Rosenberg, M. S., O'Shea, L. J., & O'Shea, D. J. (1991). *Student teacher to master teacher: A handbook for preservice and beginning teachers of students with mild and moderate handicaps.* New York: Macmillan.

Rosenshine, B. (1971). *Teaching behaviours and student achievement.* London: National Foundation for Educational Research.

Rosenshine, B. (1976). Academic engaged time, content covered, and direct instruction. *Journal of Education, 160*(3), 38–66.

Saint-John, L. M., & White, M. A. (1988). The effect of coloured transparencies on the reading performance of reading disabled children. *Australian Journal of Psychology, 40,* 403–411.

Schumaker, J. B., Denton, P. H., & Deshler, D. D. (1984). *Learning strategies curriculum: The paraphrasing strategy.* Lawrence: University of Kansas.

Smith, F. (1971). *Understanding reader: A psycholinguistic analysis of reading and learning to read.* New York: Holt, Rinehart & Winston.

Smith, J. K., & Heshusius, L. (1986). Closing down the conversation: The end of the quantitative/qualitative debate among educational inquirers. *Educational Researcher, 15,* 4–12.

Stevens, R., & Rosenshine, B. (1981). Advances in research on teaching. *Exceptional Education Quarterly, 1,* 1–9.

Strauss, A. A., & Lehtinen, L. E. (1947). *Psychopathology and education of the brain-injured child.* New York: Grune & Stratton.

Tarver, S. G. (1986). Cognitive behavior modification, direct instruction and holistic approaches to the education of students with learning disabilities. *Journal of Learning Disabilities, 19,* 368–375.

Thorpe, H. W., & Borden, K. S. (1985). The effect of multisensory instruction upon the on-task behaviors and word reading accuracy of learning disabled children. *Journal of Learning Disabilities, 18,* 279–286.

Torgesen, J. K. (1977). The role of non-specific factors in the task of performance of learning disabled children: A theoretical assessment. *Journal of Learning Disabilities, 10,* 27–35.

Ulman, J. D., & Rosenberg, M. S. (1986). Science and superstition in science education. *Exceptional Children, 52,* 459–460.

van den Honert, D. (1977). A neuropsychological technique for training dyslexics. *Journal of Learning Disabilities, 10,* 15–27.

Vygotsky, L. S. (1978). *Mind in society: The development of higher-psychological processes* (M. Cole, V. John-Steiner, S. Scribner, & E. Souberman, Eds. and Trans.) Cambridge, MA: Harvard University Press.

White, O. R., & Haring, N. G. (1980). *Exceptional teaching.* Columbus, OH: Merrill.

Whiting, P.R. (1985). How difficult can reading be? New insight into reading problems. *The Teaching of English, 49,* 49–55.

Whiting, P., & Robinson, G. R. (1988). Using Irlen coloured lenses for reading: A clinical study. *Australian Educational and Developmental Psychologist, 4,* 1–5.

Wolery, M., Bailey, D. B., & Sugai, G. M. (1988). Effective teaching. *Principles and procedures of applied behavior analysis with exceptional students.* Boston: Allyn and Bacon.

Wong, B. Y. L. (1988). Metacognition and learning disabilities. In T. G. Waller, D. Forrest, & E. Mackinnon (Eds.), *Metacognition, cognition, and human performance.* New York: Academic Press.

Changes in the Identification and Instruction of High-Risk Readers

MARY BETH MARR
University of North Carolina at Charlotte

RICHARD L. ALLINGTON
State University of New York at Albany

Key Concepts

- Reading products
- Subskill approach
- Single-setting diagnosis
- Skills first–application later approach
- Pull-out programs
- Differential instruction
- Reading process
- Informal, ungoing assessment

- Literature-based instruction
- Integrated language arts
- Strategy instruction
- Skills-through-application approach
- Curricular congruence
- Remedial instruction
- Chapter 1
- Basals
- Reading Recovery

Focusing Questions

- Define remedial instruction and its importance in teaching at-risk readers.
- Explain the Chapter 1 reading program, including its advantages and disadvantages.
- When assessing a student's ability when reading aloud, what are some things to which an examiner should pay attention? Why?
- What are some advantages and disadvantages to integrating children's literature into the reading curriculum? What does current research say?
- According to the federal mandate, who is advocated to plan an instructional program for high-risk readers? List some approaches to planning such a program.

Discussion Questions

- Reading instruction for at-risk readers is changing in significant ways. Discuss which changes you feel are most important and why.
- How are skills instruction and strategies instruction different?
- What are the advantages of the most naturalistic approaches to evaluating children's literacy development?

For over a century, the U.S. public and the education profession have engaged in public worrying about the "reading problem" in our schools. Over this time period, a variety of programs and procedures have been developed in an attempt to address these concerns. This chapter will briefly examine the traditional evaluation and instruction provided for high-risk readers and will focus on more current programs and procedures that have proved effective in meeting the needs of these students.

Traditionally, reading specialists evaluate students' reading ability through the use of standardized reading diagnostic tests. These tests consist of a series of subskills identified as necessary for success in reading. Students who perform poorly on the test are placed in remedial programs that pull students out of the classroom for instruction and consist of content predetermined by each student's test performance. The hope is that this specialized instruction will permit the student eventually to return to the classroom reading on grade level. Evaluation of these special programs and classroom observational research have shown, however, that this differentiated instruction is ineffective.

The current trend in the diagnosis and remediation of students with reading problems is to evaluate the strategies readers use during the act of reading—that is, those strategies for word recognition and comprehension that students use to extract meaning from the text and to read independently. To this end, informal and frequent evaluation of students' reading behavior is recommended. Instruction includes increased reading time both in and out of school; the use of literature-based programs; integrated reading and writing activities; and a skills-through-application focus. Research evaluating these programs has shown that students make significant gains in reading and frequently return to the classroom reading at or above grade level.

Traditional Practice

Identifying High-Risk Readers

Implicit in our evaluation of children's reading performance are underlying assumptions about the nature of reading. For quite some time, teachers and reading specialists have examined the level at which children are performing and their mastery of specific reading skills. This view of reading focuses on the product or outcome of having read a selection. It is assumed that children with proficient reading skills will be able to complete this series of tasks correctly. On the basis of this philosophy, a group of reading tests was developed that test mastery of skills believed to be essential if children are to become proficient readers. These skills might include the ability to recognize a number of words by sight, to decode words accurately, to read sentences orally with accuracy, or to answer varied types of comprehension questions correctly. These are all subtests that emphasize accuracy of performance.

At the outset of the school year, the teacher may notice students who struggle to read the grade-level text and have difficulty completing corresponding worksheets. Standardized achievement test scores such as the California Achievement Test (1987) further substantiate that a problem exists. The test reveals that grade equivalent scores in reading comprehension and vocabulary are below average. These children may then be referred for further testing to identify the nature of their problems. A reading specialist or school psychologist would typically use a diagnostic test such as the Gates-McKillop-Horowitz (1981) or the Durrell Analysis of Reading Difficulty (1980) to gather more detailed information. These tests will evaluate ability to read a short paragraph and also test a series of reading subskills such as word recognition, syllabication, sound–symbol associations, and blending. Again, grade equivalent scores on each subtest are reported to compare students' performance with that expected of an average student in their grade. These assessment data provide further evidence that a child is performing below grade level, and indicate which specific subskills need remediation.

Remedial Instruction

After children's reading difficulties have been identified, each child is then matched with a program to provide remediation. A major characteristic of traditional remedial reading programs is that the content of the program is predetermined by children's performance on a set of subskills like word attack and comprehension. Each child's tutorial consists of a series of activities that focus on these various subskills, such as cloze sentence strips to work on context clues, phonic worksheets, or word wheels to increase sight word recognition. A large portion of the tutorial is spent on these subskill activities, and the remaining minutes of the lesson are set aside for reading books. This instructional philosophy presumes that with concentrated instruction on skills, these children will then return to the classroom, apply these skills to their reading, and thus eventually begin to read on grade level. Walmsley and Walp (1990) call this a "skills first–application later" approach.

In fact, quite the opposite occurs. Yes, these children achieve subskill mastery as intended by the remedial activities. They can quickly and accurately complete activities on isolated skills. More often than not, however, they do not transfer or use this knowledge when reading books, stories, or basals. Because these skills have been heavily practiced in isolation, with only limited opportunities provided for the extended reading of text, these students are not proficient at applying this knowledge flexibly when reading. Thus, they do not make the gains in reading needed to perform at grade level in the classroom and frequently remain in remedial reading throughout much of their school career.

Chapter 1: How Effective?

Allington (1986) and others have examined the Chapter 1 reading programs and made some significant observations regarding their effectiveness. Perhaps the most notable problem was a lack of congruence or coordination between the remedial reading program and the classroom. Typically, the children were asked to read basal stories and complete worksheets in the classroom. In the reading room, they worked on skills and did a bit of reading (even using the same basal). However, the children were taught different skills and different, often conflicting, strategies to use when decoding words. For example, the classroom teacher said, "Sound it out," or "What does the word begin with?" The remedial teacher said, "Read the sentence and see if you can figure out the word by choosing one that fits with the meaning of the sentence." These different instructional cues were often confusing to already anxious and frustrated readers. They also reflected the difference among teachers in philosophy of reading instruction and knowledge of the reading process. In short, although the children were receiving reading instruction twice a day, the nature of instruction was confusing them even more and rendering the instruction ineffective.

Recent changes in Chapter 1 program regulations were adopted in an attempt to ameliorate this fragmentation of instructional experiences. Chapter 1 programs are now required to be coordinated with the instructional program offered in the regular classroom, and Chapter 1 instruction is to be designed to foster success in the classroom. However, recent evidence (Meyers, Gelzheiser, & Yelich, 1991) suggests that the required coordination is not easily achieved. Many Chapter 1 programs have moved toward providing supportive instruction that is collaboratively planned with classroom teachers, but many others remain largely separate and distinct from classroom instruction.

A second problem with compensatory education programs has to do with the nature of pull-out programs. Pull-out programs are those that remove children from the classroom to provide concentrated instruction in reading by a specialist. Removing children from the classroom attracts special attention to those children who also miss classroom instruction. When the children return, they often have to make up the missed work. Also, the classroom teacher and the specialist frequently do not discuss the content of the students' instructional programs, so neither knows what the other is covering during these children's reading periods. In addition, the amount of time it takes for these students to leave the class, arrive at the specialist's room, and set up again is approximately 15 minutes per day, resulting in 40 hours per academic year of lost instruction (Allington, 1986). In these situations, specialist teachers must be twice as effective as classroom teachers if even small achievement gains are expected. Thus, serious consideration has been given to the costs versus the benefits of traditional remedial pull-out programs.

Classroom Instruction: How Effective?

Researchers have also taken a close look at the type of instruction these high-risk readers receive in the classroom (Good, 1983). They, too, note a focus on learning the necessary skills as prerequisites to reading. Typically, the instruction of high-risk readers focuses on phonics or word analysis skills. Most of their reading is done orally, and they read much shorter texts—a couple of sentences or a small paragraph rather than a complete story. The teacher was observed to interrupt or correct the students frequently while they were reading. Cues given to assist with word attack focused on sounds rather than word meanings or the context of the sentence. The amount of time the students were engaged in real reading tasks was limited as compared with the time set aside for reading instruction. What was particularly startling about these observations was the fact that they contrasted sharply with the reading instruction provided proficient readers (Allington, 1991). Good readers read complete stories, focused on meaning or used context clues with word attack skills to decode unfamiliar words, read silently, had fewer teacher interruptions, and spent more time engaged in the act of reading than their less proficient peers. From these classroom observations came the clear realization that the nature of reading instruction provided these high-risk readers may indeed be part of the reason for their reading problem.

With the concerns regarding the illiteracy rate in the United States and the findings of classroom and remedial observational research regarding the effectiveness of our programs, a reexamination of students' needs and existing programs was in order.

Current Trends

The Reading Process: A Focus on Strategies

What occured first was a reexamination of the reading process. Just what skills are needed for children to become proficient readers? What strategies do readers use during the act of reading? Researchers and teachers began to evaluate which skills are used during reading, how flexibly children can use them, whether children understand what they read, whether they can make predictions during reading, whether they self-correct reading errors, and so on. In short, the nature of reading was reconceptualized. No longer was the focus on the products of reading, such as the number of words read correctly, the number of questions answered correctly, or the level of difficulty of material successfully decoded. Instead, the focus was on the process or act of reading to determine if children were using effective and flexible strategies to decode words and comprehend the message. This change in focus also had implications for assessment and instruction.

Identifying High-Risk Readers

Currently, it is felt that the best way to assess a student's reading ability is to listen to him or her read aloud. During the act of reading, the examiner can listen for fluency and phrasing. That is, does the child's oral reading approximate the fluency and phrasing the child shows in his or her oral language, revealing the child's knowledge of the speech-to-print relationship and his or her familiarity with reading? The examiner can also record any mistakes or miscues students make during reading. Analysis of these miscues will reveal students' knowledge and use of context clues, phonics, structural analysis, and syllabication. Also, the examiner can monitor students' self-corrections. Self-corrections reveal that a student is thinking about his or her reading and can detect inconsistencies in meaning as a result of reading errors. They also show a level of independence in the student's reading skill; that is, the student can correct his or her mistakes using alternative cues or strategies, without teacher assistance.

In short, observations during the act of reading reveal a great deal about children's knowledge of the reading process—their knowledge that the purpose of reading is to extract meaning. It also reveals their knowledge of specific strategies for decoding words and their ability to use these strategies flexibly during reading. At the very early reading stages, this type of assessment can tell us if children know to read from left to right; can use pictures to help predict what the text is about; and understand the concept of a letter word, or sentence (Clay, 1979).

Of significance is the concept that reading assessment should be informal and directly relevant to classroom instruction. This view holds that assessment can occur frequently and informally using the very materials children use in the classroom. Through the use of running records, a form of analyzing students' oral reading behavior (Clay, 1985), the teacher can record children's oral reading performance on storybooks, basals, or magazines during reading activities in the classroom. Other informal assessment measures could include book conferences, discussions with students regarding the theme, character, and plot of the book they are reading. These conferences give sound information about children's ability to remember and comprehend the story. Another measure, called a comprehension matrix (Wood, 1988) is an informal grid listing various comprehension skills the teacher feels are important, such as ability to recall main ideas or to make predictions about the story. As children informally recall what they have read, the teacher checks the corresponding box on the grid. This then becomes an informal record of comprehension performance and can be used frequently over time to examine patterns and changes. Samples of students' work and lists of books read can also be added to children's assessment files or portfolios (Valencia, 1990). In this way a more comprehensive picture, as opposed to a single-setting diagnosis, of children's knowledge of reading, abilities, and reading preferences can be obtained for instructional purposes.

Perhaps the most important change in evaluating children's reading development has been in observing performance to document what strategies each child uses rather than simply focusing on deficiencies in performance. Current evaluation emphasizes the pattern of development across time and focuses on creating instructional opportunities to foster continued development. Thus, the emphasis has shifted from what children *cannot* do and identifying the causes for these deficiencies to a focus on what children *can* do and the nature of instruction needed to further development.

Classroom Reading Instruction

With regard to instruction, significant changes have occurred in the reading curriculum and its delivery. Perhaps the first noticeable change has been the use of children's literature as the text for reading. Children's literature provides interesting stories of varied plot, characters, setting, and genre. The vocabulary is enriching for the children, who become readily involved in the stories and illustrations. Likewise, the teacher can construct a variety of activities that promote varied levels of comprehension to go along with these stories. Because the stories are so rich and meaningful, the type of activities designed to focus on different reading skills can be far more varied than those developed around the contrived texts of the traditional basal reader. Also, when they read these books at school with teacher guidance, children may more readily select other books by the same author or on a similar theme during their library and free reading time.

Characteristics of literature-based programs include time spent reading aloud to students on a regular basis, daily opportunities for sustained silent reading, self-selection of reading material by students, the use of books on audio tape, and meaningful output activities such as writing that follow the reading experiences. Research comparing the effectiveness of these programs with that of the conventional basal program has shown that students make significant gains in vocabulary and reading comprehension when using the literature-based programs (Cohen, 1968; Eldridge & Butterfield, 1986).

A note of caution is needed, however. Recently, Stahl and Miller (1989) found that these programs work less well with at-risk populations beyond kindergarten. Their synthesis of the research data revealed that these language-based programs were less efficient in teaching sound–symbol relations. They suggest that because high-risk students have limited exposure to books prior to coming to school, they take longer to learn print concepts than their middle- and upper-SES peers. While the evidence suggests that literature language-based reading programs can be very effective, there is no assurance that they will be unless we teach effectively.

A second change has been the integration of the language arts. In the past, classroom teachers set aside specific amounts of time for spelling, writing, reading, and language activities on a daily basis. Frequently, textbooks focusing on specific skills went along with each of these language arts. The skills were not matched with each other, and children showed difficulty understanding how these skills were used to learn new information. In many schools today, that no longer occurs. Instead, a period of time, 90 to 120 minutes for example, is set aside for language arts instruction. During that time, the children will be reading, writing, discussing, or listening to others share ideas on a topic, theme, or unit of study. Although the children are engaged in the various language arts skills as before, these skills now become more useful and meaningful because they are integrated. For example, the students may read *Digging Up Dinosaurs* by Aliki (1981), write a story about what it was like to live during the time of *Tyrannosaurus rex,* discuss ideas for their story with their partner, and listen to the "Reading Rainbow" video on dinosaurs. The language arts skills are integrated around a theme or unit of study. Further, the children can better understand how to use listening, speaking, reading, writing, spelling (i.e., literacy skills) to learn more about the topic. Although the concept of an integrated language arts program is not entirely new (Moffett, 1968), it has now gained more widespread support as research has underscored the importance of oral language in the development of reading and writing skills.

Even many classrooms that do not fully integrate their language arts around particular themes do integrate reading and writing activities. Again, the rationale for this integration comes from the research. Pearson and Tierney (1984) state that the two processes of reading and writing are complementary. That is, writing is the active process of creating meaning with text; and reading is the active process of extracting meaning from text. Meaning, understanding, and communication are at the core of both processes. The two processes parallel each other with regard to the cognitive skills involved, such as setting a purpose for reading or writing, accessing prior knowledge, making predictions, and evaluating. Further, we can use writing to clarify, elaborate, critique, analyze, or extend our thinking about what we read. Thus, the two processes, when used together, complement each other and promote the development of proficiency in both.

One can see the reciprocal nature of integrating reading and writing at the kindergarten level in such activities as a shared book experience using *Brown Bear, Brown Bear* (Martin, 1983), followed by drawing and writing a pattern story using invented spelling. Other examples of this integration, with older students, include the use of literature logs (e.g., "Describe how Sarah's life in North Dakota was different from her life in Maine") or dialogue journals while reading a novel like *Sarah Plain and Tall* (MacLachlan, 1985). Activities such as the "author's chair" give students an opportunity to share with others what they have read and written (Graves & Hansen, 1983). These activities, which integrate reading and writing, have resulted in increased performance in both skill areas and a better understanding of how reading and writing are tools for learning.

Educators have become increasingly aware of the amount of time actually spent reading text and its effect on subsequent reading achievement. The more children read, the better readers they become. In fact, engaged time in reading has become the single most significant factor in reading achievement (Anderson, Wilson, & Fielding, 1988). Also, early readers learn to read by reading (Smith, 1978; Clay, 1979) not by spending time learning a series of isolated subskills. Hence, what has started to occur in the classroom reading curriculum is increased time spent actually reading. This may take a variety of forms, such as teacher-directed reading (like the conventional basal lesson), independent sustained silent reading, story sharing, teacher read-aloud, and the author's chair (Graves & Hansen, 1983).

Finally, a change has occurred in the traditional basal reading program. Basals have increased their use of unadapted children's literature, reduced the number of workbook pages assigned, and reduced their emphasis on isolated skills. They have moved toward the use of children's literature, the integration of writing activities with reading, the promotion of classroom libraries, and more "authentic" assessments of student progress. Although they have retained some of their traditional basal characteristics—such as material at increasing levels of difficulty, scope and sequence charts, and teacher's manuals to guide instruction—they have tried to reflect the more current views of the marketplace, including the curricular changes noted here.

In summary, reading instruction has changed. Research has shown that literature-based reading programs that integrate reading, writing, speaking, and listening skills significantly improve students' reading performance (Tunnell & Jacobs, 1989; Walmsley & Walp, 1990). Also, with increased opportunities to read text for sustained periods of time, students make important gains in reading (Anderson et al., 1988). Overall, there has been a dramatic increase in the use of literature and in our expectations about children's reading of books. At the same time, however, most teachers still use basals in some way. Most do not use them exclusively or follow them slavishly but, instead, fall into the "basal and books" category described in Figure 4-1.

Reading Skills Instruction

Traditionally, reading skills instruction has occurred by identifying a set of subskills at various grade levels deemed appropriate for reading development. During a reading lesson, these skills would be taught using worksheets, flashcards, or word wheels. The children would then read stories designed to practice the use of these skills in context. This

---

Basal: In these classrooms, the basal (defined as a set of commercial curriculum materials) is the primary curriculum, and the basal lesson plan is followed sequentially with a skills component focus. The role of trade books is minimal, but many have SSR independently after student has finished work and teacher read-alouds. There is no literature instruction per se, although book reports may be required in upper grades. Writing is a separate lesson from reading, generally, and is focused on editing skills.

Basal and Books: In these classrooms, the basal is the core curriculum but may or may not have a skills emphasis. The basal is used regularly, and lessons proceed linearly through the series. Trade books are used in instruction, the teacher often reads to students, and student independent reading of self-selected trade books in class is common. These trade books may be linked to the basal lesson plan. Book selection for literature lessons is often teacher- or district-directed. Writing is often a combination of basal-driven and free-standing process lessons but is not a wholly integrated plan.

Books and Basal: In these classrooms, trade books are the primary reading curriculum. Reading instruction and evaluation are planned around trade books, but with regular dips into the basal for whole class instruction of a skill, for genre study, or for evaluation. The basal is often used as a benchmark for a child's progress, to provide teacher with a sense of students' development in traditional grade-level terms. Writing is often linked to trade books, but other writing activities are observed.

Books: Instruction and evaluation are planned around trade books in these classrooms. Various genres and themes are explored at appropriate grade levels. Skills and strategies are taught in the context of literature reading. Integration of reading and writing planned and frequently observed. Often there is a child-centered philosophy, with the teacher encouraging self-selection and exploration of literature. However, in some cases, selection of literature is teacher- or district-directed.

FIGURE 4-1 **A classification scheme for describing four approaches to literature implementation in elementary school classrooms**

Source: Prepared by Richard L. Allington & Kim Baker, Center on Literature Teaching and Learning, SUNY at Albany, October, 1991.

Note: Our use of the term *basal* represents a broader view than has, perhaps, been traditional. We include various commercially available sets of trade books (usually "leveled" and often with worksheets and teaching suggestions) in our use of the term.

instruction has been called a "skills first–application later" approach to reading (Walmsley & Walp, 1990).

Currently, reading skills instruction has changed to reflect an emphasis on strategies instead of isolated skill instruction. That is, the skills are viewed as strategies-in-use, those strategies used to decode and comprehend the text during the act of reading. As a result, teachers are concerned with both developing these skills and teaching children to use them effectively and efficiently while reading. This skills instruction is explicit, demonstrating to the students how, when, and why to use the strategy. This explicit strategy instruction has proved enormously successful, especially with children having reading difficulty (Duffy, Roehler, & Rackliffe, 1986).

Also consistent with this strategy emphasis is a skills-through-application approach to reading (Walmsley & Walp, 1990). As the child is reading and difficulties arise, the problems are noted and skills instruction is planned. This approach has several advantages. First, only those skills identified as needed and relevant to real reading are taught. Second, instruction and application of these skills in the context of real reading can readily occur. If instruction on the use of context clues is needed, for example, this can occur immediately as the child is reading and has difficulty, or later using text examples from the story, or as follow-up application in a second chapter or story. This approach also eliminates the problem of children who master an isolated reading skill but cannot use it in their reading. Within the classroom, skill and strategy needs can be identified and remedied with the whole class, with small groups, or on an individual basis as needed. Because these instructional changes have occurred within the classroom, they have also influenced specific programs designed for high-risk readers.

Changes in Remedial Instruction

As previously discussed, conventional remedial reading programs have not been as effective as they need to be. Perhaps this is because of a heavy subskill emphasis, perhaps because of a lack of curricular congruence with the classroom, or perhaps because of lost instructional time in pull-out programs. Now that the findings regarding classroom observational research have been shared (Good, 1983) and evaluation of existing Chapter 1 reading programs has occurred (Allington & McGill-Franzen, 1989), these programs are undergoing changes.

Program Delivery

With regard to existing pull-out programs, a federal mandate requires that specialists coordinate their instruction with that occurring in the classroom. Currently, it is advocated that a team of teachers, specialists and classroom, plan the instructional program for high-risk readers, agreeing on skill strengths and weaknesses and discussing ways to meet the child's needs. They should continue to communicate with one another about the child's progress through informal conferences or staff meetings. Also, weekly notes about content coverage may be shared (e.g., "traveling notebook"; Allington & Shake, 1986).

In an effort to better coordinate the classroom and the specialist's pull-out program, several instructional models have been tried. The most conventional approach is simply for the specialist to provide remedial students with additional personalized instruction and practice. This occurs when the specialist works alongside the classroom teacher helping the less able readers. Then, during remedial class, the students spend additional time on the same books and activities, with the remedial teacher providing supportive instruction that fosters development of important strategies.

Another approach has been to change the responsibilities of the reading specialist (Walp & Walmsley, 1989). Both teachers may share responsibility for the total language arts program, but they divide different aspects of the program. For example, the classroom teacher may teach reading skills from the basal reader, and the remedial teacher would work with children's literature on topics coordinated in the basal.

A more avant garde approach has the reading specialist come into the classroom to work with the students. This has been referred to as a *pull-in program* or an in-class model of instruction. The classroom teacher and specialist confer regarding the students' instructional needs, and the specialist comes into the classroom to work specifically with the high-risk students. The content of instruction may be slightly different from the classroom content, but on the same general topic. For example, if the class was studying whales and reading *Whales, Giants of the Sea* (Marko, 1980), the specialist might have a student complete an assigned reading from the book *Whales* (Gibbons, 1991), followed by explicit instruction on how to write a summary paragraph about the beluga whale. In this way, the student could gain additional practice reading and writing, begin to learn summarization skills, and still explore the topic of whales with the class.

Another approach would be for the specialist to work in the classroom using the same content, but working toward a different student need. For example, if the topic was mysteries and the whole class had been reading Chapter 4 in *Encyclopedia Brown Takes the Case* (Sobol, 1974), the specialist could conduct a shared reading of the same chapter and follow the reading with the teaching of a strategy for decoding polysyllabic words, using the words from Chapter 4. In this way the specialist provides much needed strategy instruction using the same material and content as the classroom teacher.

Recently, Meyers, Gelzheiser, and Yelich (1991) have studied the effectiveness of pull-in programs and found that teachers participating in the study, both classroom and specialist, met more frequently, discussed specific aspects of instruction, collaborated closely, and felt they learned from each other, in contrast to the teachers participating in the pull-out program. The authors caution that these in-class teachers chose to work with one another rather than being assigned together. They conclude that in-class remedial instruction can be a successful venture for both students and teachers.

Content Changes

Along with changes in the delivery of remedial instruction, changes have occurred in the specific content of instruction. In his review of compensatory reading instruction, Allington (1986) noted that remedial teachers spent about 33 percent of their time on management, 25 percent of their time on word recognition activities, 12 percent of their time on comprehension, and just 2 percent on silent reading. An alarming amount of time was being spent on activities that did not promote reading achievement. Currently, literature-based reading programs are being used with high-risk readers. Much more time is spent engaged in the acts of reading connected text, focusing on meaning, and combining writing activities with reading. Shanklin (1990) found that effective Chapter 1 teachers provided print-rich environments using both expository and narrative materials that also matched the students' instructional reading levels. Students were encouraged to read at home, and books were made readily available. These teachers also made efforts to complement the curricula of the classroom. Similarly, preliminary findings from the North Warren project reveal that remedial reading students are not only reading more books but also, after two years of an integrated literature and writing program, have made such gains that most are no longer eligible for remedial services (Walmsley & Walp, 1990).

Perhaps the most widely known intervention program for high-risk readers is Reading Recovery (Clay, 1985). This program is intended for young readers experiencing difficulty in their first year of reading instruction. It consists of daily lessons of thirty minutes each, which supplement classroom instruction. In a one-on-one tutorial setting, young children reread a familiar story for practice, read a second story while the teacher analyzes reading performance, work with letters and word analysis on an as-needed basis (focusing on the skills deemed necessary from the readings), write a message for a story, and begin reading a new book (Pinnell, Fried & Estice, 1990). Clay (1979) believes strongly in the philosophy that children learn to read by reading. That is, when children are engaged in reading texts, they will develop and practice their reading skills. Also, one-on-one instruction, allows teachers follow closely the children's progress toward this goal of literacy, "confirming their efforts and helping them to build a firm knowledge base regarding reading strategies" (DeFord, Lyons, & Pinnell, 1991).

The purpose of the program is to teach the children how to use a variety of reading strategies flexibly so that they can gain control over print. This inner control will then free them to read and learn independently (Clay, 1991). The goal of the program is to accelerate reading development through an intensive but brief (ten to fifteen weeks) tutorial and then return the students to the classroom reading on grade level.

This program began in New Zealand in the 1970s and was piloted in the United States in the autumn of 1984. Results from the U.S. program implementation in the first year indicated that 73 percent of those children who received at least 60 instructional lessons (approximately 12 weeks) were reading independently and thus successfully discontinued from the program. They continued to make progress and maintain these gains well into the second year (Pinnell et al., 1990). Reading Recovery has been an effective early intervention program. Through daily intensive instruction, it accelerates the reading development of young children by providing opportunities to read and write with close support from the teacher. More detail regarding the Reading Recovery program is provided in Chapter 9 of this book.

Summary

During the past decade, significant changes have occurred in the identification and treatment of high-risk readers. Traditionally, children at risk for reading failure have been given a standardized reading diagnostic test designed to identify those reading subskills in need of remediation. This philosophy of reading instruction emphasized the products or outcomes of proficient reading behavior and stressed instruction in isolated skills deemed necessary for success in reading. The reading assessment occurred in a single setting, a day and time set aside for diagnosis of the reading difficulty. Instruction then followed. Readers were assigned to a remedial reading class, which involved pulling the student out of the regular classroom for reading instruction. Instruction in skills occurred first, followed by the brief reading of text. This type of instruction differed significantly from that provided to average and above-average readers in the classroom.

As a result of classroom observational research and the evaluation of compensatory education programs, much concern was raised about the lack of progress made by these high-risk readers. These students did not maintain gains made in reading and, more often than not, read below grade placement and remained in the remedial pull-out programs throughout their school career. It was also noted that the reading instruction these students received in the classroom was not congruent with that received in their compensatory education classes, creating more confusion for these already anxious students.

Clearly, a second look at remedial instruction was needed. Currently, high-risk readers are identified from observations of their performance while reading. The specialist looks at the strategies and cues these readers use to extract meaning from text. This philosophy of reading instruction emphasizes the process of reading—that is, what readers do during the act of reading. Samples of students' reading behaviors, book preferences, and recollections of their readings are gathered informally and over time to compile a more comprehensive picture of the students' reading ability. Materials used for the assessment are those used daily, during classroom reading instruction.

Reading instruction in both the classroom and compensatory education classes has also changed. Frequently, children's literature is used as the text for reading instruction. Opportunities for sustained reading of text and for self-selection of reading materials are also provided. In addition, language arts instruction is integrated. A theme-centered approach is used whereby books are selected based on a theme, and corresponding activities involving reading, writing, speaking, and listening are conducted. This integration improves readers' reading and writing skills and helps them better understand how reading, writing, speaking, and listening are tools for learning. Skills instruction has changed in that the emphasis is now placed on strategies used during the reading of text, rather than the practice of skills in isolation. Instruction in strategies is explicit and stresses their flexible and efficient use. Frequently, students read first, then practice word analysis and comprehension strategies on an as-needed basis. This has been called a skills-through-application approach. Finally, compensatory education and classroom teachers are coordinating their reading curricula by planning together and assisting one another with reading instruction in the classroom.

Preliminary data evaluating programs designed for these high-risk readers are impressive, showing substantial and sustained gains in these readers' performance. A great deal has been learned about the needs of high-risk readers and about effective instruction. Now we need to put this knowledge to work and begin to make a difference in these children's lives (McGill-Franzen & Allington, 1991).

References

Aliki. (1981). *Digging Up Dinosaurs*. New York: Crowell.

Allington, R. L. (1986). Policy constraints and effective compensatory reading instruction: A review.

In J. Hoffman (Ed.), *Effective teaching of reading and research and practice* (pp. 261–289). Newark, DE: International Reading Association.

Allington, R. L. (1991). How policy and regulation influence instruction for at-risk learners, or why poor readers rarely comprehend well. In L. Idol & B. F. Jones (Eds.), *Educational values and cognitive instruction: Implications for reform.* (pp. 273–296). Hillsdale, NJ: Erlbaum.

Allington, R. L., & McGill-Franzen, A. M. (1989). School response to reading failure: Instruction for Chapter 1 and special education students in grades two, four, and eight. *Elementary School Journal, 89,* 530–542.

Allington, R. L., & Shake, M. C. (1986). Remedial reading: Achieving curricular congruence in classroom and clinic. *The Reading Teacher, 39,* 648–654.

Anderson, R. C., Wilson, P. T., & Fielding, L. G. (1988). Growth in reading and how children spend their time outside of school. *Reading Research Quarterly, 23*(3), 285–303.

California Achievement Test. (1987). Monterey: California Test Bureau, McGraw-Hill.

Clay, M. M. (1979). *Reading: The patterning of complex behavior, 2nd ed. Auckland, New Zealand: Heinemann.*

Clay, M. M. (1985). The early detection of reading difficulties. Portsmouth, NH: Heinemann.

Cohen, D. (1968). The effect of literature and vocabulary and reading achievement. *Elementary English, 45,* 209–213, 217.

DeFord, D. E., Lyons, C. A., & Pinnell, G. S. (1991). *Bridges to Literacy: Learning from Reading Recovery.* Portsmouth, NH: Heinemann.

Duffy, G. G., Roehler, L. R., & Rackliffe, G. (1986). How teachers' instructional talk influences students' understanding of lesson content. *Elementary School Journal, 87,* 4–16.

Durrell Analysis of Reading Difficulty. (1980). San Antonio, TX: Psychological Corporation.

Eldridge, J. L., & Butterfield, D. (1986). Alterntives to traditional reading instruction. *The Reading Teacher, 40,* 32–37.

Gates-McKillop-Horowitz. (1981). *Reading diagnostic tests.* Colchester, VT: Teachers College Press.

Gibbons, G. (1991). *Whales.* New York: Holiday House.

Good, T. (1983). Research in classroom teaching. In

L. S. Shulman & G. Sykes (Eds.), *Handbook of teaching and policy* (pp. 42–80). New York: Longman.

Graves, D., & Hansen, J. (1983). The author's chair. *Language Arts, 60*(2), 176–183.

MacLachlan, P. (1985). *Sarah plain and tall.* New York: Harper & Row.

Marko, K. D. (1980). *Whales, giants of the sea.* New York: Abingdon.

Martin, B. (1983). *Brown bear, brown bear.* New York: Holt, Rinehart and Winston.

McGill-Franzen, A., & Allington, R. L. (1991). Every child's right: Literacy. *The Reading Teacher, 45*(2), 86–90.

Meyers, J. B., Gelzheiser, L., & Yelich, G. (1991). Do pull-in programs foster teacher collaboration? *Remedial and Special Education, 12,* 7–15.

Moffett, J. (1968). *A student-centered language arts curriculum, grades K–6: A handbook for teachers.* Boston: Houghton Mifflin.

Pearson, P. D., & Tierney, R. (1984). On becoming a thoughtful reader: Learning to read like a writer. In A. Purves & O. Niles (Eds.), *Becoming readers in a complex society,* Eighty-third NSSE Yearbook. Chicago: University of Chicago Press.

Pinnell, G. S., Fried, M., & Estice, R. M. (1990). Reading Recovery: Learning how to make a difference. *The Reading Teacher, 43,* 282–295.

Shanklin, N. (1990). Improving the comprehension of at-risk readers: An ethnographic study of four Chapter 1 teachers, grades 4–6. *Reading, Writing, and Learning Disabilities, 6,* 137–148.

Smith, F. (1978). *Understanding reading,* 2nd ed. New York: Holt, Rinehart and Winston.

Sobol, D. (1974). *Encyclopedia Brown takes the case.* New York: T. Nelson.

Stahl, S., & Miller, P. (1989). Whole language and language experience approaches for beginning reading: A quantitative research synthesis. *Review of Educational Research, 59*(1), 87–116.

Tunnell, M., & Jacobs, J. (1989). Using "real" books: Research findings on literature based reading instruction. *The Reading Teacher, 42,* 470–477.

Valencia, S. (1990). A portfolio approach to classroom reading assessment. *The Reading Teacher, 43,* 338–340.

Walmsley, S., & Walp, T. (1990). Integrating literature and composing into the language arts curriculum: Philosophy and practice. *Elementary School*

Journal, 90(3), 251–274.

Walp, T. P., Walmsley, S. A. (1989). Instructional and philosophical congruence: Neglected aspects of coordination. *The Reading Teacher, 42,* 364–368.

Wood, K. D. (1988). Techniques for assessing students' potential for learning. *The Reading Teacher, 41,* 440–447.

Chapter 5

Characteristics of Students with Disabilities and How Teachers Can Help

JOHN BEATTIE
University of North Carolina at Charlotte

Key Concepts

- Students with mild disabilities
- Learning disabilities
- Communication disorders
- Mental retardation
- Behavior disorders
- Automaticity
- Restrictive classroom setting
- Strategic reading
- Decoding
- Letter clusters
- Modeling
- Articulation disorder

- Voice disorder
- Emotionally disturbed
- Direct instruction
- LEA
- Neurological impress
- Repeated reading
- Sight word approach
- Linguistic approach
- Whole language
- Directed Reading-Thinking Activity

Focusing Questions

- What are the five components of an effective reading process?
- What is the distinction between strategic reading and pleasure reading? Why is strategic reading useful?
- What is the implication of reading practice for reading comprehension?
- List and explain some communication disorders.
- List some biological/medical categories of the causes of mental retardation.

Discussion Questions

- Discuss the relationship between decoding and comprehension and its importance.
- Explain the concept of letter clusters and its relevance to a reader's comprehension.
- Suggest some ways to improve a reader's comprehension.
- What are some possible reasons for a reader having poor comprehension?
- Discuss the differences between students with communiction disorders, mental retardation, and behavior disorders.

Students with disabilities are similar to high-risk learners (described in Chapter 4) in that each group is likely to have difficulty with academic work, especially reading. High-risk learners identified in the early developmental stages often fail to meet specific standards established for students with disabilities. In other words, high-risk learners often do not qualify for special education services. These high-risk learners often continue to experience difficulty with reading. A significant number of students, however, do meet established criteria and qualify for services in special education. This chapter will describe students with disabilities and extend the previous chapter by examining the specific, unique needs of these students. Students with learning disabilities, communication disorders, mental retardation, and behavior disorders will be discussed, and the unique reading needs of each of these groups will be considered. Finally, instructional approaches will be reviewed. In general, this chapter will provide the reader with a description of the unique characteristics of students with disabilities, as well as instructional techniques proved to be effective in both the general and special education settings.

Students with disabilities constitute approximately 12 percent of the school-aged population (Ysseldyke & Algozzine, 1990). Some of these exceptional students are served in environments seen as more restrictive than the regular classroom setting. That is, these students spend all or the majority of their school days separated from students in the regular classroom setting. Students with moderate or severe/profound disabilities are usually served in self-contained classrooms (designed generally to serve one type of exceptional student), in day schools, or in residential settings. The majority of students with disabilities, however, are often served in the regular classroom setting with some time spent in resource rooms. These students are generally referred to as students with mild disabilities or high-incidence populations. Students with mild disabilities exhibit a wide array of academic and social problems.

This chapter focuses on general and specific reading problems of students with mild disabilities and discusses some effective techniques that can be incorporated into their instructional day. It is important to remember that students with mild disabilities are frequently seen in regular classrooms and less restrictive special education settings. The less restrictive an educational setting, the greater the amount of time spent with nonexceptional students. In this context, the *least* restrictive setting is the general education classroom setting. When students with disabilities have an opportunity to interact with their nonexceptional peers in the regular classroom setting, educational and social restrictions are limited. Services in a general classroom expose students with disabilities to more traditional classroom activities and behavior. For this reason, a major educational goal is to provide as many opportunities as possible for students with disabilities to receive services in this least restrictive environment.

Students with Disabilities and Reading

Most students with disabilities have some difficulty with academic components, especially with reading. It has been estimated that as many as 80 percent of students with disabilities have some difficulty with reading (Lyon, 1985). The majority of instructional time spent in special education classrooms focuses on reading, either decoding or comprehension skills.

When considered as a group, students with disabilities appear in some ways to be quite different from the remainder of the school-aged population. However, there may be more similarities than dissimilarities. Regardless of what we call them (e.g., learning-disabled, visually impaired, normal, or gifted), students learn to read in essentially the same way. They see (or touch) the letters that make up a word, they say (or sign) the sounds that represent the letters, and they hear (or see) how those sounds go together to form words and sentences. It is obvious, then, that there are only so many things that can go wrong for students to have reading difficulties. It doesn't matter if students are learning-disabled, gifted, or normal: If letters/sounds don't go together to form words and sentences, they will have difficulty with reading. Similarly, young people who have difficulty with comprehension are poor readers. Again, it doesn't matter what we call them; poor readers are poor readers (Bryan & Bryan, 1986). It is likely, however, that there are certain characteristics of students with disabilities that present unique challenges to reading instruction. The unique challenges presented by each category of students with mild disabilities will guide the remainder of this chapter.

Fundamental Assumptions

Why are some people poor readers? There may be medical reasons (neurological disorders) or environmental reasons (limited or no early stimulation, poor instruction). Regardless of the specific cause of reading failure, Anderson, Hiebert, Scott, and Wilkinson (1985) suggest that five components are basic to the effective reading process. These components should be in place if students are to be successful.

Reading Is a Constructive Process.   When any material is printed, there is a basic assumption that the reader has some background experience that provides a basic understanding of the material. Although first-time readers of *The Red Badge of Courage* will not know the specifics of the story, they must understand the concepts of *war* and *courageous acts* to appreciate the story fully. A lack of this background experience or knowledge will limit the impact of the story. Readers will have little to which to relate the story, and this will affect their understanding of it. Students with mild disabilities are frequently raised in home environments where early exposure to language and reading materials may be limited (Beattie, Algozzine, & Haney, in press). Additionally, there is often little encouragement to read, as the parents may read very little themselves. The impact on reading is obvious.

Reading Must Be Fluent.   The first step in the reading process is decoding. If the reader is unable to decode words in a smooth and fluent manner, understanding is likely to be impaired. Samuels (1973) refers to the smooth, fluent, and rapid decoding process as *automaticity*. If a reader is automatic—that is, smooth, fluent, and rapid in the decoding process—more attention can be given to understanding the meaning of the material. If the reader struggles throughout the decoding process, however, little attention can be given to understanding; it's hard enough just "reading" the words. In this instance, students remember little of what they have read because there was little opportunity to focus attention on the meaning of the words. Exceptional students frequently have poor decoding skills and lack the automaticity necessary to understand what they have read.

Reading Must Be Strategic.   Not all reading material is the same. Consequently, not all reading is the same. If you are sitting down to read the latest mass market thriller, you may not be concerned with reading every word. Your intention is to get a general understanding of the material and follow the high points of the plot. If you are reading a textbook, however, you may read each word carefully in anticipation of a test question, skim certain sections, scan for information, or preview the material by reading the end-of-the-chapter questions first. Regardless of your specific techniques, you will likely read the text differently than you would read the thriller. Poor readers, including students with disabilities who have reading problems, simply read to the best of their ability. They will likely make no adjustments in their reading techniques. Their goal is to complete reading all the words, not to understand the meaning of what they read. (Beattie et al., in press).

Reading Requires Motivation.   Most of us read because it is enjoyable. We have been somewhat successful in the process and continue to read because it brings enjoyment. In other words, we are motivated to continue. Consider, however, something in which you are not quite as successful. Maybe you have tried to play tennis. After chasing the balls all over the court and hitting most of your shots into the net, you might be inclined to say, "This isn't too much fun!" You might come back a few more times, but if the results were the same, you would likely find a different hobby. Such is the case with the poor reader. There is little motivation to read if there is no success or enjoyment in reading. Poor readers, like poor tennis players, find other things to do.

Reading Is a Lifelong Pursuit.   Each and every day, people are confronted with printed material—the newspaper, the directions on the back of some microwaveable dish, the instructions for taking a new prescription medication. It is our job as professionals to prepare students for this lifelong pursuit. Good readers and poor readers alike will be exposed to reading opportunities on a daily basis. We must try to foster success in all readers, to allow them to use these skills throughout their lives.

Reading Characteristics of Students with Disabilities

Reading is a process that involves some relationship between decoding and comprehension (Gough & Tunmer, 1986). Although an ability to decode does not ensure comprehension, an inability to decode will make comprehension much more difficult. Given that some relationship exists between decoding and comprehension, errors in either skill will likely result in some reading difficulty. Consequently, high-risk readers are those who characteristically have difficulty with decoding and/or comprehension.

Decoding Errors

For the purpose of this chapter, *reading decoding* is defined as the ability to isolate the phonemes that make up a word and the ability to blend individual phonemes into whole words. Decoding involves seeing a letter, associating a sound with that letter, and combining that letter/sound with others to form words. This task is often completed in isolation, but the true measure of decoding skills is the ability to decode in a stream of written material. Effective decoding requires the reader to make the letter–sound association in a timely fashion. Samuels (1973) refers to this as *automaticity*. The effective reader sees a letter and can *automatically* relate the symbol to a sound and combine sounds to form words. The automatic ability to decode words allows the reader to focus attention on the meaning of the word/passage and not on the pronunciation of the word. Difficulty in decoding is often reflected in reversals of letters (e.g., /*b*/ decoded for /*d*/) or words (e.g., *bag* read as *gab*), poor oral reading, or low reading rate. These errors in decoding will have a negative impact on a student's reading ability.

Students with disabilities and high-risk readers in general have a difficult time in the decoding process. This difficulty may begin as the child first becomes involved with printed material. These students may not recognize that letters have corresponding sounds. Additionally, they may not recognize that these symbols/sounds go together in specific ways to form words (Algozzine, Siders, Siders, & Beattie, 1982). Poor readers have difficulty blending individual sounds to form word parts and consequently fail to combine these word parts into words (Bryan & Bryan, 1986).

Reading has been identified as a skill process that develops in a hierarchical manner, with each skill serving as a foundation for subsequent skills (Algozzine et al., 1982). If one foundational skill remains undeveloped, the subsequent skill will likely be problematic as well. For example, students who recognize the letter–sound relationships of the letters /*d*/ and /*g*/ but do not associate the /*o*/ with its corresponding sound, will be unlikely to be able to decode the word *dog.* That is, they cannot blend the letters/sounds to form the word *dog.* The inability to blend sounds is a contributing factor to early reading failure (Hallahan, Kauffman, & Lloyd, 1985) and will likely cause future reading difficulties (Pflaum, 1980).

The recognition of printed words is a critical precursor to understanding what the words *mean.* Without understanding, frequently referred to as *comprehension,* reading is little more than an exercise in busy work. Decoding *d-o-g* without understanding that these sounds represent a four-legged, furry house pet is of limited value. Only when meaning can be attached to words is reading a truly valuable skill.

Comprehension Errors

A fifth-grade student was recently assigned a four-page reading assignment in science. After approximately five minutes, he indicated that his reading was done and that his homework was finished. His father asked him some comprehension questions about the reading. The student responded, "She said we only had to read it. She didn't say anything about understanding it, too!" Such is often the case with reading. Students focus on the decoding process but pay little attention to the meaning of the passages. Consequently, high-risk readers and students in general often fail to understand what they read.

Failure to understand the meaning of the printed word is a failure to grasp the most important aspect of reading. Decoding without understanding becomes, essentially, reading a string of nonsense words. Gaining meaning from printed material is the ultimate goal of reading. Unfortunately, many students with mild disabilities fail to gain the meaning of their assigned material.

The next section of this chapter will briefly identify several categories of students with mild disabilities. After each exceptionality is described, a brief overview of decoding and comprehension errors will be provided. This section is intended to familiarize the reader with each exceptionality and with the basic reading problems inherent in each.

Students with Learning Disabilities

Definitions of students with learning disabilities abound. It has been estimated that there are approximately forty definitions of learning disabilities currently in use (Heward & Orlansky, 1980). For the purposes of this chapter, students with learning disabilities will be defined as follows. First and foremost, they are students with some type of academic disorder. The most common academic problem seen in students with learning disabilities is a reading disorder. Approximately 80 percent of all students with learning disabilities have a reading problem (Lyon, 1985). Most students with learning disabilities, however, have some academic strengths. For example, students with reading problems may do quite well in math (except for *word* problems) or science. (Beattie et al., in press).

Nevertheless, students with learning disabilities exhibit academic difficulties that require some instructional attention. These learning disabilities may be caused by some neurological disorder, language delay, poor instruction, and/or environmental deprivation. It also appears that students with learning disabilities display above-averge intelligence, differentiating learning disabilities from other exceptionalities. Regardless of the cause, these students have difficulty in one or more academic areas. Particularly germane to this chapter is the fact that the great majority of students with learning disabilities have some difficulty with reading.

Regardless of the definition or cause, many students are identified as learning-disabled. Approximately 5 percent of all students enrolled in public schools are classified as learning-disabled (U.S. Department of Education, 1987). However, because their academic weakness is often mild or exists in only one area, the learning and social needs of students with learning disabilities are often best served in the regular classroom. In fact, 70 percent of students with learning disabilities spend at least part of their day in the general classroom (Ysseldyke & Algozzine, 1990). Given the academic nature of general classrooms, a significant portion of the students with learning disabilities (e.g., 80 percent) may experience problems in functioning as a result of their reading disorders.

Decoding

Students with learning disabilities appear to begin the development of reading skills at a disadvantage. Possibly because of a lack of exposure to reading materials and oral reading at an early age, students with learning disabilities may begin the reading process behind their peers. In the beginning stages of reading development, young readers begin to recognize relationship between letters and sounds (Algozzine et al., 1982). Students with learning disabilities, however, do not make the early connection between letters and corresponding sounds (Lovitt, 1989; Bryan & Bryan, 1986). This lack of phonological awareness limits the systematic growth that typically takes place in the reading process (Algozzine et al., 1982). The students begin to have trouble blending the letters/sounds to form words or word parts. In fact, students with learning disabilities may have difficulty recognizing that words have parts (Bryan & Bryan, 1986). Because more skilled readers recognize that individual letters/sounds are combined to form larger units, often called *letter clusters* (Samuels, 1987), they are more likely to progress to recognizing words. The failure of students with learning disabilities to recognize these letter clusters suggests difficulty with more advanced decoding activities. They may look at letters/sounds individually and struggle to combine them to form words or word parts. For example, in decoding *d-o-g,* a skilled reader immediately recognizes the combination of letters/sounds and possibly uses first-letter cues, word shape, and length to decide that these letters/sounds form the word *dog* (Samuels, 1987). Students with learning disabilities, and high-risk readers in general, often lack the skills necessary to decode *d-o-g automatically.* As a result, reading rate and the flow of reading are affected. The reading rate of students with learning disabilities is lower than that of low-achieving and regular readers (Shinn & Marston, 1985). Students with learning disabilities are also frequently dysfluent in the flow of oral reading (Lerner, 1989). Because students with learning disabilities exert so much effort in the seemingly simple process of decoding a word, these students frequently lack the skill to determine if a word is formed by the combination of the string of letters/sounds (Lovitt, 1989). As a result, students with learning disabilities are likely to have difficulty with spelling (Lovitt, 1989).

Although it appears that the delayed development of automatic reading skills is the most significant difficulty for students with learning disabilities, there are additional skill deficiencies that negatively affect reading development. For example, students with learning disabilities are more likely to reverse letters or words in their reading (e.g., *b* for *d, g-o-d* for *d-o-g*). Unfortunately, students with learning disabilities also have a difficult time recognizing their errors (Bryan & Bryan, 1986). Consequently, if *bab* is mistakenly decoded for *dad,* students with learning disabilities are less likely to recognize their error (Pflaum, 1980). It appears that these students are so intent on decoding the words that they fail to recognize their errors. because they are unsure of their skills, students with learning disabilities continue to use their fingers to point at words as they read, further lowering their reading rate (Lerner, 1988).

The impact of these limitations in decoding skills appears to be far-reaching. Students with learning disabilities are less confident in their ability to read (Loper, 1984). Because of limited confidence, they are less likely to attempt to read new material. Because of this understandable resistance to reading, skills aren't practiced and, consequently, are unlikely to improve. Thus, students with learning disabilities continue to read slowly and disfluently.

A professor in graduate school declared, "I have a ten-step process that is *guaranteed* to improve the reading skills of all students." His students, quite interested in the upcoming steps, listened intently. He went on: "Step One—get the student to read, Step Two—get the student to read. . . . Although his intentions were humorous, these "steps" make a lot of sense. Humans practice to get better: They play golf or tennis to get better at playing golf or tennis; they complete math problems to get better at math; and they read to get better at reading. Because students with learning disabilities lack many skills in reading, however, they often practice in failure and subsequently develop poor reading skills. The decoding process makes little sense to them; they read slowly, word by word. Consequently, words carry little meaning, and students with learning disabilities frequently fail to understand what they read.

Comprehension

Poor comprehension typifies the reading of students with learning disabilities. These students often read word by word, failing to grasp the meaning of the words in context. Earlier in this chapter, we discussed the advantages of automatically decoding words. Automaticity builds confidence, certainly, but it also allows the reader to focus on the meaning of the words. Students with learning disabilities frequently do not develop this automaticity. They struggle with decoding the words and, consequently, place their reading emphasis on *saying* the words, not on *understanding* the words.

Understanding what is read also requires the reader to have some background knowledge or experience with the topic. For example, reading a passage about autumn in the Midwest would have little meaning for a student from New York City. There is no experience base from which to draw conclusions or make decisions about the passage. The reader begins the assignment at a disadvantage. Such is often the case with students with learning disabilities. The home environments of these students are often lacking in materials that facilitate reading and/or encouragement to read. Additionally, there is frequently little modeling for the students to follow; their parents may not read themselves (Beattie et al., in press). Regardless of the specific reasons, students with learning disabilities frequently come to school with limited background experience. In other words, these students are less likely to assign meaning to words or passages because they lack the experiential background to provide context clues. Unfortunately, research has shown that poor readers (including students with learning disabilities) are less able to assign meaning to text where the material is read in the context of a meaningful story (Ganschow, Wheeler, & Kretschmer, 1982; Bryan & Bryan, 1986). Students with learning disabilities cannot actively use meaningful context as an aid in comprehension because they frequently lack the experiences necessary to relate the reading material to their background. because they bring fewer experiences, these students are less actively involved in the reading process than are their more accomplished peers. Additionally, students with learning disabilities are less likely to notice errors they make in the reading process (Pflaum, 1980), and consequently don't correct these errors even if these errors effect the meaning of the passage (Pflaum & Bryan, 1982).

Students with Communication Disorders

Communication disorders is a term that encompasses both speech and language disorders. Any atypical development in speech and/or language can result in a communication disorder. Communication disorders characterize the second most prevalent category of exceptional students seen in our schools. Approximately 2 to 3 percent of all students have some type of communication disorder, (Ysseldyke & Algozzine, 1990).

Speech involves the production of sound. Therefore, a speech disorder is something that disrupts the production of speech. Articulation, voice, and fluency disorders are considered to be speech problems. An *articulation* disorder is essentially a misproduction of sounds or sound patterns. Children who pronounce "wabbit" for *rabbit* are exhibiting an articulation disorder (called a substitution). So, too, are those students who omit certain sounds (e.g., "tar" for *star*) and those who distort certain sounds. A *voice* disorder may result from vocal abuse. Excessive abuse of the vocal cords results in a harsh, rough, or nasal vocal quality. Additionally, a voice disorder may result from the removal of the larynx, called a laryngectomy. The speaker no longer has a source of vibration necessary to produce sound, and this impairs vocal production. A *fluency* disorder is an interruption in the smooth flow of speech. The most typical fluency disorder is stuttering. Speech is faulty, choppy, and interrupted by repetitions of sounds and/or words or by halting moments of speech production, called *blocks*.

Language is a system unique to humans. It allows us to communicate or convey our thoughts and ideas to other humans. We do this through the production of sounds *(phonology),* and through an understanding of word meaning *(semantics)* and word order *(syntax)*. A language disorder results from any interference with this process. Children with language disorders may use words inappropriately, may display poor sentence structure, may have poor vocabulary development, or may have difficulty in understanding language in various contexts (e.g., reading, writing, or listening).

The impact of communication disorders on academic performance is tremendous. The significant majority of these students receive all or most of their academic instruction in the regular classroom setting (Ysseldyke & Algozzine, 1990). Any academic difficulty experienced by students with communiction disorders will likely manifest itself in either reading decoding or comprehension.

Decoding

Students with communication disorders, particularly those with speech disorders, often appear to have difficulty with decoding. We assume that, because their oral reading is not fluent and free from error, they do not know "how to read." In fact, they may be unable to produce oral reading because of their speech problem. They may be unable to say (i.e., read) certain words because of their speech problem. When they substitute /w/ for /r/ in *rabbit* or call out "stahwuh" for *star,* we might infer that they don't know the /r/ or /ar/ sound, when, in reality, their speech disorder might preclude the correct production. Students with speech disorders might also be unable to read because of their inability to discriminate or differentiate between sounds. For example, when learning to read, these students might be unable to differentiate between the appropriate use of the /b/ in the word *beep,* where the sound says its letter name, and /b/ in the word *big,* where the sound is not the letter name (Wiig & Semel, 1984).

Regardless of the cause, students with speech disorders tend to make more errors in oral reading than others do. They tend to be less fluent and are less likely to enjoy reading aloud (Choate & Rakes, 1987). Consequently, they are less likely to volunteer for any oral reading assignments and may be unable to comprehend material read aloud.

Comprehension

As noted before, students with speech disorders may have some difficulty understanding material that has been read aloud. They may, however, understand what they have read silently because their language skills are intact, allowing them to circumvent their speech disorder to grasp the meaning of the material.

Other students with communication disorders, however, may be unable to understand the meaning of written passages because of their language disorder. A student with poor vocabulary skills may not comprehend reading material because the words don't make sense. For example, many words in the English language have multiple meanings. In the sentence, "The boy ran onto the diamond," students with language disorders may have difficulty understanding the word *diamond.* Their basic, concrete understanding of the word is that it is a precious stone. How, then, can a boy run onto the diamond? These students' comprehension is obviously affected by their poor vocabulary development.

Students with language disorders also frequently have difficulty understanding sentence structure. Wiig and Semel (1984) provide the following example. In describing a scene from a baseball game, a child declared, "The boy was hit by the ball." A student with no language difficulties might logically assume that the batter was hit by a pitched ball or that a batted ball struck a player. But a student with a language disorder might be unable to make this distinction and assume that the boy hit the ball. The obvious impact on comprehension in these examples is representative of some of the reading difficulties experienced by students with communication disorders.

Students with Mental Retardation

Individuals classified as mentally retarded or mentally handicapped are generally identified as having IQ scores of 70 and below. In addition, this population exhibits difficulties in adaptive behavior, an inability to function within the parameters of independent self-help behaviors. Students with mental retardation are classified as mild (IQ generally 55–70), moderate (IQ 40–55), severe (IQ 25–40) and profound (IQ below 25). Students classified as mentally retarded constitute approximately 1.4 percent of the entire school population (Ysseldyke & Algozzine, 1990). Of these, roughly 85 percent are classified as mildly mentally retarded (Heward & Orlansky, 1988) and receive their education in a traditional public school setting.

Mental retardation may be caused by a myriad of possibilities. Heward and Orlansky (1988) note that over 250 causes have been identified. However, it appears that there are eight biological or medical categories of causes: (1) infections or intoxications (e.g., rubella, exposure to drugs); (2) chromosome abnormality (e.g., Down's syndrome); (3) gestational disorders (e.g., prematurity); (4) trauma and physical agents (e.g., accidents); (5) metabolism and nutrition phenyketonuria, or PKU); (6) gross brain disease (e.g., tumors); (7) unknown prenatal influence (e.g., hydrocephalus, microcephalus); and (8) poor social/familial backgrounds. Regardless of the cause, students with mental retardation are often delayed in the development of their academic skills and are below average in classroom performance. This does not suggest that this population cannot learn; they can and do learn, but through different learning styles and at different rates. In fact, many students with *mild* mental retardation spend a significant portion of their school day in the regular classroom setting (i.e., the least restrictive environment). These students generally will however, progress at a very slow rate and achieve at an academic level consistently below that of their normally achieving peers.

Students with mental retardation can and do learn to read. Their capacity to learn, however, is delayed by their limited intellectual capacity. Students with mental retardation will likely learn reading skills in a sequential manner (e.g., sounds in isolation, CV-VC patterns, CVC words). Their skill development will proceed at a much slower rate than for other low-achieving students or for normally achieving students.

Decoding

As suggested before, students with mental retardation will likely learn reading decoding skills in a sequential manner. Usually, however, students with mental retardation require extended time and instruction to master these decoding skills (Choate & Rakes, 1987). This is not to suggest that there will not be specific areas of difficulty in the development of the reading process. Students with mental retardation often experience difficulty in identifying sounds in isolation or with the blending process, or reverse letters/sounds (e.g., *p/g*) or words (e.g., *gab* for *bag*). In addition, a significant percentage of students with mental retardation have speech disorders that have a negative impact on reading production. It appears, however, that the area of reading that is most significantly affected is comprehension.

Comprehension

Students with mental retardation frequently fail to grasp the meaning of reading material. If comprehension is achieved, it will likely take an extended period of time to complete the process (Choate & Rakes, 1987). There appear to be several reasons for this difficulty.

Because of the delayed acquisition of reading skills, students with mental retardation often fail to develop automatic reading. They may struggle, reading letter/sound by letter/sound or word by word. Consequently, they give limited attention to understanding the material but, instead, focus on decoding the words. In this way, students lose the advantages of context clues; they read words individually and fail to combine them into extended ideas. As decoding skills are mastered, students with mental retardation may experience comprehension deficits for additional reasons. Although data do not exist that unquestionably link poor social/familial interactions to retardation, it is generally held that this is a major cause of mild retardation (Heward & Orlansky, 1988). Students with mental retardation begin school with limited environmental experience. Like other exceptional students (e.g., students with learning disabilities), many students with mental retardation have limited experiential learning opportunities to generalize to academic activities. Reading about other cultures or countries, for example, has little direct meaning to students with no exposure to any other culture or country. Without a concrete, hands-on knowledge base, students with mental retardation will often fail to grasp the meaning of the reading material.

Students with Behavior Disorders

Defining *behavior disorders* is extremely difficult. In fact, the category is described by many different names, such as emotional handicaps or emotional disturbances. Much of what constitutes a behavior disorder is extremely subjective; how inappropriate must a behavior be before it becomes a behavior disorder? The subjectivity appears to stem from degrees of tolerance for various behaviors. One teacher or adult may allow students to swear, whereas another may be very intolerant of that behavior. Another teacher might permit students to speak without raising a hand, which might clearly break the rules in another classroom. Teacher tolerance is an extremely important factor in identifying students with behavior disorders. Given this, the following definition of the term *seriously emotionally disturbed* from P.L. 94-142 is frequently used to identify students with behavior disorders:

> *(i) The term means a condition exhibiting one or more of the following characteristics over a long period of time and to a marked degree, which adversely affects educational performance.*
>
> *(a) An inability to learn which cannot be explained by intellectual, sensory, and health factors:*
> *(b) An inability to build or maintain satisfactory interpersonal relationships with peers and teachers;*
> *(c) Inappropriate types of behavior or feelings under normal circumstances'*

(d) A general pervasive mood of unhappiness or depression; or

(e) A tendency to develop physical symptoms or fears associated with personal or school problems.

(ii) The term includes children who are schizophrenic or autistic.

Approximately 1.5 percent of all students are classified as students with behavior disorders (Kauffman, 1985). Obviously, some behavior disorders are less severe than others. Consequently, many of these students spend a significant portion of their school day in the regular classroom with support from special education teachers. Students with behavior disorders will function appropriately in a regular classroom setting if their behavior can be controlled. This may seem an obvious statement. It is important to reiterate it in order to emphasize that these students can and do learn when their needs are met. Although they tend to have IQ scores slightly below normal, their test performance may not be truly representative of their academic aptitude or achievement (Heward & Orlansky, 1988). Providing appropriate materials, instruction, feedback, and reinforcement will assist students with behavior disorders in their efforts to reach their maximum potential.

Students with behavior disorders have significant difficulty in many academic areas, particularly in reading. It has been estimated that as many as 80 percent of students with behavior disorders have reading deficiencies and that approximately 50 percent will be unable to pass a functional literacy test (Heward & Orlansky, 1988). These reading problems are often a logical outgrowth of their behaviors (Choate & Rakes, 1987). Children who do not stay in their seats will likely not develop reading skills; those who are insecure or distracted will experience little reading growth; disruptive children prevent both themselves and other children in the class from benefiting from reading instruction. Students with behavior disorders often miss much instruction as an outgrowth of their behavior problems.

Decoding

More than those in any other category of exceptionality, students with behavior disorders present diverse reading skills. As previously suggested, the development of decoding skills is often dependent on the timing of the occurrence of the disordered behavior. If the behavior disorder disrupts a sequential skill in reading development, a cumulative effect on reading may be noticed (Choate & Rakes, 1987; Algozzine et al., 1982). For example, if the disordered behavior begins during the development of the blending skill (i.e., CV or VC combination), a long-lasting affect will occur. Subsequent development of CVC, CVCC, or CVC words might be adversely affected. The occurrence of a behavior disorder during late development will potentially have a less significant affect on the development of decoding skills.

Comprehension

Like problems of reading decoding, the reading comprehension difficulties of students with behavior disorders often reflect their behavior problems. If inappropriate behaviors have caused a delay in the development of reading decoding skills, comprehension will likely be affected. This point has been well established throughout the chapter. However, students with behavior disorders may fail to grasp the meaning of written material for several other reasons.

Comprehension often requires background knowledge and experience. Students must be physically and emotionally present to consume the information presented. Students with behavior disorders are frequently physically absent from class trips or miss hands-on experiences provided both at home and at school. Their opportunities are fewer simply because of the consequences of their behaviors; classroom punishment, time out, and restrictions at home all potentially lead to a reduction of opportunities for experience. However, there are additional concerns with this population. Simply being *physically* present does not ensure that learning is taking place. Although this statement applies to all children, it is particularly relevant to students with behavior disorders. The emotional nature of their *disorders* often causes poor attention, poor motivation, and overall poor academic performance. The impact on reading comprehension is obvious. Any interference with attention will have negative effects on understanding. A lack of motivation will reduce the effort and time spent on academic reading activities, ultimately resulting in poor academic performance.

Reading Techniques for Students with Disabilities

As you read through this chapter, reviewing the categories of students with mild disabilities, you will have seen that there are more *similarities* than dissimilarities among these students. You might even think that they are more similar to their nondisabled peers than they are dissimilar. In fact, poor readers are poor readers, regardless of what we call them (Bryan & Bryan, 1986). This is particularly important when we discuss how best to instruct students with mild disabilities. Just as there are only so many things that can cause a reading problem, there are only so many ways we can teach students to read. It doesn't matter if students are called "learning disabled," "mentally retarded," or "normal": Their reading problems must be considered individually. If students have difficulty decoding through a traditional basal approach, alternatives should be found to match their specific needs. If comprehension is difficult, attention should be given to strategies that allow the student to become more competent at understanding the meaning of the written material.

Nothing works for everyone! This statement will guide the instructional section of this chapter. Although space is limited, several techniques that have been effective with students with reading disorders—including students with learning disabilities, mental retardation, communication disorders, and behavior disorders, as well as students with no label who simply have trouble reading—will be discussed. Experience suggests that most professionals have their favorite technique for teaching reading and that this technique is the first choice in any intervention program. However, it is necessary to have alternative methods for use with exceptional students. If all students learned with the same approach, there would be no exceptional students or poor readers. Everyone would simply open the basal text and "read." Unfortunately, that doesn't happen. Consequently, there are several reading techniques that are used to teach students with mild disabilities (and high-risk readers as well). However, there are still no guarantees; as Harris and Sipay (1985) suggest, any reading approach, regardless of how carefully developed, is only as good as the teachers who use it. With this in mind, the following techniques are reviewed as they pertain to high-risk readers.

Improving Decoding

In an effort to provide a concise, systematic review of techniques designed to teach students to decode words, synopses of several techniques will be provided. Additionally, at the end of this section a table will be provided listing the advantages and disadvantages of each technique for students with mild disabilities.

Direct Instruction

Although there is no universal approach to teaching poor readers to read, it appears that if students are directly taught specific foundational reading skills, there is a greater likelihood they will learn to read (Carnine, Silbert, & Kameenui, 1990; Chall, 1989; Englert, 1984; Baumann, 1993). Direct instruction focuses on a specific hierarchical series of reading skills, the student's ability to complete these skills (based on task analysis), instruction of specific skills identified through the task analysis (rather than attention to ability deficits), and a continuous evaluation of these skills to direct future instruction (Carnine et al., 1990; Lerner, 1988). This step-by-step approach affords high-risk readers an opportunity to apply specific decoding rules to all reading occasions (see Chapters 2 and 3 for more detailed information). Several phonics approaches fall under the direct instruction format (i.e., Corrective Reading, DISTAR).

Language Experience

Although certain authors list the language experience approach (LEA) as a strategy for improving comprehension (Lerner, 1988), the LEA is often used as an approach for beginning readers. Students use their own experiences and their written text of these experiences as their reading material. The students write or dictate stories based on early experiences, field trips, guest speakers, or informed conversations. The stories are transcribed, and this text is used as the reading material. Essentially, LEA is based on the premise that students will be more interested in their own experiences and that this heightened interest will help them focus attention on the reading material. Students will be more inclined to read, and this will improve their reading. Research suggests, however, that LEA is only marginally effective as an instructional approach with exceptional students (Hallahan, Kauffman, & Lloyd, 1985).

Neurological Impress

A one-to-one approach, Neurological Impress requires the teacher and student to read in unison. The teacher sits behind and to the right of the student. As she reads with the student, the teacher concentrates on accuracy of reading, providing the student with an effective model. No phonics or word recognition skills are reviewed. The goal of Neurological Impress is fluent reading. Possibly because of the lack of phonics rule building, it appears that the Neurological Impress method is of limited value with exceptional students (Lorenz & Vockell, 1979).

Repeated Reading

The goal of Repeated Reading is to improve reading fluency. Students are presented with reading passages, typically 50 to 200 words in length, written at a level appropriate for each individual reader. The passages are read and reread three or four times until a specific rate is achieved. Repeated Reading rests on the premise that to become better, more fluent readers, exceptional students must have repeated opportunities to read. By reading the same material several times, students begin to recognize certain symbol–sound relationships, improving reading fluency. Although useful in developing decoding skills (Gearheart & Gearheart, 1989), Repeated Reading appears to have little impact on comprehension after the third reading (O'Shea, Sindelar, & O'Shea, 1987).

Sight Word Approach

Sight words are those words that may or may not follow phonic rules. For example, the Dolch list provides 220 sight words, including phonically regular words like *him, at, such,* and *put*. The list also includes words like *of, to, we,* and *one,* all phonically irregular. The key to the sight word approach is the emphasis on immediate recognition of certain words. Bender (1992) suggests that basic lists of 200 to 300 sight words may account for as much as 85 percent of the material read by most students. The sight word approach can be implemented in a variety of ways. Use of daily probe sheets and dictionary/pictionary development with sight words, games, or tape recordings are several ways these words are incorporated into the daily activities.

Linguistic Approach

The linguistic approach to teaching reading uses word families. Students learn that although there are differences between words in each family, there are many similarities as well (e.g., *kit, bit, pit*). Sentences are formed using these words (e.g., *Kit bit a pit and spit it out*). Sounds are not presented in isolation but are introduced as parts of words with regular spelling patterns. Although this appears to be an effective technique with students with mild disabilities, there is limited research to confirm the success (Hallahan et al., 1985).

Many additional reading approaches may be used with students with mild disabilities (see Table 5-1 and previous chapters). However, these techniques are infrequently used and are generally unsuccessful with students with mild disabilities.

Improving Comprehension

As mentioned previously, comprehension is the ultimate goal of reading. As professionals, we cannot assume that exceptional students will understand what is read simply because they can decode the words. Comprehension must be emphasized and taught throughout the reading process. For example, Carnine et al. (1990) provide specific direct instruction activities that focus on comprehension as a logical extension of the direct instruction decoding activities. In other words, comprehension is frequently taught as an

TABLE 5-1   Additional Reading Approaches for Students with Mild Disabilities

Technique	Description
Rebus reading	Uses pictures/symbols to represent words. A picture of a cat is used to represent *c-a-t*. Immature format.
Initial teaching	Each sound *(phoneme)* in the English language has a corresponding symbol *(grapheme)*.
VAKT	A multisensory approach requiring the student to see, hear, move, and feel letters and words in an effort to recognize these words.
Basal readers	Students are simply introduced to basal reading series texts.

extension of reading decoding. More and more effort is being directed toward this end. Professionals are recognizing that reading words is no longer sufficient. Significant emphasis is currently placed on techniques that focus on *understanding* what is read. Reading comprehension is considered a specific, unique skill and is taught accordingly.

Numerous activities may be used to enhance a reader's comprehension. Completing a story map either before or after reading helps students focus attention to specific details of the story (Idol, 1987). Using books with repetitive patterns (e.g., *Green Eggs and Ham* by Dr. Seuss) allows students to predict what will happen next in the story. The repetitive nature of the story helps students better understand the material (Gearheart & Gearheart, 1989). Bibliotherapy, using newspapers, playing Twenty Questions, writing comic strips and unscrambling sentences are all commonly used techniques in teaching reading comprehension. However, there are also several techniques that are specifically designed to teach reading comprehension. Descriptions of these techniques follow.

Metacognition / Study Skills
Essentially, *metacognition* means thinking about thinking; it is the "knowledge about cognition and the regulation of cognition" (Reid, 1988, p. 172). Metacognition helps readers by identifying a strategy and directing attention to the appropriate use of the strategy (Brown & Palincsar, 1982; Paris, Lipson, & Wixson, 1983). Students are taught to preview reading material in order to develop general understanding of the content. Specific attention is then directed to important parts of the passage, such as first and last paragraphs, and/or an enhanced (i.e., highlighted or italicized) word. Attention then is focused on monitoring the reading that has been compiled and responding to questions about the passage. Deshler and his colleagues at the University of Kansas Institute for Research in Learning Disabilities have done a significant amount of research in this area and have had great success in teaching exceptional students comprehension through a metacognitive strategy technique (e.g., Deshler & Schumaker, 1986; Deshler, Schumaker, & Lenz, 1984; Deshler, Schumaker, Lenz, & Ellis & Englert, 1984). One example of a strategy developed by these researchers is the RAP strategy (Schumaker, Denton, & Deshler,d 1984). This strategy asks students to use the acronym RAP for

each paragraph in a writing assignment. The first step is to *R*ead the paragraph. Next, students are instructed to *A*sk, "What were the main ideas and details in this paragraph." Students are finally taught to *P*ut the main idea into their own words. By using the RAP technique throughout the chapter/story, students will gain insight and understanding of the material. A significant body of information is currently available in addition to the outstanding work done at the Kansas Institute. For example, Bos (1988) suggests that comprehension of students with mild disabilities was improved using the "Spot the Story" strategy. Students are instructed to examine the *S*etting (e.g., who, what, when, where). Then they must identify the *P*roblems to be solved. After identifying the problem, the students list the *O*rder of Action, discussing the action taken to solve the problem. Finally, the students identify what happened at the *T*ail end of the story. Each of these study skill strategies is designed to focus attention on specific aspects of meaning in the target reading material.

Language Experience
Described earlier as a technique frequently used with exceptional students to teach decoding, the language experience approach (LEA) also focuses on comprehension. Students who read what they experience and subsequently write about are more likely to comprehend their reading material. As previously stated, however, the LEA appears to be of limited value with exceptional students.

Whole Language Approach
The whole language approach to reading essentially considers reading in the context of language as a whole (Lamme, 1986). It consists of reading, writing, and interaction with all forms of language. Whole language immerses children in reading material, providing opportunities for the students to reach understanding through a more or less natural development of language skills (Goodman, 1987). Emphasis is placed not on "sounding out" words but on the general context of the material (Lamme, 1986). Children listen to the reading material (one to one or via tapes), read aloud themselves, write stories, and work with their parents as much as possible. Lamme (1986) suggests that the central theme of the whole language approach is for children to love to read. Essentially, if children love reading, they will read more!

Interspersed Questions
Exceptional students often fail to comprehend reading material because of the amount of reading to be completed. Frequently, they do not remember the material read at the beginning of a story because too much information has been presented before the questions at the end of the assignment. This technique breaks long passages into smaller, more manageable sections. Students are then asked questions about the smaller amounts of material. Consequently, students are able to focus on more specific information, greatly increasing their comprehension.

Directed Reading-Thinking Activity
The Directed Reading-Thinking Activity (DR-TA) is designed as a framework for developing reading skills that are reflective, predictive, contextual, and systematic (Stauffer, 1975).

As suggested by Bos and Vaughan (1988), the DR-TA "is based on the notion that reading is a thinking process that requires the student to relate their experiences to the author's ideas, and thereby construct meaning from the text" (p. 144). In leading or facilitating the DR-TA activities, the teacher asks: (1) What do you think? (2) Why do you think so? (3) Can you prove it? (Lerner, 1988). This activity may be introduced in small groups of two to ten students or on an individual basis. The ultimte goal of the DR-TA is to help students become thinking, active consumers of a variety of reading materials. These skills are problematic with students with mild disabilities, who are less actively involved in their reading and consequently appear to be less likely to gather the intended meaning from the written text (Bryan & Bryan, 1986). One caution offered by Stauffer (1975) is that beginning reading books may have limited story lines and are therefore less effective with this procedure.

No single approach will work in all circumstances or with all students. Table 5-2 is provided in an effort to discuss some of the advantages and disadvantages of several reading approaches as they pertain to students with mild disabilities.

TABLE 5-2   Advantages and Disadvantages of Various Reading Techniques

Reading Approach	Advantages for Students with Mild Disabilities	Disadvantages for Students with Mild Disabilities
1. Decoding a. Direct Instruction	1. Effective technique for students with auditory strengths. 2. Provides a structured approach for students with little structure. 3. Provides a "code" that can be generalized to other settings. 4. Increases participation as students are successful at decoding.	1. Students with poor auditory skills may have difficulty. 2. Some people say that teaching sounds in isolation is ineffective. 3. The variance of the English language may lead to confusion.
b. Language Experience	1. Provides interesting reading material as student uses own experiences. 2. Incorporates oral language, writing, and auditory skills into lessons. 3. Can be used in a variety of settings.	1. Is limited to language skills of student. 2. Because of potential limits of student's experience, material may be somewhat limited. 3. Provides no structure or code to improve skill development. 4. Has a potentially negative impact on language skills (e.g., syntax).
c. Neurological Impress	1. Allows direct, immediate feedback from teacher. 2. Emphasizes reading accuracy. 3. Permits students with limited attentional skill to be guided by teacher.	1. Does not establish decoding rules. 2. Requires much teacher time.

Continued

TABLE 5-2 *Continued*

Reading Approach	Advantages for Students with Mild Disabilities	Disadvantages for Students with Mild Disabilities
d. Repeated Reading	1. Provides repeated exposure to specific material. 2. Assists students in development of phonic rules. 3. Achieve success in reading when never achieved before.	1. Limited exposure to variety of reading materials. 2. Has potential to be boring and repetitious for students. 3. Has little impact on comprehension after several exposures.
e. Linguistic	1. Establishes relationship between letters and sound families. 2. Provides for extensive repetition. 3. May be useful with students with limited auditory skills. 4. Incorporates spelling and reading.	1. Limited emphasis on comprehension. 2. Vocabulary is too controlled. 3. May consider the material childish because of repetition of sounds.
2. Comprehension a. Metacognition/ Study Skills	1. Provides a systematic procedure to follow. 2. Provides focus for students. 3. Lends itself to achievement in other academic areas (e.g., written expression) in many cases.	1. Must have at least a third-grade reading level. 2. Has potential to be a complicated series of steps.
b. Language Experience	1. Provides interesting reading material as student uses own experiences. 2. Incorporates oral language, writing, and auditory skills into lessons. 3. Can be used in a variety of settings.	1. Is limited to language skills of student. 2. May be limited to students' experience. 3. Provides no structure or code to improve skill development. 4. Has potentially negative impact on on language skills (e.g., syntax).
c. Directed Reading-Thinking Activity	1. Is a systematic procedure to relate reading to thinking understanding the material. 2. Is necessary for students to assume the responsibility for reading and understanding the material. 3. Active involvement in the process.	1. Not appropriate for lower level reading material. 2. Requires students to *be* self-directed.
d. Whole Language	1. Students use language constantly and are constantly exposed to reading. 2. Reading becomes fun. 3. Parental support is strongly encouraged.	1. Generally taught without phonics emphasis. 2. Parental involvement often limited, even though encouraged.

Summary

This chapter considered a variety of factors involving students with mild disabilities. These students, classified as having learning disabilities, communication disorders, mental retardation, and/or behavior disorders, are seen in a variety of academic settings. They may receive their instruction in a general education classroom, a resource room, or a self-contained setting. Regardless of the label placed on these students, there are certain considerations necessary to meet their academic needs.

Reading decoding and comprehension are clearly skills that are critical to academic development. Students with mild disabilities can and *do* learn to read if the professionals involved consider the individual needs of students and match these needs to appropriate instructional techniques. This chapter should serve merely as a beginning point; each professional will utilize a technique in his or her own unique way. Some techniques will prove quite effective; others may work with only one student. In our efforts to meet the needs of *all students,* however, even a technique that is effective with only one student is worthy of consideration.

The techniques discussed in this chapter are presented in isolation, but this is not meant to imply that they must be implemented in isolation. The *appropriate* use of whole language, for example, incorporates phonics into the lessons. Sight words can and should be introduced regardless of the other techniques used. Unfortunately, professionals often fail to consider these perspectives and tend to stay with one method regardless of the impact on their students. If all students with disabilities are to learn to read effectively, it is critical that professionals not overload the goal of reading instruction. The ultimate goal of reading instruction should always be to improve reading skills. This is true with gifted, normal, or all high-risk readers.

References

Algozzine, B., Siders, J., Siders, J., & Beattie, J. (1982). Using assessment information to plan reading instructional programs: Error analyses and word attack skills. *Reading Improvement, 12,* 156–163.

Anderson, R., Hiebert, E., Scott, J., & Wilkinson, I. (1985). *Becoming a nation of readers: The Report of the Commission on Reading.* Washington, DC: National Institute of Education.

Baumann, J. F. (1993). Implications for reading instruction from research on teacher and school effectiveness. *Journal of Reading, 28*(12), 109–115.

Beattie, J., Algozzine, B., & Haney, K. (in press). *Introduction to learning disabilities.* Boston: Allyn and Bacon.

Bender, W. N. (1992). *Learning disabilities.* Boston: Allyn and Bacon.

Bos, C. S. (1988). Process-oriented writing instructional implications for mildly handicapped students. *Exceptional Children, 54*(6), 521–527.

Bos, C. S., & Vaughn, S. (1988). *Strategies for teaching students with learning and behavior problems.* Boston: Allyn and Bacon.

Brown, A. L., & Palinscar, A. S. (1982). Inducing strategic learning from text by means of informed self-control training. In B. Y. L. Wong (Ed.), Metacognition and learning disabilities. *Topics in Learning and Learning Disabilities, 2*(11), 1–18.

Bryan, R., & Bryan, J. H. (1986). *Understanding learning disabilities,* 3rd ed. Palo Alto, CA: Mayfield.

Carnine, D., Silbert, J., & Kameenui, E. (1990). *Direct instruction reading,* 2nd ed. Columbus, OH: Merrill.

Chall, J. S. (1989). Learning to read: The great debate 20 years later—A response to "Defending the great phonics myth"). *Phi Delta Kappan, 70*(7), 521–538.

Choate, T. J., & Rakes, R. A. (1987). Reading comprehension. In T. J. Choate, T. J. Bennett, B. E. Enright, L. J. Miller, J. A. Poteet, & T. A. Rakes (Eds.), *Assessing and programming basic curriculum skills.* Boston: Allyn and Bacon.

Deshler, D. D., & Schumaker, J. B. (1986). Learning strategies as instructional alternatives for low-achieving adolescents. *Journal of Learning Disabilities, 52*(66), 583–589.

Deshler, D. D., Schumaker, J. B., & Lenz, B. K. (1989). Academic and cognitive interventions for LD adolescents: Part I. *Journal of Learning Disabilities, 17*(2), 108–117.

Deshler, D. D., Schumaker, J., Lenz, B. K., Ellis, E., & Englert, C. S. (1984). Academic and cognitive interventions for LD adolescents: Part II. *Journal of Learning Disabilities, 17*(2), 170–179.

Englert, C. S. (1984). Examining effective direct instruction practices in special education settings. *RASE, 5,* 38–74.

Ganschow, L., Wheeler, D. D., & Kretschmer, R. R. (1982). Contextual effects on reading of individual words by reading disabled adolescents with specific learning disabilities. *Learning Disabilities Quarterly, 5,* 145–151.

Gearheart, B. R., & Gearheart, C. J. (1989). *Learning disabilities: Educational strategies,* 5th ed. Columbus, OH: Merrill.

Goodman, K. S. (1987). Acquiring literacy is natural: Who killed cock robin? *Theory to Practice, 26,* 368–373.

Gough, P. B., & Tunmer, W. E. (1986). Decoding, reading and reading disability. *RASE, 7*(1), 6–10.

Hallahan, O. P., Kauffman, J. M., & Lloyd, J. W. (1985). *Introduction to learning disabilities,* Englewood Cliffs, NJ: Prentice-Hall.

Harris, A., & Sipay, E. (1985). *How to improve reading ability.* New York: Longman.

Heward, W., & Orlansky, M. (1988). *Exceptional children.* Columbus, OH: Merrill.

Idol, L. (1987). Group strategy mapping: A comprehensive strategy for both skilled and unskilled readers. *Journal of Learning Disabilities, 20,* 196–205.

Kauffman, J. M. (1985). *Characteristics of children's behavior disorders,* 3rd ed. Columbus, OH: Merrill.

Lamme, L. L. (1986). *Growing up reading: Whole language approaches to learning to read.* Paper presented at FACUC Conference, Gainesville, Florida.

Lerner, J. (1989). *Learning disabilities,* 5th ed. Boston: Houghton Mifflin.

Loper, A. (1984). Accuracy of learning disabled students' self-prediction of decoding. *Learning Disability Quarterly, 7,* 172–178.

Lorenz, L., & Vockell, E. (1979). Using the neurological impress method with learning disabled readers. *Journal of Learning Disabilities, 12,* 420–422.

Lovitt, T. (1989). *Introduction to learning disabilities.* Boston: Allyn and Bacon.

Lyon, R. (1985). Educational validation studies of learning disabilities subtypes. In B. Raukes (Ed.), *Learning disabilities in children: Advances in subtype analysis.* New York: Guilford Press.

O'Shea, L. J., Sindelar, P. T., & O'Shea, D. J. (1987). The effects of repeated readings and attentional cues on the reading fluency and comprehension of learning disabled readers. *Learning Disabilities Research, 2&2?,* 103–109.

Paris, S. G., Lipson, M. Y., & Wixson, K. K. (1983). Becoming a strategic reader. *Contemporary Educational Psychology, 8,* 293–316.

Pflaum, S. W. (1980). The practicability of oral reading behaviors in comprehension in learning disabled and normal readers. *Journal of Reading Behavior, 12,* 231–236.

Pflaum, S. W., & Bryan, T. (1982). Oral reading research and learning disabled children. *Topics in learning and learning disabilities, 1,* 33–42.

Reid, D. K. (1988). *Teaching the learning disabled: A cognitive developmental approach.* Boston: Allyn and Bacon.

Samuels, J. (1973). Effects of distinctive feature training on paired associated learning. *Journal of Educational Psychology, 64,* 164–170.

Samuels, S. J. (1987). Information processing abilities and reading. *Journal of Learning Disabilities, 20,* 18–22.

Schumaker, J. B., Denton, P. H., & Deshler, D. D. (1984). *The paraphrasing strategy.* Lawrence: University of Kansas.

Shinn, M., & Marston, D. (1985). Differentiating mildly handicapped, low-achieving, and regular education students: A curriculum-based approach. *RASE, 6*(2), 31–38.

Stauffer, P. G. (1975). Directing the reading-thinking process. New York: Harper & Row.

U.S. Department of Education. (1987). To assure the free and appropriate public education of all handicapped children. *Ninth annual report to Congress,* Washington, DC: U.S. Government Printing Office.

Wiig, E., & Semel, E. M. (1984). *Language assessment and intervention for the learning disabled.* Columbus, OH: Merrill.

Ysseldyke, J., & Algozzine, B. (1990). *Special education.* Boston: Houghton Mifflin.

What Research in Special Education Assessment Says to Reading Teachers

SUSAN S. EVANS   *WILLIAM H. EVANS*
University of West Florida

ROBERT A. GABLE
Old Dominion University

- Purposes of assessment in special education
  - Screening
  - Determining eligibility
  - Program planning
  - Monitoring student progress
  - Evaluating an educational program
- Bottom-up model
- Top-down model
- Interactive model
- Formal/norm-referenced assessment
- Criterion-referenced assessment
- Curriculum-based assessment
- Curriculum-based measurement
- Transferable comprehension inventory
- Probe
- Reading miscue analysis
- Prediction task
- Macro-cloze task
- Scrambled stories
- Sorting task
- Prereading
- Informal reading inventories
- Error pattern analysis
- Story grammar
- Story retelling
- Paraphrasing
- Multipass

Focusing Questions

- What were some historical abuses of assessment procedures, and how were these resolved and improved?
- List and explain some reading assessment models. Why are they used?
- List and explain some types of special education assessment procedures: What are some of the possible advantages/disadvantages of each and their appropriate applications?
- What are some steps recommended for developing a criterion-referenced test?
- List some possible error patterns exhibited in an oral reading performance. How can error analysis be applied to comprehension assessment?
- Explain the assessment technique known as transferable comprehension inventory. What is its function?
- Identify and explain the three categories of the multipass strategy

Discussion Questions

- Discuss the purposes of formal and informal assessment.
- Describe selected practices in reading assessment.
- Using curricular materials from an elementary classroom, design several problems that might be used to sample reading skills.
- Define and discuss reading miscue analysis, its advantages and disadvantages.
- Discuss the differences between curriculum-based assessment and data-based decision making.
- Discuss the possible applications of a problem to assess decoding skills and oral reading fluency.
- Discuss the impact and possible assessment procedures of learning environments.

Assessment is a process whereby information is gathered concerning a student's behaviors, learning characteristics, and abilities, as well as on related environmental variables that aid in instructing the student and in managing his or her learning environment. Assessment involves not only standardized test administration but also an ongoing analysis of classroom performance in order to understand fully each student's unique skills and the manner in which he or she interacts best with the learning environment. In special education, this information-gathering process is used to assist in determining educational placement and developing instructional programs that fully meet the needs of the exceptional student.

Purposes of Assessment in Special Education

The severity of the student's specific learning and behavior problems dictates the scope and type of assessment that is required (Evans, Evans, & Mercer, 1986). To the greatest degree possible, however, assessment of special needs students should be an ongoing process that occurs during every stage of instruction and is closely integrated with the classroom curriculum. According to McLoughlin and Lewis (1990), educational assessment in special education has five main purposes, including screening, determining eligibility, program planning, monitoring student progress, and evaluating programs.

Screening is a brief process used to detect students who may be at high risk for developing learning or behavior problems. An example is a readiness test that is often administered to students in kindergarten. If a student is targeted as being at risk, alternative teaching interventions may be introduced in an attempt to meet his or her needs. If the problems persist, the student may then be referred for a more comprehensive evaluation.

A second type of special education assessment involves *determining eligibility* for placement in a special program. At this stage, a more intensive individualized assessment battery is administered to identify the student's intellectual, academic, sensory, motor, behavior, and learning style deficits. Additional information is also collected from other sources, including family members, teachers, and other professionals, so that a complete picture of the student is obtained. No single source of data is sufficient in and of itself for making a decision to place a student in a special education program. Instead, the assessment data gathered are compared to preestablished criteria to determine if the student is eligible for special services. Only then is a placement decision made by a team of individuals from different disciplines, who contribute their expertise to designing the best program for a particular student.

After program eligibility is established, *program planning* takes place. The data collected from the educational assessment are used to establish long-range goals and develop an Individualized Education Program (IEP). Additional information may be gathered to determine the student's specific strengths, weaknesses, and learning preferences. Annual goals and short-term objectives are developed on the basis of the student's present levels of educational performance. Services to be provided, the extent to which the student will participate in the regular educational program, and the personnel who will provide services are also indicated on the IEP.

A fourth purpose of assessment is *monitoring student progress* in the special program. This type of assessment may be conducted periodically to determine if a short-term goal has been met; actual assessment may take the form of standardized or criterion-referenced tests or direct student observations. Often, however, student progress is determined more precisely by monitoring student performance on a daily basis. Continuous assessment procedures provide frequent measurement of learning so that subtle changes in student performance can be detected and timely changes made in the student's instructional program.

The fifth purpose of special education is *evaluating an educational program*. The effectiveness of a particular teaching program or strategy may be evaluated by using assessment procedures in a pretest/posttest format. Additionally, P.L. 94-142, the Education for All Handicapped Children Act, renamed the Individuals with Disabilities Education Act (IDEA) in 1990, requires an annual review of an IEP to evaluate the existing program and the methods used, and to determine whether services should be modified. In sum, educational assessment serves a range of purposes and comprises a variety of testing procedures.

Issues That Guide Special Education Assessment

Assessment practices in special education have been influenced by a wide variety of forces over the years. The expansion in special education services after World War II was accompanied by controversy involving assessment procedures. McLoughlin and Lewis (1990) note that many abuses of assessment accompanied growth. Assessment practices sometimes discriminated on the basis of the student's language, cultural background, or sex. Technically inadequate measures were sometimes used by untrained individuals. Finally, with the proliferation of assessment tools, labeling of students and the negative effects of labeling became major concerns and remain so today.

In 1975, the enactment of P.L. 94-142 (IDEA) significantly improved assessment practice in the schools. Through this landmark piece of legislation, guidelines were established that assisted in identifying students in need of special services. It also mandated a variety of requirements, such as accurate and nondiscriminatory assessment, development of an IEP, placement of students in the "least restrictive environment" (LRE), and procedural safeguards to ensure due process to students and their parents throughout this educational decision-making process. Current trends in service options and teaching methods used with special needs students have also been influential in shaping assessment practices (McLoughlin & Lewis, 1990). For example, assessment today places an increasing emphasis on educationally relevant information that includes evaluation of the student's learning environment. Student progress is monitored on a continuous basis, and assessment procedures are selected that reflect the close relationship between assessment and instruction. Regular education teachers are involved in observing and assessing exceptional students in their classrooms. Finally, various forms of computer technology are being introduced that facilitate the assessment process.

Assessment of Reading

Of all the academic content areas, reading difficulties are the single greatest cause of failure in school. Not surprisingly, then, reading is most often the focus of assessment of exceptional students. Although experts disagree about the nature of the reading process, most concur that the essential components of reading include decoding and comprehension. Ekwall and Shanker (1988) discuss reading in terms of a process of recognizing and analyzing words (sight word identification and word analysis skills) and of understanding words and ideas (comprehension). It follows that a problem in either area may make a student a disabled reader, necessitating assessment across each skill area.

Three models of reading attempt to describe how students use information in translating print to meaning (Vacca, Vacca, & Gove, 1987). Advocates of the *bottom-up* model believe that reading acquisition requires mastering and integrating a series of word recognition subskills. Accuracy in recognizing words is important for comprehending a selection. Advocates of the *top-down* model believe that students can comprehend a selection even when they are not able to recognize each word. Reading for meaning is emphasized. An *interactive* model suggests that the process of reading is initiated by formulating hypotheses about meaning and by simultaneously decoding letters and words.

These models serve to connect a theory or belief about the nature of reading to specific methods of reading assessment and classroom reading instruction. The bottom-up philosophy emphasizes the assessment of discrete subskills and is the basis for classroom practices involving phonics, linguistic methods, and programmed instruction. Traditional measures used in special education have focused on this approach. The top-down philosophy emphasizes the assessment of information gained through reading. Samuels (1983) suggests gathering information about the student's background experiences, awareness of text structure, and strategies he or she uses to interact with the text. Top-down advocates often use classroom practices involving the language experience approach and individualized reading. Vacca et al. (1987) note that decoding and comprehending vie for the reader's attention and that readers must learn to process graphophonic information rapidly so they are free to direct attention to reading for meaning. These authors contend that teachers of reading should reflect a strong interactive view of the reading process, which recognizes the definite interplay between the reader, the text, and the situation in which learning occurs.

Although assessment practices in special education have traditionally focused primarily on the bottom-up approach (phonics, direct instruction, programmed instruction), current methods increasingly reflect interest in portions of all three models. Moreover, the ecological perspective in special education suggests that a student's behavior is a result of the interactions between the student and all the variables in his or her environment (Evans, Evans, & Gable, 1989). Advocates of a broad-based ecological perspective of assessment argue that it should address not only the student's skills, but also the related environmental variables that may influence the reading process. Current practices in special education assessment reviewed in the next sections will reflect portions of all three models of the reading process.

Types of Special Education Assessment

A variety of reading assessment procedures are available for use with students who have special needs. These procedures may be used to carry out the different purposes of assessment that have been discussed, and they primarily revolve around two types: formal and informal assessment.

Formal Assessment

Formal assessment relies on the use of norm-referenced tests, which compare an individual's performance to that of a representative peer group. Formal tests sample a range of skills in a particular area, which are not necessarily the specific skills currently being taught in the student's classroom curriculum or those targeted on the exceptional student's IEP.

Formal tests may be administered to a group or individually. Common group-administered tests are aptitude and achievement tests that classrooms of students take at a specified time during the school year. The California Achievement Tests (1987), for example, survey several major subject areas, including reading vocabulary and comprehension. Group reading survey tests assess a general range of reading abilities. McLoughlin and Lewis (1990) note, however, that group procedures may penalize special students, who may lack skills to follow directions independently, skills that are often a prerequisite in this type of testing situation. Thus, group tests are useful primarily for initial screening and as a possible indication of the need for more comprehensive assessment.

Individually administered tests are used for diagnosis, classification, and placement of special needs students, and for making program evaluation decisions. Individual tests may also be used to assess academic achievement, aptitude, adaptive behavior, specific learning abilities, and behavior. Individual diagnostic reading tests are usually given if a student evidences a more severe reading problem.

Diagnostic reading tests sample specific reading or reading-related behaviors. These tests often include measures of decoding (reading a list of words or passage aloud) and comprehension (responding to questions after reading). Salvia and Ysseldyke (1988) note that no diagnostic reading test assesses all aspects of reading completely. Data from these tests, however, may be helpful to indicate a student's general strengths and weaknesses. The Woodcock Reading Mastery Tests—Revised (Woodcock, 1987), for example, is a norm-referenced test consisting of five reading subtests, designed for individual administration. It is used to identify a student's general strengths and weaknesses in reading skill development.

In general, formal tests are especially appropriate for use on a periodic basis for screening, determining a student's program eligibility, and for measuring long-term objectives and general knowledge. *Becoming a Nation of Readers,* Report of the Commission on Reading in 1985, states that standardized tests of reading serve a primary function of providing objective information about the success of particular children in learning to read and the success of schools in teaching reading. The report continues: "Some standardized reading tests are marketed on the basis that they provide diagnostic information and general knowledge. *Becoming a Nation of Readers, Report of the Commission on Reading* (1985), states that standardized tests of reading serve a primary function of useful. Rather, daily observation of reading behaviors gives them more detailed and trustworthy information. This report continues to state that "performance on standardized tests depends not only on a child's reading ability but also on the child's prior knowledge of the topics addressed in the test passages" (p. 98). McLoughlin and Lewis (1990) add that the ability to use reading skills is rarely assessed by formal tests. Morsink and Gable (1990) note that although traditional (formal) reading assessment is designed to pinpoint a student's reading grade level and to provide the teacher with information about the student's reading abilities and skill deficits, it does not always provide information that relates directly to the student's instructional needs.

Many reading experts have identified a need for change in the assessment of reading (Pikulski, 1989; Valencia & Pearson, 1987), for a shift toward a more dynamic type of assessment that is teacher- and pupil-centered rather than test-centered. Valencia and Pearson (1987) suggest that "the best possible assessment of reading would seem to occur when teachers observe and interact with students as they read authentic texts for genuine purposes" (p. 728). There is growing sentiment that various informal assessment strategies are best suited for this purpose.

Informal Assessment

Informal assessment procedures sample skills and behaviors relevant to the curriculum and instructional setting by means of criterion-referenced and teacher-made instruments. Informal devices are not norm-referenced and are usually administered more frequently than formal tests. Because informal procedures are generally not standardized, teachers have the flexibility to modify test procedures, administer a test several times, and observe students actually reading a variety of materials in a variety of situations.

In *criterion-referenced* assessment, a student's rate or percentage of correct responses is compared to a preselected standard or "criterion" that indicates mastery of a skill (e.g., 90 percent correct on naming consonant blends). Normative comparisons are not made; instead, data are expressed in terms relevant to classroom curricula. If a student does not master a skill, that skill or relevant prerequisite skills are targeted for classroom instruction.

Criterion-referenced tests may be commercially produced or teacher-made. The Brigance Diagnostic Inventory of Basic Skills (Brigance, 1977), for example, is a criterion-referenced test that provides subtests in readiness, word recognition, oral reading, and comprehension, word analysis, and vocabulary, in addition to other academic subtests. Caution is suggested in placing too much reliance on instruments that lack information on criterion validity.

Other criterion-referenced tests used heavily in schools are often furnished as part of an instructional material or textbook series. Basal series placement, end-of-unit, and end-of-book tests are examples of commercial criterion-referenced tests. These may employ a "skills management system" for reading instruction. Such a system contains unit objectives that are carefully specified and content of the basal tests that parallels these objectives. After instruction, children are assessed with a basal test; if they fail to master a skill or skills, instruction should continue on that skill or skills. Fuchs and Fuchs (1990) note several problems with this commonly used approach. First, when students fail to master a skills, teachers often fail to reteach the skill. Second, this type of one-shot administration does not address other sources of student error. Third, a selection response format (e.g., multiple choice) is often employed that limits qualitative information that could be gathered about a student's reading. Fourth, repeated administrations of the test generally are not feasible. Finally, the measures' reliability, validity, and sensitivity to student growth are as yet unknown. Gable and Hendrickson (1990) also note that performance standards usually are arbitrary and may lack useful predictive qualities.

Another criticism of a criterion-referenced approach to reading assessment relates to the lack of attention given to helping students to integrate all the subskills into the overall skill of reading. "Learning to read appears to involve close knitting of reading skills that complement and support one another, rather than learning one skill, adding a second, then a third, and so on" (*Report of the Commission on Reading,* 1985, p. 97). The commission states that overemphasis on performance on skill mastery tests creates an unbalanced reading program resulting in a disproportionate amount of time being devoted to workbook and skill sheet exercises thus leading attention away from the integrated act of reading itself.

McLoughlin and Lewis (1990) suggest that teachers carefully study the objectives on which criterion-referenced measures are based to ensure that the skills included are important, relevant to the student's curriculum, and immediately applicable to instruction. If criterion-referenced tests are closely linked to instructional objectives, then they may be useful not only for program planning, but also for monitoring pupil progress. To develop a criterion-referenced test, Howell, Kaplan, and O'Connell (1979) suggest the following steps:

1. *Decide what specific questions you want answered about a student's behavior. What ability (i.e., skill and/or knowledge) do you want to test?*
2. *Write a performance objective which describes how you are going to test the student. It should include (a) what the student must do (i.e., what behavior must be engaged in); (b) under what conditions the student will engage in this behavior; and (c) how well the student must perform in order to pass the test.*
3. *Use the performance objective to help you construct (i.e., write) your CRT [criterion-referenced test]. All of the necessary components of a CRT may be found in your performance objective. These components are (a) the directions for administration and scoring, (b) the criterion for passing the test, and (c) the materials and/or test items necessary.*
4. *Identify those individuals who you (or a qualified "expert") feel possess the skill being measured by the CRT. Administer the CRT to these individuals and use the minimum level of their performance as a standard for passing your test. This standard may be referred to as the criterion for acceptable performance (CAP). It is important that you consistently administer and score your CRT according to the prespecified directions. (pp. 96–97)*

Many other teacher-made informal testing devices may be developed in response to specific instructional conditions in the classroom. Informal assessment is helpful in obtaining information unavailable from other sources or to supplement available data (Harris & Sipay, 1990). A wide variety of informal procedures are used to assess reading performance. Prominent among these are observations, checklists, anecdotal records, teacher-made tests, probes, informal reading inventories, work sample error analyses, checklists, and interviews. Although not without some methodological flaws (see Morsink & Gable, 1990), many of these procedures are considered *curriculum-based assessment* measures, test strategies that facilitate determining students' instructional needs on the basis of the student's ongoing performance in existing classroom course content (Gickling & Thompson, 1985). A large body of research supports the usefulness of curriculum-based measurement for monitoring student progress and making instructional decisions (Deno, 1985; Deno & Fuchs, 1987; Fuchs & Fuchs, 1990). Various informal techniques used to assess reading performance, including curriculum-based informal measures, will be discussed in the next section.

Selected Practices in Reading Assessment

Informal Reading Inventories

The Informal Reading Inventory (IRI) is a widely used criterion-referenced method of individual reading assessment. An IRI can be either purchased or constructed by a teacher. The IRI is administered to assess decoding and comprehension skills and may be used to determine the student's instructional reading level, to decide on curricular placement in an appropriate basal, and to identify a student's reading strengths and weaknesses. Included in an IRI are a series of graded word lists, graded passages taken from selections at each reader level in a published reading series, and comprehension questions corresponding to each of the passages. The student reads from graded word lists, and performance indicates the entry point for reading the graded passages. While the student reads the passages aloud, the teacher follows along and maintains a record of the errors (e.g., hesitations, omissions). After each passage is completed, the teacher asks the student several comprehension questions.

Gillet and Temple (1986) note shortcomings of iRIs that accompany a basal series. They assert that often an IRI comprises passages from that series, passages with which students may already be familiar. Accordingly, it is not unusual for comprehension scores on those passages to be inflated. The quality of passages on various IRIs varies widely and should be examined critically before they are used. Some tests use short passages or are written in short, stilted sentences, a format that limits the amount of information available to the reader and, in turn, the number of questions that can be asked.

Although an IRI also may be constructed by the teacher, it takes a great deal of time and requires a fair amount of technical knowledge (Richek, List, & Lerner, 1989). It is often recommended that teacher-made IRIs be based on the material in which the student is being instructed. As before, however, because students may be familiar with these passages, comprehension scores are likely to be unfairly inflated. In constructing an IRI, teachers also need to develop comprehension questions. Questions generally include items from both literal and inferential categories, and should be carefully formulated because they can greatly influence IRI results. Interested readers are referred to Valmont (1972) for more detailed guidelines for question construction. McLoughlin and Lewis (1990) highlighted some of the major differences that should be evaluated when selecting an IRI for assessment. These differences include (1) the number of forms provided, (2) whether measures of listening skills and silent reading are included, (3) the number and grade levels of word lists and passages, (4) the types of comprehension questions asked, and (5) the availability of optional tests and other features.

After selecting and administering an IRI, the teacher determines three levels of reading performance based on prespecified criteria for word recognition accuracy and accuracy in comprehension: (1) independent, (2) instructional, and (3) frustration levels. A major criticism of the IRI concerns the arbitrary nature of scoring. There is little agreement regarding the criteria that should be applied to determine these functional levels (Harris & Sipay, 1990); criteria usually need to be adjusted to account for pupil-specific factors, such as limited experiential background. Finally, as Morsink and Gable (1990) note, use of an IRI to match the student with an appropriate level of reading material may be inaccurate; various studies suggest a lack of correspondence between scores derived from IRIs and actual performance in the classroom.

Although some would argue that the IRI provides useful information on reading performance, it does not measure all aspects of the reading process and therefore should not be used as the only assessment measure. Indeed, Harris and Sipay (1990) state that estimates of a child's reading level based on a series of short samples should be viewed only as approximations. They also note that some authorities suggest that students should be permitted to read passages more than once or to preread the passage silently before oral reading to obtain more reliable measures. In further cautioning against overreliance on the IRI, Gillet and Temple (1986) add that readers may fail to include information in their response to a comprehension question because to the reader it did not appear important. (Alternatives to direct questioning will be discussed in a later section.)

A child's performance on an IRI may be influenced by a number of variables and therefore may produce scores that are not necessarily truly representative of his or her actual reading ability. This is particularly true of a student with special needs, because students' performance may be greatly affected by interest in the subject, background knowledge, and textual organization (Caldwell, 1985). As Howell and Morehead (1987) point out, a student's score on postpassage questions depends not only on what he understands but on what he remembers; assessment of comprehension with postpassage questioning is really a measure of what the student retained. However, retention of information depends on motivation and interest, conditions which are not necessarily synonomous with reading comprehension. Howell and Morehead further emphasize that the process of comprehension depends on the reader's prior knowledge of the content, skill at decoding, knowledge of vocabulary, language proficiency, and application of comprehension strategies.

Despite its notable limitations, the IRI still can be a useful tool for reading assessment. During its administration, the teacher has an opportunity to observe strategies the student uses for word recognition and answering comprehension questions, and to make some judgments about student attitudes toward reading. While administering the IRI, the teacher may also use other diagnostic procedures, such as story retelling or paraphrasing, to gain additional information.

Error Analysis

Another aspect of reading assessment, the analysis of error patterns, involves careful scrutiny of a student's decoding mistakes in oral reading. Error patterns may be noted when administering a graded word list or an IRI or listening to a student read a passage from a text. As the student reads the selection, it is helpful for the teacher to tape-record the reading performance so that errors may be accurately recorded and repeatedly analyzed. Before beginning the oral reading session, the teacher should decide which errors are of instructional importance. Substitutions, omissions, and insertions are often singled out for attention (Morsink & Gable, 1990). Other error categories include mispronunciations, repetitions, reversals, hesitations, omission of punctuation marks, dialectical renditions, unknown or aided words, and self-corrected errors.

Although analysis of oral reading is a common assessment practice, there is no consensus as to what constitutes an error in oral reading. However, usually all word errors are given equal weight. Harris and Sipay (1990) recommend a scoring procedure that differentiates between serious and minor errors, as follows:

1. *Count as one error: (a) each response that deviates from the printed text and disrupts the intended meaning; (b) each word pronounced for the child after a 5-second hesitation.*
2. *Count as one-half error: each response that deviates from the printed text but does not disrupt the intended meaning.*
3. *Count as a total of one error, regardless of the number of times of behavior occurs: (a) repeated substitutions, such as "a" for "the" (except when a distinction between "a" and "the" is important to obtaining the meaning intended by the author); (b) repetitions; (c) repeated errors on the same word, regardless of the error made.*
4. *Do not count as an error: (a) responses that conform to cultural, regional, or social dialects; (b) self-corrections made within 5 seconds; (c) hesitations; (d) ignoring or misinterpreting punctuation marks. (pp. 227–228)*

Morsink and Gable (1990) have developed a method of error analysis that is designed to assist the teacher in categorizing errors in relation to three reading stages: acquisition, transition, and proficiency. After the student reads orally from graded material used in the classroom, error types are noted and confirmed by retesting and by means of a structured interview with the student. Intervention approaches are then suggested in relation to the student's identified instructional level. A sample error analysis chart for oral reading is presented in Figure 6-1.

A variation on error analysis, *reading miscue analysis* is a procedure that allows teachers to take into consideration the quality of the errors made by the student (Goodman, 1969). Errors may not be a cause for concern if they do not change the meaning of the text. The Reading Miscue Inventory (Goodman & Burke, 1972) includes nine questions used to analyze each miscue.

1. Is a dialect variation involved in the miscue?
2. Is a shift in intonation involved in the miscue?
3. How much does the miscue look like the printed response?
4. How much does the miscue sound like the expected response?
5. Is the grammatical function of the miscue the same as the grammatical function of the word in the text?
6. Is the miscue self-corrected?
7. Does the miscue occur in a structure that is grammatically acceptable?
8. Does the miscue occur in a structure that is semantically acceptable?
9. Does the miscue result in a change of meaning?

Student __Bill_____ Dates __9/21_____

Material/Level __Ginn Reading Series (H)_____

	Error Type/Number	Prioritized Instruction	
Ignore Punctuation	/		Proficiency
Hesitation			
Repetition			
Insertion	//	Work on fluency with tapes and repeated readings with intermittent praise.	Transition
Self-Correct	⊤⊬⊦ //		
Substitution			Acquisition
Teacher Aid			
Mispronounce			

Number of readings __2_____

Average number of words __122_____

Average time of readings __2 min._____

Correct rate __61_____ Error rate __5_____

FIGURE 6-1   Bill's error analysis chart for oral reading

Source: R. A. Gable & J. M. Hendrickson, *Assessing Students with Special Needs* (New York: Longman, 1990).

Wixson (1979) states that most readers make a greater number of semantically and syntactically acceptable miscues than miscues that are graphically similar to the stimuli. Less proficient readers tend to make a relatively higher percentage of miscues that are graphically similar to the stimuli. These readers make fewer attempts to self-correct, and they tend to correct acceptable and unacceptable miscues at an almost equal rate.

Although miscue analysis has served as a useful research tool for analyzing oral reading behaviors, it has significant limitations. First, it is a time-consuming process. Second, the classification of miscues varies among examiners, and not all miscue categories are equally useful. Additionally, passage difficulty can have a significant effect on a student's error patterns. If miscue analysis is used, Harris and Sipay (1990) suggest that the words on which the student erred should be presented after the test has been administered. Words that were pronounced correctly most of the time should be deleted from the analysis. Miscues should be analyzed for information about

> *(1) the use of semantic, syntactic, graphic and graphophonemic cues, as well as monitoring strategies; (2) which word-recognition and decoding skills and strategies were employed, and how well they were utilized; (3) the particular words, types of words, or word parts that may be causing problems; and (4) the impact of word-recognition errors on comprehension (Harris & Sipay, 1990, p. 245)*

The concept of error analysis may also be applied to assessment of student comprehension. Many IRIs include a variety of comprehension questions that follow the reading passages. Usually, the teacher notes the types of questions answered correctly—factual recall, vocabulary, interpretive, evaluative—and obtains a comparison of some of the components of reading comprehension. However, because of the limited numbers of questions of each type included on most IRIs, this information may be of limited usefulness. Before concluding that a student lacks particular comprehension skills, other factors may be eliminated. Carnine, Silbert, and Kameenui (1990) offer five main reasons that students may miss items in a comprehension lesson: (1) lack of effort, (2) decoding deficits, (3) lack of knowledge of critical vocabulary, (4) inability to understand directions, and (5) lack of appropriate strategy. Taking into account these factors, Morsink and Gable (1990) recommend the following procedure for identifying errors in reading comprehension:

1. Identify types of errors through direct observation of the student's performance in reading material used in daily instruction.
2. Retest errors by means of questions and the analysis of written work samples.
3. Interview the student to obtain a description of how the student attempts to comprehend written language.
4. Make a summary of the findings that integrates the stages of learning with the errors and recommended instructional procedures for remediation.

According to Morsink and Gable, this process should be viewed as a superficial analysis of comprehension errors. It does not take into account the adequacy of prior instruction, the complexities of syntax or semantics, the difficulty of the material and its motivational appeal, or the environmental variables that may influence reading performance.

Assessing Comprehension with Story Grammar, Paraphrasing, and Story Retelling

A relatively recent emphasis in reading assessment, story grammar is a description of the typical elements and their relationships imposed by writers in their narrative material. These structures are fairly consistent and predictable, and the clearer a person's idea is about story structures, the better he or she understands what is read. Elements in a story grammar usually center around a setting and plot and include the following: the setting, a beginning or initiating event, a reaction by the character(s) followed by a goal, an attempt to achieve the goal, an outcome, and a resolution. When students demonstrate an ability to follow these relationships in a reading selection, they are better able to construct meaning and distinguish important from less important ideas and events in the selection (Vacca et al., 1987). A story structure may be used diagnostically to obtain insight into a student's reading processes (Richek et al., 1989). Research has borne out that high-risk readers are less likely than good readers to be aware of such story features and may become "lost" in the passage while reading. To determine a student's understanding and recall of the events in the story, five questions may be posed (Sadow, 1982):

1. Where and when did the events in the story take place, and who was involved in them? (setting)
2. What started the chain of events in the story? (initiating events)
3. What was the main character's reaction to this event? (reaction)
4. What did the main character do about it? (action)
5. What happened as a result of what the main character did? (consequence)

To use this procedure, the teacher places these story grammar questions on the chalkboard and then reads a short story to the students. After the teacher has finished reading the story, the students fill in the story grammar. Students may check their comprehension by locating the elements of the story grammar and, in so doing, learn to identify the most important elements in a story.

Lovitt (1984) offers five additional techniques that teachers can introduce to help students understand and identify story structures:

1. *Prediction task. Have the students read incomplete stories and then say or write what they think comes next. They may read only the setting and beginning and comment on what might follow.*
2. *Marco-cloze task. In this activity an entire section (e.g., reaction) is deleted. The pupils' task is to furnish a plausible section.*
3. *Scrambled stories. Jumble the various parts of the story. Have the pupils put them in their proper order.*
4. *Sorting task. Break the story up into several sentences or phrases. Type them on strips of paper and require the pupils to sort the material for each of the elements into separate piles.*

5. *Retelling stories. Tell the children a story they know and scramble up some
of the parts (e.g., read the beginning section instead of the reaction). Have
the other pupils try to point out the misarrangements. (p. 123)*

Another way for teachers to assess student comprehension of a reading passage is
to ask a student to tell in his or her own words (paraphrase) what the passage was about.
By the very act of questioning, we shape students' comprehension, giving them cues about
what is important for them to remember (Gillet & Temple, 1986). A more systematic
approach to learning about students' comprehension is to ask them to "retell" what they
have read. Paraphrasing may be used alone or in addition to direct questioning by the
teacher. The teacher may record what the student tells or complete a checklist that contains all the information in a passage, and score each item as the student recalls it.

In further examining the area of comprehension, Lovitt (1984) presents a technique
called a transferable comprehension inventory, a form comprising comprehension features
common to many stories. Included are comprehension items at both the literal and interpretive levels. New comprehension questions do not have to be written for each story,
and a teacher can easily maintain a record of students' performances by regularly entering data on a common form. On the form, the teacher might list several features of stories
about which the student should comment. For example, literal items may consist of the
following names: names the title or author, names characters, details of the setting, details
of characters, tells plot, and gives main idea. By comparison, interpretive items may include these: tells whether fact or fantasy, predicts outcome, gives an opinion of author's
purpose, draws conclusions, infers character traits, interprets ideas, and discusses cause-
and-effect relationships. The teacher checks off features of the story as the student comments on them. After the student has responded to as many items as possible, the teacher
may remind him or her of other features and ask for additional information.

In a final example of paraphrasing, Schumaker, Denton, and Deshler (1984) have
designed a strategy for teaching paraphrasing and guidelines for scoring paraphrasing
responses. The student's oral response must be a complete thought; must contain entirely accurate information; must contain new information for which the student has not
previously been given credit; must make sense within the context of the statements the
student has previously made; must contain useful information for comprehending and
remembering the content of the paragraph; must not be the second, third, or further
global statement or sweeping generality expressed about a paragraph; and must be substantially different from any sentence in the written paragraph.

Assessing Comprehension with Prereading Systems

Techniques commonly described as "postreading" techniques have been routinely applied to the assessment of reading performance. These techniques usually involve instructing a student to answer questions orally after a passage has been read or writing
answers to questions in workbook format. Howell and Morehead (1987), however, suggest that postreading workbook exercises seldom promote comprehension and may be
a waste of valuable instructional time. Instead, critics contend that students need to be
taught to comprehend by means of a systematic prereading strategy. The recommended
procedure is to select passages with the student's decoding skills, vocabulary, and prior

knowledge in mind so that success on the passage depends only on comprehension strategies. This method may be used as a dynamic form of reading assessment that includes the following:

1. The teacher reviews previous content and presents new vocabulary prior to reading the passage.
2. The teacher asks questions that give the student a specific objective for reading the passage. The teacher may also give explicit instruction on the use of active-reading, monitoring, problem-solving, and study skills strategies.
3. After the student reads the passage, the teacher checks to see if the student found the answers.

This same prereading technique is the basis for "multipass," another strategy for comprehending (Lovitt, 1984; Schumaker, Deshler, Alley, Warner, & Denton, 1982). Multipass is based on the SQ3R (Survey Question, Read, Recite, Review) technique developed by Robinson (1946) to aid reading comprehension and is directed particularly toward helping students to comprehend content area texts. Simply put, multipass involves three substrategies—survey pass, size-up pass, and sort-out pass—each which require the student to pass through the chapter for a particular purpose. The student is tested first to determine his or her current learning style. This step involves testing the student in reading material at the level at which he or she can read and at the level at which he or she should be reading. Through this process, the teacher determines that the student is not using an appropriate strategy for studying the material and, as a result, is not recalling specific information. The next steps involve direct instruction in the learning strategy, instruction that includes a description of the strategy, teacher modeling, verbal rehearsal, practice in controlled materials, teacher corrective feedback, and additional testing and practice, if necessary.

Students may also participate in prereading activities by generating their own questions. Vacca et al. (1987) suggest two pivotal questions that students must ask as they approach a reading selection: "What do I already know about the reading selection?" and "What do I need to know?" These authors state that when students learn to ask questions before, during, and after reading, they put themselves in the strategic position of generating their own organizers for learning. With the strategy known as "Your Own Questions," students are encouraged to generate questions and then search the reading situation for answers (Vacca et al., 1987). Students first preview the title and pictures and read a beginning portion of the selection. The teacher then encourages the students to ask as many questions as they think will be answered by the selection. Students then read the selection and, after reading, discuss the questions that were or were not answered. Authorities suggest that this strategy helps students to activate background knowledge and creates a structure for comprehending reading material.

Curriculum-Based Assessment and Data-Based Decision Making

A strategy that has gained enthusiastic and widespread attention is curriculum-based assessment (CBA), which involves a careful analysis of a student's work samples using ongoing, direct, and frequent measures of a student's performance in the classroom curriculum (Blankenship & Lilly, 1981; Gickling & Thompson, 1985; Tindal & Marston, 1986). Any approach that uses direct observation and recording of a student's performance in the school curriculum as a basis for gathering information to make instructional decisions may be considered curriculum-based assessment (Deno, 1987). Gickling and Thompson (1985) note that CBA has emerged as a desirable alternative to traditional standardized assessment practices because of its focus on aligning assessment practices with what is taught in the classroom.

Curriculum-based assessment emphasizes a continuous or frequent measurement of performance over time, which allows an ongoing evaluation of specific skills taught in the instructional program. Frequently analyzing a student's reading skills allows discrete changes to be detected and immediate data-based adjustments in instruction to be made. This frequent collection of student performance data fosters more accurate and appropriate education decisions (Ysseldyke, Thurlow, Graden, Wesson, Algozzine, & Deno, 1983).

Data are commonly collected in one of two ways: (1) percentage of correct responses or (2) rate of correct and incorrect responses. Percentage measures provide an indication of accuracy of a performance and are particularly useful during initial acquisition of a skill, when accuracy rather than speed is the focus. Rate or frequency data indicate the period of time in which a behavior occurred and provide useful information related to fluency and proficiency stages of learning. Rate allows a discrimination to be made between students who have acquired skills with a high degree of accuracy but are slow, and students who are accurate and fluent or proficient in using the skill (Evans et al., 1986). After a student has reached a high level of accuracy in a particular skill, such as reading words on a word list at 100 percent accuracy, rate measures may be used to detect changes in performance.

Many students may be able to perform reading tasks accurately but not proficiently and thus may not be able to keep up with classroom tasks. Gickling and Thompson (1985) note that many low-achieving and mainstreamed students' learning rates do not correspond directly with the instructional demands in grade-level programs. As a result, many students are unable to keep pace with the curriculum of daily instruction. Student progress is adversely influenced by a rigid curriculum, with the problems characteristically being curriculum-induced. Research emanating from the Institute for Research on Learning Disabilities at the University of Minnesota indicates that rate measures allow teachers to differentiate children's performances and are very useful for making reliable assessment and instructional decisions (Ysseldyke et al., 1983).

Rate data are easy to collect and are usually gathered through the administration of teacher-made "probes" on oral reading performance. A probe is "a device, instrument, or period of time used by the teacher to sample the child's movement" (White & Haring, 1980). Probes are often used as part of a measurement system called Precision Teaching. In reading, probes are commonly used to assess decoding skills and oral reading fluency. A probe sheet may be developed by a teacher to sample reading skills; for example, the probe sheet may display a list of consonant blends, and the student is given the task of see (stimulus)–say (response) consonant blend sounds. An example of a reading probe is presented in Figure 6-2.

a	to	the	of	and
in	you	is	that	it
he	was	for	on	are
as	have	with	his	at
from	be	this	I	have

Name: _____

Date: _____

Number words correct/minute _____

Numbers words incorrect/minute _____

FIGURE 6-2   Probe: See–say high-frequency words

Proficiency standards are then used to set aims for specific reading tasks. These criteria for acceptable performance may be determined by teacher judgment, from data collected on the reading performance of regular class students performing the reading skills at an acceptable level, or from aims determined by several Precision Teaching research projects. Examples of proficiency aims from the Precision Teaching Project (Montana) for selected reading skills are as follows:

see–say isolated sounds (correct/incorrect per minute)	60–80/0
see–say words in a list (correct/incorrect per minute)	80–100/0
see–say words in text (correct/incorrect per minute)	200 + /0

The curriculum-based assessment process is described in the following steps:

1. Identify the curriculum material used in the classroom.
2. Analyze the curriculum materials to determine what will be taught (selecting and sequencing skills) and how it will be taught (teaching techniques and learning-related factors to consider).
3. Identify long-term goals of instruction.
4. Develop a curriculum-based assessment procedure. This involves writing behavioral objectives, designing the assessment material to include an adequate pool of items, planning the administration, designing a scoring and record-keeping system, and determining rules for making placement decisions.
5. Administer the CBA frequently.
6. Record performance and display the results on a graph or chart.
7. Make data-based instructional decisions.

Whereas curriculum-based assessment embraces a broad range of approaches, the term *curriculum-based measurement* (CBM) refers to a set of measurement and evaluation procedures created through a research and development program supported by the Institute for Research on Learning Disabilities at the University of Minnesota (Deno, 1985, 1986, 1987; Deno & Fuchs, 1987; Deno & Mirkin, 1977). The purpose of curriculum-based measurement is to evaluate student progress in reading, spelling, written expression, and math using systematic data collection on measures derived from curricular goals. The procedure involves four basic steps (Fuchs, 1987):

1. Identify the long-range goal, reflecting the curriculum level at which the student should be proficient within the next three to nine school months.
2. Create the pool of test items, using the curriculum as the source of material for the test item pool.
3. Measure pupil performance at least twice a week on a sample of the goal-level material.
4. Evaluate the database. Data evaluation rules are used to assess patterns in successive student performance data points in relation to an aimline or expected rate of progress.

In the area of reading, oral fluency represents the most important reading behavior to measure, as it correlates significantly more highly with the criterion reading comprehension index than do other measures of reading (e.g., question answering, recall, and cloze techniques (Fuchs, 1989). To apply CBM to reading, Fuchs (1987) and Fuchs and Fuchs (1990) use the following procedure. A teacher might first set as a year-end goal that he or she wants a student to be proficient on grade level 3 material, with a proficiency goal of at least ninety words per minute correct with no more than five errors. The pool of test items would include passages randomly sampled from the third-grade curricular text. The teacher would assess the student at least twice weekly, each time testing in exactly the same way: (1) State a standard set of directions, (2) have the student read orally for one minute from the text, and (3) score the number of words read correctly and incorrectly. Each score would be charted on graph paper and the performance criterion placed on the graph. A goal line, connecting baseline and the goal criterion, would also be drawn onto the graph.

In examining a major component of CBM, Tindal (1987) discusses various issues that relate to graphing student academic performance. Probe data recorded on graphs may indicate variability from data point to data point because students rarely perform at exactly the same level each day. Differences, sometimes referred to as "bounce," may be a result of variation in the readability of materials, administration, and scoring procedures; either within-class or outside contingencies; or student characteristics. The goal should be to reduce variability over the course of the program.

Fuchs and Fuchs (1990, p. 10) note the following advantages of curriculum-based measurement:

1. Selection of one long-term goal, instead of a series of short-term curricular steps, for monitoring student growth
2. Measurement of standard behaviors, with documented reliability, validity, and sensitivity to student growth

3. Use of prescribed measurement methods with acceptable reliability, validity, and sensitivity to student change

4. Incorporation of rules prescribing systematic procedures for summarizing and evaluating the assessment information

5. Accommodation of any instructional paradigm

Fuchs (1989) also suggests that there is a legal, a logical, and an empirical rationale for CBM monitoring. The IEP mandate from P.L. 94-142 requires an ongoing, curriculum-based approach to progress evaluation and therefore supports CBM monitoring systems. Curriculum-based measurement involves routine, systematic data collection on measures derived from curricular goals, an inductive and dynamic approach to instruction. Supported by their own research, Fuchs and Fuchs (1986) assert that use of an ongoing monitoring system can be expected to raise the typical achievement score from 100.0 to 110.5, or from the 50th to the 76th percentile.

Despite this evidence of the benefits derived from CBM, many teachers believe it requires too much of a time commitment. In response to concerns voiced by teachers, Wesson (1987) recommends several techniques to increase the efficiency of CBM, including the following:

1. Set up a measurement station.
2. Organize student graphs.
3. Routinize your random selection procedures.
4. Precount the possible number of correct responses for the random samples.
5. Have someone else administer the reading measures, so that the teacher can do something else at that time.
6. Use group administration.
7. Have the students score their own measures, or have an assistant do the scoring.
8. Score as administration takes place.
9. Make data utilization practices routine.
10. Use computer software to evaluate data.
11. Keep good records of instructional strategies.
12. Keep a list of potential instructional strategies.

A further limitation of CBM noted by Fuchs and Fuhs (1990) is that it reveals *what* needs to be taught but not *how* to teach it. Although ongoing monitoring indicates when a program change is needed and how well an instructional program is accomplishing the teacher's aims, systematic information for determining the nature of an effective program may not be provided.

In furthering considering the critics' point of view, Harris and Sipay (1990) question the use of a one-minute sample of oral reading as an effective means of monitoring overall reading growth. They state that although word recognition accuracy and speed are needed for reading comprehension, they do not assure comprehension. Frequent measures of word recognition will not necessarily lead automatically to teachers making meaningful instructional changes. In daily reading, however, CBM does seem to foster desirable gains in reading performances, perhaps in part because of variables that are often overlooked, such as students' awareness that their progress is being frequently monitored, which motivates them to stay on task.

Observation and Assessment of the Learning Environment

The bulk of the assessment procedures that we have described have been formal and informal student-centered methods of evaluating reading performance. In an instructional setting, however, it is important to recognize that assessment should also address the environmental variables associated with behavior (Evans, Evans, & Gable, 1989; Gable & Hendrickson, 1990). From an ecological perspective, a student's behavior is a product of ongoing and reciprocal interactions between the student and all the variables in his or her environment, including family, community, and school. The teacher must recognize that scores obtained from measuring classroom performance reflect far more than reading per se; indeed, a host of environmental factors that may affect a student's behavior and, in turn, reading performance. As Morsink and Gable (1990) note, all available information should be used when establishing a plan of reading instruction.

The interaction between behavior and the environment to which we refer can be examined through direct teacher observation. Students can be observed on many occasions during the day, and various behaviors may be recorded on a checklist or anecdotal format. Information can be collected concerning specific skill strengths and weaknesses within and across curricular areas. (Knowledge of free time activities and interests might facilitate selection of rewards.) Although subject to the same technical questions as any test, a reading checklist such as the "reading difficulty checklist" by Ekwall (1989) may be useful for noting common difficulties encountered by students in a reading program.

Another aspect of assessment that is often overlooked, a structured interview or questionnaire, may also be a valuable source of diagnostic data. A teacher may interview a student to determine faulty approaches to word recognition or analysis and produce information not otherwise available for designing a remedial plan of instruction (Morsink & Gable, 1990). Other information that may surface from student interviews includes: (1) self-concept, (2) students' perception of their reading problems, (3) past experiences in reading, (4) attitudes about reading, (5) reading interests, (6) reading environment, and (7) instructional techniques and materials the student has used (Ekwall & Shanker, 1988). Further, a structured or open-ended questionnaire may be used with older students to determine students' attitudes toward reading and to obtain information about recreational reading, family reading habits, books a student has read, reading strategies, and study habits. Interviews may also be used to assess students' perceptions of classroom reading tasks (see Wixson, Bosky, Yochum, & Alvermann, 1984, for a sample of an interview of assessing students' perceptions of classroom reading tasks).

Additional information that casts further light on the problems of some high-risk learners may be derived from a parent interview. Ekwall and Shanker (1988) suggest that various types of information can be derived from a parent interview: (1) parental views of a student's problems, (2) emotional climate of the home, (3) health factors, (4) reading material available at home, (5) library habits and time spent in reading, (6) study habits and study environment, (7) parental expectations, (8) social adjustment, (9) independence and self-concept, (10) duties at home, (11) sleep habits, (12) successful practices with the student, and (13) previous tutoring and results.

As indicated earlier, the classroom itself may also have a significant impact on a student's reading performance, perhaps serving as a positive learning environment for most but not all students. In this regard, McLoughlin and Lewis (1990) discuss three factors that influence reading in the context of the classroom: (1) the instructional environment, (2) the interpersonal environment, and (3) the physical environment. Assessment of the instructional environment takes into consideration the reading curriculum and instructional methods and materials used to implement the curriculum, including text style, topics, format, and readability. In the interpersonal environment, interactions between students and teachers and the social relationships among students may have an impact on reading performance. The amount of time teachers spend teaching reading and students spend actively engaged in practicing reading skills should also be considered. Finally, the physical environment of the classroom may influence reading behavior and the overall teaching-learning process. Accordingly, assessment might include an examination of the physical arrangement of the classroom and environmental factors such as lighting, temperature, and ventilation.

Taking an even broader view of assessment, it is commonly understood that a variety of environmental factors outside the classroom may have a significant impact on a student's reading performance. These variables may combine in unique ways or occur under some conditions that are not easily recognized or may not have been anticipated. Moreover, it is important to consider the following environmental conditions: (1) variables in the physiological environment such as health factors, physical impairments, and medications, (2) variables in the physical environment such as resources or conditions in the home and community, and (3) variables in the psychosocial environment such as emotional and learning impairments (Evans, Evans, & Schmid, 1989).

As we have attempted to show, it is crucial that teachers go beyond traditional student-centered assessment and consider the multitude of factors that influence a student's reading performance. As Gable and Hendrickson (1990) notes, although some of these influences are beyond a teacher's control, recognition of all the contributing factors may provide a better understanding of the teaching-learning process in reading.

As we conclude our discussion on reading assessment, it is important to point out that traditional practices may be improved by encouraging student participation in the assessment process. Indeed, experience has shown that students can take the responsibility for monitoring their own progress and/or the progress of other students. Although self-management skills are rarely taught in schools, when children learn the need for regulating their behavior in an acceptable manner, and experience the rewards for doing so, they are more likely to become responsible persons (Eaton & Hansen, 1978). Teachers have routinely given students responsibility to administer, score, and chart their own and other students' performance. To accomplish that goal, Eaton and Hanson suggest that students correct their work in a special supervised area and use different colored pens for scoring purposes. Teachers monitor the procedure through random checks of students' work habits and reinforce them for appropriate behavior (e.g., accurate and honest self-scoring).

Conclusion

Many experts have expressed a need for change in reading assessment, a change predicated on discarding test-centered assessment and moving toward a more dynamic approach to assessment. With this shift in focus, more attention is being given to determining the conditions under which a student performs reading tasks and the level of competence at which students can achieve when provided with a supportive and motivating learning environment.

Many factors should be considered when conducting assessment in reading. The assessment practices reviewed in this chapter focus primarily on special education research literature, an emphasis on curriculum-based assessment, and data-based decision making. The factors to consider in the assessment of reading include:

- Number of test items or assessment opportunities
- Manner in which the student responds to each item (modifications are made for various learning styles)
- Time considerations (repeated administrations; timed assessment; rate measures)
- Stimulus material (variety; authentic material)
- Person administering assessment (familiar teacher; student; peer)
- Place in which assessment occurs (variety of situations)
- Standard administration and scoring procedures
- Ongoing monitoring of progress
- Measurement of behaviors sensitive to student growth
- Ability to analyze errors from assessment samples
- Background knowledge, attitudes, and learning strategies
- Goals that parallel class curriculum
- Close connection between assessment and instruction
- Assessment results useful for planning instructional interventions
- Variables within the context of the classroom
- Variables outside the context of the classroom

References

Brigance, A. H. (1977). *BRIGANCE diagnostic inventory of basic skills.* N. Billerica, MA: Curriculum Associates.

Blankenship, C., & Lilly, M. S. (1981). *Mainstreaming students with learning and behavior problems.* New York: Holt, Rinehart and Winston.

Caldwell, J. A. (1985). A new look at the old informal reading inventory. *The Reading Teacher, 39,* 168–173.

California achievement tests. (1987). Monterey, CA: CTB/McGraw-Hill

Carnine, D., Silbert, J., & Kameenui, E. J. (1990). *Direct instruction reading,* 2nd ed. Columbus, OH: Merrill.

Deno, S. L. (1985). Curriculum-based measurement: The emerging alternative. *Exceptional Children, 52,* 219–232.

Deno, S. L. (1986). Formative evaluation of individual student programs: A new role for school psychologists. *School Psychology Review, 15,* 358–374.

Deno, S. L. (1987). Curriculum-based measurement. *Teaching Exceptional Children, 20,* 41–42.

Deno, S. L., & Fuchs, L. S. (1987). Developing curriculum-based measurement for special education problem solving. *Focus on Exceptional Children, 19,* 1–6.

Deno, S. L., & Mirkin, P. (1977). *Data-based program modification: A manual.* Reston, VA: Council for Exceptional Children.

Eaton, M. D., & Hansen, C. L. (1978). Classroom organization and management. In N. G. Haring, T. C. Lovitt, M. D. Eaton, & C. L. Hansen (Eds.), *The fourth R: Research in the classroom.* Columbus, OH: Merrill.

Ekwall, E. E. (1989). *Locating and correcting reading difficulties.* Columbus, OH: Merrill.

Ekwall, E. E., & Shanker, J. L. (1988). *Diagnosis and remediation of the disabled reader,* 3rd ed. Boston: Allyn and Bacon.

Evans, S. S., Evans, W. H., & Gable, R. A. (1989). An ecological survey of student behavior. *Teaching Exceptional Children, 21,* 12–15.

Evans, S. S., Evans, W. H., & Mercer, C. D. (1986). *Assessment for instruction.* Boston: Allyn and Bacon.

Evans, W. H., Evans, S. S., & Schmid, R. E. (1989). *Behavior and instructional management.* Boston: Allyn and Bacon.

Fuchs, L. S., & Fuchs, D. (1986). Effects of systematic formative evaluation on student achievement: A meta-analysis. *Exceptional children, 53,* 199–208.

Fuchs, L. S. (1987). Program development. *Teaching Exceptional Children, 20,* 42–44.

Fuchs, L. S. (1989). Evaluating solutions, monitoring progress, and revising intervention plans. In M. R. Shinn (Ed.), *Curriculum-based measurement: Assessing special children.* New York: Guilford Press.

Fuchs, L. S., & Fuchs, D. (1990). Traditional academic assessment: An overview. In R. A. Gable & J. M. Hendrickson (Eds.), *Assessing students with special needs.* New York: Longman.

Gable, R. A., & Hendrickson, J. M. (1990). *Assessing students with special needs.* New York: Longman.

Gickling, E. E., & Thompson, V. P. (1985). A personal view of curriculum-based assessment. *Exceptional Children, 52,* 205–218.

Gillet, J. W., & Temple, C. (1986). *Understanding reading problems,* 2nd ed. Boston: Little, Brown.

Goodman, K. S. (1969). Analysis of oral reading miscues: Applied psycholinguistics. *Reading Research Quarterly, 5,* 9–30.

Goodman, Y. M., & Burke, C. L. (1972). *Reading miscue inventory: Manual of procedure for diagnosis and evaluation.* New York: Macmillan.

Harris, A. J., & Sipay, E. R. (1990). *How to increase reading ability,* 9th ed. New York: Longman.

Howell, K. W., Kaplan, J. S., & O'Connell, C. Y. (1979). *Evaluating exceptional children: A task analysis approach.* Columbus, OH: Merrill.

Howell, K. W., & Morehead, M. K. (1987). *Curriculum-based evaluation for special and remedial education.* Columbus, OH: Merrill.

Lovitt, T. C. (1984). *Tactics for teaching.* Columbus, OH: Merrill.

McLoughlin, J. A., & Lewis, R. B. (1990). *Assessing special students.* Columbus, OH: Merrill.

Morsink, C. V., & Gable, R. A. (1990). Errors in reading. In R. A. Gable & J. M. Hendrickson (Eds.), *Assessing students with special needs.* New York: Longman.

Pikulski, J. J. (1989). The assessment of reading: A time for change? *The Reading Teacher, 42,* 80–81.

Report of the Commission on Reading. (1985). *Becoming a nation of readers.* (Contract No. 400-83-0057) Washington, DC: National Institute of Education.

Richek, M. A., List, L. K., & Lerner, J. W. (1989). *Reading problems: Assessment and teaching strategies,* 2nd ed. Englewood Cliffs, NJ: Prentice Hall.

Robinson, F. P. (1946). *Effective study.* New York: Harper & Row.

Sadow, M. W. (1982). The use of story grammar in the design of questions. *The Reading Teacher, 35,* 518–522.

Salvia, J., & Ysseldyke, J. (1988). *Assessment in special and remedial education,* 4th ed. Boston: Houghton Mifflin.

Samuels, S. J. (1983). Diagnosing reading problems. *Topics in Learning and Learning Disabilities, 2,* 1–11.

Schumaker, J. B., Denton, P. H., & Deshler, D. D. (1984). *The paraphrasing strategy.* Lawrence: University of Kansas.

Schumaker, J. B., Deshler, D. D., Alley, G. R., Warner, M. W., & Denton, P. H. (1982). Multipass: A learning strategy for improving reading comprehension. *Learning Disability Quarterly, 5,* 295–304.

Tindal, G. (1987). Graphing performance. *Teaching Exceptional Children, 20,* 44–45.

Tindal, G., & Marston, D. (1986). Approaches to assessment. In J. K. Torgesen & B. Y. L. Wong (Eds.), *Psychological and educational perspectives on learning disabilities.* New York: Academic Press.

Vacca, J. L., Vacca, R. T., & Gove, M. K. (1987). *Reading and learning to read.* Boston: Little, Brown.

Valencia, S., & Pearson, P. D. (1987). Reading assessment: Time for change. *The Reading Teacher, 40,* 726–732.

Valmont, W. J. (1972). Creating questions for Informal Reading Inventories. *The Reading Teacher, 25,* 509–512.

Wesson, C. L. (1987). Increasing efficiency. *Teaching Exceptional Children, 20,* 46–47.

White, O. R., & Haring, N. G. (1980). *Exceptional teaching,* 2nd ed. Columbus, OH: Merrill.

Wixson, K. (1979). Miscue analysis: A critical review. *Journal of Reading Behavior, 11,* 163–175.

Wixson, K., Bosky, A., Yochum, M., Alvermann, D. (1984). An interview for assessing students' perceptions of classroom reading tasks. *The Reading Teacher, 37,* 346–352.

Woodcock, R. W. (1987). *Woodcock reading mastery tests—Revised.* Circle Pines, MN: American Guidance Service.

Ysseldyke, J., Thurlow, M., Graden, J., Wesson, C., Algozzine, B., & Deno, S. (1983). Generalizations from five years of research on assessment and decision making: The University of Minnesota Institute. *Exceptional Education Quarterly, 4,* 75–93.

Chapter 7

Current Practices in Reading Assessment

JAMES F. BAUMANN   BRUCE A. MURRAY
The University of Georgia

Key Concepts

- Reading ability
- Reading disability
- Validity
- Reliability
- Authenticity
- Trustworthiness
- Anecdotal records
- Portfolio assessment
- Instructional reading level
- Frustration reading level

- DRP/IRI/QRI
- Informal reading inventories
- Performance-based assessments
- Intervention assessments
- Standardized assessment
- Formal assessment
- Norm-referenced
- Criterion referenced
- Scheme
- Think aloud

Focusing Questions

- Explain (dis)ability.
- *Why* assess a reader's ability? When should one make such an assessment?
- How can validity be measured?
- What is the distinction between formal and informal reading assignments? Give examples of each.

- Give some examples of performance-based reading assessments. List some examples of anecdotal notes.
- When are interviews and conferences an appropriate assessment method?

Discussion Questions

- What does it mean for an assessment to be "sound"? How are validity, reliability, authenticity, and trustworthiness related to soundness?
- What types of formal assessments would be informative when examining the reading abilities of high-risk students? Why would they be informative? What would be the limitations of formal assessments for this same purpose?
- How might an Informal Reading Inventory be used to make instructional decisions for a high-risk student?
- Select three types of informal assessments described in the chapter. For each identify its strengths and limitations when used to learn about high-risk learners' reading abilities.
- How might a portfolio assessment be useful for understanding the growth and development of a high-risk learner's reading and writing abilities? Describe a situation in which portfolios were implemented. Specify the types of materials placed in them and how that information was used by the children and teacher to guide and inform instruction and learning.

Elementary and secondary educators are in the midst of a renaissance in reading assessment.[1] Never before has there been such an interest in theoretical and practical aspects of assessing the reading abilities and performances of students, individually and in groups. This reading assessment renaissance is evident in various ways. Statewide assessments that are more compatible with current theoretical and empirical understandings of reading and writing processes are being developed and implemented (Haney & Madaus, 1989; Valencia, Pearson, Peters, & Wixson, 1989; Wixson, Peters, Weber, & Roeber, 1987), and the newest reading portion of the National Assessment of Educational Progress is more in line with our current understandings of how students read and understand text (Osborn, 1991; Pikulski, 1990; Valencia, Hiebert, & Kapinus, 1992). Further, one finds entire issues of periodicals (e.g., Brandt, *Educational Leadership,* 1989; Gough, *Kappan,* 1989; Jongsma, *Journal of Reading,* 1993; Squire, *The Reading Teacher,* 1987; Teale, *Language Arts,* 1991), recurring journal columns (e.g., *The Reading Teacher,* 1989–1993; *Journal of Reading,* 1991–1993), conferences (e.g., Language Arts Alternative Assessment Conference, August, 1990), and professional books (e.g., Harp, 1991; Johnston, 1992a; Roderick, 1991; Tierney, Carter, & Desai, 1991) devoted to assessment topics.

At the crux of this renaissance is a questioning of traditional approaches for the assessment of reading abilities, particularly standardized assessments (Graves, 1991; Johnston, 1992b; Neill & Medina, 1989; Shepard, 1989, 1991). Many critics argue that traditional standardized measures (1) are inconsistent with our knowledge of reading processes;

(2) do not capture the complexities of reading acquisition and learning; (3) require students to engage in decontextualized tasks with ecologically invalid materials; and (4) offer teachers little help in guiding and directing students' reading instructional programs in classrooms (Cambourne & Turbill, 1990; Johnston, 1987; Neill & Medina, 1989; Valencia & Pearson, 1987; Wiggins, 1989). As a result, there has been a strong call for alternative literacy assessments (Johnston, 1992a; Roderick, 1991; Valencia, 1990; Winograd, Paris, & Bridge, 1991) either as a complement to or in lieu of more traditional, standardized assessments.

In response to these criticisms of traditional assessments, teachers and researchers have developed a variety of alternative assessment procedures and techniques (e.g., Glazer, Searfoss, & Gentile, 1988; Goodman, Goodman, & Hood, 1989; Goodman, Watson, & Burke, 1987; Harp, 1991; Johnston, 1992a; Kemp, 1987; Leslie & Caldwell, 1990; Lipson & Wixson, 1991; Morrow & Smith, 1990; Paris et al., 1992; Tierney et al., 1991). These alternative assessment approaches include observational checklists, anecdotal records, intervention assessments, self-report instruments, interview and conference techniques, informal inventories, running records, process techniques, and portfolios.

Presented with this dazzling array of alternatives, how can a teacher—in particular a teacher of high-risk learners—select from among the many potential reading assessments (Farr, 1992)? Further, might there not be some conventional reading assessments that remain useful for student evaluation? What are the criteria by which reading assessments—conventional or alternative—should be judged? In short, which assessments might teachers of high-risk learners select, and how might they use them productively?

It is the purpose of this chapter to address these questions. In particular, we attempt to outline and demystify the issues involved in assessing high-risk learners and to present a framework for selecting and using reading assessments. To accomplish this, we first present our perspective on reading and high-risk learners. Second, we address two fundamental questions: "Why assess reading abilities?" and "What constitutes sound assessment?" Third, in the main body of the chapter, we provide an overview of formal and informal assessment techniques that may be useful for helping teachers understand the reading abilities of high-risk students and design appropriate instruction for them. We conclude with a brief discussion of caveats and unresolved issues in reading assessment for high-risk learners.

Reading and High-Risk Learners

Though not universally accepted (cf. Davidson, 1988), the definition of reading presented in *Becoming a Nation of Readers* (Anderson, Hiebert, Scott, & Wilkinson, 1985) nicely captures our beliefs about what is involved in skilled reading. According to this document:

- Skilled reading is constructive. *Becoming a skilled reader requires learning to reason about written material using knowledge from everyday life and from disciplined fields of study.*
- Skilled reading is fluent. *Becoming a skilled reader depends upon mastering*

basic processes to the point where they are automatic, so that attention is freed for the analysis of meaning.

- Skilled reading is strategic. *Becoming a skilled reader requires learning to control one's reading in relation to one's purpose, the nature of the material, and whether one is comprehending.*
- Skilled reading is motivated. *Becoming a skilled reader requires learning to sustain attention and learning that written material can be interesting and informative.*
- Skilled reading is a lifelong pursuit. *Becoming a skilled reader is a matter of continuous practice, development, and refinement. (Anderson et al., 1985, pp. 17–18)*

Given the analysis of skilled reading as being constructive, fluent, strategic, motivated, and a lifelong pursuit, how can practitioners understand students who are not skilled, in particular those who encounter difficulties in learning to read? In a review of research on reading disabilities, Lipson and Wixson (1986) argue that a paradigm shift in thinking about reading disabilities is in order (see Chapter 5 also).

Tracing the history of reading research, Lipson and Wixson (1986) note that early researchers (e.g., Gray, 1922; Judd, 1918) tended to locate the causes of poor reading outside the reader, in the type of instruction he or she was receiving; thus, the instruction, rather than the individual, was perceived as the source of success or difficulty in learning to read. In time, however, attention was redirected to the struggling reader himself (e.g., Monroe, 1932). Reading problems have since been seen as deficiencies within the reader, with the adoption of a medical model to describe reading *disabilities* that can be *diagnosed* and *treated,* much as organic diseases are treated.

Such a narrow focus, argue Lipson and Wixson (1986), tends to obscure many variables that affect reading performance, including prior knowledge of the topic, motivation for reading, the sociocultural background of the reader, and the demands of the task. They maintain that reading ability, far from being a fixed and static state, varies with many interacting factors, so that the reader who seems disabled in one situation may perform quite satisfactorily in another. For example, Lipson and Irwin (1984) found that less skilled readers using the strategies of examining context and rereading demonstrated greater comprehension than skilled readers who neglected these strategies.

To emphasize that reading problems are relative to the difficulty of the text and to the type of task, Lipson and Wixson (1986) use the term reading *(dis)ability*. We share this perspective that, with rare exceptions, high-risk learners and others who encounter difficulties in learning to read have no internal or constitutional limitations in acquiring reading abilities. Instead, a complex interaction of internal factors (e.g., a reader's fluency, comprehension ability, motivation) and external factors (e.g., the sociocultural context, type of text, imposed reading purpose) makes a reader "abled" in one situation and "disabled" in another.

Pearson (1992) cites Lipson and Wixson's interactive view of reading disability as one of the most astute insights in the past fifteen years:

Their view is that there are situations in which even the best of us, by virtue of low background knowledge and little interest, will find ourselves relatively "disabled." Conversely, even the lowest performers among us can and will look quite "abled" when we read something of interest or when motivation is high for other reasons. Disability, then, is not an irrevocable state but a temporary condition invoked by a particular confluence of circumstances. How much better off our low-achieving children would be if we kept this principle in mind as we seek to find ways to help them improve their reading performance. (p. 383)

Assessment tools and practices likewise should not be tailored exclusively for abled or disabled readers. Instead, the approaches that are selected for understanding a reader—high-risk or otherwise—and designing an individualized program of instruction should be chosen on the basis of their suitability for the learner's specific characteristics, abilities, and situations. Hence, any assessment tool or practice that meets standards of soundness may be potentially suitable for understanding the reading abilities of high-risk learners.

Two Fundamental Questions

Before examining current practices in assessment, two fundamental questions should be answered: "Why assess reading abilities?" and "What makes an assessment sound?"

Why Assess Reading Abilities?

Educators may administer assessments because of tradition or habit ("We administer the Iowa Tests of Basic Skills each year because we've always administered them annually"). Or educators may be so impressed with assessment plans and methods that they adopt them without tying them to educational goals ("Portfolio assessment is the latest thing, and we're a progressive district, so we should be implementing portfolio assessment"). Whether traditional or contemporary, assessment practices should be selected with a clear sense of why one is attempting to measure certain reading abilities. Assessment divorced from educational decision making is pointless (Baumann, 1988). To expend human and material resources on assessments that result in data that are quietly filed in a district office or a student's cumulative folder wastes valuable instructional time and capital.

Educational decisions resulting from assessments may take several forms (Baumann, 1988). Assessment data might lead to *administrative decisions*—for example, evaluating the efficacy of a new literature-based reading program implemented in a school district. Other assessments may lead to *parental decisions*—for example, determining whether a student should be placed in a special gifted and talented program. Most assessments, however, lead to *instructional decisions* made by teachers in schools—for example, decisions about the placement of students in instructional materials, decisions about a student's relative strengths in various reading texts and tasks, decisions about the effectiveness of specific instructional strategies for individuals or for groups, and the like. This chapter focuses on assessments that lend themselves to instructional decisions—that is, *classroom-based* assessments that teachers can use to inform and drive *instruction* for individual students (see Chapter 6 for additional discussion of purposes of assessment).

What Is Sound Assessment?

What makes the information obtained from one reading assessment useful to a teacher and information from another unhelpful or even misleading? Traditionally, the question of what constitutes sound assessment has been answered by examining an instrument's reliability and validity.

In classic test and measurement terms, *reliability* involves the degree to which an assessment represents consistent performance, a test characteristic essential for generalizing performance to other assessment and academic situations. An unreliable test is like a thermometer whose glass tube of mercury has come loose from its scale; it may read 50 degrees one minute and 110 degrees the next.

Traditionally, reliability has been broken down into several types:

- Confidence in a score, usually reported in terms of the standard error of measurement (e.g., band scores on a standardized test); such confidence reflects the internal and external factors that affect an individual's scores
- Stability of scores across time, usually reported in terms of a test–retest reliability index or an alternate form reliability index
- Consistency of test items in measuring the trait of interest, usually reported as an internal consistency index (e.g., Kuder-Richardson 20 and 21 formulas, Cronbach's coefficient alpha)
- Consistency of scorer's judgments in evaluating responses, usually reported as an interscorer or interjudge correlation

Validity, on the other hand, involves the degree to which an assessment measures what it purports to measure, not other extraneous variables. Validity may be said to indicate the truthfulness of an assessment, or the degree to which it coincides with reality (Smith, 1990). In classic test and measurement terms, validity has been defined and measured in several ways:

- *Content validity* refers to the degree that a test represents an adequate sample of the behavior in question, something usually determined by a panel of experts. For example, a group of judges might determine if items in a decoding test sampled the range of useful spelling-to-sound generalizations.
- *Criterion-related validity* refers to the degree that a test reflects concurrent achievement or predicts future performance. For example, a new test of comprehension monitoring might achieve high levels of criterion-related validity if it correlated highly with other, established indices of comprehension monitoring.
- *Construct validity* denotes the degree to which a test measures the psychological construct or trait it purports to measure. For example, one might assess the construct validity of a critical reading test by determining whether it represents a truthful measure of the construct critical reading as defined in the contemporary research literature.

Although ultimately validity—the truthfulness of a measure—is the most important characteristic of an assessment, a measure must also be reliable, as is demonstrated by the bathroom scale analogy:

Reliability is prerequisite for validity to occur. Just as a bathroom scale that is unreliable in measuring weight is useless (if your scale registers your weight at 125 pounds at 10:00 A.M. and 155 pounds at 2:00 P.M., the scale is useless), so too, an unreliable reading test is useless. However, reliability does not guarantee validity. For example, your bathroom scale may be very reliable but at the same time be consistently off by 10 pounds. Likewise, a reading test may be quite reliable but also quite invalid. (Baumann, 1988, p. 27)

What about contemporary, alternative assessments? Must they be reliable and valid, or are they so different from traditional assessments that they need not demonstrate these characteristics? Valencia (1990) argues that alternative assessments are not absolved from demonstrating qualities analogous to reliability and validity, and that all assessments—traditional, standardized measures or newer alternative assessments—must be "good" assessments. In order to be "good," an assessment must possess two qualities, *authenticity* and *trustworthiness*, analogous to validity and reliability, respectively:

First, it ["good" assessment] should be authentic; it should assess what we have defined and value as real reading. Second, it should be trustworthy; it should have clearly established procedures for gathering information (e.g., observations, written work, interviews, etc.) and for evaluating the quality of that information. As we move to more classroom-based assessments, we must be able to articulate and demonstrate that our assessments meet these criteria of "good" assessments. (Valencia, 1990, p. 60)

In other words, an authentic instrument or procedure gives a teacher insight into a student's reading behavior with a real reading task in a natural context, not an artificial task in an unnatural environment. For example, if a preschool or kindergarten teacher were interested in assessing students' early literacy development, the traditional approach would be to administer a reading readiness test. Given our understandings of emergent literacy, however, these instruments have extremely limited authenticity, since reading readiness tests are typically group-administered, paper-and-pencil tests that assess skills not directly related to early reading and writing ability (e.g., visual and auditory discrimination).

As an alternative, a teacher might rely on several informal measures of children's literacy development. For example, Sulzby's (1991) storybook reading classification scheme could be used to assess students' print awareness, book-handling skills, and understanding of print and book conventions. The authenticity of this scheme is quite high because the child is allowed to select a book of interest and then "read" it to an adult.

As Valencia (1990) notes, however, "shifting to more authentic reading tasks does not, in itself, guarantee a quality assessment" (p. 60). For example, rather than administering a group, standardized, paper-and-pencil test of decoding ability, it would be more authentic simply to listen to an individual child read orally and note the student's word identification performance through a form of miscue analysis. This is a more authentic assessment than a paper-and-pencil test because the teacher is evaluating a student's performance on the very task (reading) to which the targeted process (decoding) must be applied.

On the other hand, suppose that a teacher's oral reading coding system is so untrustworthy that he comes up with different analyses of the same child at different points in time (e.g., when coding the same audiotape at different times). Then similar miscues would be coded differently from one child to the next, or another teacher would come up with different codings and interpretations for the same student. Under these circumstances, the alternative decoding assessment scheme, no matter how authentic, becomes useless because it is untrustworthy.

Therefore, a caveat is in order: *One must be cautious in embracing and adopting alternative assessments that, though authentic, may be quite untrustworthy.* As Valencia (1990) admonishes, "we must separate the wheat [authentic/trustworthy assessments] from the chaff [the authentic/untrustworthy ones]" (p. 60).

Reading Assessment Options

Given the preceding discussions of reading and high-risk learners and sound assessment, this section deals with the nuts-and-bolts operation of sorting through some of the many assessment options available to teachers of high-risk students. First a scheme is presented for organizing reading assessments—dividing tests and procedures into formal and informal measures. Then selected examples of both formal and informal assessments that may be useful for understanding the reading performance of high-risk students are described.

Definitions and Distinctions

Reading assessment options presented and discussed in this chapter are categorized as formal and informal measures. Building on a discussion of formal and informal assessments by Garcia and Pearson (1991), these assessment types are defined as follows:

Formal reading assessments consist of a broad class of instruments that are commercially produced (they are formally printed, published, and usually sold for profit) and standardized (they have prescribed procedures for administration and scoring). Formal measures are also often norm-referenced, which means that there are statistics (norms) for comparing the performance of individuals or groups of test takers to a larger sample of comparable students. For instance, the latest version of the California Achievement Tests was normed on 300,000 pupils in kindergarten through grade 12 (Airasian, 1989). Formal tests ordinarily tap the recognition level of response through a multiple-choice format rather than requiring oral or written production of some sort. Prime examples of formal literacy measures are standardized achievement tests such as the Iowa Tests of Basic Skills (Hieronymus, Hoover, & Lindquist, 1990).

It is important to recognize, however, that by this definition not all formal reading assessments must be norm-referenced. For example, criterion-referenced tests—those that compare a student's performance to a specified standard or criterion level—are not norm-referenced, but they may be commercially produced and standardized. For example, the Criterion Referenced Curriculum—Reading (Stephens, 1982), a commercially available, standardized, and criterion-referenced but nor norm-referenced.

In contrast to formal assessments, *informal reading assessments* are carried out in the course of routine interactions with students. These measures are typically designed for use with individual students, usually are not standardized, and are rarely norm-referenced. They may be commercially produced but are often teacher constructed. When using informal measures, the examiner ordinarily looks at more extensive oral or written production for information about reading competencies, usually for the purpose of understanding the reading performance of specific students so that instruction can be individually adapted. A prime example of an informal assessment is the generic informal reading inventory (Johnson, Kress, & Pikulski, 1987), a commercial or teacher-produced individually administered procedure designed to evaluate a student's global reading levels and to provide some indication of strategies applied during word recognition and comprehension.

Formal Reading Assessments

In this section, we describe selected formal reading assessments. For teachers making classroom-based instructional decisions about individual students, formal measures are generally less useful than informal measures, which will be discussed subsequently. It is likely, however, that formal measures will be administered as part of an overall school or district assessment program or as a part of a special education evaluation. Thus, it is useful for teachers of high-risk students to be knowledgeable about these instruments and the information they provide.

We structure our discussion of formal reading assessment by first discussing two general types of formal measures, group and individual standardized reading assessments. Then we describe several specific formal measures that offer unique information about students' reading performance.

Group Standardized Reading Assessments

Group standardized reading assessments represent a class of instruments that include (1) general survey batteries, which have subtests usually in the areas of word identification or vocabulary and reading comprehension (e.g., Stanford Achievement Test, 1989); (2) separately marketed reading tests, which usually have vocabulary and comprehension subtests (e.g., Gates-MacGinitie Reading Tests; MacGinitie, 1989); and (3) tests that assess more discrete aspects of reading abilities, which may have subtests in areas such as phonic analysis, structural analysis, vocabulary, and comprehension (e.g., Stanford Diagnostic Reading Tests; Karlsen & Gardner, 1984).

Group standardized tests have the advantage of assessing a number of students simultaneously, thereby minimizing the amount of teacher and class time devoted to assessment. Further, standardized tests typically provide traditional indices of reliability and validity, giving those selecting or using a standardized instrument an opportunity to critique it for technical soundness. On the other hand, group tests usually are survey tests that assess global reading abilities; therefore, they tend to be less useful than individual assessments for providing detailed information about a specific student's reading performance.

Given standardized assessments have come under considerable scrutiny recently by individuals who promote alternative forms of reading assessments. Critics have charged that they are expensive, detract from time that could be used for instruction, have limited authenticity and construct validity, and do not provide information that leads to classroom-based decision making for individual students (e.g., Johnston, 1992b; Neill & Medina, 1989; Shepard, 1989; Wiggins, 1989).

In recent conversations with commercial test publishers, we have been informed that newer editions of group standardized reading achievement tests will include more authentic texts and assessment tasks. For instance, we have been told that new editions will include longer, unadapted excerpts from children's fiction or informational books, and pupil response modes will include open-ended tasks (e.g., written responses) in addition to traditional multiple-choice formats. If these reports are accurate, the new tests will resemble the 1992 National Assessment of Educational Progress (NAEP) reading assessment, which is considerably different in test philosophy, content, and format from prior NAEP reading assessments (National Assessment Governing Board, 1991; Valencia et al., 1992). We are encouraged to see publishers of standardized tests move toward more authentic assessments, although time will tell if these new group standardized assessments fulfill their promise.

Because group standardized reading assessments do not adequately meet the task of classroom-based reading assessment of high-risk students, interested readers may pursue discussions of such measures elsewhere in the literature elsewhere (e.g., Barr, Sadow, & Blachowicz, 1990; Baumann, 1988; Farr & Carey, 1986; Gillet & Temple, 1990; Glazer et al., 1988; Harris & Sipay, 1990; Lipson & Wixson, 1991). An important issue related to standardized testing is the interpretation of scores derived from norm-referenced tests, such as percentile ranks, stanines, and grade equivalency scores, the latter of which are particularly prone to misinterpretation and misuse (International Reading Association, 1981). Again, readers may look into other sources for information related to standardized test score interpretation (e.g., Baumann, 1988, Chapter 3; Lyman, 1991).

Individual Standardized Reading Assessments

Individually administered standardized reading tests are norm-referenced instruments used frequently in clinical reading assessment, special education assessment, or evaluations conducted by reading specialists in schools. The advantages of individual standardized tests over their group-administered counterparts is that generally one obtains more detailed, salient information when testing a student individually. The one-to-one testing format enables an instrument to be individualized, allowing the administrator to make judgments about which sections to administer and how far to proceed in an assessment. Also, the individual test makes it possible for the administrator to observe the student closely and take anecdotal records to complement the formal testing procedure.

One disadvantage of an individually administered standardized test is that it is inefficient: It may take an hour to administer such instruments, with an additional hour or two for the administrator to score and interpret the assessment. Additionally, individual standardized tests often have low levels of construct validity or authenticity, because the assessment formats and texts typically do not replicate those in normal reading situations. Nevertheless, they have been popular instruments in clinical and special education settings, and, when administered judiciously, interpreted cautiously, and used in conjunction with other sources of data, they may provide helpful data about students' reading abilities.

A large number of individually administered standardized and quasi-standardized reading tests are available (for a representative listing, see Harris & Sipay, 1990, Appendix A). Some of the more popular tests include the Diagnostic Reading Scales (Spache, 1981), the Durrell Analysis of Reading Difficulty (Durrell & Catterson, 1980), the Gates-McKillop-Horowitz Reading Diagnostic Test (Gates, McKillop, & Horowitz, 1981), the Peabody Individual Achievement Test (Dunn & Markwardt, 1989), and the Woodcock Reading Mastery Tests (Woodcock, 1987).

The Woodcock and Peabody are the most technically sound of this group, because the publishers have conducted recent, large-scale norming of the tests, and a number of reliability and validity studies have been completed on them. Both instruments provide global measures in the areas of word identification and reading comprehension, enabling users to determine how students rank relative to large numbers of peers of the same ages or in comparable grades. Further, the Woodcock contains subtests that provide more detailed information about aspects of students' word identification, vocabulary, and comprehension abilities.

The Durrell, Spache, and Gates-McKillop-Horowitz possess less rigorous norms, so the normative-type scores obtained from these instruments are not as trustworthy as those provided by the Woodcock and Peabody. However, the Durrell, Spache, and Gates-McKillop-Horowitz operate more like informal reading inventories (see the discussion of IRIs in the following Informal Reading Assessments section) and, as such, provide estimates of students' independent, instructional, and frustration reading levels (or analogues to them). These instruments also allow for the gathering and analysis of more qualitative information about students' reading performance (e.g., by analyzing students' miscues), and each possesses a collection of follow-up informal assessments.

A more detailed discussion of the strengths and weaknesses of these and other group- and individually administered standardized instruments is beyond the scope of this chapter. For this information, readers may profit from a recent collection of reviews of various reading tests (Cooter, 1989). The most comprehensive source of information on standardized tests can be found in *The Tenth Mental Measurements Yearbook* (Conoley & Kramer, 1989). (*Note:* This is the most current edition available at the time of this writing; because this source is updated periodically, however, anyone looking for reviews of published tests should refer to the most recent edition.)

Degrees of Reading Power

The Degrees of Reading Power (DRP) (1989) is a group-administered, standardized, criterion-referenced test of reading comprehension. According to its authors, Touchstone Applied Science Associates, the DRP tests:

> *measure a student's ability to understand nonfiction English prose passages at different levels of difficulty or readability. DRP test results can be used for several purposes [among others]:*
>
> * *Assess the current level of reading achievement.*

- *Determine the most difficult prose text a student can read with a specific degree or level of comprehension.*
- *Match the difficulty of materials with student ability, relative to the purposes of instruction. (College Board, 1986, p. 3)*

Each form of the DRP consists of 11 expository passages about 325 words in length, arranged in ascending order of difficulty. There are two alternate forms of the DRP at each of five levels of difficulty. The test may be used appropriately for students in grades 3 through 12.

Instead of answering questions about each passage, as is common for group-administered tests of reading comprehension, DRP readers select words from five syntactically plausible single-word options to fill seven gaps left in each passage. To supply the appropriate response, correctly, readers must carefully process the paragraph for contextual information, as is evident from the following excerpt for a sample DRP passage (College Board, 1986, p. 2):

Basscule bridges are draw-bridges with two arms that swing upward. They provide an opening as wide as the span. They are also versatile. These bridges are not limited to being fully opened or fully closed. They can be ___5___ in many ways. They can be fixed at different angles to accommodate different vessels.

5. a) *crossed*   b) *approached*
   c) *lighted*   d) *planned*
   e) *positioned*

To answer such an item successfully, a student must recognize the words in the passage, access vocabulary knowledge of some fairly infrequent words *(versatile, accommodate),* and test each answer option for semantic appropriateness in context. The most difficult passage that the reader can complete by recognizing the best-fit responses indicates the current level of reading achievement.

The publishers expressly recommend the DRP for testing reading in high-risk populations, citing (1) the availability of multiple forms for pre- and posttesting, (2) the sensitivity of the DRP to small gains in reading ability, (3) the single, easy-to-explain item format, and (4) the robustness of the test to variations in administration (the DRP is untimed). Independent researchers have noted moderate correlation (.45) with an informal reading inventory (Estes, Richards, & Wetmore-Rogers, 1989) and high correlation (.76 in fifth grade, .81 in sixth) with the Iowa Tests of Basic Skills reading comprehension subtest (Hildebrand & Hoover, 1987). Such correlations do not directly imply validity; it could be that the criterion measures have questionable validity themselves. Some critics suggest that the DRP, with its single comprehension task, tests a narrower range of comprehension than tests that require responses to a variety of question types (Hildebrand & Hoover, 1987).

In our opinion, the DRP offers a reliable measure of surface-level inferential comprehension, a necessary (though not sufficient) ingredient for deeper levels of applied or critical understanding. Additionally, the DRP seems to tap aspects of metacognition (Baumann, Seifert-Kessell, & Jones, 1992). To select a response from among other semantically and syntactically appropriate options requires monitoring one's thoughts for global levels of coherence and actively searching for strategies (e.g., rereading, withholding judgment, reading on for further cues) to gain a foothold on challenging materials. Though limited, like any group-administered standardized instrument, the DRP does provide a somewhat nontraditional glimpse of reading comprehension processes.

Integrated Literature and Language Arts Portfolio Program

The ILLAPP (Riverside, 1991) is an example of the current move to *performance-based* reading assessments, which require students to produce responses (e.g., extended writing, drawing pictures, and making diagrams) rather than simply selecting a response (e.g., filling the bubble next to the correct multiple-choice option), as has been the traditional format for group, standardized assessments. The ILLAPP, used in grades 2 through 8, requires three 45-minute periods on successive days. On day 1, students respond to an interest and experience survey, which provides useful data on students' attitudes toward reading. Next they are tested on listening comprehension, producing a variety of responses to a passage read aloud. On day 2, students read and respond to a fiction selection, and on day 3, to an expository piece.

The ILLAPP purports to deliver a deep picture of areas of strength and weakness in reading. Scores are reported for comprehension with listening, with fictional text, and with expository text; for prior knowledge, reading strategies, and vocabulary; and for levels of constructing meaning (literal, analytical, and extended) and composing responses (responsiveness to task, development and organization, and language use). Not only does the ILLAPP provide a picture of comprehension performance, it allows the examiner to look at reading performance in the light of prior knowledge, preferred reading strategies, and motivational factors (Commeyras, 1992).

Because responses to the ILLAPP are not subject to scoring by high-speed scanners, interpreting the assessment is a labor-intensive enterprise. A skilled scorer may take more than fifteen minutes to tabulate just one student's response. Scoring the ILLAPP involves thorough knowledge of the passage on which responses are based and requires frequent decisions about the appropriateness and reasonableness of variable-answer and written responses (Raju, 1991). Rubrics are provided for feature scoring, and models are given to facilitate holistic scoring. Ordinarily, individual teachers or committees of teachers at the school or district level tabulate the ILLAPP, although scoring by the publisher is also available. Accurate interpretation depends on the competence of the scorer and the quality of training.

Results of the ILLAPP yield neither firm criterion-referenced information nor norm-referenced comparisons with the performance averages of other students. Rather, they represent pieces of evidence for a literacy portfolio from a wide-ranging and carefully constructed observation. In sum, ILLAPP represents an interesting form of commercially available alternative assessment that deserves scrutiny and critique (Commeyras, 1992).

Language Arts Performance Assessment

The LAPA (Farr & Farr, 1990), a component of the Integrated Assessment System, is another example of a performance-based reading assessment (for a discussion, see commeyras, 1992). The LAPA departs even further from the formal testing paradigm. The test consists of graded *prompts* designed to engender an extended written response; each prompt consists of a reading passage and a guided writing activity. No time limits are imposed. The test can be administered in a single day or can be stretched over as many as four days. In an effort to mirror classroom instruction, the teacher is allowed to guide and encourage students as they work, and students are permitted to collaborate with peers in reviewing and critiquing their work.

Like the ILLAPP, the LAPA requires hand scoring. Evaluation of written responses is based on the dimensions of responsiveness to reading, management of content, and command of language. Rubrics are provided for primary trait assessment (to evaluate responses in the light of assigned tasks) and to facilitate holistic assessment, in which an overall score is formulated for each dimension. The instrument assesses both writing skill and reading comprehension.

Like the ILLAPP, the LAPA breaks new ground in attempting to bridge the gap between assessment and teaching and to build assessments that truly inform instruction. However, as Commeyras (1992) notes regarding these instruments, "We must be cautious about jumping on yet another education bandwagon despite the enthusiasm we may feel for the efforts underway to improve assessment. There is no quick fix to the assessment conundrum" (p. 470).

Informal Reading Assessments

In this section, we look at selected informal reading assessments that have the potential to help teachers understand the reading abilities of high-risk students and to guide teachers in designing appropriate instruction. For the most part, these assessments have been organized into categories that describe a *type* of assessment and have been grouped according to common features—for example, observational and anecdotal records. Admittedly, the categories are somewhat arbitrary and certainly not discrete; a particular assessment approach might logically fit in more than one category. Further, in two instances, specific assessment approaches, the informal reading inventory and portfolio assessment, are described in greater detail. These have been given special status because of their potential positive contributions for the assessment of high-risk learners.

Informal Reading Inventories

An informal reading inventory (IRI) is an individually administered procedure designed to estimate a student's reading levels and to assess strengths and weaknesses in word identification and comprehension. An IRI consists of a graded series of passages, progressive in difficulty, which the student reads aloud one by one (a second set of passages might be read silently). The examiner meanwhile carefully records data about word recognition. Comprehension is typically assessed by having the student respond to questions about the passage. The procedure is terminated when the student's performance falls below a criterion of success.

IRIs have two different but related purposes. First, a student's reading levels are estimated by comparing the number of words pronounced correctly and the number of comprehension questions answered correctly to certain criteria. This enables a teacher to match a student to appropriate materials for independent reading or for instruction. When a student pronounces words almost flawlessly and reveals high comprehension for a given passage, that passage is designated as being within the student's *independent reading level* range (materials a student can read without any assistance). When a student's word pronunciation and comprehension are adequate to process a passage but not perfect, that material is designated as being within a student's *instructional reading level* range (materials appropriate for use during instruction). When word recognition is poor and comprehension is incomplete for a passage, it is designated as being at a student's *frustration reading level* (materials too difficult for independent or instructional use). This process of counting words pronounced correctly and questions answered correctly is often referred to as the *quantitative analysis* portion of an IRI.

The second purpose of an IRI is to identify specific reading strengths and weaknesses in order to provide appropriate instruction in reading skills and strategies. This process is often referred to as a *qualitative analysis,* because an examiner looks at the nature of oral reading errors, or miscues, and at specific responses to comprehension questions in order to understand the strategies a reader employs.

The IRI is one of the oldest informal reading instruments. While much of its development and promotion is attributed to Emmett Betts (1946), Williams S. Gray suggested an IRI-like task as early as 1920 when he advocated that the materials used to teach reading should also be used to assess it (Jongsma & Jongsma, 1981). Extensive use of IRIs over the years has led to considerable research and increasingly sophisticated designs.

Teachers may use a commercially published IRI or construct their own. Constructing an informal reading inventory is not as simple as it may appear. The test constructor must identify a graded series of passages in an ascending order of difficulty (which typically is estimated according to a readability formula) and then formulate questions to assess comprehension on each passage. Selecting a properly graded sequence of passages and posing a balanced series of questions is difficult because of the limitations of readability formulas and variance in the type and difficulty of comprehension questions that are written (Klesius & Homan, 1985; Peterson, Greenlaw, & Tierney, 1978).

Because of the difficulties in constructing a properly graded series of passages and generating a fair and complete question set to accompany each passage, teachers who use IRIs often invest in commercially published inventories. Among the more popular instruments available are the Analytical Reading Inventory (Woods & Moe, 1989), the Basic Reading Inventory (Johns, 1991), the Classroom Reading Inventory (Silvaroli, 1986), the Ekwall Reading Inventory (Ekwall, 1986), the Informal Reading Inventory (Burns & Roe, 1989), and the Qualitative Reading Inventory (Leslie & Caldwell, 1990).

Whether a teacher-constructed or a commercially published IRI is used, IRI administration procedures typically proceed as follows. First, the examiner may use performance on graded word lists to indicate a reasonably easy text with which to begin the inventory. Next, the student is directed to read through each passage orally while the teacher codes miscues directly on a double-spaced copy of the passage. It is common practice not to offer assistance to a reader, although administration guidelines for several start IRIs suggest that the examiner occasionally pronounce a key word which, if not pronounced correctly, might seriously affect comprehension. Even for experienced IRI administrators, it is advisable to tape-record the oral reading to verify the coding later.

Although oral reading coding systems vary considerable, the following types of miscues are typically recorded:

- *Substitutions* are written directly above the words they replace.
- *Omissions* are circled.
- *Insertions* are marked with a caret and written above the text where the word was added.
- *Self-corrections* are marked with a *C*.
- *Reversals* of words are indicated with the proofreader's transpose marking.

Figure 7-1 presents a portion of an IRI passage coded according to these procedures. Other miscues (e.g., ignoring punctuation, hesitating, using dialect variants) may be marked for later analysis but typically are not counted as scorable miscues for the purpose of estimating reading levels. There is little consensus on how to score repetitions, which are counted as scorable errors in some IRIs and not counted in others.

For the frequent assessments required for Reading Recovery (Pinnell, Fried, & Estice, 1990), marking miscues on copies of text is inefficient. To facilitate continuous coding of oral reading performance, Marie Clay (1985) devised a shorthand miscue recording procedure called the *running record* (see Johnston, 1992a; Lipson & Wixson, 1991a). With a running record, the teacher codes words read accurately with check marks and indicates miscues in ways analogous to standard IRI miscue markings.

Figure 7-2 shows an example of a running record (right-hand side of the figure). Running records are useful because they require no special preparation. All the teacher needs is a blank sheet of paper to record check marks and miscues as a child reads from a trade book and the teacher checks the student's reading against the visible text. Analysis of the running record can be used to assess the readability of the text in light of the child's current ability and to gather data on the reader's use of text cues and comprehension strategies.

Returning to our discussion of conventional IRI administration, after reading the passage orally, the reader answers questions posed by the examiner. Some IRIs also include a free recall option, which invites readers to retell the passage in their own words (follow-up questions by the examiner probe for information omitted in the retelling). Inviting free recall not only breaks up the routine of the testing but also samples the reader's ability to organize the material read. Retelling was first formally introduced as a comprehension assessment in Goodman and Burke's (1972) IRI-type instrument, the *Reading Miscue Inventory,* and it remains so in the updated version, *Reading Miscue Inventory: Alternative Procedures* (Goodman, Watson, & Burke, 1987). Retelling has subsequently been incorporated into contemporary IRIs as an optional procedure. Several IRI authors also recommend that oral reading be followed with silent reading of a passage of equal difficulty to compare comprehension under oral and silent conditions.

The quantitative analysis of IRI data is achieved by comparing the percentages obtained from the oral reading and the comprehension questions to criteria for estimating

It was a ~~warm~~ *wet 1MC* spring day. The children ~~were~~ *went 2MC* going on a trip. The trip

was to a farm. The children wanted to see many ~~animals~~ *aminals 3MC*. They wanted to write

down (all) *4 MC* they saw. They were ~~going~~ *gone 5MC* to make a book for their class. On the way

the 6 to the,~~farm~~ *pumpkin 7MC* ~~the~~ bus broke (down.) *8* The children thought their trip was over.

Then a man ~~stopped~~ *stopped 9MC* his car. He helped (to) fix the bus. *10* The bus, started *won't C11* again.

The children said, "yea!" The children got to the farm. They saw *was C12* a pig. They

~~saw~~ *13 hens* a hen and cows. They liked petting the kittens. ~~looked~~ *14 MC* They learned about milking *looked 15 MC*

cows. They liked the trip to the farm. They wanted to go again. *and 16* (119 words)

The following miscues were substitutions:
  # 1, 2, 3, 5, 6, 9, 12, 13, 14, 15, 16

The following miscues were insertions:
  # 7, 11

The following miscues were omissions:
  # 4, 8, 10

The following miscues were meaning change miscues. They changed the meaning of the text or they were not self-corrected.
  # 1, 2, 3, 4, 5, 7, 9, 14, 15

FIGURE 7-1   **Example of oral reading coding from an informal reading inventory**

Source: From *Qualitative Reading Inventory* by Lauren Leslie & JoAnne Caldwell, p. 48. Copyright © 1990 by HarperCollins Publishers. Reprinted by permission.
Note: The underlining indicates words presented separately on word lists; it is not part of the coding procedure.

a student's independent, instructional, and frustration reading levels. Unfortunately, there is little consensus regarding the appropriate criteria to use for estimating these levels. Many IRI authors recommend using Bett's (1946) criteria, which require that the word recognition percentage be in the 95–98 range and the comprehension percentage be in the 70–89 range in order for performance on a passage to be designated as indicating a student's instructional level (generally, higher percentages on a passage place it at the

FIGURE 7-2   Example of a running record

Source: From *Assessment & Instruction of Reading Disability: An Interactive Approach* by Marjorie Y. Lipson and Karen K. Wixson, p. 288. Copyright © 1991 by HarperCollins Publishers. Reprinted by permission.

independent level and lower percentages at the frustration level). Other authors have argued that Bett's criteria are too rigorous and underestimate a student's performance; they recommend more liberal (lower) criteria (see Pikulski & Shanahan, 1982). This debate over criteria, coupled with the lack of consensus regarding which oral reading miscues count as scorable errors, reveals the lack of precision in estimating reading levels from IRI data.

Qualitative analysis of IRI data often involves some form of miscue analysis procedure based on the psycholinguistic model of reading advanced by Goodman (1967) and Smith (1971), in which reading is viewed as an attempt to build a text model from graphophonic, syntactic, and semantic cues. Oral miscues in the course of reading texts offer a "window on the reading process" (Goodman, 1973) through which a reader's comprehension strategies may be examined. By comparing a student's miscues to the words in the actual text, inferences can be drawn about the student's decoding ability (by examining miscues for graphophonic similarity to the word in the text) and ability to use meaning clues (by examining miscues for their syntactic and semantic acceptability). Most contemporary IRIs include some form of miscue analysis, adapting the elaborate procedures first introduced by Goodman and Burke (1972). Although miscue analysis provides considerable insight into a reader's strategies, it is quite time-consuming, even in a simplified form (e.g., Christie, 1979; Pflaum, 1979). How to score and weight miscues to reflect comprehension skill accurately may also be problematic (Sadoski & Page, 1984; Sadoski & Lee, 1986). Thus, as with the procedures employed for estimating reading levels through quantitative analysis, the qualitative analysis technique of miscue analysis likewise has its limitations (see Baumann, 1988, Chapters 6 and 7, for an in-depth discussion of these and other issues related to IRI administration, scoring, and interpretation).

A promising contemporary IRI that attempts to address the limitations of many traditional IRIs is the Qualitative Reading Inventory (QRI) (Leslie & Caldwell, 1990). It consists of word lists and passages from primer to junior high levels; because words on the lists are taken from the passages, the contrast between the same words seen in isolation and in context indicates the degree to which the reader relies on context for word recognition (see Figure 7-2). Passages on the QRI are intact texts, rather than excerpts. The rationale for the QRI explicitly recognizes that readers perform at different levels depending on the text and the task as well as on the reader's ability. For this reason, the QRI samples the reader's prior knowledge before each passage is read by means of an association task; the familiarity of the passage becomes an important factor in interpreting comprehension performance on that passage. Text structure also influences comprehension. To understand the reader's strengths with different genres, both narrative and expository texts are included at each readability level. Comprehension is tested under both oral and silent conditions, and comprehension is checked either by a balanced set of passage-dependent explicit and implicit questions or by unaided retelling. Scoring of the latter is facilitated by text maps on which the examiner can check off story elements as they are recalled. These characteristics reflect an attempt to incorporate recent research and theory about the reading process into an IRI assessment instrument.

In sum, informal reading inventories offer a time-tested means of obtaining a representative sample of reading behavior. Using appropriate means to analyze results, teachers can not only obtain a useful preliminary estimate of a student's reading levels across a variety of texts and tasks, but also get a rich source of material for arriving at deeper, qualitative hypotheses about reading (dis)abilities. Therefore, the IRI is well suited for acquiring an understanding of high-risk students' reading performance. As Lipson and Wixson (1991) note, the IRI is one of the most powerful assessment tools available to a teacher (see Chapter 6 for additional discussion).

Observational and Anecdotal Records

This cluster of assessment techniques involves the teacher recording observations of students during normal classroom learning activities. Observation is an unobtrusive means to assess students while they are engaged in natural learning tasks; therefore, observations possess high authenticity and rich detail. As Lipson and Wixson (1991) note, "no other single tool can provide such in-depth information about the learner's actual use and application of knowledge and skill as observation" (p. 109).

Observations and records can be very open ended, as in the case of anecdotal records in which the teacher writes notes in freehand concerning students' progress. The anecdotes might be observations of individual students:

> *2/15   Observed during retelling activity. A's [Aidrian's] predictions were good, his actual retelling well-sequenced, sensitive some good vocab., no punct.!!! (Cambourne & Turbill, 1990, p. 346)*

> *11/30/87 — D.J. is noticing character development in the story he's reading. In fact, it is not uncommon for him to follow me around the class reading excerpts from his book to me. (Siu-Runyan, 1991, p. 117)*

Anecdotes might also involve groups of students:

> *8/31/87 — Most of the children are struggling with their pieces. They want to write grand stories, but don't know enough about their topics to write well. They want to write fiction, and not personal narratives which is what I think would make a difference for them. (Siu-Runyan, 1991, p. 115)*

Anecdotal records can be taken in a notebook (Siu-Runyan, 1991); others have found that sticky notes (Rhodes & Nathenson-Mejia, 1992) or address labels (Pils, 1991) work well. Such notes can be affixed to students' folders or in designated sections in the teacher's three-ring binder.

Anecdotal records can be analyzed in various ways. Rhodes and Nathenson-Mejia (1992) suggest that teachers can (1) look for inferences in anecdotal records, (2) examine them for patterns, and (3) use them to identify strengths and weaknesses. Pills (1991) notes that it is easy to spot patterns and detect growth when records taken across time are reread, as in the case of her first-grade student Ben:

> *8-30 Ben: Rarely raises hand during meeting, but always attentive.*
> *9-30: Ben: "I like doing daily news because it's so easy sometimes."*
> *10-30 ben: Tells story of the Three Little Pigs to Chris.*
> *10-30 Ben: "Look, at is in my last name." (p. 48)*

The advantage of anecdotal records is that they allow a teacher to decide which literacy behaviors are to be observed and recorded, depending on the teacher's particular purpose for observing, individual students' strengths and weaknesses, and the classroom situation. As Rhodes and Nathenson-Mejia (1992) comment, "What is focused on and recorded depends upon the teacher, the student, and the context" (p. 502).

On the other hand, at times a teacher may choose to rely on an observational checklist that specifies predetermined behaviors for observation. This might be appropriate when a teacher wants to ensure that specific, key reading behaviors are observed periodically for all students. Checklists also streamline the observation process because their use reduces the amount of time teachers must spend transcribing classroom events.

There are many types of observational checklists. Most are designed for individual students. Figure 7-3 shows a portion of a fairly structured checklist designed to monitor students' oral and written language development across time. In contrast, Figure 7-4 is a more open-ended observational form to record beginning readers' development. Observational checklists can also be designed to record information about groups of students. For example, Figure 7-4 shows a literature reading checklist used by a sixth-grade middle school teacher whose class was engaged in studying a unit on time. In addition to the examples shown here, many types of literacy checklists can be found in Kemp's (1987) *Watching Children Read and Write: Observational Records for Children with Special Needs.* For additional examples, see selected sections in Au, Scheu, and Kawakami (1990), Au, Scheu, Kawakami, and Herman (1990), Cambourne and Turbill (1990), Goodman, Goodman, and Hood (1989), Harp (1991), Johnston (1992a), and Lipson and Wixson (1991).

Though observational and anecdotal records may get high marks on an authenticity (validity) scale, the reliability of the observations may be problematic. Lipson and Wixson (1991) note that the more observations a teacher makes, the more reliable or consistent the conclusions drawn from such observations: "The observations of classroom teachers may be exceptionally reliable, since teachers have many opportunities to observe student behavior" (p. 110). Regarding teachers' objectivity in observing, Lipson and Wixson suggest that teachers must continually evaluate and question the accuracy of their observations.

Finally, various observational notes and checklists become most useful when the form and function of these assessments are devised by the teachers who use them (Johnston, 1992a). For example, Paradis, Chatton, Boswell, Smith, and Yovich (1991) reported that the most effective informal assessments of students' progress in literature discussion groups were those that were developed and refined by the teachers themselves. In their attempts to implement a system of anecdotal record keeping, they learned that "kid watching is not easy and documenting what we see is even more difficult" (p. 17). In particular, the teachers found it very difficult to document strengths and weaknesses while interacting effectively with the students at the same time. They experienced a trade-off between active teaching and keeping records and experimented with various ways to circumvent this difficulty, including taping discussions and reserving an uninterrupted seatwork time immediately following discussion. Thus, the assessments presented and described here should be viewed only as models; actual anecdotal and observational recording procedures should be created and tailored by the teachers who use them.

Interviews, Conferences, Questionnaires, and Inventories

In contrast to the preceding discussion of assessments in which the teacher simply *observes* what is occurring in a classroom, this category of assessments requires a teacher to *solicit* responses or information from a student. These may be fairly open-ended, as in the case of a student interview, or more structured, as in the case of a written questionnaire. In either situation, however, the teacher has an agenda of sorts and seeks information of varying degrees of specificity from individual students or groups.

Face-to-face interviews are a simple but powerful way to obtain information about

Developing to Independent Stages

	1st	2nd	3rd	4th
Name _____ Dates				

Indicators of Developing Control and Comprehension

Code: M = Most of the time   S = Sometimes   N = Not yet

Talking and Listening | | | Code | | Comments

Talking and Listening					Comments
— Expects what is heard to make sense					
— Monitors understanding of spoken language by asking questions, seeking clarification, etc.					
— Uses a variety of speaking patterns to adjust to audience					
— Speaks confidently before a group and within the community					
— Communicates clearly and effectively					

Reading

Reading					
— Selects reading material with confidence					
— Reads for literary experience					
— Reads to be informed					
— Reads to perform a task					
— Constructs meaning, develops interpretation and makes judgments					
— Compares and contrasts, makes application					
— Understands story features—irony, humor, organization, point of view					
— Uses a variety of strategies—prediction, rate, background, information, etc.					
— Rereads for different purposes					
— Displays an expanding vocabulary					

Writing

Writing					
— Initiates writing for specific and personal purposes					
— Incorporates models from literature					
— Participates in writing conferences by asking questions and giving comments					
— Is aware of voice, sense of audience, sense of purpose					

FIGURE 7-3   Example of a structured observational checklist

Source: Reprinted by permission of Christopher-Gordon Publishers, Inc., from *Assessment and Evaluation in Whole Language Programs,* edited by Bill Harp. © 1991 by Christopher-Gordon Publishers, Inc., Norwood, MA.

Settings and Activities	Examples of Child's Activities
Story Time: Teacher reads to class (responses to story line; child's comments, questions, elaborations)	
Independent Reading: Book Time (nature of books child chooses or brings in; process of selecting; quiet or social reading)	
Writing (journal stories, alphabet, dictation)	
Reading Group/Individual (oral reading strategies; discussion of text, responses to instruction)	
Reading Related Activities Tasks (responses to assignments or discussion focusing on word letter properties, word games/ experience charts)	
Informal Settings (use of language in play, jokes, storytelling conversation)	
Books and Print as Resource (use of books for projects; attention to signs, labels, names; locating information)	
Other	

FIGURE 7-4   Example of an open-ended observational form

Source: E. Chittendon & R. Courtney, "Assessment of Young Children's Reading: Documentation as an Alternative to Testing," in D. S. Strickland & L. M. Morrow (Eds.), *Emerging Literacy: Young Children Learn to Read and Write* (Newark, DE: International Reading Association, 1989), p. 111. Reprinted with permission of Edward Chittenden and the International Reading Association.

students' reading abilities, strategies, interests, and habits. Yet they are not often employed: "Although interviews are widely used in our society for a variety of purposes, these tools are underused in the area of reading assessment" (Lipson & Wixson, 1991, p. 97). The rationale for student interviews is to use a direct means to assess students' literacy knowledge and skills—simply asking them:

> *When we evaluate children's literacy development, we are interested in finding out how the young reader/writer engages in and thinks about literate activity and about herself as a literate person. In the past we have tried many devious ways of getting this information and I can hear my mother saying to me, "Why*

Time Study Sept. '86 Literature	Read-Aloud *The Green Futures* Log Entries 3 Assigned No.	Quality	Discussion of Text	Response to Poem *J. Prufrock*	Text compared to "Back to the Future"	Film Response to Time Machine	Task: Respond to Own Lit. Re: Time
Mark	3	✓-	+	+ oral	+	+	O → +
Todd	3	✓	✓+				W ✓
Sue	3	✓	–				O
Marge	3	✓	✓-				O ✓-
Carol	3	✓	✓				O ✓-
Don	3	✓	✓+				O/W ✓
Richard	3	+	+		✓		O ✓-
Scott	3	✓-	✓-				O +
Melissa	5	✓	✓+	+W			O ✓
Darrell	2	–	–				O
Nancy	5	+	✓+	✓+W		✓	W/O ✓±
Tye	3	✓	✓	✓ O	+		W ✓+
Peter	3	✓	✓				W ✓-
Kevin	3	✓	✓-				W –
David	3	✓	✓				W ✓
Derek	3	✓+	✓+				W ✓
Dawn	3	✓-	✓-				O ✓
Maggie	5	+	+	+ W	+	+	W ✓+
Emily	3	✓-	✓-				O ✓
Darin	3	✓	✓				W ✓
Trish	3	✓	✓				W ✓
Ellen	3	+	✓+		✓		W ✓+
Jean	3	+	✓+				W ✓+
Jane	3	+	✓+		✓		W ✓+

O = Oral   W = Written

FIGURE 7-5   Example of a group observational checklist

Source: Reprinted with permission of Karen Sabers Dalrymple from "'Well, What about His Skills?' Evaluation of Whole Language in the Middle School." In *The Whole Language Evaluation Book,* edited by Kenneth S. Goodman, Yetta M. Goodman, and Wendy J. Hood (Heinemann Educational Books, Portsmouth, NH, 1989), p. 117.

didn't you just ask?" This may seem like simplistic advice, but often it is the best way to get good information. (Johnston, 1992a, p. 95)

Student interviews can be conducted for different purposes. Lipson and Wixson (1991) suggest that through an interview a teacher can obtain insight about (1) a student's knowledge about reading, including awareness of the functions of reading, goals and purposes for reading, and self-appraisal of abilities in areas such as decoding and comprehension; and (2) a student's attitude toward reading and motivation to read. An excellent source for guidance in how to conduct a reading interview is found in Johnston (1992a, Chapters 12–13); he addresses pragmatic concerns such as establishing rapport, maintaining flow during the interview, asking questions, and interpreting interview information.

Several authors have prepared scripts that might be used for conducting structured interviews. For example, Wixson, Bosky, Yochum, and Alvermann (1984) devised an elaborate reading comprehension interview script that has a student respond to the actual reading instructional materials used in a classroom, whether basal readers, trade books, or content textbooks. Lytle (1987; reproduced in Lipson & Wixson, 1991, p. 107) prepared interview questions designed to assess students' metacognitive awareness and strategies. Similar sets of questions have been prepared to probe students' reactions to literature (Cockrum & Castillo, 1991, p. 79) and to assess comprehension strategies (Baumann, 1988, p. 239). Although scripts such as these may be useful resources, they should be adapted as necessary to suit a teacher's purposes for assessment and to match the students' specific abilities and needs.

A reading conference is a specific kind of interview. A conference affords a teacher an opportunity to discuss with a student the books the child is reading, to brainstorm collaboratively what titles might be read next, and to listen to the child read in order to analyze the child's reading strategies. Conferences are usually conducted as part of an individualized or literature-based reading program. Written records of conferences are important and can take various forms. Figure 7-6 shows a fairly formal reading conference note sheet, whereas Figure 7-7 displays a more open-ended format. An excellent resource for organizing a reading program around conferences is Hornsby, Sukarna, and Parry's (1986) *Read On: A Conference Approach to Reading.*

Questionnaires and inventories provide more structured ways to assess students' reading performance. They may be conducted individually with students in an oral fashion, or, if written, can be completed independently by groups of students. Oral interviews have the advantage of allowing the administrator to follow up a student's responses with additional questions or probes; written inventories are more time-efficient because of group administration. Informal questionnaires and inventories abound (e.g., Barr et al., 1990; Baumann, 1988; Goodman et al., 1989; Harp, 1991; Harris & Sipay, 1990; Kemp, 1987; Lipson & Wixson, 1991) and vary in the aspects of reading they assess, their degree of formality, and their format. A select few questionnaires and inventories are described here as examples of this large class of instruments and procedures.

Teachers often wish to evaluate their students' reading interests and attitudes. To assess the former, a teacher might use a simple reading interest inventory to obtain some idea of the interests of students in a class (see Figure 7-8). Reading attitudes can likewise

READING AND WRITING CONFERENCE--(reading)

Name: Conference on *11/9*

* Reads during Everybody Reads time.

usually   (sometimes)   not very much
                     a little or → a lot

* Can explain how s/he chooses books.
favorite books – you read. *What I like   I ask somebody*
                                              that can read it.
* Talks about what s/he reads. (Know what s/he likes.
                                  yes)
a lot to say   some   not much to say

* Likes to read to (self--and others. *to friends if they ask me*
                    sometimes

* Reads different kinds of materials: (stories) information,
how-to, (messages) signs, poetry, pictures, (books), magazines,
(letters) plays, jokes, riddles, experiments, records, cards . .
phone numbers, menu. Happy Birthday Moon
                       Green Eggs and Ham   Didn't Frighten'm
                       Oh. Bother

* Uses illustrations to figure out words and to check meaning.

a lot   (sometimes)   not much

* Use the rest of the writing to figure out words and check
for meaning.
(quite often)   sometimes   hardly ever
I read it all over from the very beginning
and when I come to it I know the word
* Uses letters and sounds to figure out words and check for
meaning.

quite often   sometimes   (hardly ever)

* Can read words as soon as s/he sees them.

(quite a few words)   some words   just a few words

* Plans:
Just do what I'm doing. maybe read
slower so I can talk more about it.

FIGURE 7-6 Example of a scripted reading conference note sheet

Source: Reprinted by permission of Christopher-Gordon Publishers, Inc., from S. J. Reardon, "A Collage of Assessment and Evaluation from Primary Classrooms," in B. Harp (Ed.), *Assessment and Evaluation in Whole Language Programs,* p. 95. © 1991 by Christopher-Gordon Publishers, inc., Norwood, MA.

Conference Notes

Name _____ Date _____

Title of Piece _____ Type of Piece _____

Attitudes/Interests/Background

Comprehension

Fictional Text
- main idea
- details
- setting
- characters
- inferences

Informational Text
- facts
- concepts
- vocabulary

Strategies used

Further reading or extension project

FIGURE 7-7   Example of an open-ended reading conference note sheet

Source: Reprinted by permission of Christopher-Gordon Publishers, Inc., from C. J. Church, "Record Keeping in Whole Language Classrooms," in B. Harp (Ed.), *Assessment and Evaluation in Whole Language Programs* p. 184. © 1991 by Christopher-Gordon Publishers, Inc., Norwood, MA.

READING INTEREST INVENTORY

Name _____ Grade _____ Age _____

Teacher _____ Date _____

Part I: WHAT MATERIALS DO YOU LIKE TO READ?

Number the list of reading materials from 1 to 5. Put number 1 in front of the type of reading materials you like to read *most;* put number 5 in front of the reading materials you like to read *least.*

_____ newspapers   _____ hardbound books   _____ comic books

_____ magazines   _____ paperback books

PART II: WHAT KIND OF READING DO YOU LIKE?

Number the list of kinds of reading from 1 to 4. Put number 1 in front of the kind of reading you like to do *most;* put number 4 in front of the kind reading you like to do *least.*

_____ fiction   _____ poetry

_____ nonfiction   _____ plays/drama

PART III: WHAT DO YOU LIKE TO READ ABOUT?

Number the list of topics from 1 to 12. Put number 1 in front of the topic you like to read about *most;* put number 12 in front of the topic you like to read about *least.*

_____ humorous stories/jokes/riddles   _____ science fiction/fantasy

_____ famous people (biographies)   _____ stories about kids like me

_____ animals/nature/pets   _____ history/long ago

_____ science/space/airplanes   _____ poems and plays

_____ mysteries/detective stories   _____ romance/adventure

_____ sports/games/hobbies   _____ Bible/religion

FIGURE 7-8   Example of a reading interest inventory

Source: Reprinted with the permission of Merrill Publishing Company, an imprint of Macmillan Publishing Company from *Reading Assessment: An Instructional Decision-Making Perspective,* by James F. Baumann, p. 248. Copyright © 1988 by Merrill Publishing Company.

be assessed in multiple ways (see Harris & Sipay, 1990, Chapter 18). One potentially useful instrument for assessing reading attitudes is the Elementary Reading Attitude Survey (McKenna & Kear, 1990), a portion of which is reproduced in Figure 7-9. This group-administered instrument provides estimates of students' attitudes toward recreational and academic reading and has documented reliability and validity. A measure designed to assess students' awareness of strategic reading processes is the Metacomprehension Strategy

ELEMENTARY READING ATTITUDE SURVEY

School__________ Grade___ Name______________________

1. How do you feel when you read a book on a rainy Saturday?

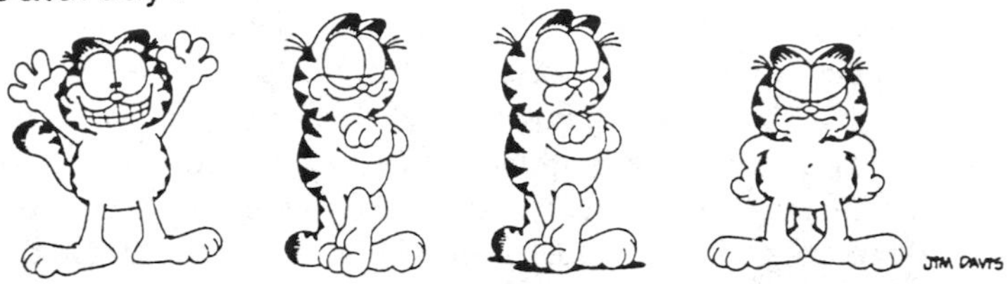

2. How do you feel when you read a book in school during free time?

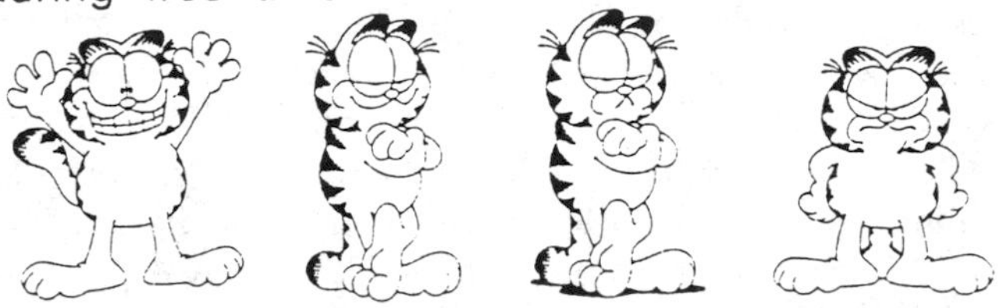

3. How do you feel about reading for fun at home?

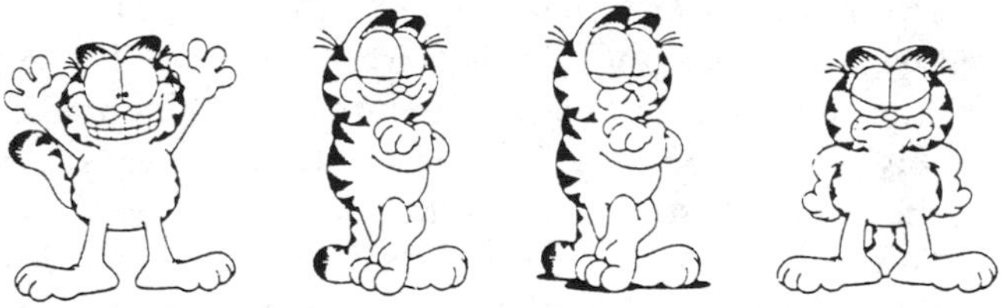

4. How do you feel about getting a book for a present?

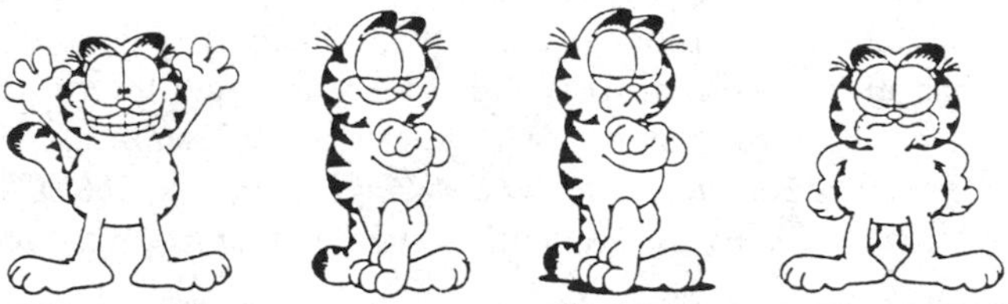

FIGURE 7-9 Example of a standardized reading attitude inventory

Source: From M. C. McKenna and D. J. Kear, "Measuring Attitude toward Reading: A New Tool for Teachers," *The Reading Teacher,* Vol. 43, 1990, p. 630. Reprinted with permission of Michael C. McKenna and the International Reading Association. The Garfield Reading Attitude Survey is reprinted with permission of United Media.

Index (Schmitt, 1990), a portion of which is reproduced in Figure 7-10. It solicits students' self-reported use of strategies such as predicting and verifying, previewing, purpose setting, and self-questioning. Like the Elementary Reading Attitude Survey, the Metacomprehension Strategy Index is group-administered and possesses reasonable technical qualities.

In any reading assessment situation, one technique or procedure should not be applied and interpreted in isolation: Additional data are needed to corroborate what is gleaned from a single assessment. For example, to supplement a reading interest inventory like that shown in Figure 7-8, a teacher might interview students individually about their reading interests and also observe them during book selection in the classroom or during a visit to the school library. These multiple data sources enhance the reliability of an assessed reading behavior, giving the teacher greater confidence in the soundness of the conclusions drawn from such assessments.

Intervention Assessments

Paratore and Indrisano (1987) devised a one-to-one comprehension strategy assessment procedure they called intervention assessment. According to this procedure, while reading a whole text, the student is asked to employ various comprehension strategies—for example, making predictions. When the student encounters difficulty with a strategy, the administrator intervenes by describing and modeling the particular strategy for the student. Then the administrator observes the student's use of the strategy. Thus, the assessment is administered in a type of teaching or intervention environment. The notion of intervention assessment exemplifies what Lipson and Wixson (1991; Wixson, 1991) refer to as diagnostic teaching, the blending of assessment and instruction.

The idea of evaluation in the form of intervention makes good sense from both an assessment and a pedagogical standpoint. Having a student engage in an authentic reading task enhances the validity of a procedure. Observing how a student responds to various prompts or tasks provides valuable insights into the reader's strategic repertoire, and these insights can guide subsequent instruction.

This section features four selected procedures that fit the concept of intervention assessment. The first two are intervention assessments for emergent or beginning readers; the latter two are comprehension assessment strategies for more advanced readers. Although the examples presented here are themselves specific and useful, they can serve as models for other adaptations of this perspective on assessment.

Marie Clay has pioneered the development of authentic forms of literacy assessment for beginning and high-risk readers. A variety of emergent or early literacy assessment procedures are contained in what she calls the Diagnostic Survey, which is included in her book *The Early Detection of Reading Difficulties* (1985). The Diagnostic Survey forms the basis for evaluating students in the Reading Recovery program (e.g., Pinnell et al., 1990).

One portion of the Diagnostic Survey is the Concepts About Print (CAP) tests, which are excellent examples of intervention assessment. In the CAP procedure, the administrator reads a special book—either *Sand* (Clay, 1972) or *Stones* (Clay, 1979)—to a young child and invites the child to help the administrator: "I'm going to read you this story but I want you to help me" (Clay, 1985, p. 28). The books are picture books with simple

Metacomprehension Strategy Index

Directions: Think about what kinds of things you can do to help you understand a story better before, during, and after you read it. Read each of the lists of four statements and decide which one of them would help *you* the most. *There are no right answers.* It is just what *you* think would help the most. Circle the letter of the statement you choose.

I. **In each set of four, choose the one statement which tells a good thing to do to help you understand a story better *before* you read it.**

1. Before I begin reading, it's a good idea to:
   A. See how many pages are in the story.
   B. Look up all of the big words in the dictionary.
   C. Make some guesses about what I think will happen in the story.
   D. Think about what has happened so far in the story.

2. Before I begin reading, it's a good idea to:
   A. Look at the pictures to see what the story is about.
   B. Decide how long it will take me to read the story.
   C. Sound the words I don't know.
   D. Check to see if the story is making sense.

3. Before I begin reading, it's a good idea to:
   A. Ask someone to read the story to me.
   B. Read the title to see what the story is about.
   C. Check to see if most of the words have long or short vowels in them.
   D. Check to see if the pictures are in order and make sense.

4. Before I begin reading, it's a good idea to:
   A. Check to see that no pages are missing.
   B. Make a list of the words I'm not sure about.
   C. Use the title and pictures to help me make guesses about what will happen in the story.
   D. Read the last sentence so I will know how the story ends.

5. Before I begin reading, it's a good idea to:
   A. Decide on why I am going to read the story.
   B. Use the difficult words to help me make guesses about what will happen in the story.
   C. Reread some parts to see if I can figure out what is happening if things aren't making sense.
   D. Ask for help with the difficult words.

6. Before I begin reading, it's a good idea to:
   A. Retell all of the main points that have happened so far.
   B. Ask myself questions that I would like to have answered in the story.
   C. Think about the meanings of the words which have more than one meaning.
   D. Look through the story to find all of the words with three or more syllables.

7. Before I begin reading, it's a good idea to:
   A. Check to see if I have read this story before.
   B. Use my questions and guesses as a reason for reading the story.
   C. Make sure I can pronounce all of the words before I start.
   C. Think of a better title for the story.

8. Before I begin reading, it's a good idea to:
   A. Think of what I already know about the things I see in the pictures.
   B. See how many pages are in the story.
   C. Choose the best part of the story to read again.
   D. Read the story aloud to someone.

9. Before I begin reading, it's a good idea to:
   A. Practice reading the story aloud.
   B. Retell all of the main points to make sure I can remember the story.
   C. Think of what the people in the story might be like.
   D. Decide if I have enough time to read the story.

FIGURE 7-10 **Example of a reading comprehension strategy questionnaire**

Source: M. C. Schmitt, "A Questionnaire to Measure Children's Awareness of Strategic Reading Processes," *The Reading Teacher, 43* (1990), p. 459. Reprinted with permission of Maribeth Cassidy Schmitt and the International Reading Association.
Note: Underlined responses indicate metacomprehension strategy awareness.

texts, but they contain several anomalies (e.g., upside-down pictures, misspellings) that enable the administrator to evaluate a child's knowledge of print and books. Through a series of questions and observations, the CAP administrator is able to evaluate the child's book-handling skills, knowledge of left-to-right and top-to-bottom conventions, letter concepts, and the like. From the CAP procedure, along with other data from the Diagnostic Survey, a teacher can make judgments about students' emergent literacy development and can provide appropriate literacy experiences and instruction.

Sulzby's (1991) Storybook Reading Classification Scheme is another informal tool that is useful for teachers of young children in assessing emergent literacy. Designed as an alternative to traditional reading readiness tests, the Scheme offers a structured observational framework for describing the child's progress from pictures to print, from commentary and monologues to wording and intonation that approximates written forms, and finally into conventional reading.

When using the Scheme, a teacher invites a child to "read" a favorite storybook to her or him and, while doing so, observes motor and verbal behaviors related to storybook reading. Figure 7-11 presents a simplified version of the Scheme, which consists of five categories of storybook "reading" behavior, ranging from a child simply describing the pictures in the book (Category 1) to attending to print and actually reading the text (Category 5). The Scheme is useful to preschool, kindergarten, and first-grade teachers assessing students' emergent storybook-reading abilities so that appropriate experiences and activities can be provided to promote their reading development.

Retelling is a powerful way to explore students' comprehension of a selection they have read or one that has been read to them. Several authors have provided elaborate procedures for soliciting retellings from students and for analyzing them in various ways.

Morrow (1988, 1989, 1990) has provided a procedure for eliciting retellings from young children after they have heard a story read aloud. Figure 7-12 presents a synopsis of the story *Jenny Learns a Lesson* (Fujikawa, 1989), a five-year-old's retelling of it, and the accompanying story retelling analysis (all from Morrow, 1988). This analysis gives the teacher a means of evaluating a child's comprehension of a specific story, understandng of stereotypical story parts, and oral language facility. This procedure can also be used following a child's independent reading of a story.

Other procedures for analyzing the retellings or free recall following the reading of a selection have also been proposed—for example, the oral retelling component of the Reading Miscue Inventory, discussed in an earlier section. Additionally, Clark (1982) has provided a procedure for quantitatively analyzing the free recall of a selection that has been read, and Irwin and Mitchell (1983) have provided a parallel technique for examining a retelling more qualitatively. Baumann (1988, Chapter 10) has incorporated these quantitative and qualitative analyses into a formal procedure for preparing, administering, scoring, and interpreting a free recall with follow-up probe questions. Figure 7-13 presents an example of a child's free and probed recall of a selection titled "A Silly Story," along with a quantitative and qualitative analysis of that recall. Retellings and recalls, though time-consuming and thus not feasible for more than a handful of students, do provide a deep and rich means of analyzing a student's listening or reading comprehension.

Another intervention assessment procedure for evaluating a reader's comprehension

1. Attending to Pictures, Not Forming Stories	The child is "reading" by looking at the storybook's pictures. The child's speech is *just* about the picture in view; the child is not "weaving a story" across the pages. (Subcategories are "labelling and commenting" and "following the action.")
2. Attending to Pictures, Forming *ORAL* Stories	The child is "reading" by looking at the storybook's pictures. The child's speech weaves a story across the pages but the wording and the intonation are like that of someone telling a story, either like a conversation about the pictures or like a fully recited story, in which the listener can see the pictures (and often *must* see them to understand the child's story). (Subcategories are "dialogic storytelling" and "monologic storytelling.")
3. Attending to Pictures, Reading and Storytelling mixed	The child is "reading" by looking at the storybook's pictures. The child's speech sounds as if the child is reading, both in the wording and intonation. The listener does not need to look at the pictures (or rarely does) in order to understand the story. If the listener closes his/her eyes, most of the time he or she would think the child is reading from print. (Subcategories are "reading similar-to-original story," and "reading verbatim-like story.")
4. Attending to Print	There are four subcategories of attending to print. Only the *final* one is what is typically called "real reading." In the others the child is exploring the print by such strategies as refusing to read based on print-related reasons, or using only some of the aspects of print. (Subcategories are "refusing to read based on print awareness," "reading aspectually," "reading with strategies imbalanced," and "reading independently" or "conventional reading.")

FIGURE 7-11   Simplified version of the Sulzby Storybook Reading Classification Scheme

Source: E. Sulzby, "Assessment of Emergent Literacy: Storybook Reading," *The Reading Teacher,* 44 (1991), p. 500. Reprinted with permission of the International Reading Association.

involves having a student describe his or her mental operations while reading. The conventional term for this is *think-aloud.* Figure 7-14 provides an example of a portion of an oral think-aloud. By analyzing the strategies a reader employs (or does not employ) during a think-aloud, a teacher can establish a program of comprehension instruction to expand a reader's range and effective use of comprehension strategies.

Various techniques have been suggested for gathering and evaluating think-alouds. For example, Wade (1990) has developed and fieldtested a fairly formal think-aloud procedure that enables an examiner to characterize a reader according to one of five types: a good comprehender, a non–risk taker, a nonintegrator, a schema imposer, or a storyteller. Davey (1983) and Brown and Lytle (1988) have proposed other techniques for examining think-alouds, and Johnston (1992a, Chapter 17) provides an elaborate description of how think-alouds and variations of them can be used to obtain insights into students' processing of texts.

PARSED STORY: JENNY LEARNS A LESSON

Setting

a. Once upon a time there was a girl who liked to play pretend.
b. Characters: Jenny (main character), Nicholas, Sam, Mei Su, and Shags (the dog).

Theme

Every time Jenny planed with her friends, she bossed them and insisted that they do what she wanted them to.

Plot Episodes

First Episode: Jenny decided to pretend to be a queen. She called her friends and they came to play. Jenny told them what to do and was bossy. The friends became angry and left.

Second Episode: Jenny decided to play dancer, with the same results as in the first episode.

Third Episode: Jenny played pirate, with the same results.

Fourth Episode: Jenny decided to play duchess, with the same results.

Fifth Episode: Jenny's friends decided not to play with her again because she was so bossy. Many days passed and Jenny became lonely. She went to her friends and apologized to them for being bossy.

Resolution

a. Jenny and her friends played together and each person did what he or she wanted to do.
b. They all had a wonderful day and were so tired that they fell asleep.

Sample Verbatim Transcription—Beth, Age 5

Once upon a time there's a girl named Jenny and she called her friends over and they played queen and went to the palace. They had to, they had to do what she said and they didn't like it, so then they went home and said that was boring . . . It's not fun playing queen and doing what she says you have to. So they didn't play with her for seven days and she had . . . she had a idea that she was being selfish, so she went to find her friends and said, I'm sorry I was so mean. And said, let's play pirate, and they played pirate and they went onto the ropes. They they played that she was a fancy lady playing house. And they have tea. And they played what they wanted and they were happy . . . The End.

STORY RETELLING ANALYSIS

Child's Name _____ Beth _____   Age _____ 5 _____

Title of Story _____ Jenny Learns a lesson _____   Date _____

General directions: Place a "1" next to each element if the child includes it in his or her presentation. Credit "gist" as well as obvious recall, counting the words *boy, girl,* or *dog,* for instance, under characters named, as well as *Nicholas, Mei Su,* or *Shags.* Credit plurals (*friends,* for instance) as "2".

FIGURE 7-12 *Continued*

SENSE OF STORY STRUCTURE

Setting

a. Begins story with an introduction   1
b. Names main character   1
c. Number of other characters named   2
d. Actual number of other characters   4
e. Score for "other characters" (c/d)   0.5
f. Includes statement about time or place   1

Theme

Refers to main character's primary goal   1
or problem to be solved

Plot Episodes

a. Number of episodes recalled   4
b. Number of episodes in story   5
c. Score for "plot episodes" (a/b)   0.8

Resolution

a. Names problem solution/goal attainment   1
b. Ends story   1

Sequence

Retells story in structural order: setting,
theme, plot episodes, resolution. (Score 2 for
proper order, 1 for partial, 0 for no sequence   1

Highest score possible: _____10_____   Child's score   8.3

FIGURE 7-12 **Example of an analysis of a child's oral retelling of a story**

Source: L. M. Morrow, "Assessing Children's Understanding of Story through Their Construction and Reconstruction of Narrative," in L. M. Morrow & J. K. Smith (Eds.), *Assessment for Instruction in Early Literacy* (Englewood Cliffs, NJ: Prentice-Hall, 1990), pp. 127–128.

As for all the procedures described in this section, gathering and analyzing an oral think-aloud is a labor-intensive and time-consuming process. However, used judiciously with students for whom a teacher needs an in-depth analysis of their comprehension processing, obtaining a think-aloud may indeed be worth the time and effort.

T: All right, Angela, now tell me as much of the story as you can remember.

A: There was this dinosaur, and he met this train (1). The dinosaur thought the train was some kind of animal, but he couldn't figure out what the animal was (2). Then the dinosaur said, "I'm going to fight you" (3). So he ran at the train (4). Then the train got afraid [inferred intrusion]. But the dinosaur said, "Hey, you can't run away from me" (5). Then he chased it (6; ½ credit). Then, at the end, the dinosaur said, "Hey, you can't fight good (7). but you sure can run faster than me" (8).

T: Good job, Angela. Is there anything else you can remember about the story?

A: Well, I think the train speeded up when the dinosaur began to chase it (9). And I think that the dinosaur was green and kind of mean to the train [inferred intrusion].

T: Is there anything else you can think of?

A: No.

T: All right. Angela, can you tell me any more about how the dinosaur looked [probe for idea number 3]?

A: Well, he was green, I think. And he was big and strong [probed credit for idea number 3].

T: Good. Do you remember what the dinosaur did after he decided to fight the train [probe for idea number 5]?

A: I think he snorted real loud [logical but unacceptable response].

T: What did the train do after the dinosaur ran at it [probe for idea number 7]?

A: It ran away [probed credit for idea number 7]?

T: Good. What did the dinosaur say to the train as it ran away [probe for idea number 8]?

A: I don't know. Maybe he said he was a big chicken [logical but unacceptable response].

T: You said that the dinosaur chased the train. How did he chase it [probe for remaining part of idea number 10]?

A: I think he ran after it down the railroad tracks [logical but unacceptable response].

T: Did the dinosaur catch the train [probe for idea number 12]?

A: No.

T: Why do you say no [follow-up probe]?

A: Well, it said something about the dinosaur being left behind on the railroad tracks [probed credit for idea number 12].

T: Thank you, Angela, you did a nice job.

A: Thanks.

FIGURE 7-13   Example of a student's free and probed recall of a reading selection

Source: J. F. Baumann, *Reading Assessment: An Instructional Decision-Making Perspective* (Columbus, OH: Merrill, pp. 226–227.

Notes: T = teacher's statements; A = Angela's responses. Numbers in parentheses refer to ideas recalled freely. Annotations are within brackets.

FREE AND PROBED RECALL COMPREHENSION

"A Silly Story"

Student _Angela Jackson_   Grade _2_

Teacher _Mr. Howell_   Date _Oct. 23_

P	F	I	
			P = Probed Recall F = Free Recall I = Importance Rating
	1	1	A dinosaur once met a train. (1)
	2	2	"I don't know what kind of animal this is," said the dinosaur, (2)
✓		3	"but it looks very strong. (3)
	3	1	I will fight it." (4)
		3	So the dinosaur put its head down (5)
	4	3	and ran right at the train. (6)
✓		1	The train began to move away. (7)
		2	"Oh, so you are going to run away, are you?" said the dinosaur. (8)
	5	2	"Well, you can't run away from me." (9)
	6($\frac{1}{2}$)	1	The dinosaur began to run beside the train. (10)
	9	3	But the train went faster and faster. (11)
✓		2	Soon the dinosaur was left behind. (12)
	7	1	"Well, you're not much good as a fighter," said the dinosaur, (13)
	8	1	"but you are a much better runner than I am." (14)
3	*8$\frac{1}{2}$*		TOTAL IDEAS RECALLED
21%	*61%*		PERCENTAGE OF IDEAS RECALLED (Total ideas/14)
	82%		TOTAL PERCENTAGE OF IDEAS RECALLED (Free % + Probed %)
	1.7		AVERAGE IMPORTANCE LEVEL RECALLED FREELY
	excellent		SEQUENCE EVALUATION (excellent, good, poor)

Elaborations
and
Intrusions

"The train got afraid." (free)
"The dinosaur was green and mean to the train." (free)
"He snorted real loud." (probed)
"He said he was a real chicken."(probed)

FIGURE 7-13   *Continued*

TEXT PORTION	STUDENT THINK-ALOUD
"The Foundling"	The Foundling. That's a funny name for a story. I wonder what a foundling is? Maybe it has something to do with found. Maybe a character has found something?
The Tilton family next door to Christopher had a new dog.	So, Christopher, who must be a boy, lives next to a family called the Tiltons. The Tiltons must have a new dog. I wonder how old Christopher is? I wonder wht kind of dog it is?
He had come through the gate one day when Christopher had got home from school.	Who came through the gate? It must be the dog. Maybe the dog was a stray, a lost dog without an owner. I wonder what grade Christopher is in?
Christopher sat down next to the puppy and scratched his head. The puppy had rings around his eyes and his dark ears.	I wonder where this is taking place? The picture shows him on a porch. It must be Christopher's house because it said the dog came through the gate. I bet it is a stray. It doesn't sound like any kind of purebred dog.
He looked the way Christopher's god, Bodger, must have looked when Bodger was a puppy. Christopher didn't remember because he had been a baby himself.	Maybe Christopher isn't too old if he was a baby when he got his dog. I wonder if Bodger is still alive? I wonder if this dog could be related to Bodger?
The puppy sniffed at Christopher's lunch box, trying to nuzzle it open. Christopher fed him the scrap of uneaten sandwich inside. After that, the puppy waited for him every day after school.	Maybe it is a stray, since he acts so hungry. But the Tiltons have him now, and I bet they take good care of him. Christopher must be in grade school. I don't think older kids carry lunch boxes. I guess Christopher and the puppy are getting to be friends, since the dog waits for him every day after school.
Bodger had been killed in an accident with a pickup truck. Still, Christopher found himself hoping every night that his bedroom door would be shoved open and Bodger's warm weight would settle on his feet. The bad dreams that came for weeks after the accident had stopped. But it was hard getting used to Bodger being gone.	Well, one question is answered: Bodger is dead. Christopher still misses him a lot. I once had a pet can run over, so I remember how sad that is. I, too, had bad dreams about that. I wonder if Christopher will get to keep the Tilton's dog? Why is this story called "The Foundling"?
Maybe it was seeing Christopher play all week with the little dog from next door that gave his father the idea. On Saturday his father came out and nodded toward the car. Christopher was bouncing a ball off the roof of the car. "Hop in. I've got a surprise for you." Christopher felt excited and wondered what the surprise could be. They stopped in front of a small building with a sign out front that said "ANIMAL SHELTER." Christopher's head snapped toward his father in panic. "We're going to get a dog," Christopher said, "Dad, I don't want another one."	I guess Bodger must have died just recently, because it seems as if Christopher's father is feeling sorry for him. Why doesn't Christopher want another dog? Maybe he really does want a dog. But why would he say that? What does the Tilton's dog have to do with this story. Will Christopher get another dog from the animal shelter? Why is this story called "The Foundling"? Will Christopher get a stray dog from the animal shelter?

FIGURE 7-14 Example of a student think-aloud.

Source: J. F. Baumann, *Reading Assessment: An Instructional Decision-Making Perspective* (Columbus, OH: Merrill, 1988), pp. 230–231.

Portfolio Assessment

The final informal assessment technique discussed here is the use of portfolios, which are collections of students' work. Because of space limitations, we can only survey the topic of literacy portfolios. For more in-depth, practical information about the implementation of portfolio assessment, we refer readers to the many sources cited here in our discussion.

Valencia (1990) provided the rationale for a reading portfolio by likening it to an artist's portfolio:

> *Developing artists rely on portfolios to demonstrate their skills and achievements. Within the portfolio, they include samples of their work that exemplify the depth and breadth of their expertise. They may include many different indicators: work in a variety of media to demonstrate their versatility, several works on one particular subject to demonstrate their refined skill and sophistication, and work collected over time to exemplify their growth as artists. Within such rich sources of information, it is easier for the critics and the teachers, and most importantly, artists themselves, to understand the development of expertise and to plan the experiences that will encourage additional progress and showcase achievements. A portfolio approach to the assessment of reading assumes the position that developing readers deserve no less. (Valencia, 1990, p. 338)*

Thus, portfolios enable and encourage teachers to draw assessments from authentic and (one hopes) trustworthy reading tasks students perform in school—and perhaps also outside of school—on a day-to-day basis.

Descriptions of portfolio assessment techniques may be found in many recent periodicals and books (e.g., Gomez, Graue, & Bloch, 1991; Harp, 1991; Johnston, 1992a; Jongsma, 1989; Lamme & Hysmith, 1991; Mathews, 1990; Mills, 1989; Paris, 1991; Rief, 1990; Tierney et al., 1991; Valencia, 1990; Valencia, McGinley, & Pearson, 1990; Wolf, 1989). As with most evolving trends in education, definitions vary. However, most conceptions of literacy portfolios describe them as collections of literacy artifacts, assembled primarily by the student, that are representative of the learner's developing literacy competencies. As Valencia (1990) notes, portfolios enable children to showcase their versatility, refined skill and sophistication, and developmental growth in literacy abilities.

Why are portfolios being touted as a viable and useful alternative to more formal or traditional assessments? Valencia (1990, p. 338) presents a four-pronged rationale for moving toward portfolio assessment:

- Portfolios include literacy artifacts that are drawn from authentic tasks, texts, and contexts.
- Portfolios promote continuous, ongoing evaluation of literacy development.
- Portfolios account for the complexity of literacy processes by drawing from multiple measures of cognitive and affective behaviors.
- Portfolios enable children, teachers, and parents to reflect collaboratively on what a learner has acquired and what remains to be done in the acquisition of literacy abilities.

Physically, portfolios vary in form, limited only by the imagination of those who construct them. (Valencia, 1990, describes their size as somewhere between a report card and a steamer trunk.) In most instances, however, portfolio contents are placed in some type of expandable folder. In their book *Portfolio Assessment in the Reading-Writing Classroom,* Tierney et al. (1991) provide a long list of potential portfolio contents (see Table 7-1). As can be seen, the variety of artifacts that might be assembled in a portfolio is almost limitless.

Although students are the "owners" of their portfolios and thus the primary contributors to them, teachers, other students, and even parents might make contributions as well. Thus, some of the informal assessments that have been discussed in this chapter would be possible contributions to a portfolio—for example, anecdotal records, conference notes, and various inventories and questionnaires. Students' self-evaluations of their efforts, their products, and their performances are also an integral part of their portfolios. There are many ways to invite students to engage in self-evaluation, including simple

TABLE 7-1   Some Possible Elements for Reading and Writing Portfolios

- Projects, surveys, reports, and units from reading and writing
- Favorite poems, songs, letters, and comments
- Interesting thoughts to remember
- Finished samples that illustrate wide writing
  —persuasive, letters, poetry, information, stories
- Examples of writing across the curriculum
  —reports, journals, literature logs
- Literature extensions
  —scripts for drama, visual arts, written forms, webs, charts, time lines, murals
- Student record of books read and attempted
- Audio tape of reading
- Writing responses to literary components
  —plot, setting, point of view, character development, links to life, theme, literary links, and criticism
- Writing that illustrates critical thinking about readings
- Notes from individual reading and writing conference
- Items that are evidence of development of style
  —organization, voice, sense of audience, choice of words, clarity
- Writing that shows growth in usage of traits
  —growing ability in self-correction, punctuation, spelling, grammar, appropriate form, and
  —

- Samples in which ideas are modified from first draft to final product
- Unedited first draft
- Revised first draft
- Evidence of effort
  —improvement noted on pieces, completed assignments, personal involvement noted
- Self-evaluations
- Writing that illustrates evidence of topic generation

Source: Reprinted by permission of Christopher-Gordon Publishers, Inc., from *Portfolio Assessment in the Reading-Writing Classroom,* by Robert J. Tierney, Mark A. Carter, & Laura E. Desai. © 1991 by Christopher-Gordon Publishers, Inc., Norwood, MA.

periodic reviews of portfolio contents or more formal checklists or self-evaluation forms. Readers may refer to Johnston (1992a, Chapters 5 and 6) for a discussion of issues related to student self-evaluation and to Tierney et al. (1991, Chapter 7) for pragmatic suggestions for student self-evaluation.

Assessment and decision making with portfolios involve a collaborative effort of the teacher and the child (and perhaps parents also). Teacher–student conferences (and occasionally teacher–student–parent conferences) are typically the vehicle for reviewing portfolio contents. Through a student's self-evaluations, the teacher's regular reviews of the portfolios, and periodic conferences, a student's progress, growth, and development in reading and other literacy abilities can be assessed. On the basis of these ongoing assessments, decisions about the focus and specific nature of literacy activities and instruction can be determined.

The primary difference between the use of portfolios and other forms of assessment we have discussed is that the *student* contributes significantly to the assessment process through portfolios. Assessment is not something that is done *to* or *for* a student; rather, the student is a full participant in the ongoing portfolio assessments. This involvement is likely to promote students' responsibility for and investment in their own learning.

Conclusion

Our survey of formal and informal reading assessments documents the current renaissance in reading assessment. Even from this limited review, it should be clear that the range of assessment options available to teachers of high-risk students is broad, if not overwhelming. How, then, does one select reading assessments? Which ones? How many? How often should they be used?

Our response is terse, simple, but we think not trite: *Assess only when the information gleaned from an assessment will lead to an educational decision.* Identify your questions about your students' literacy abilities and how answers to those questions will guide your instructional program; then select the most useful, efficient means to obtain the information you seek. In other words, administer or implement reading assessments judiciously and selectively. Like so many things done in schools, reading assessments should be used wisely, discriminatingly, and in moderation.

In addition, an earlier caveat bears reemphasis: *Be wary of assessments that may not have established soundness, whether they are alternative or traditional.* Sound assessments, as we have emphasized, demonstrate both authenticity and trustworthiness. Although we do not recommend that you refrain from sampling the many informal or alternative procedures currently available on the assessment smorgasbord until unequivocal soundness is demonstrated for all items, we do encourage you to consider soundness as you select assessments for use and to temper the conclusions you draw from instruments that may have limited authenticity or trustworthiness. The wise, selective use of assessments by sensitive, informed teachers who understand their students can compensate for our current less-than-perfect array of items on the assessment menu. The task of understanding reading progress is vital, and current instruments can at least help us locate the right instructional channel, even if they cannot of themselves fine-tune our understanding.

When a child's reading ability is explored with the patience and skill of an expert teacher, the instructional picture can be brought into focus.

Here are some of the key points addressed in this chapter:

- Reading ability, far from a fixed and static state, varies with many interacting factors, such as a reader's prior knowledge of the topic, a learner's motivation for reading, the reader's sociocultural background, and the demands of the task. A reader who seems disabled in one situation may perform quite satisfactorily in another. Thus, most high-risk students, and any who encounter difficulties in learning to read, have no internal or constitutional limitations in acquiring reading abilities. Instead, a complex interaction of internal factors (e.g., a reader's fluency, comprehension ability, motivation) and external factors (e.g., the situational context, type of text, imposed reading purpose) makes a reader "abled" in one situation and "disabled" in another.
- Classroom assessment should occur for the purpose of helping teachers plan instructional programs for individual students. In other words, for classroom purposes, assess reading abilities only when the information from an assessment will lead to an instructional decision.
- Sound assessment is both authentic (valid) and trustworthy (reliable). Be cautious when using alternative assessments that, though authentic, may be quite untrustworthy.
- Teachers can use almost any sound literacy assessment tool, procedure, or perspective to understand the reading abilities of high-risk learners. The selection depends on the instructional situation, the child's strengths and limitations, and the teacher's specific need for information.
- Traditional group formal assessment procedures yield limited information for instructional decision making for individual students.
- Some individual standardized tests (e.g., the Woodcock Reading Mastery Tests) can provide detailed information about a student's reading performance, although such measures typically have low levels of authenticity and construct validity, limiting the generalizability of results from such measures.
- Newer commercially available performance-based assessments (e.g., Language Arts Performance Assessment) show promise but have yet to provide compelling evidence of their soundness.
- Informal reading assessments give teachers many options for obtaining information about high-risk learners. Though typically receiving high marks on authenticity, such informal measures leave the user with the responsibility for establishing trustworthiness for decisions made from them.
- The Informal Reading Inventory and other variant procedures provide rich information about students' reading levels and specific word identification and comprehension strategies.
- Observational and anecdotal records enable a teacher to observe and record students' behaviors during normal classroom literacy activities for the purpose of identifying growth, areas of strength, and areas in need of further instruction.
- Interviews, conferences, questionnaires, and inventories permit a teacher to solicit

responses or information from students in order to obtain direct evidence of students' developing literacy abilities.

- Intervention assessments combine instruction and assessment, so that a teacher can observe how students react to various instruction strategies, information that guides the teacher in subsequent instructional approaches.
- Portfolio assessment provides teachers and students with a means to assemble multiple sources of data about a student's developing literacy abilities. Collaborative in nature, portfolios allow the child to engage in self-evaluation and the teacher to examine a wide range of evidence for patterns of growth or areas of literacy in need of further instruction.

Note

1. The topic of this book is reading; hence, the topic of this chapter is *reading assessment*. However, few researchers or practitioners view reading as an act isolated from its complementary process, writing, or from oral language abilities. Thus, the term *literacy* is often used in lieu of *reading* to denote this more holistic view. For simplicity and consistency, we will use *reading assessment* throughout this chapter, although it should be understood that its use does not imply that reading should be assessed (or taught, for that matter) in isolation from the other language arts.

References

Airasian, P. W. (1989). [Review of the California Achievement Tests]. In J. C. Conoley & J. Kramer (Eds.), *The tenth mental measurements yearbook*. Lincoln, NB: Buros Institute of Mental Measurements.

Anderson, R. C., Hiebert, E. H., Scott, J. A., & Wilkinson, I. A. G. (1985). *Becoming a nation of readers: The report of the Commission on Reading*. Washington, DC: National Institute of Education.

Auk, K. H., Scheu, J. A., & Kawakami, A. J. (1990). Assessment of students' ownership of literacy. *The Reading Teacher, 44,* 154–156.

Au, K. H., Scheu, J. A., Kawakami, A. J., & Herman, P. A. (1990). Assessment and accountability in a whole literacy curriculum. *The Reading Teacher, 43,* 574–578.

Barr, R., Sadow, M., & Blachowicz, C. (Eds.). (1990). *Reading diagnosis for teachers: An instruction approach,* 2nd ed. New York: Longman.

Baumann, J. F. (1988). *Reading assessment: An instructional decision-making perspective.* Columbus, OH: Merrill.

Baumann, J. F., Seifert-Kessell, N., & Jones, L. A. (1992). Effect of think-aloud instruction on elementary students' comprehension monitoring abilities. *Journal of Reading Behavior, 24,* 143–172.

Betts, E. A. (1946). *Foundations of reading instruction.* New York: American Book Company.

Brandt, R. S. (Ed.). (1989). Redirecting assessment [special issue]. *Educational Leadership, 46*(7).

Brown, C. S., & Lytle, S. L. (1988). Merging assessment and instruction: Protocols in the classroom. In S. M. Glaser, L. W. Searfoss, & L. M. Gentile (Eds.), *Reexamining reading diagnosis: New trends and procedures.* Newark, DE: International Reading Association.

Burns, P. C., & Roe, B. D. (1989). *Informal reading assessment.* Chicago: Rand-McNally.

Cambourne, B., & Turbill, J. (1990). Assessment in whole-language classrooms: Theory into practice. *Elementary School Journal, 90,* 337–349.

Chittenden, E., & Courtney, R. (1989). Assessment of young children's reading: Documentation as an alternative to testing. In D. S. Strickland & L. M.

Morrow (Eds.), *Emerging literacy: Young children learn to read and write* (pp. 107–120). Newark, DE: International Reading Association.

Christie, J. F. (1979). The qualitative analysis system: Updating the IRI. *Reading World, 18,* 393–399.

Church, C. J. (1991). Record keeping in whole language classrooms. In B. Harp (Ed.), *Assessment and evaluation in whole language programs* (pp. 177–200). Norwood, MA: Christopher-Gordon.

Clark, C. H. (1982). Assessing free recall. *The Reading Teacher, 35,* 434–439.

Clay, M. (1972). *Sand.* Auckland, New Zealand: Heinemann.

Clay, M. (1979). *Stones.* Auckland, New Zealand: Heinemann.

Clay, M. M. (1985). *The early detection of reading difficulties* (3rd ed.). Auckland, New Zealand: Heinemann.

Cockrum, W. A., & Castillo, M. (1991). Whole language assessment and evaluation strategies. In B. Harp (Ed.), *Assessment and evaluation in whole language programs.* Norwood, MA: Christopher-Gordon.

College Board. (1986). *DRP handbook.* New York: Author.

Commeyras, M. (1992). Commercially available language arts performance-based assessments. *The Reading Teacher, 45,* 468–470.

Conoley, J. C., & Kramer, J. J. (1989). *The tenth mental measurements yearbook.* Lincoln, NB: Buros Institute of Mental Measurements.

Cooter, R. B. (1989). *The teacher's guide to reading tests.* Scottsdale, AZ: Gorsuch Scarisbrick.

Dalrymple, K. S. (1989). "Well, what about his skills?" Evaluation of whole language in the middle school. In K. S. Goodman, Y. M. Goodman, & W. J. Hood (Eds.), *The whole language evaluation book* (pp. 111–130). Portsmouth, NH: Heinemann.

Davey, B. (1983). Think aloud—Modeling the cognitive processes of reading comprehension. *Journal of Reading, 27,* 44–47.

Davidson, J. L. (Ed.). (1988). *Counterpoint and beyond: A response to* Becoming a Nation of Readers. Urbana, IL: National Council of Teachers of English.

Degrees of Reading Power. (1989). Brewster, NY: Touchstone Applied Science Associates.

Dunn, L. M., & Markwardt, F. C. (1989). Peabody Individual Achievement Test. Circle Pines, MN: American Guidance Service.

Durrell, D. D., & Catterson, J. H. (1980). Durrell Analysis of Reading Difficulty. San Antonio, TX: Psychological Corporation.

Ekwall, E. E. (1986). *Ekwall Reading Inventory,* 2nd ed. Boston: Allyn and Bacon.

Estes, T. H., Richard, H. C., & Wetmore-Rogers, E. (1989). Construct validity of the Degrees of Reading Power test. (ERIC Document Reproduction Service No. ED 316 841)

Farr, R. (1992). Putting it all together: Solving the assessment puzzle. *The Reading Teacher, 46,* 26–37.

Farr, R., & Carey, R. F. (1986). *Reading: What can be measured?,* 2nd ed. Newark, DE: International Reading Association.

Farr, R., & Farr, B. (1990). Language arts performance assessment. San Antonio, TX: Psychological Corporation.

Fujikawa, G. (1980). *Jenny learns a lesson.* New York: Grosset & Dunlap.

Garcia, G. E., & Pearson, P. D. (1991). *Literacy assessment in a diverse society* (Report No. 525). Champaign, IL: Center for the Study of Reading.

Gates, A. I., McKillop, A. S., & Horowitz, E. C. (1981). *Gates-McKillop-Horowitz Reading Diagnostic Test,* 2nd ed. New York: Teachers College Press.

Gillet, J., & Temple, C. (1990). *Understanding reading problems,* 3rd ed. Glenview, IL: Scott, Foresman.

Glazer, S. M., Searfoss, L. W., & Gentile, L. M. (Eds.). (1988). *Reexamining reading diagnosis: New trends and procedures.* Newark, DE: International Reading Association.

Gomez, M. L., Graue, m. E., & Bloch, M. N. (1991). Reassessing portfolio assessment: Rhetoric and reality. *Language Arts, 68,* 620–628.

Goodman, K. S. (1967). Reading: A psycholinguistic guessing game. *Journal of the Reading Specialist, 6,* 126–135.

Goodman, K. S. (1973). Miscues: Windows on the reading process. In K. S. Goodman (Ed.), *Miscue analysis: applications to reading instruction* (pp. 3–14). Urbana, IL: National Council of Teachers of English and ERIC/RCS.

Goodman, K. S., Goodman, Y. M., & Hood, W. J. (Eds.). (1989). *The whole language evaluation book.* Portsmouth, NH: Heinemann.

Goodman, Y. M., & Burke, C. (1972). *RMI manual: Procedures for diagnosis and evaluation.* New York: Owen.

Goodman, Y. M., Watson, D. J., & Burke, C. L. (1987). *Reading miscue inventory: Alternative procedures.* New York: Owen.

Gough, P. B. (1989). Testing [special issue]. *Phi Delta Kappan, 70*(9).

Graves, D. (1991). When tests fail. In J. A. Roderick (Ed.), *Context-responsive approaches to assessing children's language* (pp. 9–19). Urbana, IL: National Conference on Research in English.

Gray, W. S. (1922). *Deficiencies in reading ability: Their diagnosis and remedies.* Boston: Heath.

Haney, W., & Madaus, G. (1989). Searching for alternatives to standardized tests: Whys, whats, and whithers. *Phi Delta Kappan, 70*, 683–687.

Harp, B. (1991). *Assessment and evaluation in whole language programs.* Norwood, MA: Christopher-Gordon.

Harris, A. J., & Sipay, E. R. (1990). *How to increase reading ability,* 9th ed. New York: Longman.

Hieronymus, A. N., Hoover, H. D., & Lindquist, E. F. (1990). Iowa tests of basic skills. Chicago: Riverside.

Hildebrand, M., & Hoover, H. D. (1987). A comparative study of the reliability and validity of the Degrees of Reading Power and the Iowa Tests of Basic Skills. *Educational and Psychological Measurement, 47,* 1091–1098.

Hornsby, D., Sukarna, D., & Parry, J. (1986). *Read on: A conference approach to reading.* Portsmouth, NH: Heinemann.

Integrated Literature and Language Arts Portfolio Program. (1991). Chicago: Riverside.

International Reading Association. (1981). Misuse of grade equivalents. Resolution passed by the Delegates Assembly.

Irwin, R. P., & Mitchell, J. N. (1983). A procedure for assessing the richness of retellings. *Journal of Reading, 26,* 391–396.

Johns, J. L. (1991). *Basic reading inventory,* 5th ed. Dubuque, IA: Kendall/Hunt.

Johnson, M. S., Kress, R. A., & Pikulski, J. J. (1987). *Informal reading inventories.* Newark, DE: International Reading Association.

Johnston, P. H. (1987). Teachers as evaluation experts. *The Reading Teacher, 40,* 744–748.

Johnston, P. H. (1992a). *Constructive evaluation of literate activity.* New York: Longman.

Johnston, P. H. (1992b). Nontechnical assessment. *The Reading Teacher, 46,* 60–62.

Jongsma, E. A. (Ed.). (1993). Assessment [Special issue]. *Journal of Reading, 36*(7).

Jongsma, K. S. (1989). Portfolio assessment. *The Reading Teacher, 43,* 264–265.

Jongsma, K. S., & Jongsma, E. A. (1981). Test review: Commercial informal reading inventories. *The Reading Teacher, 34,* 697–705.

Judd, C. H. (1918). *Reading: Its nature and development.* Supplementary Education Monographs, No. 10. Chicago: University of Chicago Press.

Karlsen, B., & Gardner, E. F. (1984). Stanford Diagnostic Reading Test, 3rd ed. San Antonio, TX: Psychological Corporation.

Kemp, M. (1987). *Watching children read and write: Observational records for children with special needs.* Portsmouth, NH: Heinemann.

Klesius, J. P., & Homan, S. P. (1985). A validity and reliability update on the informal reading inventory with suggestions for improvement. *Journal of Learning Disabilities, 18,* 71–76.

Lamme, L. L., & Hysmith, C. (1991). One school's adventure into portfolio assessment. *Language Arts, 68,* 629–640.

Languae arts alterntive assessment conference. (1990, August). Cosponsored by ERIC/RCS and Phi Delta Kappa, Bloomington, Indiana.

Leslie, L., & Caldwell, J. (1990). *Qualitative reading inventory.* New York: HarperCollins.

Lipson, M. Y., & Irwin, M. (1984, December). *Microcomputer exploration of readers' strategic processing during cloze testing.* Paper presented at the National Reading Conference, St. Petersburg, Florida.

Lipson, M. Y., & Wixson, K. K. (1986). Reading disability research: An interactionist perspective. *Review of Educational Research, 56*(1), 111–136.

Lipson, M. Y., & Wixson, K. K. (1991). *Assessment and instruction of reading disability: An interactive approach.* New York: HarperCollins.

Lyman, H. B. (1991). *Test scores and what they mean,* 5th ed. Englewood Cliffs, NJ: Prentice-Hall.

Lytle, S. (1987, May). Interviewing. In M. Y. Lipson & K. K. Wixson (Chairs), *New approaches to individual and group reading assessment: An interactionist perspective.* Institute conducted at the thirty-second annual convention of the

International Reading Association, Anaheim, California.

MacGinitie, W. H. (1989). Gates-MacGinitie Reading Tests, 3rd ed. Chicago: Riverside.

Mathews, J. K. (1990). From computer management to portfolio assessment. *The Reading Teacher, 43,* 420–421.

McKenna, M. C., & Kear, D. J. (1990). Measuring attitude toward reading: A new tool for teachers. *The Reading Teacher, 43,* 626–629.

Mills, R. P. (1989). Portfolios capture rich array of student performance. *The School Administrator, 46,* 8–11.

Monroe, M. (1932). *Children who cannot read.* Chicago: University of Chicago Press.

Morrow, L. M. (1988). Retelling stories as a diagnostic tool. In S. M. Glaser, L. W. Searfoss, & L. M. Gentile (Eds.), *Reexamining reading diagnosis: New trends and procedures.* Newark, DE: International Reading Association.

Morrow, L. M. (1989). *Literacy development in the early years: Helping children read and write.* Englewood Cliffs, NJ: Prentice-Hall.

Morrow, L. M. (1990). Assessing children's understanding of story through their construction and reconstruction of narrative. In L. M. Morrow & J. K. Smith (Eds.), *Assessment for instruction in early literacy* (pp. 110–134). Englewood Cliffs, NJ: Prentice-Hall.

Morrow, L. M., & Smith, J. K. (Eds.). (1990). *Assessment for instruction in early literacy.* Englewood Cliffs, NJ: Prentice-Hall.

National Assessment Governing Board. (1991). *Reading framework for the 1992 National Assessment of Educational Progress.* Washington, DC: U.S. Department of Education.

Neill, D. M., & Medina, N. J. (1989). Standardized testing: Harmful to educational health. *Phi Delta Kappan, 70,* 688–697.

Osborn, J. (1991, December). (Chair). *A study of the content and curricular validity of the 1992 NAEP in reading.* Symposium at the forty-first annual meeting of the National Reading Conference, Palm Springs, California.

Paradis, E. E., Chatton, B., Boswell, A., Smith, M., & Yovich, S. (1991). Accountability: Assessing comprehension during literature discussion. *The Reading Teacher, 45,* 8–17.

Paratore, J. R., & Indrisano, R. (1987). Intervention assessment of reading comprehension. *The Reading Teacher, 40,* 778–783.

Paris, S. G. (1991). Portfolio assessment for young readers. *The Reading Teacher, 44,* 680–682.

Paris, S. G., Calfee, R. C., Filby, N., Hiebert, E. H., Pearson, P. D., Valencia, S. W., & Wolf, K. P. (1992). A framework for authentic literacy assessment. *The Reading Teacher, 46,* 88–98.

Pearson, P. D. (1992). *RT remembrance: The second 20 years.*

Peterson, J., Greenlaw, J. J., & Tierney, R. J. (1978). Assessing instructional placement with the IRI: The effectiveness of comprehension questions. *Journal of Educational Research, 71,* 247–250.

Pflaum, S. W. (1979). Diagnosis of oral reading. *The Reading Teacher, 33,* 278–284.

Pikulski, J. J. (1990). The national assessments of reading: An interview with Barbara Kapinus. *The Reading Teacher, 43,* 602–605.

Pikulski, J. J., & Shanahan, T. (1982). Informal reading inventories: A critical analysis. In J. J. Pikulski & T. Shanahan (Eds.), *Approaches to the informal evaluation of reading.* Newark, DE: International Reading Association.

Pils, L. J. (1991). Soon anofe you tout me: Evaluation in a first-grade whole language classroom. *The Reading Teacher, 45,* 46–50.

Pinnell, G. S., Fried, M. D., & Estice, R. M. (1990). Reading Recovery: Learning how to make a difference. *The Reading Teacher, 43,* 282–295.

Raju, N. (1991). *Integrated literature and language arts portfolio program: Local scoring leader's handbook.* Chicago: Riverside.

Reardon, S. J. (1991). A collage of assessment and evaluation from primary classrooms. In B. Harp (Ed.), *Assessment and evaluation in whole language programs* (p. 95). Norwood, MA: Christopher-Gordon.

Rhodes, L. K., & Nathenson-Mejia, S. (1992). Anecdotal records: A powerful tool for ongoing literacy assessment. *The Reading Teacher, 45,* 502–509.

Rief, L. (1990). Finding the value in evaluation: Self-assessment in a middle school classroom. *Educational Leadership, 47*(6), 24–29.

Roderick, J. A. (1991). *Context-responsive approaches to assessing children's language.* Urbana, IL: National Conference on Research in English.

Sadoski, M., & Lee, S. (1986). Reading comprehension and miscue combination scores: Further analysis and comparison. *Reading Research and Instruction, 25*(3), 160–167.

Sadoski, M., & Page, W. D. (1984). Miscue combination scores and reading comprehension: Analysis and comparison. *Reading World, 24,* 43–53.

Schmitt, M. C. (1990). A questionnaire to measure children's awareness of strategic reading processes. *The Reading Teacher, 43,* 454–461.

Shepard, L. A. (1989). Why we need better assessments. *Educational Leadership, 46*(7), 4–9.

Shepard, L. (1991). Interview on assessment issues. *Educational Researcher, 20*(2), 21–27.

Silvaroli, N. J. (1986). *Classroom reading inventory.* Dubuque, IA: Brown.

Siu-Runyan, Y. (1991). Holistic assessment in intermediate classes: Techniques for informing our teaching. In B. Harp (Ed.), *Assessment and evaluation in whole language programs* (pp. 109–136). Norwood, MA: Christopher-Gordon.

Smith, F. (1971). *Understanding reading: A psycholinguistic analysis of reading and learning to read.* New York: Holt, Rinehart and Winston.

Smith, J. K. (1990). Measurement issues in early literacy assessment. In L. M. Morrow & J. K. Smith (Eds.), *Assessment for instruction in early literacy* (pp. 62–74). Englewood Cliffs, NJ: Prentice-Hall.

Spache, G. D. (1981). Diagnostic Reading Scales. Monterey, CA: CTB/McGraw-Hill.

Squire, J. R. (Ed.). (1987). The state of assessment in reading [special issue]. *The Reading Teacher, 40*(8).

Stanford Achievement Test, 8th ed. (1989). San Antonio, TX: Psychological Corporation.

Stephens, T. M. (1982). Criterion referenced curriculum—Reading. San Antonio, TX: Psychological Corporation.

Strickland, D. S., & Morrow, L. M. (1989). *Emerging literacy: Young children learn to read and write.* Newark, DE: International Reading Association.

Sulzby, E. (1991). Assessment of emergent literacy: Storybook reading. *The Reading Teacher, 44,* 498–500.

Teale, W. H. (Ed.). (1991). The whys, whats, and hows of literacy evaluation [special issue]. *Language Arts, 68*(8).

Tierney, R. J., Carter, M. A., & Desai, L. E. (1991). *Portfolio assessment in the reading-writing classroom.* Norwood, MA: Christopher-Gordon.

Valencia, S. W. (1990). A portfolio approach to classroom reading assessment: The whys, whats, and hows. *The Reading Teacher, 43,* 338–340.

Valencia, S. W., Hiebert, E. H., & Kapinus, B. (1992). National Assessment of Educational Progress: What do we know and what lies ahead? *The Reading Teacher, 45,* 730–734.

Valencia, S. W., McGinley, W., & Pearson, P. D. (1990). Assessing reading and writing. In G. Duffy (Ed.), *Reading in the middle school,* 2nd ed. (pp. 124–153). Newark, DE: International Reading Association.

Valencia, S. W., & Pearson, P. D. (1987). Reading assessment: Time for a change. *The Reading Teacher, 40,* 726–732.

Valencia, S. W., Pearson, P. D., Peters, C. W., & Wixson, K. K. (1989). Theory and practice in statewide reading assessment: Closing the gap. *Educational Leadership, 46*(7), 57–63.

Wade, S. E. (1990). Using think alouds to assess comprehension. *The Reading Teacher, 43,* 442–451.

Wiggins, G. (1989). Teaching to the (authentic) test. *Educational Leadership, 46*(7), 41–47.

Winograd, P., Paris, S., & Bridge, C. (1991). Improving the assessment of literacy. *The Reading Teacher, 45,* 108–116.

Wixson, K. K. (1991). Diagnostic teaching. *The Reading Teacher, 44,* 420–422.

Wixson, K. K., Bosky, A. B., Yochum, M. N., & Alvermann, D. E. (1984). An interview for assessing student's perceptions of classroom reading tasks. *The Reading Teacher, 37,* 354–359.

Wixson, K. K., Peters, C. W., Weber, E. M., & Roeber, E. D. (1987). New directions in statewide reading assessment. *The Reading Teacher, 40,* 749–754.

Wolf, D. P. (1989). Portfolio assessment: Sampling student work. *Educational Leadership, 46*(7), 35–39.

Woodcock, R. W. (1987). Woodcock Reading Mastery Tests—Revised. Circle Pines, MN: American Guidance Service.

Woods, M. L., & Moe, A. J. (1989). *Analytical Reading Inventory.* Columbus, OH: Merrill.

Teacher Effectiveness Research into Reading Practice

DOROTHY J. O'SHEA
Florida Atlantic University

Key Concepts

- Effectiveness
- Teacher expectations
- Instructional methods
- Engaged time
- Direct instruction
- Instructional organization

- Ecobehavioral factors
- Instructional setting
- Academic learning time
- Systematic processes
- Guided Discovery Learning (GDL)

Focusing Questions

- List and explain the four assumptions associated with teacher effectiveness.
- How can one create a literate environment?
- How important is the amount of time devoted to reading? Why?
- What is engagement time, and how is it monitored and managed?
- When and why would the direct instruction method be appropriate? The Guided Discovery Learning method?
- What are two ways to increase opportunities for readers' success?

Discussion Questions

- Give some examples of ecobehavioral factors and their possible effects.
- Discuss the impact teacher expectations can have on student performance and subsequent teacher effectiveness.
- List four examples of reading tasks that could be analyzed for assessment. Which assessment procedures would be best suited? Why?
- Who benefits from teacher effectiveness, and why?

Effectiveness views, including teacher, program, and school excellence issues, are in vogue for concerned teachers, parents, researchers, and program evaluators. Additionally, calls for school reform, teaching evaluations, and teacher accountability appear nationwide (Boyer, 1988; Sirotnik & Goodlad, 1988). Schools, programs, and teachers are on the front line to ensure that the needs of students from traditional backgrounds, and the large and growing number of students from poor families and culturally diverse settings, as well as those with disabilities, receive an appropriate education (Sirotnik & Goodlad, 1988; Wang, 1987; Wolman, Bruinicks, & Thurlow, 1989). Importantly, continual school and program data on teachers' and students' behaviors, and on their classroom interactions, illustrate that teachers have a great influence on why and how students learn (Baumann, 1984; Berliner, 1984; Brophy & Good, 1986; Greenwood, 1991; Kamps, Carta, Delquadri, Arraya-Mayer, Terry, & Greenwood, 1989; Robinson & Good, 1987; Ross & Kyle, 1987; Smyth, 1989). Many professionals agree that teacher effectiveness underlies the educational successes of students, teachers, schools, and programs (Baumann, 1984; Berliner, 1984; Brophy & Good, 1986; Greenwood, 1991; Kamps et al., 1989; Robinson & Good, 1987; Ross & Kyle, 1987; Smyth, 1989).

Accordingly, the purpose of this chapter is to describe how effective teachers operate, to distinguish them from peers, and to discuss why some teachers instruct in reading more effectively than others. These seemingly simple issues, debated over and over in professional circles, are not easily discernible. The chapter includes important data gleaned from literature reviews, observational reports on successful teaching, and empirical studies aimed at analyzing teaching behaviors and interactions. Figure 8-1 illustrates the key concepts to be discussed.

Teacher Effectiveness Assumptions

Four assumptions concerning teacher effectiveness are important in understanding the data presented in this chapter. These assumptions relate to effectiveness *characteristics, actions, learning,* and *desires.*

Effectiveness Characteristics.   The first assumption is that effective teachers are individuals with many characteristics. Their effectiveness is limited neither to a teaching area (e.g., special education; general education), nor to a particular setting (e.g., geographical area,

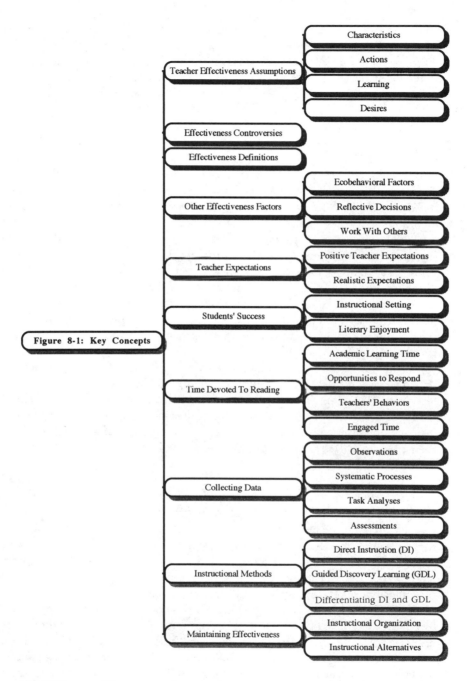

FIGURE 8-1   Key concepts

school location, classroom distance from the office). Effective teachers have varied attributes (e.g., age, gender, race, marital status, years of teaching, subject speciality). They teach students with varied characteristics (e.g., age, grade level, ability score, learning style, behavior, socioeconomic status, culture). Hence, *effective teachers are effective teachers* given a multitude of teaching conditions, individual circumstances, and diverse students.

Effectiveness Actions.   The second assumption is that effective teachers demonstrate actions similar to those of other teachers but do so more suitably to students' present needs and strengths, across people and settings, and over time. *Effective teachers demonstrate behaviors similar to their counterparts' behaviors, but effective teachers do so more appropriately.*

Quality in schools or programs and the teaching process concerns effective teachers (Lehman & Crook, 1988; Hoffman & Rutherford, 1982; Rosenshine & Stevens, 1984). Thus, high-quality reading teachers concern themselves by advocating school district conditions conducive to readers' opportunities. They seek change processes when school district conditions warrant change. They create reading activities on the basis of parent and reader input. They devise new methods and strategies for making reading fun. They help to create innovative ways of translating reading theory into alternative classroom practices (Walberg, 1984; Wang, 1987).

Many professionals concur that effective teachers make self-enhancement a focus of their teaching careers (Boyer, 1988; Rosenberg, O'Shea, & O'Shea, 1991; Sirotnik & Goodlad, 1988). Effective teachers seek and obtain updated reading content. They attend seminars, inservice workshops, or staff development trainings. They join national teaching organizations. They are members of local or state committees to help to refine their content and/or teaching knowledge and skills (Rosenberg et al., 1991).

Effectiveness Learning.   A related assumption is that *effective teaching is learned.* Teachers acquire specific instructional, management, and collaboration skills. Effective teachers do not come ready-made. They learn, practice, and refine the teaching process, suggesting that *teachers can be taught to improve* their instructional, management, and collaboration skills. Successful learning includes awareness of the "how to"s in lesson plans, reading activities, or reading assessments. Successful learning also includes classroom applications. However, teachers practice effectiveness by learning to take the teaching process further through their careful, reflective decision-making. For example, when taught by effective teachers, high-risk learners get opportunities to gain in reading achievement or literacy pleasure. Effective teachers go beyond teaching the mechanics of reading. They analyze important classroom reading conditions (e.g., the reading time schedule, readers' textbooks) and expected reading outcomes (reading achievement results, functional sight word uses). Effective teachers structure purposeful readers' behaviors (e.g., reading orally with peers, using modified audio tapes) and purposeful teaching behaviors (e.g., circulating to assist readers in new word acquisitions, reviewing often within the oral reading session). They produce reading success.

Effectiveness Desires.   The final assumption is that *successful teachers desire effectiveness.* Many teachers want to be effective. They like teaching and want to have an impact on schools and programs. Boyer (1988) reported that nearly three-quarters of the nation's teachers reported job satisfaction in their teaching careers. Most teachers predict staying with the teaching profession while seeking to upgrade their professional expertise. Effective teachers desire to learn beyond minimum requirements or basic professional competencies.

Controversy in Teacher Effectiveness

Controversy surrounds many teacher effectiveness findings (Boyer, 1988; Brophy & Good, 1986; Robinson & Good, 1987; Sirotnik & Goodlad, 1988). Many professionals do not agree on how to discriminate high-quality teaching from average teaching. They disagree on what teacher effectiveness entails. Many past effective schools researchers described effectiveness knowledge without being able to pinpoint a precise definition of effectiveness (Duffy, 1982; Fisher, Berliner, Filby, cahen, Dishaw, & Moore, 1980; Lehman & Crook, 1988). Evaluating teacher effectiveness continues to evoke strong reactions. Boyer (1988) found that nearly 25 percent of teachers describe the formal teacher evaluation process in their schools as "not very fair" (p. 52). Brophy and Good (1986). argue that effective teaching findings must be qualified by grade level, objectives, student type, and other context factors, creating dilemmas for teachers working with heterogeneous classes. Further, Robinson and Good (1987) suggested that even within a certain classroom context, all relationships (e.g., effective teacher to students) may be complex. They suggested that teacher effectiveness has boundaries. Although no professional would condone ineffective practices, Robinson and Good implied that some professionals see limits to effective teaching. Robinson and Good state that "too much of even a generally good thing is still too much" (p. 247).

Controversy exists, in part, because many professionals cannot agree on precise teacher effectiveness components (Brophy & Good, 1986; Lehman & Crook, 1988; Robinson & Good, 1987). Professionals cannot easily solve many instructional dilemmas and complexities concerning the conditions, behaviors, and results of effective practices (Boyer, 1988; Sirotnik & Goodlad, 1988). However, many professionals concur that effective teachers espouse a common theme: successful teachers operate on the basis of students' needs and strengths, conditions in and outside of the classrooms, and teachers' own professional growth and development.

Thus, many of the best teachers are student-oriented. For example, effective teachers actively "do something" to help readers learn. They assess readers' skill levels. They instruct reading. They teach despite reading errors. They look for reading strengths. They choose materials readers enjoy. They evaluate readers' progress. They collaborate with parents and peers. Effective teachers look beyond immediate teaching conditions and seek to determine how best to help readers increase their reading skills outside of that particular classroom.

Teacher Effectiveness Definitions

Although it is hard to delineate, some define *effectiveness* not only by *what teachers do in instruction* (Berliner, 1984) but also by *student behaviors:* students significantly outperforming other students in "less effective" programs when given standardized achievement tests (Baumann, 1984). In addition to students' achievement measures, many professionals use other *written products* (e.g., reading plans, worksheets, decoding and comprehension units) to verify teacher competence or to evaluate instructional success (Rosenberg et al., 1991). Researchers analyzing teacher effectiveness variables rely often on a *process–product methodology* — for example, a description of teachers' and readers' behaviors during the reading process (i.e., instruction) and on establishing relationships between the process and products (e.g., reading achievement, word recognition, reading fluency) (Duffy, 1982; Fisher et al., 1980; Rosenshine & Stevens, 1984; Sindelar, Smith, Harriman, Hale, & Wilson, 1986). Thus, important to understanding teachers' effectiveness in reading settings are teachers' behaviors, readers' behaviors, reader–teacher interactions, reading products, and process–product results. Table 8-1 illustrates examples of teachers' behaviors, readers' behaviors, reader–teacher interactions, reading products, and process-product results.

Other Teacher Effectiveness Factors

Other factors interacting within and outside classrooms (i.e., ecobehavioral factors) and within individual teachers (i.e., reflective decision-making skills) also influence teacher effectiveness. A description of ecobehavioral factors and reflective decisions is important in order to view teacher effectiveness within a whole context.

Ecobehavioral Factors

Wang (1987) suggests that school and teacher effectiveness research is still in its infancy. Many effectiveness etiologies are unknown or ill defined. Wang found that understanding effectiveness requires an in-depth look at unexplored, ecobehavioral factors. *Ecobehavioral factors* entail a systemic view of the environment in relation to behaviors, interrelationships, products, and process–products (Kaplan, 1991; Wang, 1987). Included are program features, environmental attributes, teachers' efficacy variables, students' learning productivity factors, and available adaptive instruction methods (Wang, 1987). For example program features such as room size, adult-to-student ratio, and textbook or reading material availability influence teacher effectiveness. Issues including student expected outcomes (i.e., skills mastery for functioning and further learning, ability to study, student skills in planning and monitoring learning activities, assistance from others, and enjoyment or participation in learning activities) have far-reaching implications in understanding teachers' effectiveness. These issues extend beyond teachers' instructional mechanics or applications. Some teachers may be more effective than others as a result of conditions outside of teachers' control. For example, parent involvement and readers' motivation play a role in reading results. Professionals search for solutions to complex questions, such as these:

TABLE 8-1 **Examples of Teachers' Behaviors, Readers' Behaviors, Reader–Teacher Interactions, Products, and Process–Product Result in Reading**

Teachers' Behaviors	Readers' Behaviors	Reader–Teacher Interactions	Products	Process–Product Results
Preparing decoding skills lesson plans	Listening to teachers' instruction on decoding skills use in basal reader	Implementing lesson plan on decoding skills with readers	Decoding skills lessons completed by readers at school and home	Decoding skills achievement
Introducing alphabet consonants	Using consonants in words	circulating to assist readers on deciphering consonants	Anecdotal summaries of readers' use of consonants	Consonant letters recognition
Using repeated readings to increase story comprehension	Rereading stories silently	Asking comprehension questions to determine readers' mastery of silent stories read	Reading mastery tests containing comprehension questions	Questions completed correctly
Listing word families ending in *in*	Stating word families ending in *in* (e.g., *pin, fin, win*)	Directing readers to find and circle all words ending in *in*	Practice skill sheets with word families	Word family fluency
Asking readers to read for pleasure	Checking favorite books from the library	Instructing readers to read favorite books and to write book reports	Book reports based on favorite books	Book reports read and reported per week based on favorite books

What must teachers do in order that readers at risk for problems read?

Why are some readers motivated to read more often than others?

How do teachers help readers develop independence?

How do teachers help readers generalize skills to settings other than classrooms?

How can teachers and administrators employ alternative programs and practices aimed at readers with poor progress for reading success?

Why can some teachers encourage reading when many readers have little parental modeling or community stimulation?

Reflective Decision Making

Although much is still unknown about effectiveness parameters, the answer to effectiveness questions may relate to teachers' decisions guiding self-behaviors. That is, *more successful teachers tend to be reflective in educational decisions* focusing on the teaching process, while seeking to frame experientially based problems and to identify possible solutions in the context of social, historical, theoretical, ecological, ethical, and political systems in schools (O'Shea & O'Shea, 1990; Ross, 1989; Smyth, 1989). Effective teachers reflect on their actions and act further than their immediate setting conditions. For example, they go beyond ecobehavioral factors and find different routes to teach reading to readers from poor backgrounds. Effective reading teachers do not stop at the lack of parent modeling occurring in the families of readers from traditional backgrounds. They seek other avenues to teach literary skills and enjoyment to readers with disabilities or to those from culturally diverse settings.

In reflective decision making, teachers link decision making and interventions — that is, theory and practice. What the conceptualization of reflective teachers brings to the process of melding theory/theorists and practice/practitioners is a modified sense of value for what effective teachers know through their intimate classroom experiences. Traditionally, researchers rated a special status through presumed epistemology privilege — that is, as experts with answers to complex situational problems. In contrast, practitioners required teaching guidance because they "did not know what to know or how to act." Reflective teaching expands the expectations for teachers' roles and self-evaluative behaviors from technician to empowered decision maker (O'Shea & O'Shea, 1990; Ross, 1989; Smyth, 1989). To function in this role, *effective teachers in reading analyze what they do in instruction, why they behave as they do, how effectively they instruct, and alternative ways to instruct in order that readers learn.*

Smyth (1989) summarized a reflective thinking mode that can be applied to reading instruction: Teachers consider their instruction; they consider why and how their behavior affects readers; they confront their actions by asking themselves how effects occur; and they consider alternative ways (i.e., reconstruction) to instruction. Therefore, reflective decision making reflects effective teachers who master daily technical aspects in reading but also attend to the context of how and why teachers' behaviors affect readers' responses (and thus lead to teaching modifications). *Teachers reflect on instructional, management, and collaboration issues of when, how, and why readers learn* (Smyth, 1989; O'Shea & O'Shea, 1990). Table 8-2 provides examples of reflective decisions in reading. Keys to reflective decision making in Table 8-2 are teachers' self-analyses and their interactions with readers and other adults.

Importantly, effective teachers encourage collaboration with others. For example, they are knowledgeable of reading content and teaching procedures but do not fear input from others. They use reflective decisions to seek better means of providing reading activities. They consider how teaming with others helps readers make transitions across instructional settings. Effective teachers use parent and peer suggestions to devise different ways to teach a prescribed reading plan. They consider the benefits of whole language reading approaches when they traditionally use directed reading instruction. They coordinate a literacy awareness program with community librarians, parents, general education teachers, special education teachers, school media specialists, counselors, and therapists. They ask for professional input from psychologists and counselors in writing reading goals and objectives on Individualized Education Programs (IEPs) for readers with disabilities. They encourage their readers of average abilities to participate in summer enrichment activities. They also teach self-evaluation skills or learning strategies to encourage readers' independence and problem solving skills (Ross, 1989; Smyth, 1989; O'Shea & O'Shea, 1990; Wang, 1987).

TABLE 8-2   Examples of Teachers' Reflective Decision Making in Reading

Discussing informally with other professionals instructional and management issues of when, how, and why readers learn	Self-analyzing own responses when administrators ask teachers to change reading curricula
Writing down and self-analyzing positive expectations for all readers before the school year is underway	Seeking ways readers will generalize reading skills to settings other than school by brainstorming; asking readers what they can read at home; collecting library card applications for readers without transportation to community libraries; arranging for community library book exchanges during school time
Analyzing current reading methods and procedures that may be outdated; seeking help to change even though efforts require more work after school	Modeling reading importance by showing teachers' college texts; discussing with readers how reading can be difficult even for teachers
Discussing with parents management methods to help in tutoring activities away from school—even when parents consistently ask for additional materials and examples in how to tutor reading rules and skills	Attending reading workshops, and seeking out university course work or inservice seminars on the latest reading technique or material
Making instructional decisions based on recorded class data; keeping individual data indicating readers' strengths and needs; choosing and using supplemental materials when readers' needs indicate the need for more practice	Seeking input from readers on means and methods to motivate reading; using reading materials that are challenging and fun; changing materials and activities when readers' interests wane
Making reading fun by alternating classroom routines with reading games and reader-centered activities; incorporating parents' suggestions into reading centers	Self-analyzing on the effective use of computers in the class; analyzing the need for supplemental computer-assisted instruction; seeking funding for additional classroom computers

Accordingly, *teachers work with others* to set up successful reading conditions. That is, teachers communicate with other professionals to encourage coordinated and sequenced reading programs. Teachers ask psychologists for diagnostic information useful in planning reading instruction. Teachers involve parents, for example, by asking them to prioritize their child's reading goals and objectives. Additionally, teachers set the stage for readers' skill attainment by sharing curriculum materials with others. Table 8-3 lists examples illustrating how teachers work with other professionals and parents.

Importantly, although comprehensive discussions to complex issues in reflectivity are beyond the scope of this chapter, teacher effectiveness should be viewed within a whole context (e.g., given student, teacher, program, and systemic conditions) in order to provide a more complete picture of effective teaching and quality programming. It can be said, however, that effective teachers, *skilled technicians and self-evaluators,*

TABLE 8-3   Facilitating Readers' Success When Teachers Work with Others

With Other Professionals:

Determining with counselors, psychologists, health care professionals, therapists, or other professionals their multidisciplinary views on appropriate reading goals and objectives

Structuring lessons with peer input based on reading function (short- and long-term gains) to readers

Sharing reading methods, materials, and strategies across settings

Designing, organizing, and maintaining with other professionals a variety of strategies to implement the latest reading method

Copurchasing and sharing with other professionals curricula materials

Planning and implementing with other professionals a "reading awareness night" or "literacy enjoyment month"

With Parents:

Communicating written messages and readers' progress in parents' native language

Discussing with parents family priorities for reading goals and objectives

Discussing with parents readers' skill in accuracy, fluency, and comprehension

Encouraging parents' observations in their child's reading classes

Asking for and using parent volunteers to help in class reading projects

Teaching parents tutoring skills to help in readers' generalization and maintenance of skills outside of school settings

Listing local community resources and support reading services to encourage readers' opportunities in settings other than schools; sending the lists to parents regularly

Providing to parents a list of suggested books, reading programs, or computer software packages appropriate to their child's reading skills

Lending to families reading materials and equipment to use at home

Devising a home–school management system for monitoring readers' home attempts

apply knowledge and operate in the classrooms they maintain in order to help their students succeed. They look within themselves and beyond their immediate classroom conditions. They welcome support and input from others. However, understanding teacher effectiveness also necessitates a detailed look at what effective teachers do that distinguishes them from other teachers.

Teacher Expectations

Researchers suggest that *effective teachers expect students will learn* (Brookover & Lezotte, 1979; Brophy & Evertson, 1974; Duffy, 1982) and operate on the assumption that faculty and administrators are responsible primarily for setting up positive opportunities for students' success (Baumann, 1984; Brophy & Evertson, 1974; Hoffman & Rutherford, 1982; Samuels, 1986; Venezky & Winfield, 1979). *Realistic expectations for students* also concern effective teachers (Glomb & Morgan, 1991; Commission on Reading [COR], 1984).

Positive Teacher Expectations

Brophy and Good (1986) argue that effective teachers have positive expectations and communicate those expectations to students using appropriate materials, meaningful curricula, and workable procedures and methods. Unfortunately, teacher effectiveness researchers traditionally report alarming results concerning teacher expectations of students representing groups outside classroom norms (Alves, 1983; Brophy & Good, 1970; Brophy & Good, 1974; Curci & Gottlieb, 1990; Good, Sikes, & Brophy, 1973; Richie & McKinney, 1978; Rowe, 1974; Rosenthal & Jacobson, 1968; Thompson, White, & Morgan, 1982). For example, according to Carnine, Silbert, and Kameenui (1990), teacher expectations of student achievement are often lower than is justifiable, especially for students with low achievement and/or with disabilities. Furthermore, other researchers reported that teachers treat students with atypical ability levels differently (Curci & Gottlieb, 1990), especially students of low achievement compared to average or high-achieving peers (Brophy & Good, 1974). In the early 1970s, teachers were found to criticize students of low achievement more for incorrect responses and did not often provide them feedback about oral responses (Brophy & Good, 1970). Rowe (1974) found that teachers provided the answer or called on other students rather than giving students of low achievement another chance through rephrasing or repeating questions. Curci and Gottlieb (1990) explained teachers' differential treatment on the basis of lowered expectations for students with disabilities or low achievement (Rosenthal & Jacobson, 1968; Alves, 1983).

Curci and Gottlieb (1990) found, also, that teachers directed fewer academic questions toward students with disabilities, gave them less extended feedback for their responses, and had fewer work interactions with them. Richie and McKinney (1978) and Thompson et al. (1982) suggested that teachers in general education classes behave differently toward students of normal ability than toward students with disabilities. These teachers provided students with disabilities less task involvement. Brophy and Good (1970) and Good et al. (1973) also reported less extended feedback from teachers to students with disabilities. However, Curci and Gottlieb (1990) reported that it may not be low achievement per se that is responsible for differential interaction styles directed toward students with and without disabilities. It may be a more generic desire by teachers to avoid interactions with students perceived to have problems.

Realistic Expectations

Increasing teachers' realistic expectations for students with disabilities may be related to overall programming between special education and general education classrooms. For example, there is increasing concern with the lack of successful general classroom performance by students with disabilities who are successfully served in the resource room (Epps & Lane, 1987; Glomb & Morgan, 1991; Morgan & Jensen, 1988). Part of lack of coordination may be related to teachers' beliefs about their own teaching abilities to succeed with students with disabilities. Glomb and Morgan (1991) found that to promote student success, both special education and general education teachers must receive directed training in the use of consultation and collaboration skills. General education teachers reported the need for specific help in responding to the needs of students with disabilities. Glomb and Morgan (1991) found that to promote student success, both special education and general education teachers must receive directed training in the use of consultation and collaboration skills. General education teachers reported the need for specific help in responding to the needs of students with disabilities. Special education teachers reported the need for consultation strategies with peers. Glomb and Morgan also found that both general education and special education teachers believed they should be afforded the time to engage in consultation and collaboration. However, teachers were reported to be given little or no time for consulting purposes. Accordingly, teachers believe they need training in methods to work with high-risk learners and they need time in classroom programming. More realistic expectations may occur when teachers believe they are competent to handle students' disabilities and can share strategies with others.

Despite the etiologies of expectation and treatment differences, professionals agree on the importance of teachers' expectations, their resulting teacher–student interactions, and students' successful school experiences (Commission on Reading, 1984). Teachers' beliefs can play a large role in realistic expectations and students' success in reading settings. Accordingly, effective teachers use reflective decision making to match teacher expectations and treatment of readers with varied skill levels. Effective teachers look to readers' individual strengths and needs. They ignore others' negative expectations (e.g., "readers with poor skills can't survive in general education curricula") or perceived group expectations (e.g., "all students with learning disabilities need resource rooms because they require different teaching materials").

Students' Success

Some researchers suggest that students' success relates to their responses to teachers, instructional variables, and learning conditions interacting with teacher effectiveness in instruction and students' involvement in lessons (Greenwood, 1991; Kamps et al., 1989; Ross & Kyle, 1987; Smyth, 1989). Walberg (1984) cited in Wang (1987) reported on interrelated factors found to be associated consistently with student success. Quality within the instructional setting remains consistent within their studies of student success data.

The Instructional Setting

Quality instructional experiences occur based on teachers' provision of appropriate settings. Members of the COR (1984), concluding indisputably that teaching quality makes a considerable difference in students' learning, urged teachers to *create literate environments for readers*. To do so, effective teachers prioritize reading activities by creating and maintaining classrooms that promote reading. Although Lehman and Crook (1988) reported over 40,000 children's books in print, successful teachers tend to use many reading media in their classrooms. Thus, trade books, "big books," magazines, reference texts, and multimedia (e.g., audiovisual aids, computers, language masters) help to increase literacy in school programming (Bartel, 1990; Lehman & Crook, 1988; Samuels, 1986).

Some professionals argue that *literacy* should be defined broadly not just as reading books, but as language in all its aspects—speaking, listening, writing, and reading (Symposium on Literacy and Language, 1990). Some define *literate environments* as teachers' use of diverse materials, including books representing children's literacy (Lehman & Crook, 1988), shared book experiences (Holdaway, 1982), and multiple basals matched to readers' decoding and comprehension skills (Bartel, 1990; Samuels, 1986). Reading diverse materials becomes successful as well as functional when teachers cue readers on words, phrases, and sentences across the school. Effective teachers use posters, bulletin boards, outlines, charts, graphs, and so forth in their classes to highlight key concepts, words, and phrases. To young readers, this may mean labeling classroom objects with relevant word cards. Teachers allow older readers to create and maintain reading learning centers or book clubs. If exposure to story structure facilitates prediction and comprehension, then teachers use predictable, natural-language children's books (Tompkins & Webeler, 1983). Thus, teachers facilitate readers' listening, discussions, and writings by using readers' own language and encouraging their literacy.

Additionally, teachers providing literate environments supply speaking, listening, writing, and reading opportunities throughout other daily activities. By integrating language into art, music, science, history, economics, and other subjects, teachers demonstrate the value of literacy and communicate their own positive expectations. Teachers encourage functional uses when newspapers, community reference materials, or words to favorite songs and movies appear in daily reading lessons.

Promoting Literary Enjoyment

Effective teachers *promote literary enjoyment as they model reading importance* (COR, 1984). Mandlebaum (1989) suggested that successful teachers of students with disabilities model literary importance by reading orally, participating in sustained silent reading, and demonstrating question-asking behaviors. Modeling activities encourage readers to comprehend texts and to generate additional questions demonstrating their level of text awareness. All teachers can model reading importance by reading to and with their students. For example, reading is encouraged during science classes when teachers read important passages. Modeling entails having available many supplemental books, journals, magazines, and trade books that teachers read orally. Additionally, teachers encourage researching, reporting, and writing about subject content (e.g., biology, geology, and chemistry) by demonstrating through class discussions teachers' research, reporting, and writing skills on content areas. Teachers demonstrate positive reading attitudes by daily expressions of reading importance. Teachers create bulletin boards expressing the value of reading new books or finding literacy enjoyment in old favorites. Thus, effective teachers recognize and use reflective decision making in setting up reading classrooms. Additionally, they *promote reading* as pleasurable, useful, and fun when they, themselves, model literary enjoyment.

Thus, effective teachers are cognizant of conditions leading to readers' progress.

Important research findings relevant to teachers' practices entail teachers' consideration of their own adult expectations, awareness of potentially differential treatment to students, maintenance of literate environments, and promotion of literacy enjoyment. Most important, effective teachers facilitate the instructional setting and the promotion of literacy enjoyment by allowing time devoted to reading.

Time Devoted to Reading

The COR (1984) found that in order to experience reading success, *students must spend time in reading activities. Students must receive reading instruction.* The amount of time teachers allocate to reading relates to year-to-year gains in reading proficiency, as represented by standardized tests. Approximately 30 percent of the school day in the average classroom is spent in reading instruction. Yet, reading time allocation varies enormously from one classroom to another, even within the same school. Some teachers allocate as little time as 35 minutes per day or as much as 126 minutes per day to reading. However, much of this time has been observed to be devoted to workbook pages and skill sheets, with doubtful reading value (COR, 1984).

Robinson and Good (1987) offered evidence that some teachers provide as much as 30 to 60 pecent of time devoted to reading instruction in seatwork activities. Furthermore, they reported the use of an average of 50 percent (in some classes, nearly 100 percent of seatwork assignments based on commercial products such as workbooks, dittos, and basal reading materials). Although some differences were found from class to class in seatwork assignments, their conclusions revealed that seatwork had the same format used two to five times a week (e.g., after reading the sentence, readers choose one of three to four pictures representing the sentence meaning).

Researchers working with students with disabilities also provided evidence that many teachers do not use a variety of instructional formats during reading classes. For example, Leinhardt, Zigmond, and Cooley (1981) determined that whereas teachers' reading instruction in all of its formats (e.g., silent or oral reading; discussion, listening, writing, and completing worksheets) accounted for more than one-third of the average school day for students with learning disabilities, silent and oral reading activities accounted for no more than 5 percent of the average school day. A consideration for teachers' reading practices is that students must receive reading instruction frequently. Additionally, effective teachers use a variety of instructional formats. Not only should teachers evaluate their reading schedules, but the quality of what teachers do and how readers respond during the planned time is important.

Academic Learning Time

During the 1970s, researchers defined Academic Learning Time (ALT) as time spent actively engaged in tasks completed with high success (Brophy, 1979; Fisher et al., 1980). Researchers found that the more time students spend actively engaged in tasks they complete with high success, the greater will be their achievement. Greenwood (1991) reiterated the need for teachers' consideration of Carroll's (1985) time-based model of school learning.

According to these researchers, students' degree of learning is a function of (1) the time spent in learning and (2) the time needed to learn. The time spent learning, defined as the time allocated for instruction, and the time within it during which students are engaged (e.g., Denham & Lieberman, 1980) can be controlled by teachers. Recent researchers suggested that time variables (i.e., time allocated and time engaged) have been found to be (1) positive correlates of academic achievement measures (Berliner, 1981; Rosenshine & Stevens, 1984) and (2) component processes of effective teaching practices, those producing increased levels of student achievement (e.g., Brophy, 1986; Stallings & Stipek, 1986).

Accordingly, three components of ALT include allocated time, engagement, and task success. Researcher initiated studies of ALT on students with normal abilities during mathematics and reading (Chow, 1981; Sindelar et al., 1986). Extensions of ALT research later applied to students with learning difficulties (Leinhardt et al., 1981; Sindelar et al., 1986). Observational researchers found that teaching behaviors before, during, and after instruction influenced opportunities for students' successful responding (Greenwood, 1985; Sindelar et al., 1986). Results of these observational studies underscore that teachers' behaviors affect students dramatically during instruction.

Opportunities to Respond

Researchers describing students' learning problems reported the relationship of *students' opportunities to respond (provided by teachers) as vital to students' success.* Opportunity to respond, explained by Greenwood, Delquadri, and Hall)1984) is the interaction between teachers' antecedent behaviors (e.g., reading materials presented, prompts, questions asked, signals to respond, and so forth) and teachers' success in establishing students' academic responding required by teachers or implied by materials. Kamps et al. (1989) described opportunity to respond as *teachers' careful use of stimulus antecedent procedures.* In reading activities, procedures prior to instruction (i.e., antecedents), effective teachers consider (1) scheduling sufficient instructional time relative to specific reading goals and objectives; (2) providing age- and level-appropriate reading materials that correspond directly to what or how teachers want readers to respond; (3) organizing the class's physical structure so it is conducive to academic responding in the reading environment; and (4) using teacher interaction patterns with readers (i.e., antecedents and consequences) that support academic responding at high levels.

Specific Teaching Behaviors

Table 8-4 provides an overview of teachers' specific behaviors during readers' opportunities to respond. Behaviors promoting readers' success include: *planning appropriate reading instruction, implementing reading activities,* and *evaluating reading progress.* These behaviors are important to every teacher who expects to create and maintain readers' successful learning opportunities. As can be seen from Table 8-4, these behaviors are what most teachers do as they complete their daily activities. Importantly, effective teachers demonstrate many or most of these behaviors "better" than others do.

TABLE 8-4   Examples of Teachers' Effective Behaviors and Readers' Opportunities

Planning Appropriate Reading Instruction

Writing reading curricula scope and sequence
Writing expected reading outcomes
Task analyzing reading tasks
Assessing to pinpoint readers' strengths and weaknesses
Writing out reading plans considering reading tasks and readers' levels
Matching instructional procedures to readers' reading levels
Selecting age and ability appropriate reading materials
Scheduling reading activities
Planning a variety of oral reading and written reading activities
Planning adaptations and modifications based on readers' individual needs and strengths
Planning a variety of instructional reading groups
Planning to change reading groups periodically
Planning lesson plans based on readers' skills and lesson purposes
considering instructional sequencing during all reading activities
Planning the monitoring of readers' behaviors during engaged time
Planning formative and summative reading measures

Implementing Reading Activities

Using functional reading materials
Having teaching materials organized and ready to use
Beginning reading instruction promptly
Using advanced organizers to review and link previous material or to introduce new material
Providing specific reading rules and rule applications
Modeling reading rules and rule applications
Providing readers examples and nonexamples of reading rules and rule applications
Asking appropriate number, frequency, and type of questions
Recognizing and responding to readers after teachers' directed questions
Encouraging readers with specific praise
Responding to readers' errors by cueing them about specific reading errors
Providing specific and positive reinforcement for correct demonstration of reading skills
Providing guided and independent practice for readers' skill automaticity
Analyzing engaged reading time to allow readers to practice skills
Managing and monitoring reading activities
Eliminating dead reading time
Reviewing to increase readers' skills and understandings
Reteaching when necessary

Evaluating Reading Progress

Observing readers read
Collecting and maintaining systematic reading data
Assessing reading abilities using formative and summative procedures
Linking assessment and curricula decisions
Making warranted instructional changes based on evaluation data

Engagement Time

Engagement time is found to have a stronger relationship to student achievement than time allocation alone (Berliner, 1984; Fisher et al., 1980). Engagement time also includes appropriate stimulus procedures teachers use (Kamps et al., 1989). Stimulus procedures establishing high rates of correct academic responding by the most students are those providing the greater opportunity to respond and have the likelihood of producing more learning in less time (Greenwood, 1985; Greenwood et al., 1984; Kamps et al., 1989). Researchers found that opportunity to respond is confirmed by the extent to which academic behavior is successfully produced under the procedures provided by teachers. Thus, the probability that a response occurs more frequently under some procedures used by teachers than others, or the "functional covariation" of a response with procedures, is essential to the opportunity to respond (Kamps et al., 1989).

Accordingly, *engagement reading time* is the amount of time readers spend actively performing the academic tasks presented to them during instruction. Effectiveness researchers found that, the greater the proportion of engaged time to allocated instructional time, the greater the academic performance of learners (Rosenberg et al., 1991). Unfortunately, differences in teachers' use of engagement time are widespread. For example, Greenwood (1991) reported a longitudinal analysis of time, engagement, and achievement in high-risk versus nonrisk students (i.e., students from poor, urban settings versus students from suburban settings). Greenwood found that nonrisk students in suburban schools spent on the order of 5 percent more of their prime instructional time per day in academic instruction than did the high-risk controls. The activities to which this extra instructional time was devoted included more time in reading and language. High-risk students in urban schools were not only at increased risk for academic delay compared with their suburban peers, but this risk was reported to be in part a function of time devoted to instruction and of students' engagement in lessons. Students in urban schools were obtaining less instruction and engagement time in basic academic subjects.

When *teachers engage readers actively during reading instruction geared to appropriate levels,* readers will attend to and participate in reading tasks (e.g., attending to teachers' skill instruction, reading aloud or silently, completing skills sheets, working a computer reading program, reading independently) as opposed to their nonacademic engagement—for instance, transition times, talking, time out of their seats, and so forth. In effective reading programs, teachers allocate enough time for reading engagement. When readers are off task, overtly or covertly performing nonacademic tasks, they are not working toward mastery of reading skills.

Effective teachers maximize engaged time by using instructional time efficiently, monitoring the rates of engagement reading time, and avoiding readers' "dead time" (Rosenberg et al., 1991). Dead time occurs when teachers delay the start of reading instruction or do not have necessary reading materials ready and close at hand, when readers take unnecessary time to make transitions within reading activities, and when discussions go off reading during instruction to unrelated tangents. Effective teachers are aware of engagement time importance. By using their reflective decision making, successful teachers monitor the rates of reading engagement activities. Effective teachers engage readers productively in reading tasks.

Additionally, effective teachers monitor engagement time activities and make changes based on their monitoring results. Effective teachers purposely make the reading environment conducive to learning and monitor the learning environment effects during instruction by moving through materials at an appropriate pace, stimulating and sustaining readers' attention, and arranging for high rates of success (Bartel, 1990; COR, 1984; Rosenberg et al., 1991; Samuels, 1986).

Importantly, interaction analyses during engaged time suggest specific teacher actions. For example, Chow (1981) reported that engagement by students with disabilities was related to three teacher behaviors: (1) explaining assignments, (2) providing academic feedback, and (3) structuring and directing lessons. Thus, through teachers' specific behaviors, even high-risk learners can be engaged in reading activities. Dead reading time can be eliminated. Table 8-5 depicts examples of teachers' actions in engaged reading time and dead reading time.

Collecting Data on Reading Levels

In order to plan and implement appropriate instruction, more successful teachers are proficient at collecting data on entry reading levels. Effective teachers *master observing and analyzing readers' problems and noting individual strengths and needs* (Bartel, 1990; Polloway, Patton, Payne, & Payne, 1989; Rosenberg et al., 1991). Effective teachers also *collect systematic data on readers' present educational levels* before, during, and after instruction to help to determine reading progress. Effective teachers make behavioral or program changes based on analyzed data (Bartel, 1990; Carnine, Silbert, & Kameenui, 1990; Carnine, 1977; Polloway et al., 1989; Rosenberg et al., 1991). Table 8-6 illustrates examples of problem reading behaviors that teachers would observe and analyze in systematic data collection processes. These examples relate to problems in decoding skills, word recognition skills, comprehension skills, and functional reading skills. Readers with normal reading achievement and those at high risk for reading problems may display some or many of the problems listed.

Observation and Data Collection

Carnine, Silbert, and Kameenui (1990) reported that when teachers are aware of reading levels through observations and continual data collection, they can implement appropriate interventions. Thus, *teachers work actively to ameliorate and/or prevent further difficulties through well-planned lessons* (Carnine, 1977). *Teachers also use quality planning to maintain and increase reading strengths.* Carnine reported that teachers can encourage high-quality work from readers at risk for reading problems by seeking out techniques that will bring about success, rather than looking for excuses to explain reading failure. Some readers have many reading problems. Most have some reading problems. However, teachers' behaviors can do much to help to prevent or ameliorate long-lasting effects. Bartel (1990) found that effective teaching of readers with persistent problem reading behaviors includes teachers' use of daily data collection procedures. Effective reading teachers base educational decision making on systematic data collection. Thus, effective

TABLE 8-5   Examples of Engaged and Dead Reading Time

Examples of Engaged Reading Time	*Examples of Dead Reading Time*
The bell rings to begin reading class and readers move quickly and quietly into their reading groups. The teacher begins reading instruction within one minute of the readers' entry into class.	The bell rings to begin reading class and readers remain in the hallway for the first six minutes of class. Once in the room, it takes the teacher three additional minutes to quiet the readers to begin reading instruction.
The readers have all necessary reading materials (e.g., textbook, word cards, pencils, paper) organized and ready to use prior to the teacher's instructions to begin.	The readers need the first five minutes of class to locate all necessary reading materials (e.g., textbook, word cards, pencils, paper) after the teacher's instructions to begin.
The teacher models the first two reading workbook examples after instructing readers on sentence comprehension skills. The readers complete the rest of the 20 items on the workbook page independently while the teacher circulates to assist individual readers.	The teacher passes out the reading workbook after instructing readers on sentence comprehension skills. The teacher tells readers to read the directions on their own to complete the 22 items on the workbook page. Readers do not understand how to complete the workbook page independently. They get out of seats to ask for the teacher's individual help in completing the assignment.
Readers make a smooth and orderly transition to two separate activities during reading. The teacher moves from discussing an overhead with readers' new vocabulary words to readers using the vocabulary words in complete sentences. The teacher passes out paper and pencils for readers and instructs them to use their standard reading procedure for "saying the word and definition silently, and then using the word correctly in a written sentence."	Readers make a disorderly transition to two separate activities during reading. The teacher discusses an overhead with readers' new vocabulary words in complete sentences. The teacher searches for paper and pencils, but cannot find the materials. The teacher tells half of the readers to "go to the board to complete the reading procedure for saying the word and definition silently . . . and then" use the word correctly in a written sentence." The other half of the group does not have the materials to complete the assignment so the teacher tells them: "You can complete this assignment later."
Tomorrow is the class field trip, and readers are instructed to have all reading assignments completed before they may go on the field trip tomorrow. Readers get right into the reading assignments and all are finished before the bell rings to end class.	Tomorrow is the class field trip and readers are instructed to have all reading assignments completed before they may go on the field trip tomorrow. Readers start to ask the teacher what time they will be leaving in the morning and whether they can take "souvenir money" with them. Ten class members out of sixteen have not completed all reading assignments before the bell rings to end class.
When readers complete the daily sustained silent reading period for fifteen minutes after lunchtime, they place the chosen library book back into their desks. Then, they take out scissors and paste to begin their usual word search puzzle game using magazines and today's new vocabulary words.	When readers are asked to complete the daily sustained silent reading period for fifteen minutes after lunchtime, they interrupt the teacher. Silent reading is hard to maintain. Readers want to know where to place the chosen library book, what the next reading activity is, and what time reading will be over today.

TABLE 8-6   Examples of Readers' Problem Behaviors

Problems in Decoding Skills
*Fails to notice distinctive features of letters and words (e.g., *b* and *d; pig* and *dig*)
*Fails to note differences of letter and word configurations
*Cannot recognize upper- and lower-case letters of alphabet
*Focuses only on certain characteristics (e.g., word beginnings, letter typography)
*Cannot verbalize phonetic sounds when shown graphic symbols: (i.e., consonant sounds, short
    vowel sounds, long vowel sounds, consonant blends, consonant digraphs, regular vowel
    combinations, *R*-controlled vowel combinations, hard and soft sounds of *g* and *c,* vowel
    diphthongs)
*Has problems in blending sounds to form words

Problems in Word Recognition Skills
*Does not recognize common, irregular words on sight (e.g., *was, to, come*)
*Cannot rhyme words
*Does not recognize words through contextual clues
*Does not make use of structural analysis for identification: (i.e., compound words; common word
    endings—noun, verb, and adjective forms; common prefixes; common suffixes; syllables within a
    word)

Problems in Comprehension Skills
*Cannot recall main idea of written material
*Does not recall sequence of events and/or ideas
*Cannot locate/recall answers to detail questions from written material
*Does not follow written directions
*Does not follow simple cause and effect relationships
*Cannot make predictions (e.g., possible ending of words, phrases, or sentences; expectations or
    predictions concerning the direction or main idea of a passage)
*Cannot make inferences based on materials read
*Does not recognize absurdities
*Does not recognize factual versus fictional material
*Does not use book components appropriately (e.g., table of contents, index, charts, graphs)
*Cannot apply multiple meanings to words
*Cannot shift attention readily to reading comprehensions

Problems in Functional Reading Skills
*Often reads because required, rather than self-motivation
*Fails to choose age or ability appropriate materials
*Fails to relate reading content to his or her own background
*May aproach all reading tasks the same way rather than shift speed and approach to the type and
    reading purpose
*Does not use reading materials functionally
*Demonstrates limited resource, library, or media skills
*Has a limited repertoire of audiovisual media awareness

Source: Based on Bartel (1986) and Polloway, Patton, Payne, and Payne (1989).

teachers employing systematic data collections would (1) use task analyses to help
pinpoint readers' strengths and weaknesses, (2) conduct teacher assessment of readers'
current skills, and (3) match instructional procedures to lesson purpose and readers'
levels.

Task Analyses and Teachers' Assessments

Task analyses entail the breakdown of reading tasks into small, sequenced steps specifying reading behaviors (Bartel, 1990; Polloway et al., 1989; Rosenberg et al., 1991). For example, rather than expecting readers to use all letter sounds when first introduced, teachers would use a task analysis to break letter sounds into the smaller, sequenced behaviors involved in their use (e.g., letter recognition, sound recognition, letter–sound associations, discriminations of letter–sound associations, and so forth). Teachers would then use a variety of assessment procedures (e.g., formal reading tests, informal letter–sound tests, rating scales, teacher-made checklists, observation systems) to determine where to begin reading instruction. The choice of instructional methods evolves from data analyzed on reading behaviors and reading tasks. When readers display difficulty in reading skills, assessment data from task analyses provide information to teachers about important points to begin instruction. These data help to determine present education levels in reading and become the focus of teachers' lesson plans.

Thus, teacher actions in observations, data collection, task analyses, and assessments help to *determine reading levels.* Data collection activities provide teachers much information in order to specify instructional methods, lesson objectives, or reading materials. Additionally, teacher actions help to pinpoint adaptations and modifications for individual readers within reading groups. Teachers' maintenance of records denoting readers' progress helps to disseminate information to peers, administrators, readers, and parents. Table 8-7 illustrates steps of teachers' behaviors in determining readers' strengths and weaknesses. Importantly, systematic data collection, used frequently, helps teachers to implement appropriate reading methods.

Results of setting decision research, ALT, opportunities to respond, task analyses, reading assessment, and systematic data collections pose important practice considerations to teachers using reflective decision making. Teachers practice effectiveness research by asking themselves a number of questions. First, they analyze the reading setting and the amount of time devoted to reading instruction. Are readers given ample opportunities to respond in a conducive reading setting? Are readers engaged successfully in productive reading activities? Has the teacher task-analyzed reading tasks by breaking skills into small, sequenced reading behaviors (i.e., specifying the steps of the task analysis)? Has the teacher conducted numerous assessment analyses in order to know where to begin readers' instruction? Are other data collection systems needed (e.g., discussions with formal teachers, review of formal or standardized reading assessments, additional creation of teacher-made reading scales)? Do teachers' interpretations of data specify adequate information about current reading levels? Are more data needed? Answers to these questions can help teachers *decide appropriate methods to use* during reading instruction. Figure 8-2 represents steps in the process of deciding which reading methods to use.

Instructional Method Choice

Bartel (1990) suggested the major competing positions on the nature of reading can be characterized as *bottom up* models, *top-down* models, and *interactive* models that

TABLE 8-7 Determining Reading Levels

Consider the purpose of assessing readers' skills (i.e., problem behaviors and reading strengths).

Measure attitude toward reading by asking readers and observing readers' interactions with printed materials.

Task-analyze reading tasks into small, sequenced reading behaviors.

Establish a basis of reading level by using informal oral reading or informal reading inventories.

Access specific reading skills:
  Use standardized, formal reading tests.
  Use teacher made word recognition tests.
  Use teacher-made reading comprehension tests.
  Use curriculum-based assessment inventories.

Analyze oral reading miscues:
  Count the number of omissions of letters, word(s), and punctuation.
  Determine the number of reversals.
  Record the number of substitutions.
  Record the quality of dialect differences (i.e., teacher judgment).
  Count the number of insertions of words or letters.
  Count the number of nonword substitutions.
  Record the duration of word-by-word reading or long pauses.
  Count the number of repetitions that corrects a previously incorrect word.
  Count the number of repetitions that abandon a previously correct word.
  Record the number of repetitions of incorrect substitutions.
  Record how often readers asks for assistance.

Analyze all data collected systemtically.

Determine readers' reading levels based on reading behaviors exhibited in task analysis.

Match instructional method to analyzed data.

Devise lesson plans highlighting purposeful and sequenced lessons.

Begin reading instruction.

Consider modifications/adaptations for readers within the group.

Use appropriate materials.

Use appropriate instructional method based on reader's skill level.

Observe reader's use of method to determine reading comprehensive levels:
  Record reader's use of method after silent reading.
  Record reader's use of comprehension questions.
  Analyze reader's frequency of comprehension responses.
  Analyze reader's quality of comprehension responses.

Observe the quality of reader's interactions with reading materials independently (i.e., without adult assistance).

Compare and contrast readers interactions in varied formats (e.g., with adults, peers, small groups, independently).

Monitor reading progress daily and over time.

Consider alternatives to traditional interventions.

Make reading intervention changes as warranted.

Use graphing and charting techniques for data dissemination.

Source: Adapted from Bartel (1986).

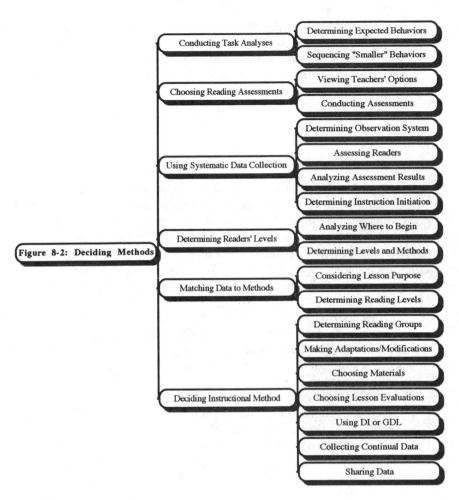

FIGURE 8-2   Deciding methods

combine features of both (see Chapter 6 for additional discussion). Bottom-up models emphasize that reading begins when readers must discriminate and organize words, sentences, and, finally, meaningful paragraphs. Top-down models emphasize that reading begins when readers are set to hypothesize, sample, and predict concerning the nature of what they are about to read. Interactive models assume efficient readers move back and forth, or simultaneously attend to both what is in their own minds (predicting or hypothesizing) and what's on the page (attending to specific letters and words).

Recent researchers have reported that teachers should aproach reading instruction by treating reading as an interactive process, first helping readers use their attention on beginning decoding and comprehension skills and then helping readers shift their attention to refinement in comprehending written discourse (Bartel, 1990; Samuels, 1986;

Stanovich, 1986; Stanolivich, Nathan, & Vali-Rossi, 1987). According to these researchers, reading success depends on patterns of semantics and syntax enhanced through careful selection of instructional methods. Effective teachers facilitate readers' discovery of patterns in their reading materials and through their own use of appropriate teaching methods. Two teaching methods used frequently by effective teachers are Direct Instruction and Guided Discovery Learning.

Effective Reading Instruction

Two sets of instructional methods found to relate to effective reading instruction include *Direct Instruction* (DI) and *Guided Discovery Learning* (GDL) (Rosenberg et al., 1991). Reading teachers using DI focus on readers' skills in mastering specific curriculum content. The outcome of DI is seen as the demonstration of specific skills and knowledge about reading (e.g., being able to sound out words and knowing facts about word families). Basic teacher behaviors in DI reading include demonstrating, guiding readers to practice, and allowing readers' independent activities (i.e., "model, lead, and practice" format).

Teachers using GDL focus on the importance of readers learning procedures for problem solving and learning how to learn. GDL is seen as the demonstration of skills and knowledge about the process of learning (e.g., how to implement steps for solving problems in reading or how to use study skills) (Rosenberg et al., 1991).

Direct Instruction

DI researchers suggested specific teaching procedures and highly structured curriculum materials that help teachers systematically direct students in making accurate responses (Becker, Englemann, & Thomas, 1971; Englemann & Carnine, 1982). For example, during reading instruction, teachers model target reading responses, lead readers in making the response, and periodically test readers' skills to respond without teacher cues (Rosenberg et al., 1991).

Teachers manipulate classroom variables in the reading setting using DI methods in order to provide appropriate physical facilities, promote engagement, use functional and interesting materials and activities, pace lessons briskly, employ contingent management techniques, structure effective transitions, provide multiple opportunities for learning (e.g., massed and distributed opportunities to read), capitalize on naturally occurring events and routines, and communicate expectations (e.g., use of rules in word formations). Teachers using DI promote a general scientific-empirical approach to problem solving in the reading process (Rosenberg et al., 1991; Wolery, Bailey, & Sugai, 1988).

Thus, teachers using DI in reading are taught to use a diagnostic approach by first identifying curricular goals, next collecting baseline data to determine readers' present educational levels (e.g., task analyses and assessments in systematic data collections), and then distinguishing the configuration of environmental variables affecting instruction. After careful consideration of all assessment results, and based on these data in systematic data analyses, teachers then specify the learning objectives and plan and implement intervention programs. Finally, teachers monitor and evaluate reading progress on a formative basis (Lewis, 1983; Wolery et al., 1988; Rosenberg et al., 1991). Links from teacher effectiveness research are obvious.

Important to independent practice, the third step in DI, are readers' skill development and teachers' effective classroom management. Teachers can work with other groups of readers while one group practices independently. Second, readers must be making accurate responses so they can truly work without the teachers' assistance. Independent practice activities require teachers' careful preparation and progress monitoring. *Management behaviors linked to effective reading instruction* include thorough preparation by the teacher, a brisk pace of instruction, minimal transition time, unambiguous rules and procedures, and ability to prevent misbehavior (Anderson, Evertson, & Brophy, 1979; Duffy, 1982). Additionally, *teachers' monitoring* is related to reading achievement (Anderson et al., 1979). Monitoring involves teachers' ability to check readers' understanding, provide corrective feedback, reteach when necessary, and ensure that assigned work is completed.

Rosenberg et al. (1991) identified a typical independent practice sequence important for teachers using reflective decision making in DI reading activities: Give instructions for reading activities; lead readers in completing example tasks; provide timelines for completion; circulate and assist as needed; and review readers' responses to activity tasks. Table 8-8 provides a summary of DI steps and specific teacher behaviors within a DI reading format.

TABLE 8-8 Summary of Direct Instruction During Reading Instruction

Demonstration	• Teacher models target responses for readers. • Teacher relates response to performance of an academic rule. • Teacher discusses relationship of response to the formation of concepts.
Guided practice	• Teacher poses questions to readers. • Teacher leads groups of readers in making the desired response (e.g., performs the desired response simultaneously). • As readers demonstrate accurate responses, teacher gradually fades his degree of leading. • Instead of making the response with readers, teacher presents the stimulus and has the readers responding (e.g., unison responding). • Teacher monitors the response of individual readers in the group. • Teacher tests by calling on readers to make individual responses. • As readers become more accurate in their responding, teacher shifts the performance criterion to fast and accurate responding. • Teacher provides numerous opportunities to practice the responses while the teacher leads readers.
Independent practice	• Readers perform responses accurately without cues or prompts. • Teacher provides readers numerous opportunities to practice response accuracy and speed independent of the teacher.

Source: Based on Rosenberg, O'Shea, and O'Shea (1991).

Guided Discovery Learning

In contrast, steps in DGL instruction provide less direct teacher involvement. Readers make decisions about what they learn and how learning proceeds. Teachers use few specific teaching behaviors, and do not use prearranged or highly structured reading content and materials (Rosenberg et al., 1991). Bruner's (1966) "cognitive structure," or students learning the structures and relationships of structures of a field of study, are important in a GDL choice. According to Bruner, students can learn independently when teachers provide generic problem-solving and information-processing techniques. In the purest form of Bruner's model, school curricula should contain courses that transcend subject matter content and teach critical thinking skills (Ausubel, Novek, & Hanesian, 1978; Beihler & Snowman, 1982). Gagne (1970), however, suggested that teachers using the GDL model should guide students through a logical series of problem-solving sequences to facilitate learning specific content better. Gregory (1985) proposed teachers' use of guided discovery methods in which students actively participate in lessons first using examples and nonexamples arranged by the teacher. The teacher then allows students to problem-solve. Teachers encourage students' participation by arranging for students to work in various capacities as part of a group.

In a reading group assignment, for example, teachers using GDL would assign readers or ask volunteers to record answers to reading questions or research other sources of information. The purpose of active participation in GDL is to *ensure readers' involvement* in the process of solving problems, classifying information, or establishing rules (Rosenberg et al., 1991). Table 8-9 provides GDL steps that effective teachers often implement during reading instruction.

TABLE 8-9   Summary of Guided Discovery Learning during Reading Instruction

Concept or rule assembly	• Teacher assembles concepts or rules examples. • Teacher assembles well-chosen nonexamples to present one at a time. • Other target concept stimuli (from the same class) are presented to readers.
Comparisons concept	• Readers examine irrelevant features. • Teachers provide readers cues to assist in induction or rule identification. • Readers make comparisons, identify patterns, and identify the concept or rule that links examples. • Contrasts are emphasized by identifying and comparing the distinctive features of like concepts.
Problem solving	• Teacher guides reader through a logical series of problem-solving steps to facilitate learning specific content. • Readers make comparisons to distinctive features. • Teacher encourages readers to make informed guesses by using information they have identified as the basis for asking questions that lead to further information about concepts. • Teacher encourages readers to problem solve independently. • Teacher encourages active participation by arranging readers to work in various capacities as part of a group.

Source: Based on Rosenberg, O'Shea, and O'Shea (1991).

Differentiating Direct Instruction and Guided Discovery Learning

Researchers reported differential achievement results with normal students versus students with low-achievement and/or disabilities when teachers choose either DI or GDL. For example, Sindelar et al. (1986) found that time spent in teacher-directed reading instruction using DI was the single best predictor of reading achievement gain for elementary level students with mild learning or mental disabilities. According to these researchers, time spent in "teacher questioning" was the single best predictor of achievement gain. Other classroom observational researchers investigating DI usage (Korinek, 1987; Zigmond, Sansone, Miller, Donahoe, & Kahnke, 1986) reported a positive relationship between teacher questioning and student responding. Korinek (1987) found that questioning sessions within DI formats provided students opportunities to become actively involved in instruction. Zigmond et al. (1986) found question use and higher involvement in teacher-directed instruction positively correlated with increased student achievement in mathematics and reading.

However, Stallings (1980), Leinhardt et al. (1981), and Sindelar et al. (1986) found that time spent in students' independent instructional activities during reading was unrelated to achievement gain, a noted difference from results reported in research with students of average abilities. For example, Fisher et al. (1980) reported that average students' independent work was related to student engagement (and through engagement to student achievement). One explanation for the difference between readers of average abilities and those with disabilities is that the more difficulty readers have in learning, the less they benefit from working independently (Sindelar et al., 1986). Teachers' practical consideration of effectiveness research, then, is to consider whether readers are familiar with required tasks before assignments are given. Teachers determine whether readers understand assignments independent of teachers' directions by (1) asking readers for clarification questions, (2) having readers repeat directions before initiating independent tasks, and (3) observing readers' work in examples practiced with the teacher. Accordingly, effective teachers use information on readers' skill levels prior to deciding to use DI or GDL procedures. They also determine readers' ability to work independently on assigned activities.

Other researchers reporting evidence that *teachers' selection of the most efficacious instructional method to use is dependent in large part on reading levels* were Ross and Kyle (1987). They found that many effective teachers use multiple methods (e.g., GDL variations) to teach reading but that, during low-level primary skill lessons, DI appeared more applicable and very well suited to readers of average ability. During reading comprehension and writing sessions, however, DI appeared less applicable (Ross & Kyle, 1987, p. 41). Many researchers observing students with disabilities noted teachers' use of DI procedures and successful reading progress in word analysis skills (e.g., Idol-Maestas, 1981, and Pany, Jenkins, & Schreck, 1982, both cited in Bartel, 1990). More recently, teachers focusing on reading comprehension skills and DI procedures reported promising results (Bartel, 1990).

Samuels (1986) reiterated that teachers' choice of instructional method is dependent on readers' needs and strengths and on the lesson's purpose. He found *teachers should* provide to all students learning sequences entailing well-planned lessons and instructional sequencing. Importantly, effective teachers afford to all readers (1) activities that begin with an introduction to the new reading lesson, (2) organized and structured reading assignments, (3) a variety of reading formats, (4) an appropriate instructional method dependent on students' independence in reading tasks, (5) conclusions to every reading lesson, and (6) reading activities interspersed throughout other daily activities. Table 8-10 lists examples of learning sequences in reading activities based on lesson plan considerations and instructional sequencing.

Maintaining Teacher Effectiveness

Readers' independent skill levels, interacting with lesson purposes, cue teachers' decisions in appropriate instructional methods. Additionally, during reading instruction, observational researchers continue to confirm that more successful teachers *use a variety of instructional organizations in order to maintain effectiveness* with students (Robinson & Good, 1987; Rosenberg et al., 1991; Samuels, 1986). For example, small-group instruction is reported to be necessary for teaching reading, especially in highly heterogeneous classes (Anderson et al., 1979). Anderson et al. found that when readers work in homogeneous groups (usually achievement-level groups), achievement is greater than when they work independently on learning packets or centers. However, the COR (1984) also reported that more successful teachers are able to maintain effectiveness when readers periodically are offered alternatives to traditional forms of instruction. That is, they found that ability grouping in reading may slow the progress of high-risk learners. As suggested by the COR, some of the problems with ability group assignments can be alleviated by teachers deciding to switch reading group assignments, use criteria other than ability for group assignments, and periodically increase the time devoted to whole-class instruction.

Alternatives to traditional instruction (Kamps et al., 1989; Wang, 1987) also are pertinent to teachers' maintenance of effectiveness. When traditional reading instruction fails, effective teachers seek and use diverse reading interventions. For example, teachers consider computer technology to motivate readers through animation, sound, or color. They use systemwide reading models with other teachers to share reliable and interesting reading materials. Teachers arrange opportunities so that even the hardest-to-reach readers (e.g., those with severe reading disabilities, or readers from poor, urban schools with diverse backgrounds) periodically tutor younger children and experience success as reading tutors. Effective teachers co-team reading practice sessions with parents. Importantly, effective teachers demonstrate reflective decisions geared to diversity in today's schools and programs.

Conclusion

Researchers of the last twenty years focused on clarifying teachers' behaviors, their interactions with students, and successful practices. In this chapter, findings were examined as they affect special education teachers and general education teachers in reading.

TABLE 8-10   Examples of Learning Sequences Provided by Teachers

- Introduce the new reading lesson:
    Provide an overview of the reading activities.
    State the purpose of the new lesson.
    Tell readers the lesson's objectives.
    Use advance organizers.
    Describe how the work of the new lesson relates to previous work.
    Review key concepts and key vocabulary.

- Provide readers organized and structured reading assignments:
    Provide well-managed reading procedures.
    Routinize reading procedures.
    Tell readers what is expected.
    Tell and show materials to be used.
    Lead readers through examples of reading materials.
    Review and link all examples to previous lesson components.

- Use a variety of reading formats (e.g., unison responding, repeated readings, sustained silent reading; choral readings):
    Monitor readers' success with reading formats.
    Change reading formats consistently.
    Assign procedures for distribution and collection of reading assignments.

- Provide Direct Instruction for readers requiring adult assistance:
    Model and discuss with appropriate pace.
    Use cues and prompts as necessary.
    Use guided practice to involve readers actively.
    Use teacher-directed questions.
    Provide feedback to readers' responses.
    Begin to fade adult assistance when readers demonstrate some task independence.

- Provide independent reading activities for readers at practice level:
    Strive for automaticity in reading only through practice (e.g., ask readers to read orally a passage with expression that has not been previewed; ask readers to read orally passages with expression and describe what was read).

- Consider Guided Discovery Learning as readers demonstrate independence:
    Set up independent silent or oral reading activities.
    Provide readers problem-solving activities.

- Conclude each lesson:
    Summarize what was learned that day.
    Ask for readers' feedback and questions to monitor mastery and lesson retention.

- Intersperse reading activities throughout other daily activities.

Indicators of effective teaching, as confirmed by teacher effectiveness data, include teachers' successful applications of teaching mechanics and teachers' demonstration of reflective decisions. *Points to ponder* to generate further discussion on teacher effectiveness include the following:

1. How can ineffective teachers become effective? What can be done and who should do it?

2. What can be taught in preservice and inservice education to help teachers recognize and use reflective decision making?
3. Do effective teachers leave the profession despite success with their students? If so, why?
4. Given increasing calls for school reform, teacher evaluations, and educational accountability, what can administrators and parents do to encourage teacher effectiveness? What are administrators' and parents' responsibilities in school reform, teacher evaluations, and educational accountability?
5. How do teachers with diverse student populations and varied teaching conditions begin the processes of consultation and collaborations with others? What can be done and who should do it?

What teachers can learn from effectiveness research is that successful teachers in reading—in fact, all professionals who interact with students—work to maintain and update their knowledge and professional expertise. Teacher effectiveness should not be viewed as a given in view of teachers' varying degrees of experience, diverse student populations, and varied teaching conditions. Today's educational system demands that teachers increase and maintain teaching proficiency in order to be successful.

The most practical implication of teacher effectiveness research in reading practices would have to do with teachers' efforts in reaching their diverse readers. The influx of high-risk students and students with disabilities places high demands on an already strained educational system (Wolman et al., 1989). To succeed in responding to the challenge of ensuring that readers from both traditional and diverse settings receive appropriate reading instruction requires that all teachers' be effective.

Effective teacher researchers found a direct relationship between the length of reading periods and reading achievement (Berliner, 1984; Fisher et al., 1980) and the quality of activities provided (Bartel, 1990; Samuels, 1986). Practical implications for teachers who want to increase opportunities for readers' success are to (1) devote instructional time to reading and (2) provide quality reading activities. Research findings confirm that successful teachers integrate reading throughout other subjects. Effective teachers use a variety of instructional formats. They monitor reading procedures and materials choices. They analyze whether reading classes promote literacy enjoyment. Effective teachers seek alternative interventions when other reading approaches fail. They act reflectively.

When teachers strive for effectiveness in their school or program performances, everyone benefits. Effective teachers examine, enhance, and redefine their professional responsibilities. They promote self-assessment, job enhancement, empowerment, and professional renewal (Boyer, 1988; Sirotnik & Goodlad, 1988). They affect parents, administrators, and other school professionals. Most importantly, effective teachers reach students and make a difference in their lives.

References

Alves, A. J. (1983). *Classroom interactions of the teacher with mainstreamed handicapped students and their nonhandicapped peers.* Unpublished doctoral dissertation. New York University. (University Microfilms).

Anderson, L., Evertson, C., & Brophy, J. (1979).

An experimental study of effective teaching in first grade reading groups. *Elementary School Journal, 79,* 193–222.

Ausubel, D., Novak, J., & Hanesian, H. (1978). *Educational psychology: A cognitive view.* New York: Holt, Rinehart and Winston.

Bartel, N. R. (1990). Teaching students who have reading problems. In D. D. Hammill & N. R. Bartel (Eds.). *Teaching students with learning and behavior problems,* 5th ed. Boston: Allyn and Bacon.

Baumann, J. F. (1984). Implications for reading instruction from the research on teacher and school effectiveness. *Journal of Reading, 28,* 109–115.

Becker, W. C., Englemann, S., & Thomas, D. R. (1971). *Teaching: A course in applied psychology.* Chicago: Science Research Associates.

Beihler, R. F., & Snowman, J. (1986). *Psychology applied to teaching,* 5th ed. Boston: Houghton Mifflin.

Berliner, D. C. (1981). Academic learning time and reading achievement. In J. T. Guthrie (Ed.). Comprehension and Teaching: Research Reviews. newark, DEL: International Reading Association.

Boyer, E. L. (1988). *The condition of teaching.* Princeton, NJ: Princeton University Press.

Brookover, W. B., & Lezotte, L. W. (1979). *Changes in school characteristics coincident with changes in student achievement* (Occasional Paper No. 17). East Lansing: Institute for Research on Teaching, Michigan State University.

Brophy, J., & Evertson, C. M. (1974). *Process-product correlations in the Texas teacher effectiveness study: Final Report* (Report No. 4004). Austin: Research and Development Center for Teacher Education, University of Texas at Austin.

Brophy, J. E., & Good, J. E. (1974). *Looking in classrooms.* New York: Harper & Row.

Brophy, J., & Evertson, C. M. (1976). *Learning from teaching: A developmental perspective.* Boston: Allyn and Bacon.

Brophy, J. E. (1979). Teacher behavior and its effects. *Journal of Educational Psychology, 71,* 733–750.

Brophy, J. E. (1986). Teacher influences on student achievement. *American Psychologists, 41,* 1069–1077.

Brophy, J. E., & Good, T. (1970). Teachers' communication on differential expectation for children's classroom performance: Some behavioral data. *Journal of Educational Psychology, 61,* 365–374.

Brophy, J. E., & Good, T. L. (1986). Teacher behavior and student achievement. In M. C. Wittrock (Ed.), *Handbook of research on teaching,* 3rd ed. (pp. 328–376). New York: Macmillan.

Bruner, J. S. (1966). *Toward a theory of instruction.* New York: Norton.

Carnine, D. W. (1977). Phonics versus look-say: Transfer to new words. *Reading Teacher, 30,* 636–640.

Carnine, D., Silbert, J., & Kameenui, E. J. (1990). *Direct instruction reading,* 2nd ed. Columbus, OH: Merrill.

Caroll, J. B. (1985). The model of school learning: Progress of an idea. In C. W. Fisher & D. Berliner (Eds.), *Perspectives on instructional time* (pp. 29–58). New York: Longman.

Chow, S. H. L. (1978). *A study of academic learning time of mainstreamed learning disabled students.* San Francisco: Far West Regional Laboratory for Educational Research and Development.

Commission on Reading. (1984). *Becoming a nation of readers: The report of the Commission on Reading.*

Curci, R. A., & Gottlieb, J. (1990). Teachers' instruction of noncategorically grouped handicapped children. *Exceptionality, 1:* 239–248.

Denham, C., & Lieberman, A. (Eds.). (1980). *Time to learn.* Washington, DC: National Institute of Education.

Duffy, G. G. (1982). Teacher effectiveness research: Implications for the reading profession. In M. L. Kamil (Ed.), *Directions in reading: Research and instruction. Thirtieth yearbook of the National Reading Conference.* Washington, DC: National Reading Conference.

Engleman, S., & Carnine, D. (1982). *Theory of instruction: Principles and applications.* New York: Irvington.

Epps, S., & Lane, M. (1987). Assessment and training of teacher interviewing skills to program common stimuli between special- and general-education environment. *School Psychology Review, 16*(1), 52–68.

Fisher, C., Berliner, D., Filby, N., Marliave, R., Cahen, L., & Dishaw, M. (1980). Teaching behaviors, academic learning time, and student achievement: An overview. In C. Denha & A. Lieberman (Eds.),

Time to learn (pp. 7–32). Washington, DC: National Institute of Education.

Gagne, R. M. (1970). *The conditions of learning,* 2nd ed. New York: Holt, Rinehart, and Winston.

Glomb, N. K., & Morgan, D. P. (1991). Resource room teachers' use of strategies that promote the success of handicapped students in regular classrooms. *Journal of Special education, 25*(2), 232–235.

Good, T., Sikes, J., & Brophy, J. E. (1973). Effects of teacher sex and student sex on classroom interaction. *Journal of Educational Psychology, 65,* 74–87.

Greenwood, C. R. (1985). Settings or setting events as treatments in special education: A review of mainstreaming. In M. L. Wolraich & D. K. Routh (Eds.), *Advances in developmental and behavioral pediatrics* (Vol. 6, pp. 205–239). Greenwich, CT: JAI Press.

Greenwood, C. R. (1991). Longitudinal analysis of time, engagement, and achievement in at-risk versus non-risk students. *Exceptional Children, 57*(6), 521–536.

Greenwood, C. R., Delquadri, J., & Hall, R. V. (1984). Opportunity to respond and student academic performance. In W. Hewaqrd, T. Heron, D. Hill, & J. Trap-Porter (Eds.), *Behavior analysis in education* (pp. 58–88). Columbus, OH: Charles E. Merrill.

Gregory, J. (1985). *The concept teaching model.* Unpublished manuscript.

Hoffman, J. V., & Rutherford, W. L. (1982). *Effective reading programs: A critical review of outlier studies.* Paper presented at the National Reading Conference, Clearwater, FL.

Holdaway, D. (1982). Shared book experience: Teaching reading using favorite books—Theory into practice. *Education, 17*(2), 108–112.

Kamps, D. M., Carta, J. J., Delquadri, J. C., Arreaga-Mayer, C., Terry, B., & Greenwood, C. R. (1989). School-based research and intervention. *Education and Treatment of Children, 12*(4), 359–390.

Kaplan, J. S. (1991). *Beyond behavior modification. A cognitive-behavioral approach to behavior management in the school.* Austin, TX: PRO-ED.

Korinek, L. (1987). Questioning strategies in special education: Links to teacher efficacy research in general education, *Journal of Research and Development in Education, 21*(1), 16–22.

Lehman, B. A., & Crook, P. R. (1988). Effective schools research and excellence in reading. A rationale for children's literature in the curriculum. *Childhood Education, 64*(4), 235–242.

Leinhardt, G., Zigmond, N., & Cooley, W. W. (1981). Reading instruction and its effects. *American Educational Research Journal, 18,* 343–361.

Lewis, R. B. (1983). Learning disabilities and reading: Instructional recommendations from current research. *Exceptional Children, 50*(3), 230–240.

Mandlebaum, L. H. (1989). Academic curricular content: Reading. In G. A. Robinson, J. R. Patton, E. A. Polloway, & L. R. Sargent (Eds.), *Best practices in mild mental retardation* (pp. 87–108). Reston, VA: Council for Exceptional Children.

Morgan, D. P., & Jensen, W. R. (1988). *Teaching behaviorally disordered students.* Columbus, OH: Merrill.

O'Shea, D. J., & O'Shea, L. J. (1990). Theory-driven teachers: Reflecting on developments in reading instruction. *Learning Disabilities Forum, 16*(1), 80–91.

Polloway, E. A., Patton, J. R., Payne, J. S., & Payne, R. A. (1989). *Strategies for teaching learners with special needs,* 4th ed. Columbus, OH: Merrill.

Richie, D., & McKinney, J. (1978). Classroom behavior styles of learning disabled children. *Journal of Learning Disabilities, 11,* 297–302.

Robinson, R., & Good, T. L. (1987). *Becoming an effective reading teacher.* New York: Harper & Row.

Rosenberg, M., O'Shea, L. J., & O'Shea, D. J. (1991). *Student teacher to master teacher: A handbook for beginning and preservice level teachers in special education.* New York: Macmillan.

Rosenshine, R., & Stevens, R. (1984). Classroom instruction in reading. In P. D. Pearson (Ed.), *Handbook of reading research.* New York: Longman.

Rosenthal, R., & Jacobson, L. (1968). *Pygmalion in the classroom: Teacher expectation and pupils' intellectual development.* New York: Holt, Rinehart, and Winston.

Ross, D. D. (1989). First steps in developing a reflective approach. *Journal of Teacher Education,* 22–30.

Ross, D. D., & Kyle, D. W. (1987). Helping preservice teachers learn to use teacher effectiveness research. *Journal of Teacher Education, 38*(2), 40–44.

Rowe, M. (1974). Wait-time and rewards as instructional variables, logic and fate control: Part 1.

Wait-time. *Journal of Research in Science Teaching, 11,* 81–94.

Samuels, S. J. (1986). Why children fail and what to do about it. *Exceptional Children, 53*(1), 7–16.

Sindelar, P. T., Smith, M. A., Harriman, N. E., Hale, R. L., & Wilson, R. J. (1986). Teacher effectiveness in special education programs. *Journal of Special Education, 20*(2), 195–207.

Sirotnik, K. A., & Goodlad, J. I. (1988. *School–university partnerships in action: Concepts, cases, and concerns.* New York: Teachers College Press.

Smyth, J. (1989). Developing and sustaining critical reflection in teacher education. *Journal of Teacher Education, 11,* 22–30.

Stallings, J. A. (1980). Allocated academic learning time revisited, or beyond time on task. *Educational Researcher, 9*(11), 11–16.

Stallings, J. A., & Stipek, D. (1986). Research on early childhood and elementary school teaching programs. In M. C. Wittrock (Ed.), *Handbook of research on teaching,* 3rd ed. (pp. 727–753). New York: Macmillan.

Stanolivich, K. E., Nathan, R. G., & Vali-Rossi, M. (1987). Developmental changes in the cognitive correlates of reading ability and the developmental lag hypothesis. *Reading Research Quarterly, 21*(3), 267–283.

Stanovich, K. E. (1986). Matthew effects in reading: Some consequences of individual differences in the acquisition of literacy. *Reading Research Quarterly, 21,* 360–406.

Symposium on Literacy and Language. (1990). *Freedom through literacy.* The Orton Dyslexia Society 41st national conference, Washington, DC. Washington, DC: National Academy of Education, National Institute of Education, Center for the Study of Reading.

Thompson, R. H., White, K. R., & Morgan, D. P. (1982). Teacher–student interaction patterns in classrooms with mainstreamed mildly handicapped students. *American Educational Research Journal, 19,* 220–236.

Tompkins, G. E., & Webeler, M. B. (1983). What will happen next? Using predictable books with young children. *The Reading Teacher, 35,* 498–502.

Venezky, R. L., & Winfield, L. (1979). *Schools that succeed beyond expectations in teaching reading.* Technical Report No. 1. Newark: Department of Educational Studies, University of Delaware.

Walberg, H. J. (1984). Improving the productivity of America's schools. *Educational Leadership, 41*(8), 19–30.

Wang, M. C. (1987). Toward achieving educational excellence for all students: Program design and student outcomes. *Remedial and Special Education, 8*(3), 25–34.

Wolery, M., Bailey, D. B., & Sugai, G. M. (1988). Effective teaching. *Principles and procedures of applied behavior analysis with exceptional students.* Boston: Allyn and Bacon.

Wolman, C., Bruinicks, R., & Thurlow, M. L. (1989). Dropouts and dropout programs: Implications for special education. *Remedial and Special Education, 10,* 6–20.

Zigmond, N., Sansone, J., Miller, S. E., Donahue, K. A., & Kahnke, R. (1986). Teaching learning disabled students at the secondary school level: What research says to teachers. *Learning Disabilities Focus, 1*(2), 108–115.

Reading Recovery: Widening the Scope of Prevention for Children at Risk of Reading Failure

JANET S. GAFFNEY
University of Illinois at Urbana-Champaign

Key Concepts

- Observation survey
- Reading readiness
- Primary, secondary, and tertiary forms of prevention
- "Roaming around the Known"
- Teacher training
- Regular Education/Special Education Initiative (REI)

Focusing Questions

- List and define the six observational procedures within the Diagnostic Survey.

The author is grateful to Dr. Marie Clay for her comments on an earlier draft of this chapter. The author acknowledges the contribution made by Dianne Napolitano for the successful completion of this chapter.

- List three functions of the Diagnostic Survey.
- Differentiate between primary, secondary, and tertiary forms of prevention. Give examples of each.
- What are the two goals of the Reading Recovery[1] program?
- Describe a typical Reading Recovery lesson.
- What does a Reading Recovery training course entail?

Discussion Questions

- Discuss the concept of reading readiness.
- Discuss the benefits of preventive versus remedial intervention.
- What is the function of "Roaming Around the Known"?
- Brainstorm to develop a Reading Recovery lesson plan.

The first time I observed Juan, his desk was placed alone in a corner of the first-grade classroom. The teacher stated that he was unable to concentrate on any tasks and that he completed no work. He had been referred for possible placement in special education by his teacher, who strongly suspected that he was a child with an attention-deficit disorder. The school faculty had requested that he be placed on Ritalin. He was on a waiting list for a comprehensive evaluation.

The first-grade teacher was concerned about Tina's reading after the first few days of school. She was considering putting Tina back into a Transition Room so that she would have time to develop some readiness skills for reading.

Amanda was absent eighteen days in the first two months of first grade in her new school. The information in the cumulative file revealed that she had attended kindergarten at a previous school only thirty days, had transferred to a school in a metropolitan area, and had then returned to the school from which she left. A two-month gap was unaccounted for by the records.

For different reasons, these three young children were at high risk for experiencing reading failure early in school. Each of these first-graders, however, was reading and writing at the average level of their peers after participating in Reading Recovery for less than three months. As the result of a referral made prior to Juan's participation in Reading Recovery, he received a comprehensive evaluation for possible placement in special education and was found "not eligible." His classroom teacher observed him reading "little books" for twenty minutes during an indoor recess while Nerf balls passed over his head and noise filled the room.

Tina was moved to an average reading group after twenty-seven lessons. A few weeks after Reading Recovery teaching had been discounted, Tina was moved to the highest reading group.

After starting Reading Recovery in February, Amanda was absent only two days for the remainder of the school year. Her participation in Reading Recovery had ended in April.

In this chapter, Reading Recovery is described as a way of increasing the possibility of literacy success for all children by providing specialized instruction within the general education system for the lowest achieving children. Distinctions that contribute to the success of Reading Recovery are highlighted. The relationship between Reading Recovery and special education is discussed within the context of the Regular Education/Special Education Initiative (Will, 1986). The implications for the reorganization of schools and for teacher education programs are presented as a shared responsibility of educators of children and of teachers to be accountable for the effectiveness of interventions with children.

Description of Reading Recovery[2]

Reading Recovery, a system intervention designed to reduce the incidence of reading failure in a community, was developed in New Zealand by Clay, who worked closely with competent teachers of young children to develop an array of procedures that could be used effectively to support the acquisition of reading and writing by children who are making inadequate progress after one year of school (Clay, 1985). Reading Recovery was developed over two years, followed by one year of field-trial research (1976–1978). The program expanded in the education system until 1983, when it was adopted as a national program in New Zealand (Clay, 1990b). Reading Recovery is currently being implemented in five countries (Australia, Canada, England, New Zealand, and the United States).[3] Forty-seven states and four provinces now have some level of implementation of Reading Recovery.

Early Identification

Clay (1987b) contends that even in quality school programs, some children will not benefit from sound instruction. Every program has biases that place different demands on children. Given the different response histories of children, the adjustment required for a successful transition to a particular program varies for each child. "Children in a learning programme adjust to the demands of the programme and different programmes bias children's response patterns in different ways" (Clay, 1987b, p. 163). In Reading Recovery, at the beginning of first grade, teachers are asked to identify the children who are experiencing the greatest difficulty in learning to read and write. Selection is inclusive of children being taught in ordinary classrooms. Exceptions are not made for any reason, including for children of lower intelligence, possible learning disability, or limited English proficiency (Clay & Cazden, 1990).

The Observation Survey (Clay, 1993), which is separate from Reading Recovery but is used in the program, is administered to children who, according to teachers, are performing at below-average levels in reading and writing. The Observation Survey is a set of six individually administered observation procedures that collectively provide a triangulated assessment of a child's reading and writing performance (Gaffney, 1991b). The six observational procedures are: (1) Letter Identification, (2) Word Test, (3) Concepts about Print, (4) Writing Vocabulary, (5) Sentence Dictation, and (6) Running Record of Text Reading. Administering the Observation Survey to more children than can initially be served in Reading Recovery corroborates the teacher's judgment in the identification of the lowest children and reveals patterns across children's response profiles.

The following overview explains how each task works:

Letter Identification
A child is asked to identify 54 letters, including upper- and lower-case characters plus the alternative forms of *a* and *g*. Children may respond with the name of the letter, the sound of the letter, or a word beginning with the letter.

Word Test
A child is invited to read a sample of high-frequency words that have been drawn from the "corpus of words that the child has had the opportunity to learn" (Clay, 1985, p. 31) in the classroom reading program. A word list compiled by the faculty at The Ohio State University is used in the United States (Clay, 1993, Pinnell, DeFord, & Lyons, 1988).

Concepts about Print
While the teacher reads aloud a little book that has been specifically developed for this purpose, a child is asked to indicate particular features of the text. For example, the child is asked to locate the front of the book, where one starts reading, capital letters, and a word. An observer records whether or not the child notices changes in line, word, and letter order in text and if the child knows the purposes of common punctuation marks.

Writing Vocabulary
A child is asked to write down all known words in ten minutes. The teacher may prompt the child by suggesting words from the child's basic vocabulary or categories of words (e.g., names of animals, things to eat).

Dictation
A child is read a story of one to two sentences and asked to write down the words in the story. The child may be prompted to "say them slowly and think how you would write them" (Clay, 1985, p. 38).

Running Record of Text Reading
After being told the title of a selection and given a brief orientation to the story, the child is asked to read the text orally while the teacher records the child's reading behaviors. Running records of text reading reflect what a child is saying and doing "on the run" in a task like that expected in the classroom. The running record provides a lens that reveals the operations or processes the child is using while interacting with texts of varying levels of difficulty.

The Observation Survey is used to select the children who performed the lowest on these tasks so that they may be served in Reading Recovery. The results reflect the teaching emphases relative to each classroom program as well as the literacy learning of individual children. The Observation Survey also provides a systematic means for teachers to inventory what a child knows and for teachers to view *how* a child solves problems during reading and writing tasks in order to inform their teaching decisions. Finally, the results of the Observation Survey are a way of measuring changes in a child's performance over time.

The combination of teacher judgment with these systematic procedures for observing children's early literacy behaviors reduces error that Fedoruck and Norman (1991) have found may result from first-grade teacher judgment alone. Fedoruck and Norman content that teachers differ vastly in prerequisite competencies that they require in first-grade classrooms and that, therefore, the ecological validity of predictive indices must be considered.

This situational variability is expected and accounted for in the process of selecting children for Reading Recovery. Teachers, not specialists, are trained to administer and analyze the results of the Observation Survey and to make selection decisions based on the profile of scores. The first-graders who are the lowest achievers in reading and writing are selected for Reading Recovery. (Clay (1991b) notes that the lowest scorers in one school might be better than some of the average scorers in another school. The point is that personnel in each school have made the decision to increase the performance of the low-progress readers in their school. In addition, the Observation Survey, unlike nationally standardized tests, enables teachers and administrators to examine closely the patterns of performance that children in their systems are developing in response to specific program emphases.

Readiness: A System Responsibility

The term *readiness* is most often used to refer to a young child's preparation for literacy learning upon entry to school. In this context, one hears statements such as "Tina is not ready to read," "Carlo needs more time," "Jared is missing some prerequisite skills," and "Wayne is too immature." The assumption underlying this idea of readiness is that there is one path to literacy that is entered through a gate represented by absolute standards of prerequisite skills or abilities. In this conceptual picture, Teale and Sulzby (1986) point out that children are not reading or writing until they pass through the gate. The implication is that children's readiness for reading varies as a result of different rates of maturation and, therefore, that reading instruction for slow-progress children would be premature. In this passive notion of readiness, development precedes learning (Kagan, 1990).

An alternative view proposed by Clay (1979, 1991a) is that the formal demands of school, in general, and of reading instruction, in particular, present challenges for young children in which they must transform prior ways of responding to respond to novel situations. "The need to transform preschool competencies into new ways of responding creates the developmental discontinuity, masks the early reading success a product of learning, and discredits the adequacy of a maturation concept of learning" (Clay, 1991a, p. 21). To withhold literacy instruction, waiting for maturation, is to deprive children of the very learning opportunities that they need to progress. Consistent with Vygotsky, Clay and Cazden (1990) state that in Reading Recovery "instruction supports emergent development rather than waiting for it. (p. 220)" Clay suggests that children will vary widely in patterns of progress and lengths of transition periods during their first years at school. If this perspective prevails, "the school's programme must go to wherever each child is and take his learning on from that point" (Clay, 1991a, p. 19). As posited by Kagan (1990), the burden of proof of readiness is transferred "from children to schools, making readiness a condition of the institution, not of the individual. . . . The concern should focus not on whether children are ready for schools, but on whether schools are ready for children" (p. 274).

Purpose of Intervention: Prevention versus Remediation

Reading Recovery is a preventive rather than a remedial intervention, which may be implemented by a school system in order to respond to children who are experiencing significant difficulties in making the transformations that are essential for successful transitions to formal schooling and to literacy programs. Early identification enables a school system to implement an appropriate preventive intervention before children fail. Serious concerns have been expressed about the use and abuse of screening procedures and special interventions at the kindergarten level (Martin, 1988; Shepard, 1991), but early identification is critical to offering an effective preventive intervention. Clay (1985, 1991a) asserts that children should receive one year of quality instruction that supports them during the transition period prior to the identification of children who might be at risk of reading failure for participation in an intensive intervention. Clay (in press) concurs with Martin and with Shepard that "we should not be eager to predict failure before exposure to the opportunity to learn. . . . We should not try to identify which children will fail in reading and writing before they have been given the opportunity to succeed in a good programme" (p. 3).

Kagan (1990) argues that school entry is individualized by screening out or "siphoning off" children who are not ready into extra-year classes but, once children enter the system, services are homogenized. Like Clay (in press), Kagan claims that it is the school's responsibility ("response-ability") to adjust to individual differences. Without preventive services, the lowest-achieving children would fall farther and farther behind their peers until it was determined that they have failed and a remedial intervention could be implemented. Remediation, therefore, requires a long-term intervention because a large gap has developed between the performance of the children who are failing and their peers, and the children have practiced inappropriate ways of responding to print for long periods of time. In the United States, first grade appears to provide a window of time within which teachers may closely observe children's response repertoires, assess the trajectory of progress of individual children, and intervene before inefficient response patterns are habituated, leading to failure and the subsequent need for long-term remediation.

Prevention as a System Intervention

Pianta (1990) proposes a preventive schema as a viable means for a school system to organize and implement delivery of special services that are responsive to individual children. Pianta uses the framework proposed by Caplan (1961) of three forms of prevention: primary, secondary, and tertiary. Pianta differentiates the three forms of prevention as follows.

1. Primary prevention actions are designed either to reduce the rate of occurrence of a particular problem or to strengthen the well-being of the individuals in the population as a form of inoculation against the causes of subsequent problems. These interventions are made available to the entire population and are targeted specifically toward groups and individuals who have not yet been identified as having the problem to be prevented (pp. 306–307). Inoculation of school-age children for measles for example, is a primary prevention.

2. Secondary prevention programs provide services to a select group of the population who have the highest likelihood of experiencing the target outcome (a high-risk group) to keep problems from becoming debilitating and to diminish the effect of early identified dysfunction. . . . These programs are usually offered in the absence of primary prevention or if the individual did not benefit from primary prevention services (p. 307). Dropout prevention and prereferral interventions are examples of secondary prevention programs.

3. Tertiary prevention consists of intervention after a negative outcome has been attained—that is, after the child has failed. Tertiary prevention (or remediation) seeks to reduce the residual effects or adverse consequences of disorder or failed outcome (Cowen, 1980). Tertiary prevention is the *most* common form of formal intervention services delivered in the public schools (p. 308). Remedial and special education programs are examples of tertiary prevention programs.

Remediation and special education have been the dominant mode for delivery of services to meet the individual needs of children. As tertiary interventions, both systems require that children fail before services may be rendered. Compounding the formidable gap between failing and successful children, the effectiveness of both service delivery systems has been challenged (Allington & McGill-Franzen, 1989; Lipsky & Gartner, 1989; Reynolds, Wang, & Walberg, 1987; Stainback & Stainback, 1984; Ysseldyke et al., 1983). Pianta suggests that preventive services be given consideration as viable additions to remedial programs, thus reserving remedial programs for children with the most severe needs.

Reading Recovery is a way for a system to intervene for the purpose of preventing reading and writing failure within a school or district. Within Pianta's conceptualization, Reading Recovery is a secondary prevention that provides a second chance for success for first-grade children who, after one year of quality instruction, are already showing a trajectory of progress that is falling away from that of other children in the class. Children who are unable to attain average levels of reading and writing performance in their classrooms after approximately twenty weeks of participation in Reading Recovery may be referred to specialist services (tertiary prevention), such as remedial and special education programs. Clearly, Reading Recovery widens the scope of prevention that a school or district may offer under the auspices of general education.

Achieving Full Implementation

A goal of full implementation is crucial to the success of a preventive intervention. Full implementation of Reading Recovery means that every first-grade child within an educational system who is not achieving at average levels in reading and writing has the opportunity to participate in a complete, individual program. An educational system may be a district, a consortium of districts, a region, or a state. For most systems, full implementation is a gradual process that must be planned for and successively achieved in each classroom, in every school, within an educational system that has chosen to participate in Reading Recovery.

A primary consideration for establishing full implementation is the number of children within a first-grade cohort and the proportion of children who may be in jeopardy of not learning to read at a level commensurate with their average classmates. Research has shown that approximately 10 to 20 percent of young children fall into this range. The proportion of children who require an intensive intervention will vary across systems and may be less than 10 percent or may well exceed 20 percent. The actual percentages of children who are served in Reading Recovery will depend on the allocation of personnel resources, the quality of training, the effectiveness of the implementation, and the successful communication of the value of early, preventive interventions (Clay, 1987a, 1990b).

The value of full implementation cannot be minimized when policy decisions are being made regarding the implementation of preventive interventions such as Reading Recovery. With partial implementation, children who need services and are unable to receive them have an increased likelihood of failure due to the widening of the gap between the lowest achievers and their average peers. Long-term planning must also take into account maintenance of the current level of implementation as well as expansion. Continuing support of trained personnel and expected teacher attrition requires a continuous training scheme. Clay (1990b) cautions decision makers to be aware that effective prevention programs destroy the very evidence that led to their creation, and the results may be taken for granted. The medical field is fraught with examples of preventive procedures that, once discontinued, led to the resurgence of a disease that had been eradicated.

Changing Each Child's Trajectory of Progress

Reading Recovery has a two-pronged goal: (1) to assist children who are the lowest achievers in reading and writing to perform at levels commensurate with their average peers in the least amount of time and (2) to have these children continue to improve at about an average rate upon discontinuation of Reading Recovery teaching. These goals are a clear statement of the level of competency that is needed to discontinue services to children relative to their educational system. In addition, the elusive goal of generalization of learning, which is always sought and seldom achieved, is incorporated into these statements as an expected outcome.

For those who are developing and implementing secondary preventive interventions, the concept of "change over time" is critical. The effects of an intervention, especially for persons who have the probability of experiencing negative outcomes in a significant aspect of their lives, must be profound and swift in order to counteract the likelihood of failure. The standard of competency restricts the period that is available for changing the trend of performance. Logically, programs designed to reduce the percentage of children who drop out of high school have a greater latitude in the period of intervention than does a program intended to reduce kindergarten retention. Clearly, the upper limit of twenty weeks recommended by Clay (1990a) for a child's participation in Reading Recovery restricts the interval in which change can be affected. To bring the lowest children to average levels of literacy within this time period requires dramatic change in the "trajectory of each child's progress" (p. 63).

> *I assumed that an acceptable trajectory of change over time was that described by the original longitudinal data for children making successful progress. This gave us models of average and high progress, and explicit in our model of change was that we aimed to teach the poor readers to use the strategies observed in successful readers on the assumption that to be competent in literacy low achieving children would need to learn to do what good readers did. This has not been a common assumption in remedial programs. (Clay, 1990a, p. 10)*

Because this is a short-term intervention, Reading Recovery teachers attend to both the direction and rate of change in each child's performance. A rapid rate of change is referred to as accelerated progress. Without an appropriate intervention, the gap between the lowest achievers and their average peers continues to expand. Accelerated progress is essential if the lowest achievers are to catch up and perform within the average range of their peers on reading and writing tasks. "Such a goal runs counter to the expectations of many educators but it has been reached by a high proportion of Reading Recovery children" (Clay, 1990b, p. 63).

Research in New Zealand, Australia, and the United States has demonstrated that children are able to perform at levels commensurate with their average peers after an average of twelve to eighteen weeks of instruction (Clay, 1985, 1990b; Pinnell, DeFord, & Lyons, 1988; Wheeler, 1986). In addition, these children are able to continue to make progress in reading and writing through their regular classroom program (Clay, 1990b; Pinnell et al., 1988; Slavin & Madden, 1989).

Facilitating Accelerated Progress

Although the systemic nature of the intervention cannot be overemphasized, the overall effectiveness of Reading Recovery is achieved one child at a time. Children are actively engaged in reading texts and writing stories during an intensive, one-to-one tutorial session for thirty minutes daily by a teacher who has been specially trained to design and to implement a different, individual program for each child. The teacher creates the program moment by moment during a lesson through informed interaction with a child.

The specialized training that the teachers receive enables them to reconstruct a framework for observing and responding to children. Through the training, teachers develop new understandings about the relationships between children's reading and writing behaviors and the processes underlying those behaviors. Different behaviors become salient for the teachers as they deepen their understanding about the behaviors that represent forward thrust on the paths of progress of successful readers. Children's responses that previously went unnoticed now become indicators of significant change in a child's performance. For example, a teacher acknowledges a child's inclusion of a new word in a story that he is writing even though the response was only partially correct. The teacher values this approximation because of the *process* the child used to construct the response, not because of the accuracy of the response.

Gradually, teachers recognize the value of partially correct responses as indicators of children's emerging control over processes. Partially correct responses give a teacher a way of analyzing a child's current level of performance on a specific task in order to support the child's new learnings. A Reading Recovery teacher works in partnership with a child to encourage reading and writing work at the "cutting edge of the child's competencies" (Clay & Cazden, 1990, p. 219). The teaching needs to be adjusted continually to enable the child to problem-solve on more difficult tasks. The more finely calibrated the teaching, the more robust are its effects. The effects of powerful teaching are leaps by the child that are a result of the child's control of nascent skills or processes. Powerful teaching helps the child make leaps by facilitating a child's learning of *how to* perform a new task rather than requiring the cumbersome acquisition of knowledge, item by item. Traditionally, the way that educators have adapted instruction for special education students has been to limit the curriculum. In the five models for limiting curriculum, described by Howell (Howell, Kaplan, & O'Connell, 1979), the curriculum is viewed as an accumulation of items that are deemed to be unnecessasry within each model, thus depriving low-progress children access to information available to other children. In Reading Recovery, acceleration is achieved by fostering the child's control of *processes* through the teacher's "selection of the clearest, easiest, most memorable examples with which to establish a new response, skill, principle, or procedure" (Clay, 1985, p. 53).

> *There is an important assumption in this approach. Given a knowledge of some items, and a strategy which can be applied to similar items to extract messages, the child then has a general way of approaching new items. We do not need to teach him the total inventory of items. Using the strategies will lead the reader to the assimilation of new items of knowledge. (Clay, 1985, p. 14; emphasis in original)*

Creating the Opportunity to Learn from Classroom Teaching

Reading Recovery supplements literacy instruction in the first-grade classroom. An important advantage of simultaneous participation in both instructional contexts is that children have the opportunity to apply new behaviors learned in the tutorial setting to reading and writing tasks in group settings. Through the precise interactions of the Reading Recovery teacher and the child, children gain more independence in the construction of meaning while reading increasingly difficult texts and in the written construction of their own messages. Consistent with the constructivist view of learning, children are viewed as active, constructive, and generative architects of their own understandings (Wood, 1988, p. 116). Thus, the vehicle for transfer of information across instructional settings is the child. Transfer will occur only when a child is actively engaged in meaningful tasks at an appropriate level of difficulty. Reading Recovery teaching is discontinued when a child is observed to be benefiting from instruction commensurate with the average of the classroom. The child's reading and writing behaviors in context are then double-checked with the child's performance on the Observation Survey. Evidence that the child is using appropriate strategies is necessary for the discontinuation of Reading Recovery services. These latter criteria establish the ecological or social validity of Reading Recovery.

Observing and Teaching Children: Identifying Children's Strengths

In a previous section, the use of the Observation Survey for the purpose of selection of children was thoroughly explained. For those children who are selected to receive Reading Recovery services, the Observation Survey affords the teacher a lens for observing the child's use of strategies on letters, words, and text during reading and writing tasks. More important than scores are the opportunities the teacher has for observing the ways that a child interacts with print on a variety of tasks. The strengths that a low-progress child exhibits are particularly noteworthy. They form the basis from which the child's program is initiated. Because each child has a different repertoire of strengths, a different program needs to be developed for each child.

A tool, like the Observation Survey, yields information from which to launch a child's program. More information is gained during a two-week period called "Roaming around the Known." During this period, the teacher has the opportunity to observe a child on a large array of reading and writing tasks that are designed to be easy based on child's strengths. The teacher engages children in reading texts and writing stories in such a way that they experience success and increase their willingness to take risks. Gradually, the teacher addresses the needs of the child and introduces more challenging tasks into Reading Recovery lessons.

In a typical Reading Recovery lesson, the child rereads several familiar books; independently reads a book read for the first time the previous day; if necessary, works with letters or words; creates and writes a story; reassembles the story after the teacher has cut it up; and reads a new book following an orientation by the teacher. These components form the skeletal framework of a lesson; within this framework, however, the teacher creates an individual program for each child utilizing the specialized Reading Recovery procedures. The teacher's skillful use of these procedures promotes a child's accelerated progress. Just as a bowl being shaped on a potter's wheel must be centered each time, so must teaching be recalibrated with each response of the child. The child's reading and writing behaviors provide "teachers with feedback which can shape their next teaching moves. Teaching then can be likened to a conversation in which you listen to the speaker carefully before you reply" (Clay, 1985, p. 6).

Education of Reading Recovery Teachers

A key to successful implementation of Reading Recovery is a staffing scheme in which *trainers of teacher leaders,* who are specially trained university faculty members, conduct training for *teacher leaders,* who in turn conduct training for *teachers* (Gaffney, 1991a). This staffing scheme assures that the replications of Reading Recovery will be consistent across districts and across generations of training. The evidence of quality control is the consistent success, as measured by children's progress, of the program across educational settings. This description will be limited to the training of teachers. For further information regarding the training of other Reading Recovery personnel, see Clay (1987a, 1991b) and Jongsma (1990).

The success of Reading Recovery is contingent upon a teacher's skill in designing and implementing a "superbly sequenced programme determined by the child's performance, and to make highly skilled decisions moment by moment during the lesson" (Clay, 1985, p. 53). Experienced teachers of young children volunteer to participate in an intensive, year-long training course that includes: (1) assessment training in the use of the Observation Survey, prior to the beginning of school; (2) a weekly inservice session; (3) daily teaching of a minimum of four children; and (4) school visits by a teacher leader.

Each week, as part of the inservice session, two teachers conduct a thirty-minute lesson with a child whom they are currently teaching. The other participants observe the lessons through a one-way mirror. The teacher leader engages the participant-observers in a discussion of each lesson while it is occurring. According to Gaffney and Anderson (1991), the teachers

> *discuss the child's behavior, teacher–child interactions, and the teacher's implementation of procedures. They are challenged to form hypotheses about the child's performance, to present evidence from the lesson unfolding in front of them that supports or disconfirms their hypotheses, to provide rationales for the teacher's decisions, and to suggest alternative instructional procedures. (1991, p. 191)*

Following the two lessons, the teacher leader engages the group in a discussion of important aspects of the lessons. The teachers, who have just completed the lessons and who have the most intimate knowledge of the response histories of the children, are now available to participate in the discussion. During the "on-line" discussions, behind the one-way mirror and in the group immediately following the lessons, teachers engage in the process of problem solving about the individual needs of children. The discussions about their teaching decisions are grounded in their developing knowledge of the successful performance of good readers and writers. The teacher–child interactions form the essential content of teacher training. Without the concurrent teaching of children, there would be no thread to weave into the fabric of inservice sessions (Gaffney & Anderson, 1991).

Convergence of Reading Recovery and Special Education

A goal of the Regular Education/Special Education Initiative (REI) is that school services to children be provided by one system rather than our current dual system of special and regular education. In a dual system, the two service options are general education and remedial or special education. The child must fail in the context of the regular classroom in order to be eligible for specialized, remedial services. The rationale for this dual delivery system is that in large-group instruction, teachers are unable to respond to children who are functioning at the extreme ends of the normal curve; therefore, special services must be provided to respond to the individual needs of these children. Traditionally, the responsibility for the children is determined by which system is delivering the services. Failing children, therefore, are not perceived as being the responsibility of general education.

The intent of the REI is to respond to the variability among children by offering a continuum of services within one educational system. In this scheme, educators are able to respond flexibly to the individual strengths and needs of children. In contrast to the dual system, which is limited to general education and remedial/special education alternatives, the REI would add preventive interventions to the range of service options provided by *the* educational system. Rather than shifting responsibility for low-functioning children from general education to remedial or special education, accountability for the progress of all children is the charge of one domain—*the* educational system.

Reading Recovery is an option for preventive intervention by an educational system. When *special education* is defined as the use of exceptional instruction rather than the instruction of exceptional people (Howell, 1983), Reading Recovery falls under the rubric of special education in the form of a secondary, preventive intervention. Some of the ways that Reading Recovery instantiates the preventive function of special education are represented by the following concepts:

1. Reading Recovery may operate as a prereferral intervention. A small number of children who do not make accelerated progress through the short-term, intensive, and individual Reading Recovery service are legitimate candidates for referral to special education. Thus, Reading Recovery serves a preventive function prior to referral for placement in remedial or tertiary interventions.

2. Reading Recovery is taught by teachers who are trained to use these specialized procedures. Teachers who have experience in primary classrooms where they have had the opportunity to observe a range of children and know the course of average progress participate in the inservice training. Most Reading Recovery teachers spend half of the day teaching Reading Recovery children and the other half of the day in kindergarten or first-grade classrooms or other group instruction settings.

3. In Reading Recovery, the focus is on observable behaviors of children on classroom reading and writing tasks, rather than on special education labels. Behaviors are viewed as signals that reflect the child's inner control of reading and writing processes (Clay, 1991a).

4. The instructional emphasis is on alterable variables. The teacher is not concerned with conditions that cannot be modified. The effectiveness of instruction is measured by the progress of children—that is, by changes in a child's behavior over time.

5. Teachers closely observe the reading and writing behaviors of children moment by moment to inform their next teaching decision. In Reading Recovery, observation and teaching are inextricably linked; they occur nearly as a simultaneous event, in contrast to an assessment–instruction sequence.

6. The goal of instruction is successful and independent reading and writing performance in the first-grade classroom. Reading Recovery children typically achieve this goal within twelve to eighteen weeks. In addition, the expectation is that children, through the flexible use of strategies, will continue to improve as they encounter new and more difficult tasks.

Conclusion: Implications for Reorganization of Schools and Teacher Education

Full implementation of Reading Recovery in a system has implications for personnel, programs, and curriculum. Roles and responsibilities of the teaching personnel are redefined as a result of implementing a range of services within a unitary system. First-grade teachers who are trained in Reading Recovery deliver specially designed instruction, formerly the role reserved for special educators. Some effects of the operation of Reading Recovery in a district are: (1) the redirection of Chapter 1 resources, (2) the reduction of referrals to special education, (3) a reduced rate of retention in kindergarten and first grade. Curriculum changes in the primary grades include a reconceptualization of readiness, increased sophistication of teachers' knowledge of text characteristics and text difficulty, and greater emphases on children's writing and on the reciprocity between reading and writing at the time of acquisition of these literacy skills.

Teacher education is frequently criticized for the discontinuity between the university course work and field experiences (Joyce & Clift, 1984). The inservice component of Reading Recovery bridges this gap between theory and practice. The two-tiered scaffolding model was developed by Gaffney and Anderson (1991) to explain the interactive relationship between the teaching and learning of teachers and of the children whom they teach. This model depicts the complex interactions that occur on the first tier (teacher–child) with the interactions that occur on the second tier (teacher educator–teacher). In Reading Recovery, the child is the driving force for activities on both tiers. The effectiveness of the teaching of the children is contingent upon the effectiveness of the training of the teachers. Rarely has teacher education been able to demonstrate such direct accountability for the impact of teacher training on the performance of children as in Reading Recovery. Programs that are initiated for the purpose of training teachers or for teaching children must be evaluated by the effectiveness of the implementation on both tiers. Ultimately, the value of any intervention rests on its effectiveness with children.

Notes

1. The name Reading Recovery is a trademark of The Ohio State University. The trademark is used to assure the quality of program implementation in the interest of high success for children. All Reading Recovery Programs that have met the requirements established by Marie M. Clay and other designates of The Ohio State University have been granted a royalty-free license to use in conjunction with their program. The University of Illinois at Urbana-Champaign is an officially licensed program.

2. A written description does not provide sufficient information for effectively implementing Reading Recovery. Participation in the specialized training is necessary to adequately support the implementation of this complex intervention.

3. The terminology used in this chapter corresponds to the implementation of Reading Recovery in school systems in the United States. Although there is only one version of Reading Recovery, policymakers in different countries incorporate the program into the framework of their educational systems. For example, in New Zealand, most children start school on their fifth birthday rather than a cohort of children starting kindergarten on the same day, as is done in districts in the United States. Also, a New Zealand tutor is comparable to a teacher leader in the United States.

References

Allington, R. L., & McGill-Franzen, A. (1989). School response to reading failure: Instruction for Chapter 1 and special education students in grades two, four, and eight. *Elementary School Journal, 89,* 529–542.

Caplan, G. (1961). *Prevention of mental disorders in children.* London: Tavistock.

Clay, M. M. (1979). *Reading: The patterning of complex behaviour,* 2nd ed. Auckland, New Zealand: Heinemann.

Clay, M. M. (1985). *The early detection of reading difficulties,* 3rd ed. Auckland, New Zealand: Heinemann.

Clay, M. M. (1987a). Implementing Reading Recovery: Systemic adaptations to an educational innovation. *New Zealand Journal of Educational Studies, 22,* 35–58.

Clay, M. M. (1987b). Learning to be learning disabled. *New Zealand Journal of Educational Studies, 22,* 155–173.

Clay, M. M. (1990a). *Reading Recovery in the United States: Its successes and challengesd* (Report No. CS010122). Auckland, New Zealand: University of Auckland. (ERIC Document Reproduction Service No. ED 320 125)

Clay, M. M. (1990b). The Reading Recovery Programme, 1984–88: Coverage, outcomes and Education Board district figures. *New Zealand Journal of Educational Studies, 25,* 61–70.

Clay, M. M. (1991a). *Becoming literate: The construction of inner control.* Portsmouth, NH: Heinemann.

Clay, M. M. (1991b). Why is an inservice programme for Reading Recovery teachers necessary? *Reading Horizons, 31,* 355–372.

Clay, M. M. (1993). *An observation survey of early literacy achievement.* Portsmouth, NH: Heinemann.

Clay, M. M. (in press). *Increasing success in literacy learning: The Reading Recovery programme.* Unpublished manuscript, University of Auckland, Department of Education, New Zealand.

Clay, M. M., & Cazden, C. B. (1990). A Vygotskian interpretation of Reading Recovery. In L. C. Moll (Ed.), *Vygotsky and education: Instructional implications and applications of socio-historical psychology* (pp. 206–222). New York: Cambridge University Press.

Cowen, E. (1980). The Primary Mental Health Project: A summary. *Journal of Special Education, 14,* 133–154.

Fedoruk, G. M., & Norman, D. A. (1991). Kindergarten screening predictive inaccuracy: First-grade teacher variability. *Exceptional*

Children, 57, 258–263.

Gaffney, J. S. (1991a). Reading Recovery: Getting started in a school system. *Reading Horizons, 31,* 373–383.

Gaffney, J. S. (1991b). Reading Recovery: How to observe and analyze the reading and writing behavior of young children. *Communique, 19*(6), 10.

Gaffney, J. S., & Anderson, R. C. (1991). Two-tiered scaffolding: Congruent processes of teaching and learning. In E. H. Hiebert (Ed.), *Literacy for a diverse society: Perspectives, programs and policies* (pp. 184–198). New York: Teachers College Press.

Howell, K. (1983). *Inside special education.* Columbus, OH: Merrill.

Howell, K. W., Kaplan, J. S., & O'Connell, C. Y. (1979). *Evaluating exceptional children: A task analysis approach.* Columbus, OH: Merrill.

Jongsma, K. S. (1990). Questions & answers: Training for Reading Recovery teachers. *The Reading Teacher, 44,* 272–275.

Joyce, B., & Clift, R. (1984). The phoenix agenda: Essential reform in teacher education. *Educational Researcher, 13,* 5–18.

Kagan, S. L. (1990). Readiness 2000: Rethinking rhetoric and responsibility. *Phi Delta Kappan, 72,* 272–279.

Lipsky, D. K., & Gartner, A. (1989). *Beyond separate education: Quality education for all.* Baltimore, MD: Paul H. Brookes.

Martin, A. (1988). Screening, early intervention, and remediation: Obscuring children's potential. *Harvard Educational Review, 58,* 488–501.

Pianta, R. C. (1990). Widening the debate on educational reform: Prevention as a viable alternative. *Exceptional Children, 56,* 306–313.

Pinnell, G. S., De Ford, D. E., & Lyons, C. A. (1988). *Reading Recovery: Early intervention for at-risk graders.* Arlington, VA: Educational Research Service.

Reynolds, M. C., Wang, M. C., & Walberg, H. J. (1987). The necessary restructuring of special and regular education. *Exceptional Children, 53,* 391–398.

Shepard, E. A. (1991). Negative policies for dealing with diversity: When does assessment and diagnosis turn into sorting and segregation? In E. H. Hiebert (Ed.), *Literacy for a diverse society: Perspectives, programs, and policies* (pp. 279–298). New York: Teachers College Press.

Slavin, R. E., & Madden, N. A. (1989). What works for students at risk: A research synthesis. *Educational Leadership, 46,* 4–13.

Stainback, W., & Stainback, S. (1984). A rationale for the merger of special and regular education. *Exceptional Children, 51,* 102–111.

Teale, W. H., & Sulzby, E. (1986). Introduction: Emergent literacy as a perspective for examining how young children become writers and readers. In W. H. Teale & E. Sulzby (Eds.), *Emergent literacy: Writing and reading* (pp. vii–xxv). Norwood, NJ: Ablex.

Wheeler, H. G. (1986). *Reading Recovery: Central Victorian field trials.* Unpublished manuscript, Bendigo College of Advanced Education, Bendigo, Australia.

Will, M. C. (1986). Educating children with learning problems; A shared responsibility. *Exceptional Children, 52*(5), 411–415.

Wood, D. (1988). *How children think & learn.* Cambridge, MA: Basil Blackwell.

Ysseldyke, J. E., Thurlow, M., Graden, J., Wesson, C., Algozzine, B., & Deno, S. (1983). Generalizations from five years of research on assessment and decision-making: The University of Minnesota Institute. *Exceptional Education Quarterly, 4,* 75–93.

Instructional Techniques for Making Subject Area Materials More Comprehensible for Readers at Risk

ROBERT B. COOTER, JR.
Texas Christian University

D. RAY REUTZEL
Brigham Young University

Key Concepts

- Global coherence
- Content analysis
- Facts
- Concepts
- Generalizations
- Graphic organizer

- Content-focused melodrama
- SQ3R
- Three-level guide
- Anticipation guide
- Semantic web

Focusing

- Define expository text. List five possible text structures. Give examples of each.
- What steps are involved in developing a graphic organizer?
- How can study guides help metacognition? Give examples of some specific study guides.

Discussion Questions

- Discuss some specific strategies to improve vocabulary.
- Create your own study guide using the SQ3R system.
- Create a lesson plan based on content-focused melodrama.

As students begin to investigate the world of print, they discover that there are two major forms of text structure with which they have to cope in the elementary school—*exposition* and *narration.* Narrative text is a structural form of writing in which the author relates a story, either fact or fiction, in prose or verse (Harris & Hodges, 1981). Expository text is a structural form of writing that has the primary purpose of explanation. It is a form that poses significant obstacles for readers who experience difficulties comprehending text (Baumann, 1981). It is precisely because younger students in the elementary school spend the preponderance of their time reading narrative texts that students encounter great difficulty reading in content area textbooks. McCormick (1987) indicates that concept density—the number of new ideas, words, and concepts found in expository text—also contributes to students' difficulty in reading content area materials. She states that, without explicit instruction, readers with special needs (i.e., high-risk readers) do not always recognize how text structure contributes to comprehension. Varnhagen and Goldman (1986) assert that readers with special needs, especially those with comprehension problems, benefit from instruction that helps them understand the relationships and structures found in expository text.

Teaching students to read content area texts successfully is mainly concerned with helping them work out the meaning of expository text structures. Hence, it is the prime role of teachers of content area subjects to help students understand the unique characteristics and demands of differing expository texts.

Getting Ready to Teach: Analyzing the Characteristics of Expository Text for Effective Instruction

The successful teaching of expository text requires extensive preparation and planning on the part of the teacher. Two major concerns that should be addressed when planning for instruction are the *organizational structure of text* and *the completion of a content analysis* (Reutzel & Cooter, 1992). In this section, each of these topics is discussed from the point of view of what teachers must do to prepare for instruction.

Organizational Structures of Text

A great deal of research has been conducted in recent years on *global coherence* (Armbruster, 1984), the overall structure or organization of types of text. Narrative text has been described using *story grammars,* which include such common elements as *setting, theme, characterization, plot,* and *resolution.* Expository text, however, is quite different.

The structure of expository text tends to be much more compact, concept-dense, and explanatory in nature (Heilman, Blair, & Rupley, 1990). In research similar to the story grammar research for narrative text, Meyer and Freedle (1984) have described five common expository text structures: *description, collection, causation, problem/solution,* and *comparison.*

Teachers in preparing to teach units in the content areas, need to establish which expository text structures are utilized and organize for instruction accordingly. This extra step can be most beneficial in aiding comprehension for readers with special needs. Each of Meyer and Freedle's (1984) five expository text patterns is described next, along with examples taken from content textbooks.

- *Description:* Explains something about a topic or presents a characteristic or setting for a topic:

  ***Decimals** are another way to write fractions when the denominators are 10, 100, and so on. (From* Merrill Mathematics *[Grade 5], 1985, p. 247)*

- *Collection:* A number of descriptions (specifics, characteristics, or settings) presented together:

  ### Water Habitats

  . . . Freshwater habitats are found in ponds, bogs, swamps, lakes, and rivers. Each freshwater habitat has special kinds of plants and animals that live there. Some plants and animals live in waters that are very cold. Others live in waters that are warm. Some plants and animals adapt to waters that flow fast. Others adapt to still water. (From Merrill Science *[Grade 3], 1989, p. 226)*

- *Causation:* Elements grouped according to time sequence with a cause–effect relationship specified:

  ### America Enters the War

  *On Sunday, December 7, 1941, World War II came to the United States. At 7:55 A.M. Japanese warplanes swooped through the clouds above **Pearl Harbor.** Pearl Harbor was the American naval base in the Hawaiian Islands. A deadly load of bombs was dropped on the American ships and airfield. It was a day, Roosevelt said, that would "live in infamy." Infamy (IN-fuh-mee) means remembered for being evil.*

  The United States had been attacked. That meant war. (From The United States: Its History and Neighbors *[Grade 5], Harcourt Brace Jovanovich, 1985, p. 493)*

- *Problem/solution:* Includes a relationship between a problem and its possible cause(s) and a set of solution possibilities, one of which can break the link between the problem and its cause:

Agreement by Compromise
(events that led to the Civil War)

For a while there was an equal number of Southern and Northern states. That meant that there were just as many Senators in Congress from slave states as from free states. Neither had more votes in the Senate, so they usually reached agreement on new laws by compromise. (From The United States and the Other Americas *[Grade 5], Macmillan, 1980, p. 190)*

- *Comparison:* Organizes factors on the basis of differences and similarities; comparison does not contain elements of sequence or causality:

Segregation—Segregation laws said that blacks had to live separate, or apart, from whites. Like whites, during segregation blacks had their own parks, hospitals, and swimming pools. Theaters, buses, and trains were segregated.

Many people said that the segregation laws were unfair. but in 1896, the Supreme Court ruled segregation legal if the separate facilities for blacks were equal to those for whites. "Separate but equal" became the law in many parts of the country.

But separate was not equal. . . . One of the most serious problems was education. Black parents felt that their children were not receiving an equal education in segregated schools. Sometimes the segregated schools had teachers who were not as well educated as teachers in the white schools. Textbooks were often very old and out-of-date, if they had any books at all. But in many of the white schools the books were the newest ones. Without a good education, the blacks argued, their children would not be able to get good jobs as adults.

Finally in 1954, the Supreme Court changed the law. (Adapted from The American People *[Grade 6], American Book Company, 1982, p. 3264)*

Conducting a Content Analysis

Perhaps the best way to begin planning for instruction in any of the content areas is to perform a *content analysis.* The purpose of a content analysis is to help teachers identify the important *facts, concepts,* and *generalizations* presented in a given unit of study. This is an essential process for establishing curriculum objectives and learning activities for children (Martorella, 1985). By carefully analyzing a new unit of study, the teacher is able to locate important information, disregard trivia, and know which areas of the unit will require further development for students. The end result of this process is a cohesive unit of study that is constructed in such a way as to build new schemata or memory structures for students. In explaining the significance of analyzing units for these mental building blocks, Martorella (1985) stated:

What we regard as an individual's knowledge consists of a complex network of the elements of reflection. The fact of our date of birth, for example, is linked in some way to our concept of birthday. As further reflection occurs, we incorporate the new information into our network and it becomes related with the old knowledge. (pp. 69.70)

Facts are individual bits of information, or details, presented in a unit under study. In a science unit dealing with the human body some of the facts to be learned might pertain to the *brain, heart, liver, intestine, lungs,* and *stomach. Concepts* are categories into which we group facts or phenomena, anything of which we are aware, within our experience (Martorella, 1985). In the example of a unit about the human body, the *stomach, liver,* and *intestine* could be grouped into a single concept called the *digestive system.* Concepts are usually stated in a simple phrase, word, or sentence that captures the main idea. *Generalizations* are very simple statements summarizing what the unit of study is about. These are teacher-generated and should be written in simple, concise language. Generalizations organize a large amount of information, often an entire unit. A generalization should be expressed in a complete sentence or two, in language that children in the class can understand. Two examples of generalizations follow:

1. There are many different parts in the human body, which function together to allow us to move, grow, eat, breathe, and reproduce the species.
2. Comets are like dirty snowballs traveling through space.

Once the facts, concepts, and generalizations have been identified, the teacher might organize them into some sort of graphic depiction. This could take the form of a traditional outline, semantic web, structured overview, or some other form. Arranging information in a graphic organizer allows the teacher to help students size up the unit and develop a structure for remembering new information. An example of a finished content analysis is depicted in Figure 10-1. Notice this takes the form of a schema map.

Characteristics of Effective Instruction for Planning the Unit

Once analysis of the content has been completed, unit plans can be constructed. It is important to remember *how* students learn and *what* the teacher's role is in promoting comprehension of expository text. Some considerations include the following:

Learner Responsibility and Collaboration.   Once students understand the requirements for a given unit of instruction, they should progress toward completion of those requirements at their own pace (within reason) and be held accountable for their assignments. Also, important are collaborative experiences in which children help each other to succeed. "Buddy systems" reduce the unnecessary feelings of competition and promote the acquisition of new knowledge in the content area(s).

A Strong Writing Component.   The reciprocal nature and value of writing and reading in the content areas cannot be denied. Writing helps *new* knowledge become *known* knowledge. Creative experiences in writing help foster stronger interest and understanding mass: is the measure of the amount of matter.

microscope: device used to observe small things.

direct evidence: information collected while observing matter.

indirect evidence: set of clues scientists use to make logical guesses.

hypothesis: a logical guess based on evidence.

Scientific methods help us better understand matter.

atom: tiny particles that make up matter. The basic unit of matter.

nucleus: center part of an atom.

protons: tiny packed particles that make up the nucleus.

neutrons: tiny packed particles that make up the nucleus.

electrons: tiny particles that travel around the nucleus.

Atoms are the building blocks of matter.

Matter is what makes up all things around us.

elements: matter that is made up of only one kind of atom.

92 natural: number of elements that occur in nature.

17 man-made: number of elements that man has created.

symbols: short way to write the name of an element.

compounds: substance formed when more than one element combine.

molecules: simplest particle of many compounds.

formulas: group of symbols and number that stand for a compound.

Matter is divided into different elements and compounds with their individual symbols.

FIGURE 10-1   Partial content analysis on matter

Source: Provided by David Harlan, fifth-grade teacher, Sage Creek Elementary School, Springville, Utah.

of the content. For learners with special needs, this component is especially important to help them make crucial connections between the reading and writing modes of language.

A Strong Supplemental Reading Component.   Too often content teachers rely on text-book readings alone to teach new content information. Most school systems have an abundant supply of fiction and nonfiction print materials that can provide rich reading experiences for students. Children need to be immersed in quality reading materials, not just for narrative reading experiences during reading workshops, but also during the content instructional periods.

Intensive and Applied Themed Investigations.   Children often become engrossed in content area instruction when it centers around interesting themed investigations. For example, one sixth-grade class in Bowling Green, Ohio (and many other schools as well), each year work through a fascinating unit called *The Voyage of the Mimi.* The unit uses materials of the same name provided by the Public Broadcasting Company and has to do with a group of children who live aboard a renovated ship for a period of time. They investigate aspects of navigation and marine biology. The class learns much because they are excited about the learning process.

Allow for Creative Expressions of Student Achievement.   Many content teachers seem to fall into a lecture–test scenario for unit instruction. Both teacher and students quickly become bored and apathetic with the same old routines. Many other avenues of expression for student achievement are available. Instead of assigning book reports about famous scientists, why not let children dress up as the scientist they have chosen and be interviewed in a talk show format before the class. The same research is needed, but the product is much more stimulating!

In the next section, a step-by-step process for teaching content area units is discussed.

Teaching Successful Content Area Units for Readers with Special Needs

Planning

Interesting, informative, and compelling content area units do not come together by accident. They require deliberate planning and certain key elements. These key elements are developed naturally from the content analysis and help special needs students build lasting memories of the content material. They include *graphic organizers, key vocabulary and concepts, study guides,* and *content knowledge extension projects.*

Step 1: Graphic Organizers
A *graphic organizer* is essentially a map or graph distributed to students prior to beginning a new chapter or unit of study representing information to be learned. It provides

a means for presenting new technical vocabulary in the unit of study, showing relationships of vocabulary to larger concepts and generalizations, and helping content teachers clarify teaching goals (Tierney, Readence, & Dishner, 1990). Graphic organizers vary in appearance, but they always show vocabulary in relation to more inclusive vocabulary or concepts (Vacca & Vacca, 1989).

Graphic organizers are generally used as an introductory instrument to begin a unit of study, are referred to regularly during the course of the unit, and are used as a review instrument near the end of a unit of study. Although they are very instructive, graphic organizers should never be viewed as the mainstay of a content area program (Earle & Barron, 1973; Tierney et al., 1990).

Procedures for Constructing Graphic Organizers.   Constructing the graphic organizer is simple once the content analysis (described earlier in this chapter) has been completed. All that needs be done is to simplify or condense the facts, concepts, and generalization in the unit by reducing each to a single word or phrase, then arranging them graphically in the same hierarchical pattern as the content analysis. If a thorough content analysis is not possible, however, use the following steps to develop a graphic organizer (adapted from Barron, 1969):

1. Identify all facts and vocabulary you feel are essential to understanding the unit under study. This forms the bottom layer of information, or subordinate concepts (Thelen, 1984). For the sake of consistency with the content analysis idea discussed earlier in the chapter, we refer to these subordinate concepts as *facts.*
2. After listing the preceding information, group related facts into clusters. These clusters form a second layer of understanding in the unit, which we refer to as *concepts.*
3. Finally, concepts that relate to each other should be grouped under the major heading for the unit we refer to as a *generalization.* Usually there will be only a single generalization for the unit, but occasionally there may be a need for two or more generalizations for large or complex units. This is a professional decision best made by the teacher.

Formats.   Teachers may wish to use a variety of graphic formats to depict the different units covered each year. One style is not better than another, but using a different style for each unit may help hold the attention of special needs students. Figures 10-2 through 10-5 show several popular formats for a unit pertaining to cancer taken from an article by Frager (1984, p. 160).

Step 2: Teaching Key Vocabulary and Concepts
A fundamental challenge for every elementary teacher is attempting to add previously unknown concepts and new vocabulary to students' permanent memory structures (schemata). New vocabulary comprises the words or "labels" that represent concepts (Vacca & Vacca, 1989). Vocabulary knowledge is developmental and is based on background experiences (Heilman et al., 1990). There are four types of vocabulary knowledge through which teachers will need to escort their students if new content or specialized words are to become part of their permanent vocabulary—listening, speaking, reading, and writing.

I. Cancer
   A. 1. Carcinomas
         a. Skin cancer
         b. Oral cancer
         c. Breast cancer
      2. Sarcomas
         a. Bone cancer
         b. Stomach cancer
         c. Lung cancer
      3. Lymphomas
         a. Leukemia
         b. Hodgkin's disease
   B. How cancer spreads
      1. Infiltration
      2. Metastasis
   C. Treatment
      1. Surgery
      2. Radiation
      3. Chemotherapy

Figure 10-2 Traditional outline

Listening vocabulary, the largest of the four vocabularies, is made up of all words people can hear and understand. This includes not only the words we use in our everyday speech, but also those words we are capable of understanding only when they are used in context. For instance, while listening to an evening news report, a child in sixth grade may hear about the latest breakthrough in cancer research. Although the youngster may be able to hear and understand the news report, it is probable that she would not be able to reproduce the specialized medical terms used in the report (e.g., *carcinomas, metastasis, chemotherapy*). While exact estimates of just how large the listening vocabulary may be for elementary students vary, some have speculated that entering first-grade students may have a listening vocabulary of upwards of twenty thousand words! Estimates for special needs learners have not been made to date.

The second level of vocabulary knowledge is called the *speaking vocabulary* and consists of words we not only are able to hear and understand but also can use at will in our everyday speech.

A third level of vocabulary knowledge is called *reading vocabulary.* These are words we are able to hear and understand, use at will as part of our speech communications, *and* recognize in print. The final level, *writing vocabulary,* is made up of words we can understand on all the preceding levels—listening, speaking, and reading—and also use in our written communications. In teaching new technical vocabulary like that found in typical content readings (also referred to as *expository text*) the goal is to bring students through each of these levels of vocabulary knowledge.

A better way to teach children with special needs about new ideas is through concrete or hands-on experience. For example, if one wanted to teach children from rural Wyoming about life in New York City, the most effective way to do so would be to

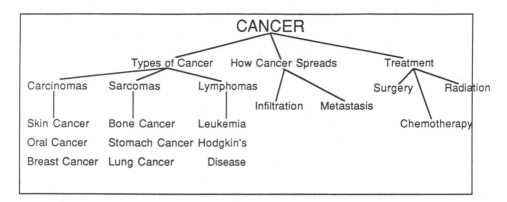

FIGURE 10-3   Structured overview

take them there for a visit. Similarly, the best way to teach children about the space shuttle would be to put them through astronaut training and send them into space on some future mission! Obviously, neither of these experiences is feasible in today's public schools, so we must seek the best concrete experiences within our reach as teachers.

Some educators (Dale, 1969; Estes & Vaughan, 1978) have suggested hierarchies for typical classroom activities ranging from concrete to abstract experiences. Such hierarchies help prospective teachers select more concrete concept and vocabulary development activities and help practicing teachers review their past practices for evaluative and

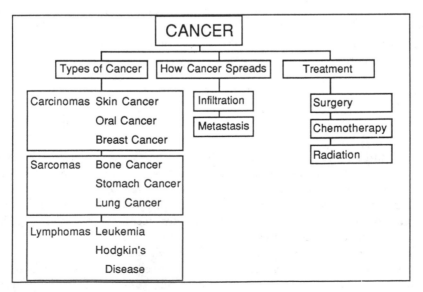

FIGURE 10-4   Pyramid outline

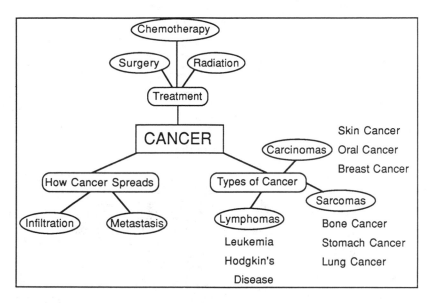

FIGURE 10-5 Semantic web

curriculum redesign purposes. A composite version of these hierarchies is presented in Figure 10-6 (Reutzel & Cooter, 1992). Notice that, as one ascends toward the top of the pyramid, the activities become more concrete and thus easier for children to assimilate.

According to recent studies of vocabulary development (Nagy, 1988), effective instruction in content classes seems to include three important properties: (1) *integration* of new words with known experiences and concepts, (2) sufficient *repetition* so that students will recognize words as they read, and (3) *meaningful use* of new words brought about through stimulating practice experiences. In light of this, we offer several examples of vocabulary development activities for whole group and individual teaching situations.

Whole Group.   When teaching in large or small group situations, the primary vehicle for integrating new vocabulary with known experience, discussed earlier in this chapter, is graphic organizers. Graphic organizers (e.g., semantic web, pyramid, etc.) can be used to introduce and review new words throughout the unit. Because of their schematic nature, they are ideal for this type of learning situation.

Another way of approaching vocabulary instruction is through *whole group vocabulary demonstration*. The idea is to involve the entire class in an activity that demonstrates the meaning of new vocabulary. Whole group vocabulary demonstration will not work with all new vocabulary but may be helpful occasionally. The idea is to provide concrete understanding for abstract ideas. An example for fifth-graders learning about the basic components of an atom is shown on page 259.

∧

**Concrete
Experiences**

Perform a
"Hands-on"
task or Activity

Stage a Simulation
of the Concept Under Study

Literature Response Activities--

(Student Dramas, Construct

Games, Dioramas, etc.)

Experiment, Demonstrate, or Investigate

Role Play or Dramatization

Field Trips

Participate in a Debate

Related Independent Readings--

(Fiction / Non-Fiction)

Participate in a Discussion

Read for Information in a Textbook

Write a Summary of Readings and Research

Complete a Categorization Exercise

Watch a Demonstration on Video

Listen to a Guest Speaker

View Still Pictures

Listen to an Audio Recording

Have a Question-and-Answer Session

Read and Answer Questions

Look up Vocabulary Words

**Abstract
Experiences**

FIGURE 10-6 Pyramid of classroom experiences

Individual Instruction.   There are a number of creative ways teachers can help children with special needs acquite content vocabulary on an individual basis. Here are two examples. First, Holdaway (1979) discusses a procedure called *word masking* by which students can gain practice using context clues to rehearse new words. In his example the teacher (1) makes an overhead transparency of the desired page of text and (2) using a long strip of cardboard, blocks out some of the words. The students read the uncovered words and sentences to guess the covered word(s) by using context. This activity can be done easily on an individual or peer tutoring basis for vocabulary review. Simply set up the overhead projector in a corner of the classroom with the necessary materials. It can serve as one of the class centers through which students rotate.

Atomic Kid Power!

Step 1: The teacher introduces key information about atomic structure (e.g., nucleus made up of protons and neutrons, electrons orbiting the nucleus, etc.).

Step 2: The teacher takes the class out to the play area and assigns children to a role-playing situation wherein they take turns being subatomic particles (e.g., protons, neutrons, electrons). protons could wear a special hat for the occasion that is colored purple, neutrons wear a white hat, and electrons wear a bright orange hat.

Step 3: A circle is drawn with chalk on the playground surface large enough for approximately six children to stand within. Several children are assigned to play the part of the nucleus and the appropriate number of children will be the electrons.

Step 4: Finally, the nucleus children will stand together in the circle, hopping up and down to simulate a live atomic nucleus, and the electron child or children will run around the nucleus, keeping about a twenty-foot distance at all times. For extra instructional benefit, a parent helper could stand on a ladder (or perhaps the roof of the building) and film the simulation using a video camcorder. The teacher could replay the film to the class later for review purposes.

A second approach for helping students with special needs increase their vocabularies is suggested by Thelen (1984) in her book *Improving Reading in Science*. She suggests that categorizing new facts or concepts into categories will help "students relate newly learned verbal associations to familiar and emphasized relationships" (p. 36). The format for this categorizing activity is shown in Figure 10-7.

Functions of Cells: Vocabulary Review

Name _____

1. _____
   neutrons
   protons
   electrons

2. _____
   light reaction
   chlorophyll
   nutrients from soil

3. _____
   diffusion osmosis
   active transport
   pinocytosis

4. _____
   metabolish
   respiration
   homeostasis

Answers: 1. atoms, 2. photosynthesis, 3. transport, 4. cell functions

FIGURE 10-7 Vocabulary reinforcement: Functions of cells

Step 3: Making and Using Study Guides

A major purpose for making and using study guides is to help students with special needs improve their *metacognition,* or comprehension monitoring. Metacognition has to do with helping students "know what they know" or "know what they are learning." Research on the differences in the strategies used between good and poor readers generally show that good readers are able to describe their methods for reading and getting meaning, whereas poor readers seem virtually unaware of deliberate strategies that can be employed (Brown, 1982). Smith (1967) found that poor readers fail to adjust their reading behavior when reading for different purposes, such as reading for specific details versus general impressions. Therefore, it may be said that a crucial role for the content area/reading teacher is to help students (1) become aware of their own reading comprehension abilities and needs *(metacognitive awareness),* and (2) learn specific strategies that can be used to monitor and adjust reading behaviors to fit their own comprehension needs.

A tetrahedral model for teaching students metacognitive processes has been developed by Brown (1982) and includes the following four steps:

- *Consider the nature of the material to be learned.* Students should review the text, say using the previewing method described earlier in this chapter, to learn what kind of material it is (narrative, expository, etc.). Most content area texts and materials in each of the subject areas follow a fairly well-defined pattern. Understanding the pattern involved at the outset helps the reader to anticipate reading demands and expectations.
- *Consider the essential task involved.* Students need to understand what they are studying for in the text. Specifically, what is the critical information that will likely appear on tests and other assessment activities? Anderson and Armbruster (1980) indicate that when students modify their study plans accordingly, they tend to learn more than if the criterion task remains vague.
- *Consider your own strengths and weaknesses.* As Brown (1982) points out some students are "good at numbers" or "have a good rote memory," whereas others may have trouble remembering details or learning new languages (foreign, computer, scientific, etc.). In general, the task is to make new, abstract ideas familiar and memorable. Learners need to assess their own strengths and weaknesses in each of the content fields they study in preparation for the final phase of the four-step sequence.
- *Employ appropriate strategies to overcome learning weaknesses.* Once students understand where they have specific learning difficulties, remedial action to overcome these weaknesses is essential. Such strategies as look-backs, rereading, reading ahead, highlighting, note-taking, summary writing, webbing, and outlining, when taught in connection with this new self-awareness on the part of the reader, suddenly become of great interest to students.

One way to implement these recommendations is to use study strategies and study guides. Research has made available a number of study strategies helpful to elementary students in their content area pursuits. It seems that when students understand *what to study, how to study quickly and efficiently,* and *why the information is pertinent to their world,* classroom performance is improved. We have chosen some of the most popular study strategies for brief discussion in this section.

Survey Question Read Recite Review (SQ3R).   Perhaps the most widely used study system is SQ3R (Robinson, 1946). Especially effective with expository text, SQ3R provides students with a logical progression of study and multiple encounters with the new material to be learned. Many students also find that they can trim their study time using SQ3R and earn better grades.

SQ3R is best taught initially through teacher modeling, followed by a whole class walk-through. The steps and explanation for each step of SQ3R are listed here:

Survey.   To survey the chapter, students read and think about the title, headings and subheadings, captions under any pictures, vocabulary in bold print, side entries on each page (if there are any), and summary.

Question.   Next, students should use this information, particularly headings and subheadings, to write anticipatory questions about what they are about to read. Students frequently need teacher assistance the first few times they use SQ3R in developing questions that will alert them to important concepts in the unit.

Read.   The third step is for students to read actively (Manzo & Manzo, 1990) looking for answers to their questions. They should also attend to boldface type, graphs, charts, and any other comprehension aid provided by the author(s).

Recite.   Once the material has been read and the questions answered fully, students should test themselves on the material. That which is difficult to remember should be rehearsed aloud or recited. This multisensory experience helps the difficult material to move into short-term and, with practice, into long-term memory.

Review.   The final step is periodically to review the information learned. This can be done orally with a peer, through rewriting notes from memory and comparing to the students' master set of notes, or with mock quizzes developed by a peer or the teacher.

Three-Level Guide.   A three-level guide (Herber, 1978) is a popular study guide in that it leads students from basic levels of comprehension to more advanced levels (Manzo & Manzo, 1990). The first level *(literal)* of the guide helps students understand *what the author said,* the second level *(interpretive)* helps students understand *what the author means,* and the third level *(applied)* helps students understand *how this information can be applied* (Manzo & Manzo, 1990). Although three-level guides have traditionally been constructed using declarative statements, we feel that it might be just as appropriate to use a *questions* or *problem-solving* format. This decision, however, is best left to the teacher's discretion.

We suggest the following guidelines in constructing a three-level guide, which have been adapted from Vacca and Vacca (1989):

1. Begin constructing your study guide at the second or interpretive level by determining what the author means. Write down what you feel are inferences that make sense and fit your content objectives. Revise your statements so that they are simple and clear. Now you have Part II of the guide.
2. Next, search the text for explicit pieces of information (details, facts, and propositions) that support inferences you have already chosen for the second part of the guide. Put these into statement, question, or problem form. Now you have Part I of the guide.
3. Now develop statements, questions, or problems for the applied level of the guide, Part III. They should represent additional insights or principles that may be drawn when analyzing Parts I and II of the guide. Part III should help students connect what they already know with what they have learned from the study of the unit.

When using a three-level guide, be flexible. Vary the format from unit to unit to help hold students' attention. It may also be a good idea to put in occasional distractor items (items not directly pertinent to the subject). Distractors sometimes prevent students from focusing indiscriminately on every item and prompt them to focus on the information search more carefully (Vacca & Vacca, 1989).

Finally, we recommend that teachers include page numbers in parentheses following each question, problem, or statement where answers may be found. This alerts students to key ideas found on each page and enables them to screen out irrelevant information.

Anticipation Guides.   Anticipation guides are prereading activities used to survey students' prior knowledge and attitudes about a given subject or topic. They usually consist of three to five teacher-prepared declarative statements that students read and react to before reading. The statements may be either true or false. The important factor is for students to respond to the statements on the basis of their own experiences (Wiesendanger, 1986). Figure 10-8 shows a sample anticipation guide for "Our Picture of the Universe" (Hawking, 1988).

Step 4: Going Beyond the Text

Elementary teachers of content area subjects in the 1990s are finding themselves attempting to create *transition* classrooms (Reutzel & Cooter, 1992). That is, they are moving away from the typical *lecture–filmstrip–test* modes of teaching of the past and blending elements of whole language into the content classroom. The previous three steps of the process approach for teaching successful content area units of instruction represent a good start, but a final integrating exercise, "real-world application projects," is needed for a more complete content area unit plan.

Real-World Application Projects.   The idea here is to involve students in extensive projects that require them to apply new knowledge in novel ways. Borrowed from the progressive era of American education, real-world projects require students, in groups of

---

Our Picture of the Universe

Directions: Read each statement below and decide whether you agree or disagree with the statement. If you agree with a statement, put an "X" in the *Before I Read* blank before that statement. If you disagree, put an "O" in the blank. After you have finished reading "Our Picture of the Universe" complete the blanks labeled **Hawking's View,** indicating how you think the author would answer those same questions.

Before I Read   **Hawking's View**

_____ Many of the early scientists, like Aristotle (340 B.C.),   _____
believed the earth was round instead of flat.

_____ The universe was created at some point in time in   _____
the past more or less as we observe it today.

_____ An expanding universe theory (big bang) does not   _____
preclude a creator.

_____ Knowing how the universe came about millions of   _____
years ago can help mankind to survive in the future.

FIGURE 10-8   Anticipation guide based on "Our Picture of the Universe" from Stephen W. Hawking's 1988 book *A Brief History of Time*

three to five, to take and apply new knowledge acquired in steps 1 through 3 described earlier in the chapter. As with most teaching, these project ideas are limited only by the imaginations and resources of the classroom teacher and his or her students. The example shown in Figure 10-9 illustrates the spirit of real-world application projects.

This project (Reutzel & Cooter, 1992) is intended for sixth-grade students who have been learning about bacteria and how they cause disease. The nature of their project is to solve the following health problem for a depressed rural community known as Eagleville.

The wonderful thing about real-world projects is that they require students to read and learn beyond material covered in class. These projects involve students with library research skills, foster supplemental reading, encourage learner responsibility and collaboration, and result in creative applications of new learning.

Writing Projects.   One of the most important elements of holistic teaching is the writing process. We know that reading and writing are reciprocal processes and that as we help high-risk learners to become better writers, they automatically improve as readers. Writing projects in the content areas do all this *and* help students internalize new knowledge about the content area. Because much of what is learned in the content areas is rather abstract, writing can be an important addition to our curriculum. Listed next are several writing projects that may be helpful in content classrooms.

Cooter and Chilcoat (1990–1991) describe a procedure whereby students in U.S. history classes can write and perform their own melodramas based on nonfiction texts. The procedure, *content-focused melodrama*, is as follows:

PROBLEM: Eagleville relies on well water for most of its drinking and cooking needs. Because of the large number of outhouses in Eagleville, the underground water supply is rapidly becoming contaminated, resulting in a number of epidemics. Students in this group are to find answers to the following:

1. What bacteria and diseases are likely to emerge as the groundwater is contaminated by the outhouses? Name at least three bacteria and three diseases. Explain or justify your responses.
2. What can the community do for the immediate future (one to two years) to solve this problem? Develop a plan that could be presented to the city council for action.
3. Design a long-term plan for doing away with outhouses, which includes a new state-of-the-art sewage system. *Note:* Use the map of Eagleville provided to draw in your new sewage system.

FIGURE 10-9   Sample application project: "Outhouses are out!"

1. Implementation of content-focused melodramas in history classes begins with the teacher identifying important issues in the unit. For example, in a unit dealing with events that led up to the American Civil War, some relevant issues might be *slavery, economic differences between states in the North and South,* and *political figures of the period.*

2. During the first day or two of the unit, the teacher should introduce the topics to the class through the use of video productions, guest speakers dressed in clothing of the period, or readers' theater productions. Book talks are a stimulating way to introduce topics (Fader, 1976; Donelson & Nilsen, 1985). They involve dramatic readings from fiction or nonfiction books about important historic events. For example, with the pre–Civil War theme, the teacher could use *The Drinking Gourd* (Monjo, 1970) or *The Slave Dancer* (Fox, 1973) to introduce the issue of slavery.

3. Once the topics have been introduced, students should be allowed to choose topics of interest. Self-selection creates a sense of ownership of the process, improves learner attention, increases motivation, and tends to reduce disciplinary problems. To avoid conflict, some teachers have students write their first and second choices of topics on a slip of paper and turn it in anonymously.

4. Once the teacher has collected and collated the topic requests, he or she is ready to form groups based on the student choices. In this unit, there might be several groups of students interested in the slavery issue, some interested in politicians of the era, and so on. We recommend that none of the groups exceed six members so as to keep the group discussions productive and manageable.

Groups will need some training and direction when first implementing melodramas. There should be an elected group leader and a recorder. Ground rules for group behavior and expectations should be discussed, with role playing of positive and negative group behaviors. In the end, the class should develop their own group etiquette rules. Collaboration and cooperation within the group are the ultimate goals.

5. Production of the melodrama is the chief task of the group. The first time the teacher introduces melodrama in the classroom, it is desirable to offer some examples of various elements of melodrama, perhaps by showing the class an old movie in which features of melodrama are easy to identify. Some examples include *It's a Wonderful Life,* starring Jimmy Stewart and Donna Reed, or *The African Queen* with Humphrey Bogart and Katharine Hepburn. One of the great silent film classics, such as *Wings,* may also be a good choice.

The production of the melodrama involves writing the plot, developing characterization, and making scenery. We recommend that in developing the script, students follow the writing process format (Graves, 1983; Atwell, 1987). This means that students will go through (1) a *prewriting* stage where they research the topic thoroughly, organize facts, and develop the characters; (2) a *draft* of the script; and (3) a revising and editing stage where the students, sometimes with the aid of the teacher, polish and perfect the script (p. 275).*

Once students have created their melodrama scripts and rehearsed the play, it is performed for the class. Following the performance, the teacher should lead a class discussion to compare and contrast the melodramatized version of the facts with history as we know it. This will reduce the possibility of learning erroneous information.

Conclusion

In this chapter, we have suggested several steps teachers can take to help readers who experience difficulties comprehending content area reading materials. We suggested that students who experience unusual difficulties comprehending content area materials may not be able to determine the type of expository text patterns authors use. Hence, we suggested that teachers determine the dominant text pattern the author has used and make this information available to the reader through explicit instruction. Next, we proposed that teachers carefully examine the conceptual load found in content area materials. Finally, we described a four-step instructional scaffolding for making content area texts more comprehensible for struggling readers. We began by using graphic organizers to help students get a sense of the structural patterns of the text and how the various concepts presented in the text relate to one another. Second, we offered several strategies for teaching unfamiliar vocabulary concepts that directly affect the comprehensibility of the text. Third, we suggested that students learn and use simple but effective study strategies to improve their comprehension of content materials. Finally, we noted that students should participate in integrative activities designed to extend and deepen their understanding of the content materials. This means inviting students to write, discuss, conduct experiments, or dramatize what they have read. Although the instructional scaffolding proposed

*Adapted with permission of the International Reading Association from R. B. Cooter and G. W. Chilcoat, ''Content-Focused Melodrama: Dramatic Renderings of Historical Text,'' *Journal of Reading,* Vol. 34, No. 4, 1990. 1991, pp. 274. 277.

admittedly entails a great deal of effort on the part of both teachers and students, we have found that the potential benefits for high-risk students who frequently experience much difficulty reading and comprehending content materials more than offset the acknowledged disadvantages.

References

The American people (Grade 6). (1982). Miami, FL: American Book.

Anderson, T. H., & Armbruster, B. B. (1980). Studying. In P. D. Pearson (Ed.), *Handbook of reading research*. New York: Longman.

Armbruster, B. B. (1984). The problem of "inconsiderate text." In Duffy et al. (1984). (Eds.), *Comprehension instruction: Perspectives and suggestions*. New York: Longman.

Atwell, N. (1987). *In the middle: Writing, reading, and learning with adolescents*. Portsmouth, NH: Heinemann.

Barron, R. F. (1969). The use of vocabulary as an advance organizer. In *Research in reading the content areas: First year report*, H. L. Herber & P. L. Sanders (Ed.), Syracuse, NY: Reading and Language Arts Center, Syracuse University.

Baumann, J. F. (1981). Effect of ideational prominence on children's reading comprehension of expository prose. *Journal of Reading Behavior, 13*(1), 167–177.

Brown, A. (1982). Learning how to learn from reading. In J. A. Langer & M. T. Smith-Burke (Eds.), *Reader meets author: Bridging the gap*. Newark, DE: International Reading Association.

Cooter, R. B., & Chilcoat, G. W. (1990–1991). Content-focused melodrama: Dramatic renderings of historical text. *Journal of Reading, 34*(4), 274–277.

Dale, E. (1969). *Audiovisual methods in teaching*, 3rd ed. New York: Holt, Rinehart and Winston.

Donelson, K. L., & Nilsen, A. P. (1985). *Literature for today's young adults*. Boston: Scott, Foresman.

Earle, R. A., & Barron, R. F. (1973). An approach for testing vocabulary in content subjects. In H. L. Herber & R. F. Barron (Eds.), *Research in reading in the content areas: Second year report*. Syracuse, NY: Reading and Language Arts Center, Syracuse University.

Estes, T. H., & Vaughn, J. L. (1978). *Reading and learning in the content classroom*. Boston: Allyn and Bacon.

Fader, D. N. (1976). *The new hooked on books*. New York: Berkley.

Fox, P. (1973). *The slave dancer*. New York: Bradbury.

Frager, A. M. (1984). An "intelligence" approach to vocabulary teaching. *Journal of Reading, 28*(2), 160–165.

Graves, D. (1983). *Writing: Teachers and children at work*. Portsmouth, NH: Heinemann.

Harris, T. L., & Hodges, R. E. (1981). *A dictionary of reading and related terms*. Newark, DE: International Reading Association.

Hawking, S. W. (1988). *A brief history of time: From the Big Bang to black holes*. Toronto: Bantam.

Heilman, A. W., Blair, T. R., & Rupley, W. H. (1990). *Principles and practices of teaching reading*. Columbus, OH: Merrill.

Herber, H. L. (1978). *Teaching reading in the content areas*, 2nd ed. Englewood Cliffs, NJ: Prentice-Hall.

Holdaway, D. (1979). *The foundations of literacy*. Portsmouth, NH: Heinemann.

Manzo, A. V., & Manzo, U. C. (1990). *Content area reading: A heuristic approach*. Columbus, OH: Merrill.

Martorella, P. H. (1985). *Elementary social studies*. Boston: Little, Brown.

McCormick, S. (1987). *Remedial and clinical reading instruction*. Columbus, OH: Merrill.

Merrill Mathematics (Grade 5). (1985). Columbus, OH: Merrill.

Merrill Science (Grade 3). (1989). Columbus, OH: Merrill.

Meyer, B. J. F., & Freedle, R. O. (1984). Effects of discourse type on recall. *American Educational Research Journal, 21*(1), 121–143.

Monjo, F. N. (1970). *The drinking gourd*. New York: Harper & Row.

Nagy, W. (1988). *Teaching vocabulary to improve*

reading comprehension. Unpublished manuscript, Champaign, IL. Center for the Study of Reading.

Reutzel, D. R., & Cooter, R. B., Jr. (1992). *Teaching to read: From basals to books.* New York: Merrill Publishing Company—An Imprint of Macmillan Publishing.

Robinson, F. (1946). *Effective study.* New York: Harper Brothers.

Smith, D. E. P. (1967). *Learning to learn.* New York: Harcourt Brace Jovanovich.

Thelen, J. N. (1984). *Improving reading in science.* Newark, DE: International Reading Association.

Tierney, R. J., Readence, j. E., & Dishner, E. K. (1990). *Reading strategies and practices: A com-*

pendium. Boston: Allyn and Bacon.

The United States: Its history and neighbors (Grade 5). (1985). San Diego, CA: Harcourt Brace Jovanovich.

The United States and the other Americas (Grade 5). (1980). New York: Macmillan.

Vacca, R. T., & Vacca, J. L. (1989). *Content area reading,* 3rd ed. Glenview, IL: Scott, Foresman.

Varnhagen, C. K., & Goldman, S. R. (1986). Improving comprehension: Causal relations instruction for teaching handicapped learners. *The Reading Teacher, 39,* 896–904.

Wiesendanger, W. D. (1986). Durkin revisited. *Reading Horizons, 26,* 89–97.

Chapter 11

Peer-Mediated Instruction for High-Risk Students

LARRY MAHEADY

BARBARA MALLETTE
GREGORY F. HARPER
State University of New York College at Fredonia

KATHERINE C. SACCA

DAVID POMERANTZ
State University of New York College at Buffalo

Key Concepts

- Peer-mediated instruction
- Cooperative learning
- Group goals and individual accountability
- Free rider effect
- Positive student interdependence
- Cross-age and reverse-role tutoring
- Implementation requirements
- Point inflation
- Jigsaw
- Classwide Peer Tutoring (CWPT)

- Procedural efficiency
- Social acceptability
- Student Teams Achievement Divisions (STAD)
- Teams-Games-Tournaments (TGT(
- Team-Assisted Individualization (TAI)
- Cooperative Integrated Reading and Composition (CREC)
- Learning Together Approach

Focusing Questions

- List the steps necessary to utilize the cooperative learning approach. What are some important considerations?
- Why are *group goals* critical to the cooperative learning approach?
- Describe the free rider effect and its possible impact on cooperative learning methods.
- List and briefly explain four methods developed utilizing the concept of student team learning.
- Explain the four basic elements to Johnson and Johnson's cooperative learning approach, and their Learning Together Approach.
- What is Jigsaw and how does it work?
- Differentiate between cross-age tutoring and reverse-role tutoring.

Discussion Questions

- What is peer-mediated instruction?
- What components of peer-mediated instruction make it effective with high-risk learners?
- What are the two essential ingredients of any effective cooperative learning approach, and how does one incorporate such components into one's own peer teaching system?
- What are the primary advantages and disadvantages of using peer-mediated instruction with high-risk learners?
- Briefly describe some possible guidelines for selecting appropriate cooperative learning and peer tutoring techniques.
- Discuss some of the major implementation requirements inherent in the use of peer-mediated instruction and some possible techniques for evaluating their effectiveness.
- List three or four common problems involved in the use of either cooperative learning or peer tutoring programs, and suggest some possible solutions.
- Aside from the documented academic benefits inherent in the use of peer-mediated instruction, what possible social benefits may also accrue from the use of these procedures?

One of the most common complaints heard among teachers today is that many students just don't get into the material being taught. They are simply not interested in acquiring the knowledge deemed essential in the respective disciplines, and often they appear unwilling even to try. Such complaints are voiced most often about those students who do not perform particularly well in school. Some of these students have been labeled disabled, and a growing number of others have simply been referred to as *high-risk pupils.* The challenge facing classroom teachers is, indeed, formidable. They must somehow get these increasingly large numbers of students interested enough in disciplinary knowledge to put forth the effort to read, discuss, and reflect on the information being processed. This challenge becomes much more formidable when teachers must work with youngsters who have specific reading disabilities and/or long histories of poor academic performance in school. In such instances, teachers face both skill and motivational deficits. The question then becomes: How does one motivate students enough to try and yet get around their substantial reading difficulties. One possible solution may lie in the use of peer-mediated instruction.

Peer-mediated instruction refers to an alternative teaching arrangement in which students serve as instructional agents for classmates and/or other children (Strain, 1981). Peer teaching roles can be either direct or indirect in nature, and can focus on fellow students' academic or social behavior (Kalfus, 1984). In recent years, two general peer-mediated approaches, *cooperative learning* and *peer tutoring,* have emerged as appealing instructional alternatives for improving the academic performance of children with mildly disabling conditions, as well as other lower performing students (see for example, Delquadri, Greenwood, Whorton, Carta, & Hall, 1986; Johnson & Johnson, 1986; Slavin, 1990). In this chapter, we will briefly describe a few cooperative learning and peer tutoring programs that have been used effectively with high-risk students; discuss the relative advantages and disadvantages of these methods as compared to traditional teacher-led instruction; and propose a variety of ways in which practitioners may use peer-mediated instructional methods in their own classrooms (see Chapter 13 as well).

Before we begin, however, a number of caveats are in order. First, our review is intended to be illustrative, not exhaustive. There are other similarly effective peer approaches that we are unable to review at this time (e.g., Palincsar & Brown, 1984; Piggott, Fantuzzo, & Clement, 1986; Piggott, Fantuzzo, Heggie, & Clement, 1985). Second, our peer mediation "review" will focus primarily on school-aged pupils with mildly disabling conditions (i.e., learning disabilities, behavior disorders, and those with mentally retardation who are considered educable) and other low-achieving, peers without disabilities (e.g., compensatory education and high-risk learners). Again, other excellent peer-mediated systems have been developed for more severely involved individuals at the preschool (e.g., Odom & Strain, 1984; Strain & Odom, 1986) and young adult (see Gaylord-Ross & Haring, 1987) levels. Finally, our discussion regarding the uses of peer-mediated instruction will focus mainly on how these approaches can be used to remediate basic skill and factual knowledge deficits. Although we are aware of the recent interest in teaching "higher-order" cognitive skills, we remain convinced that equal attention must be given to existing deficits in basic skills.

Peer-Mediated Instructional Approaches

The use of peers as instructional assistants is certainly now new. As Gerber and Kauffman (1981) noted, peer teaching programs have been around since the early 1800s in public education. It was not until the past few decades, however, that peer-mediated instructional approaches were studied in a rigorous, systematic fashion (Strain, 1981). The two primary peer-mediated approaches that appear most frequently in the current

TABLE 11-1   Major Cooperative Learning and Peer Tutoring Methods

Cooperative learning approaches

Learning Together	(Johnson & Johnson, 1989)
Simple Structures	(Kagan, 1985)
Jigsaw	(Aronson et al., 1978)
Group Investigation	(Sharan et al., 1980)
Student Team Learning	(Slavin, 190)

- Student-Teams-Achievement Division (STAD)
- Teams-Games-Tournaments (TGT)
- Team-Assisted Individualization (TAI)
- Cooperative-Integrated-Reading-Composition (CIRC)

Peer tutoring approaches

Cross-age peer tutoring	(Scruggs et al., 1985)
Reverse-role tutoring	(Top & Osguthorpe, 1987)
Classwide peer tutoring	(Delquadri et al., 1986)

literature are cooperative learning and peer tutoring. Table 11-1 shows some of the major instructional methods available within both the peer tutoring and cooperative learning literature. As seen in Table 11-1, numerous methods have been developed within both peer teaching literatures to work with high-risk learners. Interestingly, there is seldom cross-referencing between the peer tutoring and cooperative learning literatures. This is unfortunate in that readers may come away from their readings with only part of the story. This chapter may provide practitioners with a more complete representation of the instructional options available to them when working with high-risk learners. It should also be noted that some methods contained in Table 11-1 appear to be more effective for facilitating the acquisition of factual knowledge, whereas others seem better suited for enhancing "higher order" cognitive functioning. The important implication for practitioners is that they should select those methods that are most compatible with their existing instructional objectives.

Cooperative Learning Approaches

Cooperative learning refers to a class of peer-mediated practices in which small groups of three to six students work together in order to earn rewards based on the collective performance of the group (Greenwood, Carta, & Kamps, 1990). A wide variety of cooperative learning methods have been developed. Perhaps the two most widely recognized approaches are *Learning Together* (Johnson & Johnson, 1986) and *Student Team Learning* (Slavin, 1990). Together, these approaches probably account for over 80 percent of all empirical studies conducted on practical cooperative learning (Slavin, 1990). Additional cooperative learning methods include *Jigsaw* (Aronson, Stephan, Sikes, Blaney, & Snapp, 1978), *Simple Structures* (Kagan, 1989–1990), and *Group Investigation* (Sharan & Sharan, 1976).

Regardless of which cooperative learning approach is selected, classroom teachers usually begin by dividing their classes into a number of small (three- to six-member), heterogeneous learning groups. Each group should be composed of students who differ in ability level (i.e., high, average, and low ability), as well as sex, race, and/or ethnic background. Next, group members are given a common instructional goal—that is, to work together to ensure that everyone on the team learns important curricular content. Finally, team members are rewarded or recognized on the basis of their collective group performance. In cooperative learning systems, students are dependent on one another for their success. They must learn to work together effectively if everyone is to succeed (for a more extensive review, see Bohlmeyer & Burke, 1987; Johnson & Johnson, 1989; Kagan, 1985; Slavin, 1985, 1990).

Notwithstanding the commonalties across cooperative learning approaches, certain critical differences do exist among individual methods. To date, at least four different schemes have been used to classify and differentiate among cooperative learning approaches (i.e., Bohlmeyer & Burke, 1987; Kagan, 1985; Sharan, Hare, Webb, & Hertz-Lazarowitz, 1980; Slavin, 1990). Although a complete discussion of these varied classification schemes is beyond the scope of this chapter, some comment can be made on the most recent analysis. Slavin (1990) noted, for example, that cooperative learning practices may differ along six principal dimensions: (1) group goals, (2) individual accountability, (3) equal opportunities for success, (4) team competition, (5) task specialization, and (6) adaptation to individual needs. Perhaps the two most critical dimensions, however, are *group goals* and *individual accountability*. As Slavin (1990) noted, "cooperative learning methods can be an effective means of increasing student achievement, but only if they incorporate group goals and individual accountability" (pp. 31–32).

Group goals usually require the classroom teacher to establish team standards or preset levels of performance that the entire group must achieve if the team is to be rewarded. For example, the teacher might say that all teams that earn an 85 percent average or above on the Friday quiz will be given a "Great Team" certificate; those teams with 90 percent averages and higher will earn "Super Team" certificates, and so on. Group goals are designed to stimulate teamwork. They prompt team members to help one another so that the whole group reaches its goal. Research suggests, however, that simply placing students in groups, providing some interesting materials or problems to solve, and allowing free discovery of information is *not* an effective instructional alternative (Slavin, 1989–1990). Allowing groups to work together to produce a single product or solution appears to be equally ineffective. For cooperative learning to work, students must strive toward group goals and earn recogition based on their collective group performance.

By the same token, effective cooperative learning methods also require individual accountability. This can be achieved in at least two ways (Slavin, 1990). One is by adding individuals' quiz scores and other assessments into a team total. In this way, each member's test score contributes to the overall group performance. If students perform well, the team benefits. When individuals fail, the team's performance is adversely affected. A second way to achieve individual accountability is by giving each group member unique responsibility for one part of a group task. How well the group performs is then determined by how well each team member masters his or her individual part. Again, the success of the whole is dependent upon the sum of the individual parts.

Building individual accountability into cooperative learning methods also appears to be an effective means for minimizing the free rider effect (Kerr & Bruun, 1983; Slavin, 1990). The *free rider effect* refers to a situation in which some group members do all or most of the work while others do little or none. This scenario is familiar to anyone who has worked on or assigned group projects or papers throughout the years. Slavin (1990) suggests that free rider effects are most likely to occur when a group has a single task or product to complete. To hold students individually accountable for their work in cooperative learning groups, the teacher can simply give quizzes and tests individually, require all students to turn in their own papers, and/or call on students randomly from each team to complete problems or provide relevant answers to discussion questions. Grades earned on these individual demonstrations are then put into the grade book for that particular student and assignment.

A few cooperative learning methods may hold particular relevance for those interested in teaching high-risk learners. In this section, we will examine briefly, four cooperative learning approaches: (1) *Student Team Learning* (Slavin, 1990), (2) *Learning Together* (Johnson & Johnson, 1986), (3) *Jigsaw* (Aronson et al., 1978), and (4) *Simple Structures* (Kagan, 1989–1990).

Student Team Learning

Student Team Learning methods, developed by researchers at Johns Hopkins University, consist of four separate methods. The first method, *Student Teams-Achievement Divisions* (STAD), assigns students to four-member, heterogeneous learning teams. Following teacher presentation of lessons, students work within their teams, typically using study guides/worksheets, to make sure that everyone has mastered the newly introduced content. All students take individual quizzes on the content, and their scores are compared to their previous test averages. If students meet or exceed their earlier performances. they are awarded individual points. These individual points, in turn, are summed to form team scores. Teams that meet or exceed predetermined criteria earn recognition certificates or other rewards. Slavin (1990) suggests that STAD can be used in every imaginable subject and across most, if not all, age levels. STAD appears to be most appropriate, however, for teaching well-defined objectives with single correct answers. According to Newmann and Thompson (1987), STAD has been the most consistently successful cooperative learning technique used in secondary content area courses. In eight of nine experimental studies, students using STAD have significantly outperformed comparison groups in such content areas as language arts, world geography, and general mathematics.

The second Student Team Learning method is *Teams-Games-Tournaments* (TGT) (DeVries & Slavin, 1978). TGT uses the same teacher presentation and team practice format as STAD. Instead of taking weekly quizzes, however, students in TGT participate in weekly tournaments. Following team practice each week, students are assigned to three-person tournament tables where they compete against other team members of comparable ability. Students earn points for their teams by performing well during these weekly competitions. Because students at each table have comparable skills, competition is usually fair. Moreover, because point values for "winning" are the same regardless of the table at which a student performs (high- versus low-ability), low and high achievers have equal opportunities for success, a situation that rarely occurs in traditional, teacher-led instruction (Slavin, 1990). TGT has been used in at least eight empirical studies involving content area courses. Significant positive outcomes have been found in six of these investigations and have included subject areas such as language arts, general math, U.S. history, and science (Newmann & Thompson, 1987).

Team-Assisted Individualization (TAI) is the third Student Team Learning method. TAI (Slavin, Leavey, & Madden, 1986) is a combination of cooperative learning and individualized instruction, designed specifically to teach mathematics to students in third through sixth grade, although it has also been used in higher grades. Students are placed initially into an individualized math sequence based on placement test results. They then proceed through the prescribed curriculum at their own pace. They complete daily practice sheets, which are then checked by other team members, and they take final unit tests individually. Students earn points for their respective teams by passing final tests, completing multiple units, and handing in homework assignments and "perfect" papers. Slavin (1990) notes that TAI is most appropriate for developing firm conceptual mastery of algorithms and for applying mathematical ideas to solve real-life problems. To date, seven field experiments have been conducted on the effects of TAI (see Slavin & Stevens, 1991). For the most part, children who received TAI instruction significantly outperformed their control peers in terms of their math computational skills, displayed more positive attitudes toward mathematics, and were rated more favorably on a variety of behavior rating scales.

The Student Team Learning method that may be of most interest to readers of this text is *Cooperative Integrated Reading and Composition* (CIRC) (Madden, Slavin, & Stevens, 1986; Stevens, Madden, Slavin, & Farnish, 1987). CIRC is a comprehensive program for teaching reading and writing in the upper elementary grades. Essentially, teachers continue to use existing basal readers and reading groups. In addition, however, they assign students to teams composed of pairs of students from different reading groups. While the teacher works with one reading group, students in the other groups work in pairs with teammates on prescribed activities. Prescribed instructional activities include: (1) partner reading; (2) story-structure tasks (e.g., identifying and describing story characters, settings, and problems, predicting story endings, and summarizing main ideas and events); (3) story-related writing; and (4) practice spelling, decoding, and vocabulary. During language arts sessions, students draft, edit, and revise one another's work and prepare to "publish" team books (Slavin, 1990).

CIRC instruction follows a regular mastery cycle of teacher presentation–team practice–independent practice–peer assessment–individual testing. Partner checking is an integral part of the mastery cycle. Team members initial their partner's papers if the latter's performance is satisfactory. Additional practice is assigned if performance is unacceptable. Team members receive points based on individual performances on all quizzes, compositions, and book reports. Slavin (1990) recommends using CIRC when one wants to: (1) increase students' daily opportunities to read aloud, (2) improve students' reading comprehension skills, and (3) enhance students' writing abilities. Two recent studies (Madden et al., 1986; Stevens et al., 1987) indicated that CIRC-instructed students earned significantly higher scores on the reading and language

Achievement Test than did controls. Moreover, CIRC students performed better on measures of oral reading and written expression.

Learning Together

Perhaps the most widely disseminated cooperative learning method, Learning Together, was developed by David and Roger Johnson and their colleagues at the University of Minnesota (Johnson, Johnson, Holubec, & Roy, 1984). Johnson and Johnson (1986) described four basic elements in their cooperative learning approach: (1) face-to-face interaction, (2) positive student interdependence, (3) individual accountability, and (4) interpersonal and collaborative skill building. Like Student Team Learning, Learning Together places students into small, heterogeneous groups and instructs them to work together to ensure that everybody on the team learns critical curricular content. Learning Together differs from the Johns Hopkins' methods, however, in that it emphasizes team-building activities and allocates substantial time for group members to reflect on their collaborative efforts. The Learning Together model assumes that students must be "taught" how to work together and that they can benefit from discussing how well they performed as a group.

The Johnsons have also developed methods for engaging students in what they call "cooperative controversy." Students are assigned to four-member teams and are given study materials on a controversial topic (e.g., the fairness of the verdict in either of the trials of Los Angeles police officers for beating Rodney King; protection of the spotted owl). Two team members take one side of the issue, the other pair takes an opposing perspective. They then switch roles and argue the other side. Finally, the entire group must reach consensus on their particular issue. Students are given seven "collaboration" rules to follow while they debate various topics (see Table 11-2). The Johnsons report that collaborative controversy is more effective than either traditional debate or individual study methods in increasing retention of information and influencing students' attitudes (Johnson & Johnson, 1989). Newmann and Thompson noted as well that the Learning Together model has been used effectively in eight of eleven empirical studies conducted in secondary content area courses. Most successful applications have occurred in seventh- through ninth-grade science and geography classes.

TABLE 11-2 Classroom Rules for Use During Collaborative Controversy

1. We can be critical of ideas, but not other team members.
2. We must remember that we are all in this together.
3. We make sure that everyone in the group gets to participate.
4. We listen to everyone's ideas, even if we don't agree.
5. We restate what someone else has said if it is not clear.
6. We must try to understand both sides of each issue.
7. First we bring out all the ideas, and then we put them together.

Note: Rules are adapted from those proposed by Johnson and Johnson (1989).

Jigsaw

Jigsaw was developed and described by Aronson and his colleagues as early as 1978. In this system, students are assigned to heterogeneous, six-member learning teams to work on academic content that has been divided into a comparable number of parts. For example, a biography on Eleanor Roosevelt might be divided into six distinct sections covering her early years, the White House years, the post-Franklin years, and so on. Each team member receives a unique set of information on their particular parts. Students read their parts and then meet in "expert groups" with members from other teams who were assigned similar sections. They then discuss the content in their expert teams, identify the most important information, and return to their original teams to instruct their teammates about their sections. After peer instruction occurs, students are assessed individually on all six parts of the jigsaw topic. Since students can learn about other parts only by listening carefully to their teammates, they tend to be motivated to support and show interest in each other's work (Slavin, 1990).

Slavin (1990) suggests that Jigsaw is one of the most flexible of all cooperative learning methods. It can be used in a variety of subject areas and can be adapted in numerous ways to meet particular learning objectives. Slavin notes further, however, that the original Jigsaw method poses considerable material development demands. Because each content unit must be written so that it is comprehensible by itself, existing curriculum materials typically cannot be used. Instead, one must prepare Jigsaw sections by rewriting existing materials. Given the substantial demands already placed on teachers' time, preparation requirements may make Jigsaw a less appealing instructional alternative. It should also be noted that Newmann and Thompson (1987) found little empirical support for the use of Jigsaw in secondary content area courses. Statistically significant outcomes were reported in only one of six empirical studies (eighth-grade science).

Simple Structures

Simple Structures refer to a variety of procedures for organizing the social interactions among students. According to Kagan (1989–1990), classrooms can be structured in many ways. Some structures elicit competitive interactions among students, others encourage pupils to cooperate with their classmates. The most common classroom structure is one in which students sit passively while teachers lecture to them. Another common structure is Whole Group, Question–Answer. Here, the teacher directs a question to the entire class, students who think they know the answer raise their hands, and the teacher calls on one of them. Kagan (1989–1990) argues that such competitive structures set students against one another. Because only one person can be called on, everyone competes to be that person. Those who are not called on are disappointed or, worse yet, don't care at all. In contrast, the use of a cooperative structure, Numbered Heads Together, in this situation typically results in more favorable reactions among students. Numbered Heads Together is a simple procedure for actively engaging *all* students during teacher-led lectures and discussions. The class is divided into heterogeneous teams with one high-, two average-, and one low-achieving student on each tearr Students within each team are assigned numbers from 1 to 4. Teachers continue to assess comprehension by directing questions to the entire class, but now they add, "Put your heads together, come up with the best answer(s) you can, and make sure everybody knows." This added directive prompts students to discuss questions immediately, listen to others' points, and evaluate possible responses. The teacher than says, "All number __ [1, 2, 3, or 4] who know the answer, please raise your hands." The number selected is varied with each succeeding question. Because students can never predict which number will be picked, they are motivated to ensure that all "numbers" know the answer. After a randomly selected student responds to the question, the teacher asks, "How many other number __ agree with that answer?" Recognition and/or game points can then be given to all teams that respond correctly and/or agree with a correct answer. The teacher can even use bonus points to reward those teams that come up with creative, unusual, and/or higher order responses.

Recently, we compared the instructional effects of Numbered Heads Together to Whole Group, Question–Answer on third-graders' on-task rates and their performance on daily social studies quizzes (Maheady, Mallette, Harper, & Sacca, 1991). Under Heads Together conditions, students' daily quiz scores were approximately 17 percentage points higher (87 percent versus 70 percent) and their on-task rates were almost doubled. Moreover, no student failed any quizzes when using Heads Together. In contrast, two to three pupils consistently failed exams when a whole group questioning technique was used. Kagan (1989–1990) has described fourteen other Simple Structures that can be used to promote cooperative as opposed to competitive interactions among students.

In summary, a variety of cooperative learning approaches have been used effectively with high-risk learners. Although many of these techniques share a core set of common characteristics, they also differ enough in specific procedural intent and application that teachers should familiarize themselves with each individual approach. Some general guidelines for selecting and implementing specific peer teaching approaches are provided in subsequent sections of this chapter (more general approaches to cognitive learning are discussed in Chapter 13).

Peer Tutoring Approaches

The use of peer tutoring programs with students experiencing academic difficulties is certainly not new (Gerber & Kauffman, 1981). For years, higher achieving students have tutored their lower achieving classmates in an attempt to improve the latter's academic performance. Most recently, peer tutoring has become a frequently recommended strategy for facilitating mainstreaming efforts. Here, we will describe three innovative peer tutoring approaches (cross-age, reverse-role, and classwide peer tutoring). Each system is unique in that it has employed high-risk students as academic *tutors*.

Cross-Age Tutoring

Cross-age tutoring refers to peer teaching programs in which older students with mild disabilities instruct younger, similarly labeled pupils. In two reviews, Osguthorpe and Scruggs (1986) and Scruggs, Mastropieri, and Richter (1985) described over twenty-five studies in which cross-age tutoring was used. An analysis of these studies revealed some interesting findings. First, older students with mild disabilities consistently learned important tutoring behaviors (e.g., structured task presentation formats and immediate corrective feedback strategies). This suggests that such students are, indeed, capable of learning important instructional procedures. Second, younger tutees with similar disabling conditions consistently improved their academic performance as a function of their tutoring involvement. This added a measure of effectiveness to the tutors' teaching skills. A third important outcome was that the older tutors made significant academic gains while functioning in their tutoring roles. This demonstrated that instructional benefits accrued to those who taught as well. Finally, "social" improvements were often associated with the use of cross-age tutoring. For example, Maher (1982, 1984) reported decreases in absenteeism and disciplinary referrals among adolescents with behavior disorders while they tutored younger children enrolled in classes for the mildly mentally retarded. Franca (1983) found more positive social interactions between tutors and tutees with behavior disorders as a function of their tutoring experiences. Similarly, Lane, Pollock, and Sher (1972) reported significant decreases in disruptive behavior among adolescents with behavioral problems following their tutoring experiences with younger students with learning disabilities. Finally, Csapo (1976) noted an increase in positive remarks between high-risk tutors and their tutees during tutoring sessions.

Questions still remain regarding the exact nature of the social benefits that accrue from cross-age peer tutoring (cf. Scruggs et al., 1985; Scruggs, Mastropieri, Veit, & Osguthorpe, 1986). It is clear, however, that no detrimental effects have been reported to date. In addition, most cross-age tutoring programs have emphasized basic skill instruction in reading, math, and spelling. Comparable tutoring arrangements involving content area instruction would substantially increase the utility of this method.

Reverse-Role Tutoring

Because students with academic/behavioral difficulties have proved to be effective tutors for younger, similarly labeled children, some speculated that they might be equally successful with younger, *nondisabled* pupils (Top & Osguthorpe, 1987). A presumed advantage to this new approach was that high-risk students' self-esteem and social acceptance may be enhanced even further if they can demonstrate their competence with "normal" pupils. Top and Osguthorpe (1987) examined the academic and social effects of "reverse-role" tutoring (i.e., older, disabled students tutoring younger, nondisabled peers) on both tutors' and tutees' performance. Using a nonequivalent control group design, the authors demonstrated that (1) both tutors with mildly disabling conditions and regular class tutees made statistically significant gains in reading achievement, and (2) tutors, as compared to controls, improved significantly in their perceptions of their academic competence. No statistically significant improvements were found, however, in experimental subjects' general self-concepts.

Despite the nonsignificant effects on high-risk students' general self-concepts, the present study has important implications. First, the authors demonstrated once again that students with serious learning/behavioral difficulties could function effectively in teaching roles. While functioning in these roles, they were able to make substantial academic gains themselves. Furthermore, the researchers demonstrated that learners with disabilities may actually become *instructional assets* for general education teachers. By providing assistance to those failing students whom the general educator cannot teach individually, high-risk learners may offer an instructional resource that is sorely needed but has been greatly underutilized to date. Moreover, by providing "effective" remedial assistance, students with disabilities may help to dispel many of the negative stereotypes that have persisted about such disabilities among general educators and their children alike. Clearly, much more work must be done with reverse-role tutoring. However, these procedures hold great potential not only for improving the academic performance of pupils with and without disabilities, but also for dispelling many of the myths that have controlled special education students for years.

Classwide Peer Tutoring

A third innovative peer tutoring system was developed by researchers at the Juniper Gardens Children's Project in Kansas City, Kansas. Classwide Peer Tutoring (CWPT) was designed to improve the basic skills performance of low-achieving, minority students and/or those with mildly disabling conditions (Delquadri et al., 1986). CWPT consists of four major components: (1) weekly competing teams, (2) highly structured tutoring procedures, (3) daily point earning and public posting of scores, and (4) direct practice of functional academic skills. Each week, the class is divided randomly into two competing teams. (Students may draw colored slips of paper from a covered box to determine team membership.) The teacher then assigns students *within each team* to tutoring pairs. One student in each pair serves as tutor for ten or fifteen minutes while the other child is the tutee. After the established time limit has expired, the tutoring pairs reverse roles for an equivalent amount of time.

While students work in tutoring dyads, they follow prescribed instructional procedures. That is, the tutor presents an instructional item (e.g., vocabulary term, math problem, social studies question) and the tutee must "say and write" the response. If the answer is correct, the tutor awards two points. If the tutee responds incorrectly, the tutor: (1) provides the correct response, (2) requires the tutee to write the answer three times, and (3) gives one point if the tutee corrects the mistake. If tutees fail or refuse to correct their answer, no points are awarded. The more items students complete, the more points they earn for themselves and their team.

While peer tutoring is in effect, the teacher moves about the classroom and awards bonus points for good tutor and tutee behavior. Behaviors that are reinforced include: (1) clear and succinct presentation of materials, (2) appropriate use of points, (3) use of the error correction procedure, and (4) supportive comments and assistance. Immediately after the tutoring session, students total their daily points and record them on a laminated scoreboard in the front of the classroom. Tutoring sessions usually occur two to three times per week in content area courses and are followed by a weekly test or quiz (e.g., social studies quiz, math facts review). Tests are administered *individually,* but students receive five points for each correct answer. At the end of the week, all points, including bonus and test points, are totaled, and the "winning team of the week" is announced. Weekly results and outstanding individual efforts are usually printed in classroom or school bulletins or announced via achievement certificates.

To date, classwide peer tutoring has been shown to be effective across subject areas (e.g., reading, spelling, math, social studies) (Bell, Young, Blair, & Nelson, 1990; Delquadri, Greenwood, Stretton, & Hall, 1983; Greenwood et al., 1984), age levels (Maheady & Harper, 1987; Maheady, Sacca, & Harper, 1988), and instructional settings (i.e., general, special, and compensatory education classrooms) (Delquadri et al., 1983; Maheady & Harper, 1987; Maheady, Harper, & Sacca, 1988). For a more complete review of empirical studies involving CWPT, readers are referred to Greenwood et al. (1990) and Maheady, Harper, and Mallette (1991).

Recently, CWPT procedures were combined with features of Slavin's Teams-Games-Tournaments (TGT) to form an intervention called *Classwide Student Tutoring Teams* (CSTT). CSTT was implemented across six secondary math classes containing 28 adolescents with disabilities and 63 nondisabled peers (Maheady, Sacca, & Harper, 1987). Findings revealed that students' weekly math quiz scores increased by approximately 20 percentage points during CSTT instruction. High-risk pupils' academic gains closely paralleled and often exceeded improvements of "regular" students. No students with mild disabilities earned any failing grades on their report cards while CSTT was in effect. In contrast, these pupils routinely failed under traditional teacher-led instructional conditions.

Summary

Collectively, findings from the cooperative learning and peer tutoring literatures are quite encouraging. Consistent positive academic benefits have been reported across varied populations of high-risk learners, in a diversity of instructional settings and in numerous subject areas. In addition, there is ample evidence that interpersonal relationships among students with disabling conditions and their nondisabled peers may be improved, and that high-risk pupils' self-concepts and attitudes may be enhanced as a function of their involvement in peer teaching procedures. In the following section, we turn our discussion to why peer-mediated instruction may work for high-risk learners. We also comment briefly on what types of difficulties may arise when one decides to use a peer teaching system and how to go about solving many of these commonly occurring problems.

Advantages and Disadvantages of Peer-Mediated Instruction

In a recent chapter on peer-mediated instruction, Greenwood et al. (1990) described the relative merits and limitations of peer teaching approaches. They noted that, in general, peer-mediated systems (1) created more favorable pupil/teacher ratios, (2) increased pupils' time on task, (3) offered students more opportunities to respond, (4) increased the opportunity for and immediacy of error corrections, (5) enhanced student motivation, and (6) increased students' opportunities for receiving individualized help and encouragement. Individual classroom teachers are limited in the amount of individualized instruction they can provide. With the help of trained peer assistants, however, teachers can offer the diversified and systematic types of instruction that high-risk learners need.

In general, cooperative learning and peer tutoring systems simply create a different instructional arrangement in classrooms, one in which *students* must take more responsibility for their own and others' learning. These systems require *active* student involvement in academic activities, a critical element in effective teaching practice (see Chapter 8). Moreover, since peers monitor and provide immediate feedback for one another, it is much more likely that student responding will be successful, another key ingredient of "effective instruction." Teachers' roles change as well when peer-mediated instruction is used. In essence, the teacher assumes the role of monitor rather than disseminator of information. Teachers move among students, provide feedback regarding the accuracy of pupils' academic performance, comment on the appropriateness of their social interactions, and offer additional instruction to those who encounter difficulty. This differs substantially from the teacher's role in traditional, teacher-led instruction, in which teachers' opportunities to monitor individual student responding are less frequent and often limited to only a few pupils.

One should not assume, however, that peer-mediated instruction has no disadvantages. Ironically, many limitations inherent in the use of peer teaching approaches stem from trying to use them appropriately. For example, Greenwood et al. (1990) noted that the most effective peer-mediated strategies are those that *systematically* train students in their teaching roles and monitor their instructional accuracy (i.e., fidelity) *on an ongoing basis.* Unfortunately, systematic peer training and ongoing monitoring require additional teacher time, a demand that is not present in teacher-led instruction. Another potential disadvantage is the time required to make curricular adaptations. To our knowledge, no commercially available curricula (with the exception of TAI and CIRC materials) exist specifically for use with peer-mediated approaches. Therefore, materials such as weekly study guides, Jigsaw sections, and practice worksheets must be developed from existing curricular texts. Again, this may place additional time demands on teachers, especially in the beginning.

Other issues may arise from the actual operation of peer teaching sessions. For example, classroom noise levels may rise significantly when students are actively involved in peer teaching arrangements. Similarly, students may complain initially about their peer partners and/or refuse to work together. When individual and team points are used, the probability of cheating and "point inflation" may also increase (Maheady & Harper, 1987). Finally, the use of peer teaching arrangements presents unique ethical concerns for teachers. These concerns include: (1) the issue of accountability, (2) peer competence, and (3) informed consent (for complete discussion, see Greenwood, 1981; Greenwood et al., 1990). In general, users of peer-mediated instruction must ensure that *all* (high-, average-, and low-achieving) students benefit from peer instruction, that students are trained properly to carry out their teaching responsibilities, and that all involved are aware of the effects their teaching may have on their relationships with classmates.

Notwithstanding the potential drawbacks associated with peer-mediated instruction, these procedures still offer teachers effective instructional options for working with high-risk learners. The next section describes a variety of ways in which these systems may be used with students having academic and/or motivational difficulties.

Potential Applications for Peer-Mediated Instruction

Having decided to use peer-mediated instruction, one now faces a number of implementation questions—for example, which peer-mediated method to use; when, how often, and for how long to use a particular approach; how to set up, implement, and evaluate a peer-mediated program; and what to do if and when problems arise. In this concluding section, we will address each of these implementation concerns and suggest some possible directions for future applications of peer-mediated instruction.

Selecting Peer-Mediated Options

Teachers have a number of instructional options to select from once they decide to use a peer teaching arrangement. Only a few of those options were described here. Some general guidelines are provided in Table 11-3 to facilitate the selection of appropriate peer teaching approaches. Perhaps the best rule of thumb is to select a method that is consistent with your instructional objectives. For example, if your goal is to increase students' factual knowledge in content area courses, then the Student Team learning and classwide tutoring systems would be the methods of choice. On the other hand, if your goal is to teach students how to work together, reach consensus on controversial issues, and/or settle disputes in a nonaggressive fashion, then the Learning Together model may be most appropriate. Finally, if your goal is to improve relationships between general and special educators and to dispel myths surrounding disabilities, then reverse-role and cross-age tutoring may be the methods of choice.

Additional criteria for selecting a peer-mediated approach should include (1) documented effectiveness, (2) procedural efficiency, and (3) social acceptability. All peer teaching systems are not equally effective; you must select those methods that have the most empirical support. Similarly, you should choose those procedures that are feasible to implement under existing instructional conditions. Material development demands, student training requirements, and ease of daily implementation should be taken into consideration when deciding which system to use. Finally, teachers should select methods that they and their students will enjoy. In assessing satisfaction, teachers might consider their level of agreement with a particular system's *goals,* the acceptability of the recommended *procedures,* and their satisfaction with the *outcomes* produced by that specific method.

TABLE 11-3 **Guidelines for Selecting Peer-Mediated Instructional Approaches**

1. Select methods that are consistent with your specific instructional objective(s) (i.e., academic and/or social goals).
2. Select methods that are feasible to implement given existing demands on your instructional time (i.e., start small, with clearly defined instructional methods).
3. Select methods that have documented evidence of effectiveness with high-risk learners.
4. Select methods that you and your students will enjoy.

Logistical Considerations

After having identified a particular method of choice, teachers must decide when, how much, and for how long to use peer-mediated instruction. Again, some specific guidelines are offered in Table 11-4 to facilitate teachers' decision making regarding the implementation of specific peer teaching procedures. When to use these systems should be determined on an individual basis. Certainly, peer-mediated instructions should not be viewed as *the* solution to all the academic and behavioral problems teachers face. Rather, it is more appropriate to view these methods as *one set of instructional options.* In general, peer-mediated approaches seem to be most appropriate as alternative *practice* activities that can be used instead of independent seatwork. In other words, these systems should *supplant* existing instructional arrangements instead of being "add-on" activities. Moreover, it seems most appropriate to use peer teaching methods *following* initial teacher-led instruction. It is not clear, empirically or ethically, that peers should be involved in the initial instruction of "new" curriculum content.

Other logistical concerns are *how much* peer-mediated instruction to use, and *how long* to continue using these systems. Again, the final decision should be made on an individual basis. The Johnsons suggest that their cooperative learning systems should be used up to 60 percent of the school day (Edwards & Stout, 1989–1990). Kagan (1989–1990) recommends using Simple Structures whenever teachers want their students to work cooperatively rather than competitively and/or individualistically. Greenwood et al. (1990) advocate the use of classwide peer tutoring for 90 minutes per day at the elementary level. Our experience suggests that students rarely get tired or bored with peer teaching arrangements, even when they use them three times per day throughout an entire school year. Interestingly, when asked why they did not get tired of CWPT,

---

TABLE 11-4   Guidelines for Implementing and Evaluating Peer-Mediated Instructional Approaches

---

1. Use peer-mediated instruction on an "as needed" basis (i.e., when students need to improve their academic and/or social performance).
2. Use peer-mediated instruction *in place* of existing instructional activities (e.g., independent seatwork), rather than as an add-on to the existing schedule.
3. Use peer teaching methods *following* teacher-led instruction on new curricular topics.
4. Use peer-mediated instruction in conjunction with teacher-led and student-managed instructional arrangements.
5. Continue to use peer-mediated instruction as long as pupils are responsive to these methods.
6. Prepare relevant instructional materials in advance and establish a regular schedule for using peer-mediated instruction.
7. Train pupils directly in how to use specific peer teaching methods (i.e., model, role-play, and provide feedback on important instructional components of the method).
8. Monitor the effectiveness of peer-mediated instruction using ongoing curriculum-specific outcome measures (e.g., weekly quizzes, unit exams, CBA data, etc.).
9. Adjudt procedures to improve the effectiveness and/or efficiency of implementation.

---

one secondary student responded, "What's the alternative, work by ourselves or listen to the teacher? We've been doing that stuff for years." We recommend using a combination of teacher-led peer-mediated, and student-managed approaches throughout the school year. Ultimately, student responsiveness to peer-mediated procedures should dictate the frequency with which such methods are used.

Implementation Requirements

Although a considerable amount has been written about the characteristics and effects of peer-mediated instruction, very little attention has been directed toward implementation requirements. As Greenwood et al. (1990) and Slavin (1989. 1990) have noted, however, using peer-mediated instruction *correctly* will require additional time and effort, at least initially. One might conceptualize these implementation requirements in terms of three, distinct phases: (1) *preparation,* (2) *actual implementation,* and (3) *evaluation.*

Preparation requirements include developing appropriate instructional materials, teaching students to use the system, and scheduling events to fit the existing regularities in the classroom. The amount of preparation time will vary as a function of which method is selected, how often it will be implemented, and how much existing material can be used. In a recently completed study using classwide peer tutoring (Maheady, Mallette, Harper, & Winstanley, 1991), teachers rated preparation demands associated with CWPT as comparable to those involved in "normal" instructional routines.

Regarding actual implementation requirements, one must consider the amount of time it will take to use peer-mediated instruction on a daily basis. Initial implementation requirements will include: (1) a verbal explanation of the peer teaching procedures and their rationale, (2) modeling demonstrations using individuals or the entire class, and (3) role-playing with corrective feedback. Once students have been trained, the only daily implementation requirements will involve distributing materials, monitoring students' performance, and evaluating their daily products. Again, the amount of implementation time required will vary depending on the complexity of the system and content being taught, as well as the teacher's fluency in carrying out the selected methodology. Maheady et al. (1991) found that, on average, it took about two hours for each of eight, elementary teachers to use CWPT unassisted with at least 90 percent accuracy in their own classrooms. Our experience with other cooperative learning systems such as Simple Structures suggests that significantly less time is required to use these methods.

To ensure that peer-mediation is "working," teachers should also monitor students' performance on an ongoing basis. Program evaluation, therefore, is an integral part of the implementation requirements associated with the use of peer teaching arrangements. We do not see a need for an elaborate evaluation process. Rather, teachers may collect data on "naturally occurring," curriculum-based measures (e.g., weekly quizzes and chapter or unit exams). These data can be plotted on simple line graphs and contrasted with student performance under teacher-led instruction. Naturally, one should not continue to use ineffective methods. Careful observations of *how* students use the procedures, however, may often reveal reasons for some procedural ineffectiveness. We recommend that the teacher collect data primarily on those students who are of most concern to them. Moreover, it is often beneficial to have the students collect and graph their own data. This not only saves teacher time but also gives the pupils important visual feedback on their own rates of progress.

Problem Solving

Like any other innovative instructional practice, one may encounter problems when implementing peer-mediated systems. Throughout the years, three common difficulties have surfaced in our work with peer-mediated instruction. These common problems, as well as some possible solutions are depicted in Table 11-5. Without question, noise levels will increase in classrooms that use peer teaching arrangements. Part of this noise increase results from actively engaging more students in academic-related talk, while the rest stems from students' excitement about using these procedures. This increased noise level may become problematic for those who teach in open space classrooms or settings separated only by plastic dividers. To control noise levels, we developed three simple rules (speak only during the tutoring session, speak only to your tutoring partner, and use your inside voices), provided rewards for those who complied with the rules (e.g., bonus points or teacher attention), and administered aversive consequences for those who failed to comply. The most effective aversive consequence used to date involves a brief "time out from reinforcement." All students must stop working and not receive any points for fifteen seconds. Once noise levels subside, students can begin earning points again.

Student complaints about tutoring partners and/or teammates are common problems in the initial phases of peer-mediated instruction, especially at the secondary level. Such

TABLE 11-5   Common Problems Associated with the Use of Peer-Mediated Instruction and Some Possible Solutions

1. *Increased noise levels*
   - Post and review "good work" rules.
   - Recognize and reward those who comply with good work rules.
   - If necessary, use brief (i.e., fifteen-second) time out from point earning when noise levels become unacceptable.

2. *Student complaining and/or bickering:*
   - Use as an opportunity to teach students that complaining/bickering are unacceptable behaviors.
   - Ignore complaints while simultaneously recognizing and reinforcing the "cooperative" working groups.

3. *Student cheating (e.g., point inflation):*
   - Move among cooperative groups; monitor and interact with groups as needed.
   - Publicly or privately acknowledged those groups that are working well together.
   - To maintain high accuracy for pointr totaling, randomly schedule "surprise day" checks of students' worksheets. Randomly select one paper from each team, score it publicly, and provide 100 bonus points for "matching totals." Conduct "surprise day" checks of students' point totals.

complaints are understandable given that students are assigned to heterogeneous groups in the first place. We use these occurrences as opportunities to teach students that complaining about classmates is an unacceptable behavior. We ignore their complaints and instead focus our attention on those who begin to work without bickering. On occasion, we have used bonus points to reinforce those who work cooperatively. Our experience dictates that once students learn that complaining and bickering won't work, they settle into cooperative working relationships.

One final problem we have encountered is student cheating. Most often, this has involved "point inflation" in systems that provide points for correct responding on practice activities (e.g., CWPT and CSTT). Typically, students will record more points on the top of their papers than they earned within the body. To discourage this practice, we recommend: (1) "surprise day" checks (i.e., random announcements that the teacher will rescore everyone's paper and award bonus points to all those with correct totals) and/or (2) random, daily selection of one practice sheet from each team, with public rescoring and awarding of bonus points for matching the correct total.

Conclusion

The 1990s pose unique instructional challenges for all educators. Significant among these challenges will be the ability to create and apply instructional technologies that are capable of accommodating increasingly diverse student populations in less restrictive settings. The characteristics of these instructional technologies are not entirely clear, nor are the procedures for carrying them out fully developed and validated (Greenwood, Maheady, & Carta, 1991). Nonetheless, several methods have been employed recently that hold promise in this regard. We see peer-mediated instruction as one set of promising alternatives.

The purpose of this chapter was to familiarize practitioners with an exciting set of instructional options, describe the relative advantages and disadvantages of such procedures, and discuss some potential applications with high-risk learners. Our intent was to stimulate interest in applying these methods with lower achieving and unmotivated youngsters. Clearly, much more work of this nature must be done. It would be inappropriate to conclude, however, that peer-mediated instruction will only work with those who are experiencing academic and/or motivational deficits. On the contrary, there is clear evidence that such approaches work with better performing students as well. We would like to see additional applications of peer teaching systems across other content areas and with even more reluctant learners. In particular, applications with students enrolled in grades 10 through 12 and those focusing on higher order cognitive outcomes are sorely needed. We know that such efforts will not be easy, but there is some solace in knowing that our students will be the primary beneficiaries of our attempts.

References

Aronson, E., Stephan, C., Sikes, J., Blaney, N., & Snapp, M. (1978). *The Jigsaw classroom*. Beverly Hills, CA: Sage Publications.

Bell, K., Young, K. R., Blair, M., & Nelson, R. (1990). Facilitating mainstreaming of students with behavioral disorders using classwide peer tutoring.

School Psychology Review, 19, 564–573.

Bohlmeyer, E. M., & Burke, J. P. (1987). Selecting cooperative learning techniques: A consultative strategy guide. *School Psychology Review, 16,* 36–49.

Csapo, M. (1976). If you don't know it, teach it! *Clearinghouse, 12*(49), 365–367.

Delquadri, J. C., Greenwood, C. R., Stretton, K., & Hall, R. V. (1983). The peer tutoring spelling game: A classroom procedure for increasing opportunity to respond and spelling performance. *Education and Treatment of Children, 6,* 225–239.

Delquadri, J. C., Greenwood, C. R., Whorton, D., Carta, J. J., & Hall, R. V. (1986). Classwide peer tutoring. *Exceptional Children, 52,* 535–542.

DeVries, D. L., & Slavin, R. E. (1978). Teams-Games-Tournaments (TGT): Review of ten classroom experiments. *Journal of Research and Development in Education, 12,* 28–38.

Edwards, C., & Stout, J. (1989–1990). Cooperative learning: The first year. *Educational Leadership, 47*(4), 38–41.

Franca, V. M. (1983). Peer tutoring among behaviorally disordered students: Academic and social benefits to tutor and tutee. *Dissertation Abstracts International, 44,* 459A.

Gaylord-Ross, R., & Haring, T. (1987). Social interaction research for adolescents with severe handicaps. *Behavioral Disorders, 12,* 264–275.

Gerber, M., & Kauffman, J. M. (1981). Peer tutoring in academic settings. In P. S. Strain (Ed.), *The utilization of classroom peers as behavior change agents* (pp. 155–187). New York: Plenum Press.

Greenwood, C. R. (1981). Peer-oriented behavioral technology and ethical issues. In P. S. Strain (Ed.), *The utilization of classroom peers as behavior change agents* (pp. 327–360). New York: Plenum Press.

Greenwood, C. R., Carta, J. J., & Kamps, D. (1990). Teacher- versus peer-mediated instruction: A review of educational advantages and disadvantages. In H. Foot, M. Morgan, & R. Shute (Eds.), *Children helping children.* Chichester, Sussex, England: Wiley Ltd.

Greenwood, C. R., Dinwiddie, G., Terry, B., Wade, L., Stanley, S. O., Thibadeau, S., & Delquadri, J. C. (1984). Teacher- versus peer-mediated instruction: An ecobehavioral analysis of achieve-

ment outcomes. *Journal of Applied Behavior Analysis, 17,* 521–538.

Greenwood, C. R., Maheady, L., & Carta, J. J. (1991). Peer tutoring programs in the regular education classroom. In G. Stoner, M. R. Shinn, & H. Walker (Eds.), *Interventions for achievement and behavior problems.* Washington, DC: National Association for School Psychologists (NASP).

Johnson, D. W., & Johnson, R. T. (1986). Mainstreaming and cooperative learning strategies. *Exceptional children, 52,* 553–561.

Johnson, D. W., & Johnson, R. T. (1989). *Cooperation and competition: Theory and research.* Edina, MN: Interaction Book Company.

Johnson, D. W., Johnson, R. T., Holubec, E. J., & Roy, P. (1984). *Circles of Learning.* Alexandria, VA: Association for Supervision and Curriculum Development.

Kagan, S. (1985). *Cooperative learning.* Riverside, CA: University of California, Riverside.

Kagan, S. (1989–1990). The structural approach to cooperative learning. *Educational Leadership, 47*(4), 12–15.

Kalfus, G. R. (1984). Peer-mediated intervention: A critical review. *Child and Family Behavior Therapy, 6*(1), 17–43.

Kerr, N., & Bruun, S. (1983). The dispensability of member effort and group motivation losses: Free rider effects. *Journal of Personality and Social Psychology, 44,* 78–94.

Lane, P., Pollack, C., & Sher, N. (1972). Remotivation of disruptive adolescents. *Journal of Reading, 15,* 351–354.

Madden, N. A., Slavin, R. E., & Stevens, R. J. (1986). *Cooperative Integrated Reading and Composition: Teacher's manual.* Baltimore, MD: Johns Hopkins university, Center for Research on Elementary and Middle Schools.

Maheady, L., & Harper, G. F. (1987). A classwide peer tutoring program to improve the spelling test performance of low income, third and fourth grade students. *Education and treatment of Children, 10,* 120–133.

Maheady, L., Harper, G. F., & Mallette, B. (1991). Peer-mediated instruction: A review of potential applications for special education. *Reading, Writing, and Learning Disabilities International, 7*(2), 75–103.

Maheady, L., Harper, G. F., Mallette, B., &

Winstanley, N. (1991). Implementation requirements associated with the use of a classwide peer tutoring system. *Education and Treatment of Children, 14*(3), 177–198.

Maheady, L., Harper, G. F., & Sacca, M. K. (1988). Classwide peer tutoring programs in secondary self-contained programs for the mildly handicapped. *Journal of Research and Development in Education, 21*(3), 76–83.

Maheady, L., Mallette, B., Harper, G. F., & Sacca, K. (1991). Heads Together: A peer-mediated instructional option for improving the academic performance of heterogeneous learning groups. *Remedial and Special Education, 12*(2), 25–33.

Maheady, L., Sacca, M. K., & Harper, G. F. (1987). Classwide Student Tutoring Teams: Effects on the academic performance of secondary students. *Journal of Special Education, 21*(3), 107–121.

Maheady, L., Sacca, M. K., & Harper, G. F. (1988). Classwide peer tutoring with mildly handicapped high school students. *Exceptional Children, 55*, 52–59.

Maher, C. A. (1982). Behavioral effects of using conduct problem adolescents as cross-age tutors. *Psychology in the Schools, 19*, 360–364.

Maher, C. A. (1984). Handicapped adolescents as cross-age tutors: Program description and evaluation. *Exceptional Children, 51*, 56–63.

Newmann, F. H., & Thompson, J. (1987). *Effects of cooperative lerning on achievement in secondary schools: A summary of research.* Madison: University of Wisconsin, National Center on Effective Secondary Schools.

Odom, S. L., & Strain, P. S. (1984). Peer-mediated approaches to promoting children's social interaction: A review. *American Journal of Orthopsychiatry, 54*, 544–557.

Osguthorpe, R. T., & Scruggs, T. E. (1986). Special education students as tutors: A review and analysis. *Remedial and Special Education, 7*(4), 15–26.

Palincsar, A. M., & Brown, A. L. (1984). Reciprocal teaching of comprehension-fostering and comprehension-monitoring activities. *Cognition and Instruction, 1*(2), 117–175.

Pigott, H. E., Fantuzzo, J. W., & Clement, P. W. (1986). The effects of reciprocal peer tutoring and group contingencies on the academic performance of elementary school children. *Journal of Applied Behavior Analysis, 19*, 93–98.

Pigott, H. E., Fantuzzo, J. W., Heggie, D. L., & Clement, P. W. (1985). A student-administered group-oriented contingency intervention: Its' efficacy in a regular classroom. *Child and Family Behavior Therapy, 6*(4), 41–65.

Scruggs, T. E., Mastropieri, M., & Richter, L. L. (1985). Tutoring interventions with behaviorally disordered students: Social and academic benefits. *Behavioral Disorders, 10*, 283–298.

Scruggs, T. E., Mastropieri, M., Veit, D. T., & Osguthorpe, R. T. (1986). Behaviorally disordered students as tutors: Effects on social behavior. *Behavioral Disorders, 12*, 36–44.

Sharan, S., Hare, P., Webb, C. D., & Hertz-Lazarowitz, R. (1980). Introduction. In S. Sharan, P. Hare, C. D. Webb, & R. Hertz-Lazarowitz (Eds.), *Cooperation in education* (pp. 7–13). Provo, UT: Brigham Young University Press.

Sharan, S., & Sharan, Y. (1976). *Small-group teaching.* Englewood Cliffs, NJ: Education Technology Publications.

Slavin, R. E. (1985). An introduction to cooperative learning research. In R. E. Slavin, S. Sharan, S. Kagan, R. H. Lazarowitz, C. Webb, & R. Schmuck (Eds.), *Learning to cooperate, cooperating to learn.* New York: Plenum Press.

Slavin, R. E. (1989–1990). Research on cooperative learning: Consensus and controversy. *Educational Leadership, 47*(4), 52–54.

Slavin, R. E. (1990). *Cooperative learning: Theory, research, and practice.* Englewood Cliffs, NJ: Prentice-Hall.

Slavin, R. E., Leavey, M. B., & Madden, N. A. (1986). *Team Accelerated Instruction: Mathematics.* Watertown, MA: Charlesbridge.

Slavin, R. E., & Stevens, R. J. (1991). Cooperative learning and mainstreaming. In J. W. Lloyd, N. N. Singh, & A. C. Repp (Eds.), *The Regular Education Initiative: Alternative perspectives on concepts, issues, and models* (pp. 177–191). Sycamore, IL: Sycamore Publishers.

Stevens, R. J., Madden, M. B., Slavin, R. E., & Farnish, A. M. (1987). Cooperative Integrated Reading and Composition: Two field experiments. *Reading Research Quarterly, 22*, 433–453.

Strain, P. S. (1981). *The utilization of peers as behavior change agents.* New York: Plenum Press.

Strain, P. S., & Odom, S. L. (1986). Peer-social

initiations: Effective interventions for social skills development of exceptional children. *Exceptional Children, 52,* 543–552.

Top, B. L., & Osguthorpe, R. T. (1987). Reverse-role tutoring: The effects of handicapped students tutoring regular class students. *Elementary School Journal, 87,* 413–423.

Chapter 12

Motivating High-Risk Learners to Think and Act as Writers

NANCY FARNAN

JAMES FLOOD
DIANE LAPP
San Diego State University

Key Concepts

- Learned helplessness
- Instructional constraints
- Procedural facilitation
- Substantive facilitation
- Portfolio assessment

Focusing Questions

- How does the phenomenon of learned helplessness affect a learner?
- Give examples of instructional constraints and how these would impede a burgeoning writer.
- What are some ways to heighten students' awareness of the writing process?
- What is a portfolio assessment, and how does it function?

Discussion Questions

- Discuss some ways for teachers to facilitate students' processing of ideas for exposition and narration.
- Utilize the concept of a Planning and Writing Card in a lesson plan.
- Why is feedback important to writers?
- Discuss the importance of evaluation with regard to writing.

As Mrs. Flores discussed a composition assignment with her students, they verbally punctuated her explanation:

> "I hate writing!"
> "I can't write."
> "I don't have anything to say!"
> "Do we have to do this?"

Unfortunately, such comments are heard in many classrooms, and, as most of us who have taught writing can testify, these are not sentiments exclusive to high-risk learners and students with learning problems. Writing is not a "friendly" process for every student, and, for several reasons, it may be particularly difficult for students identified as having learning disabilities. For one thing, students with learning disabilities are often passive learners, who fail to use efficient strategies (Johnston & Winograd, 1985) and who tend to attribute their success and failure to elements outside of their control (Diener & Dweck, 1978; Johnston & Winograd, 1985), a phenomenon referred to as *learned helplessness* (Seligman & Maier, 1967). When students lack a sense of control, they tend to display behaviors and attitudes of avoidance. Such feelings are not entirely without logic. Why keep trying if one is powerless to prevent failure? When it comes to writing, this learned helplessness interferes with writers' inclinations to be proactive in their engagement with writing process — that is, in the active planning, generating, and organization of ideas and in writing and rewriting.

In addition, students with learning disabilities, as well as many novice writers who have no disabilities, tend to lack insights about what strategies they can employ in order to become effective writers. As a result, many students become what McGuire (1990) refers to as "writing-resistant." They view writing not as an acquired skill but as a congenital feature; either you have it or you don't. Lacking their own strategies for effective writing, and without any insights about writing processes to aid them, these students too often conclude that they simply don't.

Writing is a cognitively demanding process, what Flower and Hayes (1980) have described as a juggling act. Unskilled writers need help to avoid confusion and frustration, to avoid what amounts to cognitive overload. The demands can feel excessive as writers are faced with accessing topical knowledge, organizing that knowledge, taking audience and purpose into account along with associated rhetorical requirements, paying attention to linguistic features of written text, and managing the motor skills required to get words onto paper (or typed into a computer).

In order to teach students with learning disabilities, who also have characteristics seen in many novice writers, strategies must be designed that will help them overcome feelings of passivity, helplessness, and frustration. In this chapter, we use the term learning-disabled, unskilled, and novice writers interchangeably. This represents a philosophical stance grounded in the belief that learning-disabled students, who are also novice writers, are not so different from other unskilled writers and should be treated similarly. From our perspective, the goal is to help children learn to write, and effective instruction represents what amounts to productive engagement for all less skilled writers. The goals of such instruction are myriad: to demystify writing processes; to make writing manageable, providing control strategies that will lead to genuine success; and to let students know that what they are doing is useful and meaningful.

The purpose of this chapter is to examine how teachers can help students with learning disabilities gain the skill and experience necessary to develop as writers. This is similar to one of the major goals of school reading programs—that students come to view themselves as lifelong readers, not merely readers of school-related materials but readers who want to read, who incorporate the reading habit into their lives beyond the classroom.

Voices of Experienced Writers

Comments from practicing writers are instructive as well as motivating, since writers report that writing is an integral part of their lives. Robert Frost offers an example in his comment: "You know, I've often said that every poem solves something for me in life. I go so far as to say that every poem is a momentary stay against the confusion of the world." Similarly, E. B. White comments: "I haven't told why I wrote the book *[Charlotte's Web]*, but I haven't told why I sneeze either. A book is a sneeze (Murray, 1990, p. 9)." Likewise, Doris Lessing reports: "I write because I've always written, can't stop, I'm a writing animal. The way a silk-worm is a silk-producing animal (Murray, 1990, p. 6)

These experienced writers speak of writing as a way to clarify thoughts—as a natural, and even necessary, part of their lives. Of course, it may not be particularly surprising that highly successful, practicing writers reflect such dedication and interest. Neither, perhaps, is it particularly surprising that students' attitudes would be different from those expressed by these writers. After all, experienced writers choose to write and are motivated in their craft.

Does this mean that writing is easier for these folks? The following writers' self-reports belie that assumption:

> *The fact is that blank pages inspire me with terror. What will I put on them? Will it be good enough? Will I have to throw it out? (Margaret Atwood, in Murray, 1990, p. 72)*

> *The blank page is there every day; that's what keeps you humble. That's what keeps your feet on the ground. No one can do it for you; and the page can*

be terrifyingly blank. As much as there is joy in writing, there's always the little bit of terror to keep you on edge, on your toes. (Robert Cormier, in Murray, 1990, p. 72)

I got so discouraged, I almost stopped writing. It was my 12-year-old son who changed my mind when he said to me, "Mother, you've been very cross and edgy with us and we notice you haven't been writing. We wish you'd go back to the typewriter. . . ." (Madeleine L'Engle, in Murray, 1990, p. 74)

Inherent in each of these writers' reports is a range of feelings, including intrigue and discomfort associated with writing, particularly with the intimidating aspect of a blank page. Students, such as those quoted at the beginning of the chapter, are expressing similar avoidance feelings. Expert writers, however, have understandings about writing in general, and, in particular, about their own writing, which many novices do not. Such insight is apparent in Pulitzer Prize winner Toni Morrison's comment:

When you first start writing—and I think it's true for a lot of beginning writers— you're scared to death that if you don't get that sentence right that minute it's never going to show up again. And it isn't. But it doesn't matter—another one will, and it'll probably be better. And I don't mind writing badly for a couple of days because I know I can fix it—and fix it again and again and again, and it will be better (Murray, 1990, p. 75)

Obviously, writing is difficult for experienced writers, even as it is for novices; but there are distinct differences, one of which relates to insights, skills, and strategies that expert writers develop by virtue of the time they spend engaged in actual writing. Another difference relates to the value and satisfaction that experienced writers obviously associate with the task. Such perspectives from expert writers could be cited endlessly, from collections such as Pamela Lloyd's (1987) and Donald Murray's (1990) and from *Writers at Work: The Paris Review Interviews* (1963). Clearly, expert writers garner insights about composition over time, by virtue of their effort, energy, and commitment. It is these insights and experiences, shared through self-reports, that can inform novice writers and their teachers, just as the insights and behaviors of skilled readers are instructive for the less able.

The instructional issue, then, is to help students feel like writers, to support their efforts so that they, too, develop useful strategies and insights about composing processes. The goal is to inculcate in our students the sense of efficacy that associates with experience and success in writing—or, for that matter, in any endeavor.

In the remainder of the chapter, we first identify some methods of writing instruction that may actually constrain, rather than encourage, writing. Second, we offer strategies that we believe will enable students to become effective writers. Finally, we offer insights into how teachers can support students' processes and skills and can motivate them to be practicing, lifelong writers.

Instructional Constraints

Instructional constraints, which often provide actual roadblocks to learning, can be detrimental to all students, but particularly to the novice. In thinking of writing, we can look at reading as a parallel process. Referring to reading instruction, Harste and Carey (1984) refer to "instructional constraints" as something in the teaching–learning environment that limits what is learned. These constraints include such things as emphasizing word correction rather than meaning; asking questions only to test memory and not to support comprehension during reading; and asking only literal questions to the exclusion of those that require students to make connections, consider relationships, draw conclusions, think critically, and so forth (May, 1990). It is easy to see that these constraints represent potential obstacles for all students' active engagement with print, especially for those students who are struggling to engage in language processes in ways that are meaningful and productive.

The concept of instructional constraints has direct parallels in writing instruction. We will discuss three that have direct implication for writing instruction.

Emphasis on Surface Features of Writing

An obvious constraint occurs when writing instruction focuses primarily on teaching surface features, such as handwriting, spelling, grammar, and punctuation (Bridge, Hiebert, & Chesky, 1983). Consequently, writing too often feels like what Britton, Burgess, Martin, McLeod, and Rosen (1975) refer to as "dummy runs," whose purpose is to display writers' knowledge and skill of the mechanics rather than the total process of writing.

In a classroom, one sees students engaged in practicing sentences and paragraphs. During such instruction, the primary emphasis tends to be on how students display the surface and structural features of writing, with the teachers' evaluations tending to focus on how correctly their students manipulate written forms (indentations, number of sentences, etc.) and conventions (standard spelling, sentence structure, punctuation).

This does not mean students should never practice writing as a craft. But when everything students write is merely in preparation for something else, writing begins to feel like an exercise without purpose, merely another practice session to get through. It's a little bit like taking seventh grade simply so you'll be ready for eighth, or studying your social studies chapter merely so you can do well on the test. Such ploys have a hollow ring — that is, if we prescribe to the idea that learning objectives should be aligned with students' active construction of knowledge and with engendering excitement and motivation for learning. When school-related writing tasks are reduced to one "dummy run" after another, the agenda of the writer, in this case the student, is ignored.

Such instruction may be seen throughout the grades, beginning very early when young children are told that correct spelling precedes effective writing. Accompanying this view might be a statement similar to the following: "My children can't write until they learn to spell." Many teachers are beginning to question such statements because of their knowledge of whole language processes and research findings from studies on emergent literacy, and by virtue of their understandings of literacy development. Effective teachers of writing design instruction that centers on a different perspective, one that in the primary grades emphasizes the expressive, functional, and communicative nature of writing and honors developmental aspects of spelling displayed in children's invented spellings. We must be careful not to adhere to writing instruction that involves isolated drill and practice on grammar (subjects, verbs, direct objects) and punctuation, and use of spelling worksheets, to the near exclusion of active engagement in the creative process of productive writing.

The point here is not to set up an either-or proposition. Writing instruction should include student engagement in activities that focus on content and purpose, on ideas and the organization of ideas. In addition, it is necessary to pay attention to the craft of writing, here referring to the mechanics and conventions that support students' ability to develop their ideas in print clearly. The problem arises when the surface features (mechanics and conventions) become the exclusive or near exclusive objective of writing instruction. It is not surprising that when the instructional focus is on the creation of grammatically and mechanically perfect pieces of writing rather than on one's thoughts and ideas, students tune out and turn off, feeling inadequate and uninspired by this activity called "writing."

Emphasis on Writing-as-Formula

Another instructional constraint occurs when content and form are inappropriately taught, resulting in what Fortune refers to as "the gap between the simple formulations and the real demands of writing" (1990, p. 134). Students become "weighted down with text-book exercises and formulations that simplify the task of writing to the point of making it a poor imitation of the real thing" (Fortune, 1990, p. 133). For many students, the essay is defined, not by its content and rhetorical considerations (solve a problem, persuade someone else to agree with you, report on information obtained through thoughtful and thorough inquiry, etc.), but by instructional directives that mandate such things as five-paragraph essays with a first-paragraph thesis statement, three supporting paragraphs, and one concluding paragraph; five sentences per paragraph, one of which is a topic sentence and one a clincher; five references for research reports; and so forth.

Newkirk (1989) points out that when structures such as the five-paragraph essay — or, as he terms it, the thesis-control paper — and the hamburger paragraph (a sequence of topic sentence, supporting sentences, concluding sentence) are taught as ends in themselves, they become counterproductive exercises for both experienced and less able writers. Good writers learn how simply to "fill in the blanks" with enough information to support what they stated in the introduction as, essentially, a conclusion. Less able writers are called upon to put aside their uncertainties, to know what they are going to say before they say it, to have a conclusion and support formulated before the writing actually begins. Such a reductionistic process leads skilled and unskilled writers alike to believe that composition processes can be boiled down to counting sentences and paragraphs.

Such formulas for writing run counter to some commonalities among individuals who actually write. From practicing writers, it is evident that writing is a thinking process, not simply a recording of thoughts; that it is through the writing itself, through the evolving text on the page, that ideas for writing develop. Nowhere do we find experienced writers speaking of writing in terms of numbers of sentences and paragraphs and formulas.

The following writers' comments support the absurdity of knowing before writing whether they will capture their ideas in one, five, or twenty sentences:

> *A poem can be said to have two subjects, the initiating or triggering subject, that which starts the poem or "causes" the poem to be written, and the real or generated subject, that which the poem comes to say or mean, and which is generated or discovered in the poem during the writing. (Richard Hugo, in Murray, 1990, p. 85)*

> *I don't really know what I'm going to say. In the end it's a process of discovery, rather than of putting something in that I know beforehand. (Saul Bellow, in Murray, p. 96)*

> *How do I know what I think until I see what I say? (E. M. Forster, in Murray, 1990, p. 101)*

> *I write out of ignorance. I write about the things I don't have any resolutions for, and when I'm finished, I think I know a little bit more about it. I don't write out of what I know. It's what I don't know that stimulates me. I merely know enough to get started. (Toni Morrison, in Murray, 1990, p. 109)*

The similarity of their sentiments is unmistakable and leads to a question that is useful to ask (and one that students, particularly our unskilled writers, frequently ask). That is, why write, anyway? Newkirk (1989, p. 15) expands the question:

> *What in the act of writing can give the writer pleasure? To be sure we can name external rewards—promotion, publication, graduation. But if writing is to be more than a duty—like going to the dental hygienist—we need to speculate on the pleasure that writers find in the act of writing itself . . . if writing became merely an act of transcription, of carrying out detailed plans—its appeal would vanish. Without the lure of uncertainty and surprise, writing would be drudgery.*

It is this experience, of writing as discovery, as ideas evolving from an actively engaged writer, that characterizes classrooms where effective writing instruction occurs.

Emphasis on Stage-Bound Process

Related to the constraint just discussed, which occurs when content is subjugated to form, is that which occurs when sequential notions of process dominate writing instruction. Such notions are often represented in posters that adorn classroom walls and which enumerate writing processes in five or seven sequential and linear steps. These charts may be in text, such as the following:

1. *Prewriting*—generating ideas
2. *Writing*—putting ideas on paper

3. *Rewriting* — revising your ideas
4. *Editing* — checking for spelling, grammar, and punctuation errors
5. *Postwriting* — publishing your work

Or these charts may represent writing process in the form of a schematic, similar to the following:

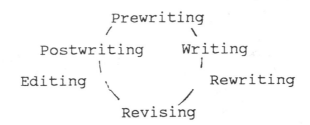

Regardless of the format, what each chart suggests is that writing process is a formula, that a recipe exists that all students can use to create a gourmet composition. When this does not happen, students become discouraged, perhaps even feeling betrayed by teachers whose instuction suggests that this is the way writing is supposed to work, when, in fact, it does not.

Again, reports from experienced writers eschew a linear sequence for writing process. Certainly, something must go on before writers write (a time we label "prewriting"). However, ideas for writing are also generated *during* the process. In essence, what we typically think of as prewriting — that is, the generation of ideas — is fundamental to the drafting process itself, as emerging text sparks ideas for content, organization, and words that had not previously been considered. Although writing involves all of the process elements represented on the wall charts, when we enumerate them and teach them as a composition lesson plan, we never give students a chance to experience writing which Bereiter and Scardamalia (1987) describe in the following way: "Thoughts come into existence through the composing process itself, beginning as inchoate entities ('driblets') and gradually, by dint of much rethinking and restating, taking the form of fully developed thoughts" (p. 10).

Instruction that treats writing as a recipe ignores research evidence (Flower & Hayes, 1980; Bereiter & Scardamalia, 1987) and insights from experienced writers, evidence that suggests that writing cannot be reduced and coded as a sequence of steps, and that writing is idiosyncratic, not only to the individual, but to the context or type of writing that is being done. Robert Cormier, for example, talks about having an outline in his head but never written down; Seymour Simon talks about the importance of extensive reading and research before he writes, particularly since he writes nonfiction; Beverly Cleary talks about doing research only during the writing, if the need arises; and Jane Yolen talks about the importance of a connection occurring between an idea outside herself and an inner emotion before she can write, thus emphasizing the significance of affect. It is clear from these and many other writers' self-reports that there is no one way to write; there is no such thing as *the* sequential writing process. It should not be surprising, then, that classroom instruction that implies otherwise has tremendous potential for causing consternation among our students.

The question is: What can we do to make classroom writing experiences productive for students? In the next section of this chapter, we look at some ways to avoid setting up constraints and, instead, support students' writing development.

Effective Writing: Avoiding Traditional Pitfalls

Using Procedural Facilitation in Narration

Bereiter and Scardamalia (1987) use a term, *procedural facilitation,* that is useful to think about as we discuss how to support the development as writers of novice writers and children with learning problems. Defined as "ways to ease the executive burden of writing in some particular respect, without providing any substantive help such as suggestions of content or form" (p. 57), this is not a way to teach specific strategies or concepts but, rather, a way to help students set complex writing processes in motion so they can ultimately develop their own strategies based on the knowledge they already have. The role of the teacher in procedural facilitation is clear: "the facilitator, be it live teacher or inanimate set of cards, functions somewhat as conductor to soloist, but neither as puppeteer to puppet nor as partner in a duet" (p. 256). The message is obvious: Writers (in this case our students) must retain responsibility for writing; if, instead, it becomes a collaborative act between teacher and student with each doing a share of the work, then the teacher no longer facilitates but takes over processes that should be the domain of the writer.

Although it is well substantiated that most children come to school with knowledge of stories and their structures, students with learning disabilities, as well as most novice writers, have difficulty accessing this information for their writing. That is, less able writers have more difficulty than skilled writers in accessing and ordering the knowledge they already have. Related to this is the difficulty less skilled writers have in planning. Whereas skilled writers tend to plan globally for ideas and organizations that will guide their writing, less able writers tend to get bogged down by planning that fixates at the surface level of word and sentence. Whereas for most beginning writers little difference exists between their planning and the text they produce, as writers become more skilled, planning and content can, at times, be entirely separate; that is, writers' plans begin to include schemes for organization that support their composition goals. In addition, as we mentioned earlier, good writers tend to plan as they write, altering their approach as necessary as their writing unfolds, a process in which unskilled writers rarely engage (Flower & Hayes, 1980).

Graves, Montague, and Wong (1990) found they could facilitate students' processes of accessing and ordering ideas for story writing by providing them with story grammar clues and metacognitive prompts and, in the process, could promote the story-writing skills of students with learning disabilities. The following suggestions have been adapted from their work:

1. Give students cue cards on which are written story grammar elements (setting, characters, problem, ending). Go over these elements with students, relating them to stories and books that they have read.
2. Students need some time to plan their stories, but the time should not be strictly mandated. Encourage them to talk with you and with others about story ideas. Encourage discussion about how writers often begin their stories — that is, with characters talking, by describing a character, with a specific happening, or by describing a place. If a student seems stuck on the planning/thinking time, encourage him to begin and to see what develops as he writes. Also, discuss the idea that characters in stories have thoughts and feelings, just as real people do.
3. Encourage students to use their cue cards and to check off the story grammar elements as they use them in their stories.

Even though students with learning disabilities and other high-risk learners are familiar with story grammar elements, left to their own devices, they may be unable to access this knowledge effectively and apply it to the planning and writing of their stories. Suggestions 1 through 3 and other similar activities have been shown to support these cognitive behaviors for unskilled writers.

Using Procedural Facilitation in Exposition

In another example of procedural facilitation, Flood, Lapp, and Farnan (1986) addressed students' common difficulty in writing exposition. Incorporating what Bereiter and Scardamalia (1987) refer to as substantive facilitation, the teacher alleviates some of the cognitive burden associated with students' generation of text. In this process, teachers support students not only in procedures for developing a well-formed expository paragraph, but also in procedures for developing the substance and organization of their writing. For this activity, students complete a form (see Figure 12-1) on which they plan their writing. This form contains the following four components:

1. First, the teacher asks children what they would like to write about. After students choose their topics, the teacher helps them explore those topics by asking relevant questions. For example, if a child said "sports," the teacher might ask questions about which sport was the child's favorite, why, what the rules were, what equipment was involved, and whether the child liked playing it or watching others play. At this point, students have generated some ideas related to the topic and are ready to move to look outside themselves for additional information.
2. Students document relevant information they have gathered. At this point, they also organize their information into the different categories represented. For example, if the sport chosen was soccer, information collected might fall into categories of famous players, rules, championship teams, origin of the sport, and so forth. Also, as part of this step, students choose one category and write one statement (main idea) that relates all of the information.
3. Students write their main idea statement and select and write ideas they think will expand upon it.
4. Finally, students organize their ideas into an expository paragraph.

Step 1. Teacher helps student select topic and list background knowledge

Topic: _____

         Facts I already knew   1. _____

                                 2. _____

                                 3. _____

                                 4. _____

                                 5. _____

Step 2. Student turns to other sources of information

Facts I have learned about the topic	Source	Fact
	1. (reference material, (e.g., encyclopedia) _____	1. _____
	2. (reference material) _____	2. _____
	3. (teacher) _____	3. _____
	4. (other informed adult or child) _____	4. _____
	5. (miscellaneous) _____	5. _____

Step 3. Student plots the paragraph

Theme or main idea _____

   Supporting details 1. _____

                          2. _____

                          3. _____

                          4. _____

                          5. _____

Step 4. Student writes the expository paragraph

My final paragraph:

_____

_____

_____

_____

_____

FIGURE 12-1 Writing an expository paragraph

Note: To help children focus on the task, the teacher will want to start by putting the blank form for each step on a separate piece of paper and handing them out to be used one step at a time.

Flood, Lapp, and Farnan (1986) suggest a feedback step to help students evaluate their writing, which we modify slightly here. Students meet a partner and read their paragraphs to one another, leaving out the main idea sentence. In turn, both partners write on a sheet of paper the main idea statement they think would fit the ideas in the paragraph. The writers then compare this to their sentence. Students can discuss their partners' findings in terms of ideas that do not seem relevant or that might need to be added. We suggest that teachers model this process by reading a paragraph of their own, minus the main idea sentence, and encouraging students to write and discuss what they think would be appropriate sentences, and why.

Self-Instructional Strategy Development

Similar to the notion of procedural facilitation, strategy instruction has as its goal "to help students learn to carry out the planning, writing and revising processes that underlie effective writing" (Graham & Harris, 1990, p. 15). Making the point that students with learning disabilities do not tend to discover effective strategies on their own, Graham and Harris (1990) designed a teaching approach that they refer to as "self-instructional strategy development." This approach involves three components: (1) developing knowledge of strategies, (2) ensuring mastery, and (3) developing self-regulation necessary for independent use.

In writing instruction for students with learning disabilities, such strategy development centers on three basic elements. The first encourages student writers to think about their audience and their purpose for writing, both crucial for effective writing; the second prompts students to plan what they will say; and the third encourages students to elaborate, to add more details that might have been sparked by the content already written. Let's see what this would look like in Mr. Wheeler's fifth-grade classroom.

A Look Inside

First, Mr. Wheeler gives his students what Graham and Harris (1990) call a Planning and Writing Card, which looks something like this:

Processes Associated with Planning and Writing
1. THINK
    WHO?
    WHY?
2. PLAN
3. WRITE AND SAY MORE

Mr. Wheeler begins by discussing planning and its role in the writing process—that is, its effect on what students say and how it is organized. Then he asks students to look at their Planning and Writing Cards, covering up all but the first point. Together, he and his class discuss why this is important.

"O.K., let's assume you're going to write about an exciting summer canoe trip you took with your family. If you're writing just for yourself, it would be like a diary entry. What would that be like?"

Mr. Wheeler solicits students' input. He asks how this writing would be different if it were a letter to a friend, or a true story written for lots of people to read. As students volunteer different ways of thinking about their writing, Mr. Wheeler tells them that what they are doing is setting goals for their writing. He says that, for example, if they are writing in their diaries, they probably wouldn't worry too much about whether or not their entries were fully understandable to a reader. On the other hand, if they were writing their experience into a story to be shared with their classmates, they might want it to sound exciting and fun, and it would be important to describe what happened clearly, so readers could picture in their minds what the writer experienced.

Mr. Wheeler asks students to uncover number 2 on their card, the Plan. He tells his students that when they think about writing their experience, they will need to think about how to begin in order to interest their readers in what they have to say. He asks them what else they will want to consider. Through discussion, the class concludes that they will need to tell who was involved, where the incident took place, and why it was so much fun. Why, after all, is this something even worth writing about? What makes it a special memory worth sharing?

Finally, Mr. Wheeler tells students they're ready for number 3: "When writers write, they often think of new ideas while they're writing. They often stop and reread what they have written and ask themselves questions like, 'What else could I say?' and 'What might I change to make my writing better?' Writers don't hesitate to add new ideas or to make changes."

Graham and Harris (1990) suggest asking students to debrief this activity by reading the three parts aloud and telling in their own words what they mean. Also, they suggest that it might be productive for students to memorize these three elements, taking turns naming them rapidly without looking at the cue card.

What all of the activities in this section of the chapter have in common is providing instruction that can help students effectively engage in various aspects of writing (planning, generating content, organizing ideas, elaborating, and rethinking their work) without reducing writing to either a formula or a standardized process.

In the remainder of the chapter, we will discuss four additional ways to support processes and skills of novice writers with learning problems. These ways include helping students gain insights into their composing processes; helping them learn the difference between effective and ineffective feedback, and how to give feedback that is direct and functional; providing opportunities for self-evaluation; and supporting students' improvement in the craft associated with independent, proficient writing.

Developing Independent, Lifelong Writers

Insights into Composing Processes

High-risk learners often know very little about writing, and much of what they know is dominated by confusion and misconceptions. They may assume that only the most creative people are able to be writers, that good writing is the result of some mystical inspiration that visits only a blessed few, that good writers always know what they want to say and how they want to say it, and that writing is effortless for good writers. Experienced writers' self-reports, which we have already discussed in this chapter, offer insights for children into these and other misconceptions. Nystrand (1990) suggests that students can benefit if we raise their consciousness about writing, letting them in on experiences of practiced writers and modeling for them our own composing processes. The objective is to help students see writing more realistically, to understand that effective writing is an attainable goal that requires hard work and is related to the effort invested in actually writing.

A Metacognitive Approach

It is important that students realize "experienced writers spend most of their time involved in it [writing process]" (Nystrand, 1990). What this means is that writers immerse themselves in the process, spending a great deal of time thinking, rethinking, writing, and rewriting. In fact, for experienced writers, the thinking processes might be more important than the text itself, an idea that is probably foreign to most of our students. The following self-reports illustrate how writers articulate their immersion in the process of writing. Notice that their approaches to these processes are as varied as the individuals themselves. It is evident that there is no single correct way of approaching writing. Allan Baillie, writer of realistic fiction and adventure stories, shares his experience:

> *The writing starts off from the moment I start thinking about the ideas. I find that if I fiddle around before I start, too many wasted ideas get tossed around. So I just start writing, forcing and pushing the thoughts out, because I know that I'm going to take two, three or four drafts to write the book. It doesn't matter how bad the writing is. What matters is that it's all down. (Lloyd, 1987, p. 14)*

Simon French says it another way:

> *My writing tends to weave in and out of my other daily activities because I don't write all the time. . . . My ideas often come "on the run"—when I'm stuck in a traffic jam, flat out at work, or at home reading the paper. I think about whatever story I'm working on much of the time, and from this come sparks for new ideas. . . . I really have to concentrate to write. If I've an idea that's mapped out and ready to be written down, I have to do it straight away. (Lloyd, 1987, p. 15)*

Unlike these writers, novices tend to lack understanding of their composing processes. They tend to focus on the text as finished product, spending little time engaging in processes that are crucial to the production of effective written work; they spend little time planning, drafting, rethinking, and redrafting, even though these are the processes that take center stage for experienced writers. Instead, novices tend to think of writing as sequential steps, beginning with an idea, followed closely by writing, and perhaps—if they are forced or cajoled — by rewriting. As Sommers (1980) has reported, unskilled writers' revision strategies and rewriting tend not to go beyond reworking of superficial and mechanical elements of writing, such as spelling, punctuation, and grammar. Unfortunately, as many teachers can testify, revision often means simply rewriting a piece in better handwriting. In contrast, for experienced writers, writing tends to focus not on an end product but, rather, on processes of thinking, planning, and generating ideas, which happen, sooner or later, to result in a product.

In addition to sharing reports from expert writers, students' consciousness can also be raised by asking them to talk and write about their own composing processes. They can write about what did and didn't work for them when they were working on a piece of writing. How did they come up with their ideas, and what thoughts did they have while they were writing? Did they do anything after they had finished a draft? What did they not do, which, on reflection, they think might have been helpful? Students can keep a log that helps them reflect on their writing processes not only in relation to one composition, but across several pieces on which they have worked. Do their processes differ depending on what they are writing? Can they make generalizations about what works best for them and what causes them problems? Whole-class sharing of these logs has the potential for offering numerous insights. Students' reactions to these discussions might range from feeling good about having what they do affirmed in someone else's report to gaining new ideas that they might want to incorporate in their approach to writing.

Using Think-Alouds

Another way to heighten students' awareness is for teachers to model their own writing processes. This can only be done as one writes and is similar to think-alouds that have been used during reading so that teachers can model for students the processes involved in comprehending text. In order to model writing processes, teachers can choose a topic (or, better yet, ask their students to suggest one) and model what occurs from the beginning (at topic selection) through the production of a completed piece of writing. Through this process, the teacher writes on an overhead transparency or chalkboard and talks aloud about what she is thinking as she writes. How does she get started? How are ideas for writing developed and pursued? Why are certain words and certain punctuation marks chosen (for example, the use of a semicolon instead of a period)? When does she stop to reread, and why? What happens during the rereading? Are revisions made during the writing? If so, why? Do new ideas develop as a result of the writing itself? What sparks these ideas? Does the teacher ever get stuck or have problems? If so, what are they and how are they solved?

Opportunities for Timely and Productive Feedback

Myriad instances in educational literature suggest that writing is a social phenomenon, that it is basically a social act. Murray (1990) offers another perspective. He suggests in fact, that,

> *most of writing is not collaborative, that we write alone to an individual reader who hears our words alone. Those of us who live our lives as writers accept and,*

*if we are honest, secretly delight in solitude, in those hours of the day when
we are alone with our developing texts. But after the day's hours—or pages—
are done, we need the fellowship of other writers. It helps to share the problems,
attitudes, skills, successes we have experienced alone at our desks. (p. xiii)*

We need to allow student writers both opportunities—that is, both time alone to
write and time to share and conference with other writers. Murray (1990) speaks of the
importance of such collegial interactions, interactions not unlike those our students solicit
constantly from their peers (albeit perhaps not always about writing). In addition, problems of learned helplessness can better be countered through cooperation than through
competition. It is more difficult to expect failure in a cooperative, supportive environment. Frequent and functional feedback provides writers with opportunities to control
and direct their own writing; and, through peer conferences and writing workshops,
teachers can give students opportunities for such sharing and feedback.

One problem is that children don't always know intuitively how to give productive
feedback to one another. However, students can be taught the difference between feedback that is direct and functional and that which is weak and nonconstructive (Farnan
& Fearn, 1990). Through modeling, teachers can illustrate weaknesses in often-heard
feedback comments like the following: "That's good." "I liked that." "Wow!" "Good
description." "It was O.K." Students may not realize that such comments, though ego-
stroking, are virtually worthless when it comes to helping a writer improve a text.

Often, students also express the fear that they might give feedback that will hurt
someone's feelings. Students should be taught the difference between feedback that is
destructive and that which is critical yet constructive, even positive. Obviously, feedback
that attacks the writer or a writing ("That was stupid!" "How dumb." "That didn't make
any sense to me.") is counterproductive. On the other hand, comments that are constructive address directly what the reader likes, in addition to what he might find confusing or troubling about a writing. Functional feedback includes comments like the
following:

"I liked the way you started your story. I like the picture you created in my mind
when you talked about where the main character is at the beginning."

"I was confused by the ending. I don't know what happened to Eric when he walked
in to talk to his dad about the broken window."

"When your characters were talking, it wasn't clear to me who was saying what."

"I wasn't sure exactly why you didn't like the new school rule."

"You started almost every sentence with 'he was.' You might use his name, or say
something like 'When he woke up, he was still sleepy' instead of 'He was still sleepy
when he woke up.'"

There are specific characteristics that make these instances of feedback potentially
productive. Though not necessarily ego-stroking, they provide something valuable to
writers, something that vague comments cannot. That is, they tell exactly what the listener

or reader likes or does not like, and even what the writer might do to improve the writing. Feedback can also include conversations with the writer about what she wanted to accomplish (purpose). Was it accomplished? If not, valuable input might evolve from conference discussions and notes. We suggest that in their writing portfolios, which we will discuss next, students have a section where they keep feedback notes to be used for self-evalution.

Writing and Self-Evalution

Schools are about the business of evaluation, and for good reason. We measure and assess in order to know where we've been and where we are. One of the authors of this chapter talks about her twelve-year-old's twice yearly reminder that it's time to stand up against the molding that frames the door from the garage into the house and have his height marked. Each mark, for the past eight years, has been etched into the wood and dated. He then stands back with anticipation, pointing with pride to how far he has come and projecting where he might go. He has been known to say things like, "Wow' Look how tall I am! Last year I sure was little."

Human beings have a need to receive feedback, to measure and record, to evaluate and muse upon the significance of where they have been, where they are, and where they are going. Schools have, by and large, reduced this need to a shred of reportable evidence, to a number. The idea of the "bottom line" reflects a mind set in our society. Those who make the most money have the best jobs; those who score the highest are the best learners. When everything is neatly quantifiable, we can label and categorize and feel we know what really counts: the bottom line.

The question is, "What do we actually know?" We may be able to categorize a worker or a child with a number; we may be able to compare the worker or the child with like individuals in the rest of the population; but the question remains unanswered. What do we know? More explicitly, what do we know about the individual?

Let's focus on the child as learner by first looking at a practicing gymnast. In the Olympics, expert gymnasts' performances are evaluated according to a number system, with the explicit purpose of comparing them to other competitors. At this point, that's all that matters. The question is, "Who's best?" However, the picture is quite different in the years prior to the Olympic competition. These years are filled with practice and work that refine movements and skills. If we could eavesdrop on a coach during those years, we might hear such things as "Good tight pike," "Tuck tighter and rotate faster," "Don't release your hands from the bar until your hips are above your head," and "Your height on the release was exceptional." The feedback is explicit, informative, and focused on process as well as product. These is a sense that the feedback is crucial, perhaps potentially life-saving. After all, a gymnast who flies off the high bar during a giant swing is apt to be severely injured or even killed. The stakes are high. If gymnasts' feedback consisted only of numbers, it's doubtful that they would know enough to improve their routines significantly or even protect their lives.

Are the stakes any less high in school? Is a child's literacy learning not crucial to his life? Of course, we think the answer is "yes"; literacy is critical. Like the gymnastics coach, we must ask ourselves, "What is important?" We must know what we value and how to evaluate it. Farr and Carey (1986) describe important insights that have emerged relative to evaluation over the past decade or so. First, evaluation should be conducted for the purpose of decision making; second, it must acknowledge the importance of both process and product; third, evaluation must occur on a variety of fronts, allowing information to be gathered continuously and from multiple perspectives.

Also, as with our gymnast, evaluation information is not collected for the sole benefit of someone else forming a judgment about the individual, whether the judge be a coach or teacher. As a sole objective, this limits the potential of evaluation, for a great deal of its power lies in opportunities for self-reflection. One way to broaden the scope of evaluation is through the use of portfolios, which we will describe by answering the following questions suggested by Lapp and Flood (1991) that may be useful in promoting your use of portfolios.

What Is Portfolio Assessment?

In writing, portfolios offer a way to design evaluation that goes beyond a bottom-line assessment and addresses what students and teachers value — in other words, what they think is important (see Chapter 7). Teachers use colorful plastic folders, manila folders, or large portfolio binders in which students organize their portfolio materials. Whatever system the teacher chooses will be sufficient as long as a variety of writings (compositions, lists, notes, etc.) can easily be inserted and removed.

There is no magic set of criteria that dictates how portfolios *should* be designed or what they *should* include. Rather, teachers and students must decide what snapshots they want to take, what questions they want to answer, what materials are worth keeping and for what reasons. Therefore, one of the characteristics of portfolio assessment is that it is fluid and ongoing, providing multidimensional profiles of students' progress. This latter point is important in relation to all students, but it is particularly significant when working with students with learning problems. A problem with single-test assessments is that they evaluate all children similarly, according to predetermined standards that are blind to individual differences. Portfolios, with their multidimensional perspective on students' development, set the stage for evaluation of students as diverse and unique individuals, rather than according to present standards (Flood & Lapp, 1989).

Additionally, portfolios allow students and teachers to gather information that will promote students' self-monitoring of their own development and learning. This is crucial, particularly for high-risk learners, who often do not have a sense of control over their progress and achievement. When students document and reflect on their progress, they can gain insights about their learning often denied to students. Through these insights, students can develop strategies that will give them a sense of control over their future learning and an opportunity to overcome feelings of learned helplessness.

In portfolios, students collect information that is related to their growth over time as well as to their achievement at any given moment. Portfolios do not simply measure a bottom line, a product. Instead, they address the process of writing development and offer feedback that informs both teacher and students.

What Should a Portfolio Contain?

As we have already suggested, there are many ways to design writing portfolios, each one dependent on what teachers and students decide is important to record. Farnan and Kelly (1991) suggest the following several components that might be incorporated into students' portfolios.

1. *Writing samples.* It is one of the most productive functions of portfolios that students use them to keep track of their writing by saving drafts of their work (both unfinished and final). These drafts can be organized in a variety of ways, with works-in-progress and final drafts put in separate portfolios or with all drafts of a particular composition filed together. Regardless of how they are organized, these drafts, which should be labeled and dated for later reference, can serve a variety of functions. For instance, teachers can promote self-evaluation in their students by asking them to choose the best and worst piece they have written over a specified period of time. Students then write their own evaluations of these works, comparing one to another, discussing what makes one piece stronger than the other, and reflecting on the growth they have experienced as writers. These self-evaluations can occur quarterly, twice a year (comparing writings from the beginning of the year to those at the end), or on whatever schedule students and teachers deem productive. At the end of a set period of time, perhaps a semester or a school year, students can go back over their compositions and write a self-evaluation that includes an overview of all their work over time. Questions to ask themselves include: Have I improved? In what areas? Are there some types of writing or certain elements of the process, such as topic selection or revision, that have been especially difficult? Such questions explicitly focus students on their progress as writers.

Another benefit to keeping drafts of their writing is that students can, periodically, go back through their works, choosing one to revise and refine. As they reconsider a work, they must be attentive to issues of content, organization, and conventions (grammar, spelling, and mechanics), asking questions such as "What should I change, and why?" Again, such activities serve to raise students' consciousness about their developing skills and expertise. Teachers can conference with students about what revisions they made, and why; equally instructive would be to consider what remained unchanged, and their insights about why.

2. *Writings completed and in progress.* Students can keep a list of works they have written and their titles. These works can be categorized according to genre (autobiography, letters, poetry, report, story, biography) in order to give students an accounting of the various modes of discourse they have experienced. If never documented, such knowledge is easily lost. Through documentation, students have a chance to reflect not only on what they have written, but also on how prolific they have been as writers. Not recording such information is a little like jogging a couple of times a week over the course of a year without ever paying attention to distance, speed, or frequency. The jogger knows she has gotten some exercise, but it will be nearly impossible for her to evaluate her progress.

3. *Learning in progress.* Students can keep records in their portfolios in the form of simple checklists to document their progress. One example is a two-column list. On one side of their paper, students keep notes under the heading "What I Do Well"; on

the other side they record "What I Need to Work On." During conferences, teachers can collaborate with their students as they add and revise items under each heading.

4. *Writing topics.* When students are treated as individuals working to develop their writing skills, topics for writing should not always be teacher-imposed. Students have to take ownership for their writing, and one way this can be encouraged is through their self-selection of topics. Teachers can guide this process by encouraging students to become observers, tapping into daily happenings for writing ideas. Calkins (1991) suggests that children keep notebooks in which they take notes on conversations, events, and observations that might spark topic ideas. Teachers can also help students by modeling how they might choose a topic for writing. Where does a writer find topics? Ideas can come from an incident, a news item, a song on the radio, a television show, a book, or a tory. Occasionally, students can share their topic lists with one another and have new ideas triggered by comments from other students. When students consistently choose the same topics, teachers can guide them in other directions through teacher–student conferences. Over time, students' self-selected writings will take on purposes beyond pleasing the teacher. Writing will become functional and meaningful. This meaning-centered approach supports a major principle of language acquisition: language learning occurs in contexts that are authentic, rather than contrived and with no inherent purpose.

The contents of portfolios will change regularly, depending on students' needs and classroom orientation. Teachers and students may decide to include research projects, responses to what they have read, and journal entries. Whatever the format, portfolios should reflect a variety of literacy endeavors and active student involvement. One model might look like the one shown in Figures 12-2 or 12-3.

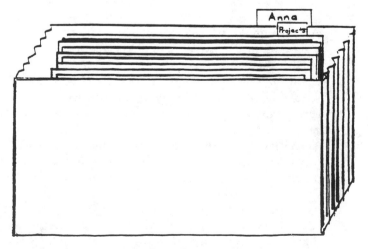

FIGURE 12-2   A model portfolio folder

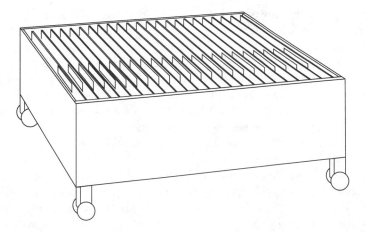

FIGURE 12-3   Another model portfolio folder

How Is Portfolio Assessment Different from Traditional Assessment?

Lapp and Flood (1991) discuss five dimensions on which traditional assessments and portfolio assessment differ. A major difference is that portfolios have appropriate instruction as a primary goal, whereas traditional assessment rarely includes instructional improvement as an overt goal. In addition, portfolios reflect a wide range of literacy endeavors, whereas traditional assessments focus on only a limited set of objectives and texts. In other words, portfolios allow for evalution of a variety of tasks, rather than being limited to a single task. Further, portfolios encourage student involvement, whether as scorers, self-evaluators, or decision makers. This is a crucial element missing from traditional assessments. Finally, portfolio assessment allows for collaborative partnerships among students, whereas traditional assessment is noncollaborative.

Whom Does Portfolio Assessment Inform?

One of the strengths of portfolio assessment is the wealth of information it makes available. Unlike most tests, which provide limited data to the limited number of individuals who can interpret the numbers, portfolio data can inform at least seven potential audiences: the students themselves, their current teachers, their future teachers, their parents, site administrators, district administrators, and legislators. This is a scope much broader than that offered by traditional assessments.

Promoting Craft in Writing

The term *craft,* as applied to writing, can have multiple meanings, including selection of appropriate content, sufficient elaboration, and effective organization. Craft in writing, as we discuss it here, relates to surface features of writing that are often troublesome for students with learning problems. Those features include attention to mechanics and grammar. Earlier in the chapter we cautioned against reducing writing instruction to drill and practice on these features because, in fact, subjects, verbs, commas, and capital letters are not the essence of writing; ideas are. However, effective written communication is dependent on clarity, much of which depends in turn on avoiding superficial errors that distract readers and cause confusion and ambiguity.

A report based on two national assessments of writing proficiency (Applebee, Langer, Mullis, & Jenkins, 1990) produced some interesting results about students' errors in grammar, sentence structure, and punctuation. These results were partially summarized as follows: "Generally, the errors that were most frequent for a particular group of students or at a particular grade level were found in the papers written by only a small proportion of those students" (p. 58). This suggests that certain individuals or groups of individuals might need specific instruction in a particular convention of written language, whereas others might not. Just as writing is an idiosyncratic process, the errors students make are also idiosyncratic. All students do not have difficulty with identical areas of mechanics and grammar. Thus, whole-class drill may not always be useful to the majority of students in a class.

Instead, teachers can discover, through their students' writing, where individual problems lie. Then, in individual and small-group conferences, those difficulties can be addressed directly with those students who have the problems. If teachers notice that many students are having difficulty with a particular item—for instance, writing complete sentences—then instruction and practice in those areas can occur in mini-lessons directed toward the entire class.

What might this look like? Too often, practice in conventions of writing takes place through the use of worksheets where students are asked to label parts of speech and to insert capital letters and punctuation marks in prewritten sentences. The problem with this method is that it is far removed from the reason students learn these conventions— that is, from writing. For example, students who have difficulty with sentence structure need additional practice in sentence writing, not in defining subjects and verbs. Fearn (1983) suggests a method that focuses on direct application of conventions to actual writing. Such instruction might look like the following interchange between Mrs. Warren, a third-grade teacher, and her students:

"All right, I would like everyone to write a sentence that uses the word *friend.* Take a couple of seconds to think of your sentence. Don't write; just think."

Students then share their sentences—for example, "My best friend is Alice"; "I have lots of friends"; "Maryann is a good friend of mine." At this point, the syntax of effective sentences has been modeled numerous times by students themselves.

Next, Mrs. Warren says, "All right, this time, I want you to think of a sentence that contains the word *friend* and the word *game.*" After students think for a couple of seconds, she continues. "Now, I want you to write your sentence."

The process continues; this time, however, students share what they have *written.* Also, the teacher asks that, as students read their sentences, they tell where they have put capital letters and punctuation marks. She walks around the room as students read, checking individual students' work and giving immediate feedback when she notices sentence errors. Meanwhile, students are again hearing many oral models.

Next, Mrs. Warren says, "Think about your favorite pet." After a couple of seconds she says, "Now, write one sentence about this pet."

Tommy reads his sentence: "My new puppy."

His teacher comments, "What about your new puppy, Tommy?"

He responds, "He likes to sleep with me."

"Oh, that's terrific. Rewrite your sentence to tell us about that."

Tommy gets busy, and in a few minutes raises his hand. He reads, "My new puppy likes to sleep with me."

"Wonderful sentence," his teacher replies.

Mrs. Warren could have launched into a lesson on sentence fragments with Tommy, telling him that sentences contain a complete thought with a subject and verb. This information would not be wrong, it simply would not help him become a proficient writer of sentences; for in order to become proficient, students must have a sense of how sentences sound, they must write sentences, and they must get immediate feedback on their work. At some point, it might be productive for this student to learn about subjects and verbs, but the immediate concern is for his writing, which can only be addressed productively through writing itself. Such practice does not violate the nature of writing as a process of meaningful communication. Instead, it supports what students must do to communicate effectively—that is, write in ways that are conventionally accurate and unambiguous.

Conclusion

In this chapter we have discussed some factors that can promote the development as writers of students with learning problems. Practicing writers have developed insights and strategies that novices and high-risk learners do not have. We hope that the ideas in this chapter will help support your students' writing development so they have both the ability and the inclination to think and act like writers.

References

Applebee, A. N., Langer, J. A., Mullis, I. V. S., & Jenkins, L. B. (1990). *The writing report card, 1984–1988: Findings from the nation's report card.* Princeton, NJ: National Assessment of Educational Progress.

Bereiter, C., & Scardamalia, M. (1987). *The psychology of written composition.* Hillsdale, NJ: Erlbaum.

Bridge, C., Hiebert, E., & Chesky, J. (1983). Classroom writing practices. In J. A. Niles & L. A. Harris (Eds.), *Searches for meaning in reading/language processing and instruction.* Thirty-second yearbook of the National Reading Conference. Rochester, NY: National Reading Conference.

Britton, J., Burgess, T., Martin, N., McLeod, A., & Rosen, H. (1975). *The development of writing abilities.* London: Macmillan Education.

Calkins, L. M. (1991). *Living between the lines.* Portsmouth, NH: Heinemann.

Diener, C., & Dweck, C. (1978). An analysis of learned helplessness: Continuous changes in performance, strategy, and achievement cognitions following failure. *Journal of Educational Psychology, 36,* 169–182.

Farnan, N., & Fearn, L. (1990). *Cooperative/Collaborative Writing and Whole Language.* San Diego, CA: San Diego State University, Developmental Writing Institute.

Farnan, N. J., & Kelly, P. R. (1991). Keeping track: Portfolio assessment in reading and writing. *Journal of Reading, Writing, and Learning Disabilities*

International, 7, 255–269.

Farr, R., & Carey, R. F. (1986). *Reading: What can be measured,* 2nd ed. Newark, DE: International Reading Association.

Fearn, L. (1983). *Developmental writing in the elementary and middle school.* San Diego, CA: Kabyn Books.

Flood, J., & Lapp, D. (1989, March). Reporting reading progress: A comparison portfolio for teachers. *The Reading Teacher, 42,* 508–515.

Flood, J., Lapp, D., & Farnan, N. (1986). A reading-writing procedure that teaches expository paragraph structure. *The Reading Teacher, 39,* 556–563.

Flower, l. S., & Hayes, j. R. (1980). The dynamics of composing: Making plans and juggling constraints. In L. W. Gregg & E. R. Steinberg (Eds.), *Cognitive processes in writing* (pp. 31–50). Hillsdale, NJ: Erlbaum.

Fortune, R. (1990). Literature as writing. In G. Hawisher & A. O. Soter (Eds.), *On literacy and its teaching: Issues in English education* (pp. 128–141). Albany: State University of New York Press.

Graves, A., Montague, M., & Wong, Y. (1990). The effects of procedural facilitation on the story composition of learning disabled students. *Learning Disabilities Research, 5,* 88–93.

Graham, S., & Harris, K. R. (1990, Fall). Self-instructional strategy development. *LD Forum, 16,* 15–22.

Harste, J., & Carey, R. F. (1984). In J. Flood (Ed.),

Promoting reading comprehension (pp. 30–47). Newark, DE: International Reading Association.

Johnston, P., & Winograd, P. (1985). Passive failure in reading. *Journal of Reading Behavior, 17,* 279–301.

Lapp, D., & Flood, J. (1991). *Teaching reading to every child,* 3rd ed. New York: Macmillan.

Lloyd, P. (Ed.). (1987). *How writers write.* Portsmouth, NH: Heinemann.

May, F. (1990). *Reading as communication: An interactive approach,* 3rd ed. Columbus, OH: Merrill.

McGuire, B. S. (1990, February). Where does the teacher intervene with underachieving writers? *English Journal,* 14–21.

Murray, D. M. (Ed.). (1990). *Shoptalk: Learning to write with writers.* Portsmouth, NH: Heinemann.

Newkirk, T. (1989). *Critical thinking and writing: Reclaiming the essay.* Urbana, IL: National Council of Teachers of English.

Nystrand, M. (1990). Writing as a verb. In G. Hawisher & A. O. Soter (Eds.), *On literacy and its teaching: Issues in English education* (pp. 144–158). Albany: State University of New York Press.

Seligman, M. E. P., & Maier, S. F. (1967). Failure to escape traumatic shock. *Journal of Experimental Psychology, 74,* 1–9.

Sommers, N. (1980). Revision strategies of student writers and experienced adult writers. *College Composition and Communication, 31,* 378–388.

Writers at Work: The Paris Review Interviews, 2nd series. (1963). New York: Viking Press.

$C\ h\ a\ p\ t\ e\ r$ *13*

Using Cooperative Grouping to Meet the Needs of High-Risk Learners

KAREN D. WOOD

BOB ALGOZZINE
University of North Carolina at Charlotte

Key Concepts

- Cooperative learning/grouping
- Group retellings
- Associational
- Cybernetic sessions
- Buddy system
- Dyadic learning
- Research grouping
- Interest grouping
- Mumble reading
- Whisper reading
- Four-way oral reading
- Cloze procedure and oral reading

- Tutorial grouping
- Random grouping
- Ability grouping
- Needs grouping
- Social grouping
- Team/competitive grouping
- Group communal grouping
- Interactive Reading Guide (IRG)
- Paired/assisted reading
- Imitative reading
- Choral reading

Focusing Questions

- List five grouping strategies. Explain each.
- How does the Interactive Reading Guide facilitate cooperative learning?
- How can grouping be used with other instructional methods? Give examples.
- What guidelines facilitate the use of cooperative grouping methods?

Discussion Questions

- Discuss some of the recorded advantages of cooperative language.
- Create a lesson plan utilizing a grouping strategy with another instructional method.
- Discuss the guidelines for cooperative learning. What are the strengths of these? Any disadvantages?

Imagine the following scenarios:

Classroom A: Students are seated at their desks in rows. They have been assigned these seats since the beginning of the year. The teacher stands at the front of the room and asks questions about the assignment. As students raise their hands, the teacher calls on them one at a time to answer.

Classroom B: The desks are arranged in groups of four throughout the room. In one corner, students are cutting and pasting. In another area, four students are composing a paper. Throughout the room, groups of two pairs of students are reading and retelling stories to each other.

In the latter situation, the teacher has not lost control of the classroom. On the contrary, the teacher is employing *cooperative learning/grouping,* the practice of grouping and pairing students for the purpose of accomplishing assigned tasks.

Cooperative learning is an educational method that elicits both praise and concern. Although almost everyone recognizes it as a necessity, much needs to be learned about how to apply cooperative learning techniques effectively in the classroom. The threat of chaos is one of the reasons offered for the absence of cooperative learning in many classrooms today. For too long, straight rows and assigned seats—the proverbial "quiet classroom"—have been associated with effective teaching. Yet, learning cannot take place without some noise—the purposeful hum of students deciding on a group science project, retelling a selection, or working out the solution to a problem in long division.

It is the purpose of this chapter to alleviate the concerns associated with placing students in cooperative groups and to demonstrate specific ways to implement cooperative grouping techniques to meet learners' diverse educational needs. The chapter is organized in a question–answer format, dealing with typical concerns of (1) reviewing the research on cooperative learning for high-risk learners, (2) identifying specific strategies for grouping, and (3) developing guidelines for merging grouping with other methods of instruction.

Does Research Support Cooperative Learning with High-Risk Learners?

There is ample research in the professional literature to support the use of cooperative learning in the classroom for students with disabilities as well as for their peers who are not experiencing learning problems. Research on these teaching methods and on relations between students with disabilities and their regular classroom peers generally shows that "cooperative learning can overcome barriers to friendship and interaction between these students. Further, these improvements can be obtained while achievement is being enhanced for all students in the class" (Slavin, 1990, p. 43).

Students of all ability levels can benefit from participation in cooperative learning. Several studies have compared the effects of cooperative learning on relationships between academically disabled students and their nondisabled peers. Johnson and Johnson (1982) compared the effects of cooperative learning versus individualized instruction on relationships between students with and without disabilities. They found that in classrooms where cooperative learning was practiced, students engaged in more positive cross-disability interactions than did students in individualistic learning situations. Nondisabled students became actively involved with their disabled peers, offering encouragement and assistance. These positive effects carried over to noninstructional free time as well. Other studies support the finding that cooperative learning improves the social acceptance of students with disabilities (Johnson & Johnson, 1982; Slavin, 1990). Such studies have obvious implications for the mainstreaming of special needs students into the regular education classroom.

There is further evidence to support the use of cooperative learning with special needs students, especially in mainstream programs. In a study involving 21 learning-disabled and 24 low-achieving elementary and secondary students, participants receiving instruction in regular classrooms where cooperative learning was employed exhibited significant achievement gains in reading comprehension as well as in mathematics computation and reasoning over those in the control group who received traditional instruction in resource room settings (Carlson, Ellison, & Dietrich, 1984). Putnam and Markovchick (1989) describe a staff development and research project implemented in Ganderin, Maine, for the promotion of the social integration of special needs students into the mainstream. Staff development for the program provided extensive training in using cooperative learning as well as support throughout the school year. By the end of the year, students in cooperative learning groups had experienced decreased alienation from school and peers and increased positive interdependence with classmates. Nondisabled students in cooperative classrooms rated each other and their academically disabled peers more favorably than did students who did not participate in cooperative learning.

It is evident that cooperative learning programs can play an important part in the mainstreaming of special needs students. The primary goal of mainstreaming is to involve students with disabilities in constructive relationships with their nondisabled peers. Cooperative learning can facilitate the accomplishment of this goal, with the added advantage that students will gain in achievement, motivation, and self-esteem as well (Johnson & Johnson, 1985).

In summary, the benefits of cooperative learning are varied and numerous. Reviews of the research by Lehr (1984), Johnson and Johnson (1985, and Slavin (1987) have demonstrated that, among its many advantages, cooperative learning does the following:

1. It promotes higher achievement across the subject areas, from language mechanics to math problem solving.
2. It improves race relationships.
3. It increases students' self-esteem and their tolerance for others' opinions, values, and interests.
4. It positively affects students' views of mainstreamed and disabled individuals.
5. It motivates students to want to learn and undertake assignments.
6. It improves students' attitudes toward their teachers and their assignments.
7. It fosters independence.
8. It helps students to view the intentions of classmates more positively.

What Types of Grouping Techniques Are Available?

Many types of cooperative grouping methods have been described in the professional literature. This portion of the chapter is devoted to synthesizing and describing some techniques with relevance to reading instruction so that classroom teachers will have a wide variety of options from which to choose. Although many of the techniques presented here have been recommended for use in middle- and secondary-level classrooms (Wood, 1987), they are particularly appropriate for basal and subject area instruction at the elementary level as well.

Group Retellings

One way to encourage peer interaction is through the use of group retellings. Students might be assigned to heterogeneous groups of three, where each group member is given a different assignment to read. The material, though topically related, may come from varied sources and may even reflect multiple reading levels. In this way, the lower ability students in the class can be given shorter and easier material to read. Students are instructed to read the material silently and retell it in their own words to other group members. At any point, group members may interject with a similar fact from their reading or elaborate with information from their background knowledge. A sample science lesson on "volcanoes" might include the following information sources for a group reading assignment:

1. An excerpt from the encyclopedia on types and causes of volcanoes
2. A newspaper article detailing a recent volcanic eruption

3. A portion from the earth science textbook dealing with volcanoes
4. A magazine article on life after an eruption

Associational Dialogues

The associational dialogue is part of a broader strategy called free associational assessment (Wood, 1986), which uses student free recalls as a means of evaluation. The dialogue portion can be used independently as a method for reviewing significant concepts to be learned and retained.

The teacher begins by preparing a list of the key concepts from a unit of study. Students are to take notes from class demonstrations or the textbook and add new content from their own experiences until they have "associational clusters" of information relevant to these key concepts. The students should be encouraged to use anecdotal information and analogies as mnemonic devices. With the original list unmarked, the students study by looking at each word and mentally or subvocally reciting the appropriate information until the concept is comfortably associated with its content. The entire process can be done in class or partially at home if preferred. Ample class time should be permitted for students to work in pairs engaging in an associational dialogue—that is, discussing each concept in their own words. Partners should feel free to elaborate and/or add their own contributions, thereby broadening the depth of each other's learning. As a final step, prior to evaluation, the teacher can discuss the topic with the class as a whole, eliciting their contributions and filling in gaps where needed. For example, an excerpt of a list of history concepts on the topic of "The Lone Star Republic" is illustrated in Figure 13-1. Shown also are two associational clusters on "Sam Houston," which resulted from a synthesis of material from varied sources. Notice how both students demonstrated sufficient recall and undertaking, although their responses are different. Imagine, too, how restricted their responses would be with a typical fill-in-the-blank task such as "Sam Houston defeated _____ at _____."

Buddy System

Developed by Fader (1976), the buddy system is a methodical way of forming heterogeneous groups that possess some elements of homogeneity. To begin, the teacher ranks the class on the basis of "how prepared" they are for that particular subject area, with student number 1 as the "most prepared" and student number 30 as the "least prepared." This list is then divided into three groups: high (1–19), middle (11–20), and low (21–30). Next, the teacher groups the top student from the high group, the top student from the middle group and the top student from the low group together (#1, #11, and #21) and so on, until the last group consists of students #10, #20, and #30. This results in a grouping arrangement in which the differences in preparation are not so disparate as to cause feelings of boredom or intimidation. Instead, the students, though different in terms of ability, are sufficiently similar to help each other and benefit from their varied backgrounds.

The major requirement, as outlined by Fader, is that students are buddies; that is, they are responsible for each other's learning. They consult one another before asking

List of Concepts, Events, People

President Adams
President Jackson
Mexico City
Santa Ana
The Alamo
Davey Crockett
Jim Bowie
February 23, 1836
Sam Houston
San Jacinto

Student Free Recalls or "Association Clusters"

Sam Houston

Student A—Defeated the Mexican Army; took Santa Ana as a prisoner; president of the Republic of Texas.

Student B—Rode on horse as head of Texas army; helped free Texas from Mexico; Houston, Texas, named for him.

FIGURE 13-1   "The Lone Star Republic"

the teacher, edit each other's work, and read fellow group members' assignments before they are handed in to the teacher. The buddy system is especially useful for writing assignments. The simple directive, "Move into your 'buddy system' groups and write a descriptive paragraph on what you visualize on a Sioux reservation," can be the catalyst for a rewarding cooperative learning experience.

Cybernetic Sessions

In Masztal's (1986) cybernetic sessions, small groups of students respond to preplanned questions within a limited period of time. The four phases of cybernetic sessions can be readily adapted and simplified for use in elementary-level classrooms. The phases will be described by applying them to an introductory lesson on plants designed for primary grade students.

In the *preplanning* phase, put one question on each piece of posterboard and hang them around the room. Carefully worded, thought-provoking questions that may elicit misconceptions are most useful here. Some examples might be: "Where do plants come from?," "In what ways are plants useful to use?," and "How do plants live?"

During the *response-generating* phase, students are grouped in fives or sixes around each posted question. When instructed by the teacher, students contribute as many answers as possible while a group recorder writes them down on a separate sheet of paper.

After the allotted time, the groups move to another question station and the process is repeated. Each time a new recorder is chosen.

The next phase involves *data synthesizing,* wherein class members pool their responses to each question. This phase occurs after each group has had the chance to circulate around the room and answer all questions. The teacher, or an appointed student, writes the class's responses under each posted question. In the *final presentation* phase, the posters may be placed on bulletin boards, typed as handouts, or reread later as a form of review.

Cybernetic sessions appeal to students because of their novelty and also because this form of grouping capitalizes on their inherent need to be active. In this method, students have the opportunity to move around the classroom every ten minutes or so with no repercussions from the teacher.

Dyadic Learning

Dyadic learning (Larson & Dansereau, 1986) is based on recent research on (1) metacognition, which suggests that students need help monitoring their own comprehension, and (2) elaboration, which demonstrates the utility of creating images and making analogies while reading. In this technique, students are instructed to work in dyads (pairs) to read and learn subject area material. One partner, assuming the role of "recaller," orally summarizes the material read; the other partner becomes the "listener/facilitator," correcting mistakes and adding information. Students are instructed to read a designated number of paragraphs or pages silently and then switch roles. They may put their heads together to draw pictures or diagrams or make outlines depicting the major concepts in the selection. In a history lesson, students may be grouped in dyads to read about the Civil War. They may choose to depict the location, dates, and outcomes of each battle via a map or similar illustration. Likewise, in a science lesson on weather, they may choose to draw pictures illustrating the various cloud formations.

Research Grouping

Research grouping can be employed in any subject where the teacher feels a topic or issue warrants further study. Students who have just read a nonfiction basal story on seeing-eye dogs may choose to investigate related areas, such as training schools, commands, or types of dogs used. Such an assignment may involve answering a simple question or conducting an in-depth investigation and report on a related area.

The subject areas of science, health, social studies, and even math provide appropriate avenues to engage students in research grouping. Students may want to seek out biographical information about explorers in the New World, or they may choose to examine the habits of various arthropods. In any case, library skills are a prerequisite, and teachers will want to ensure that either they, or the school media specialist, have demonstrated and modeled the research abilities needed to complete such assignments.

As with many other cooperative learning techniques, the teacher may choose to "group within the group" by combining students of varied ability levels. The buddy system grouping technique previously described is especially appropriate for this purpose.

Interest Grouping

Many methods are available to assess students' interests, but few give suggestions on what to do once the data are gathered. Teachers can also easily design inventories that give clues regarding students' likely reading preferences. A structured, directed response type of inventory that requires the marking of hobbies or other areas of interest would be helpful. From these data, teachers can direct students who have a preponderance of activity-oriented interests to adventure or how-to books. Those who display an interest in more sedate activities might find biographies, romances, or fantasy stories enjoyable, whereas students with pets might prefer books about animals.

Stations can be set up around the room for sharing particular types of books. A favorite book from each variety (adventure, animal, fantasy, biography, etc.) can be chosen and shared with the class. Then students can be given the option of changing stations to read a new type of book or selecting one of the class favorites for free reading time.

Interest grouping is not limited to the language arts period. Teachers can prepare a list of choices in social studies on China, for example, with categories ranging from ancient dynasties to mode of dress. Students who share a common interest in any area can be grouped together and can merge their resources to generate a project, model, demonstration, play, or report.

Tutorial Grouping

Tutorial grouping can be employed when the teacher feels that students will benefit from one-on-one assistance. Similar to the buddy system described previously with groups of three, tutorial grouping involves two students working together to assist and be *responsible* for each other's learning. Teachers may tell students to pair up in their preassigned tutorial groups for a basal skills assignment, math word problems, or an end-of-the-chapter activity. These pairs should be made up of students who are similar in terms of ability and yet sufficiently disparate academically and or socially to benefit from each other's assistance. In some cases, a teacher may assign the majority of the class the textbook reading while other students are working in topically related alternative materials under a tutorial grouping arrangement. These may be ESL, learning-disabled, or other high-risk students who are often unable to handle the grade-level textbook material.

When used in this latter sense, a tutorial program can be adopted by an entire school system, complete with resources, teacher and student training, and recognition for the participants. Plaques, certificates, and badges are excellent ways to recognize tutorial program participants without distinguishing between the tutor and the tutee.

Random Grouping

In the interest of time, it may be necessary to engage in random grouping. Here, the teacher may direct class members to move their desks together in groups of two or three in order to facilitate the retelling of a film's events, check each other's math problems, or share the reading of individual compositions. Counting off by ones, twos, threes, or more, depending on the size of the group desired, is another way of randomizing the groups.

Ability Grouping

When used properly, the practice of dividing students according to ability levels has some merit. For example, when multilevel texts and materials are available, students can use them and be grouped according to their reading proficiency. In math, it may be beneficial to divide students according to their respective abilities for small-group learning and specific demonstrations.

However, teachers must be careful not to overuse ability grouping, especially in the case of the reading circle with "its buzzards, bluebirds and goldfinches" (Wood, 1987). Informal observations have shown that students are assigned to such groups early in their schooling and are often locked into their original status throughout their elementary school careers. This results in the phenomenon of "basal labeling" (once a buzzard always a buzzard) and "basal tracking," whereby students are automatically placed in the next year's basal level, regardless of possible gains in performance (Wood, 1984).

Needs Grouping

It is often necessary to group students on the basis of their strengths or weaknesses in a specific area. Without a systematic plan for ongoing assessment, these discrete needs and abilities are sometimes not recognized until the first comprehensive test. Some methods for determining students' needs are (1) the content inventory, (2) pre- and post-testing, and (3) arranging assessment tests topically.

Originally developed for use with secondary-level material, the *content inventory* can be readily adapted for upper elementary use. Constructed by the classroom teacher for use at the beginning of the year, it is based on the textbook used in the class. The content inventory assesses students' abilities in three areas: reading and study aids, vocabulary knowledge, and comprehension. Thus, the teacher has information early on regarding the specific needs of the class, as well as which students may have difficulty reading the science, social studies, or health textbooks.

Pretests can be developed on, for example, a language arts textbook to determine students' preexisting knowledge of such skills as letter writing, proper nouns, or subjects and predicates. Likewise, they can be designed to preassess students' math computation skills. This practice eliminates the unnecessary teaching of material students already know and provides a method for assisting those in need. *Posttests* used after the instructional lesson help the teacher determine who has and has not mastered the skill taught.

Arranging chapter tests topically is another method for evaluating what students have learned and what they still need to know. A health test arranged topically would group all items related to the various body systems together (e.g., respiratory, excretory, nervous, digestive). Then the teacher can determine if additional explanation of given subtopics is needed for the class as a whole or for specific students (see Wood, 1985).

Social Grouping

There are times when allowing students to work with peers of their own choosing can be advantageous. Rewarding students with the prospect of working with their chosen peer group can motivate them both behaviorally and academically. Students can list three peers with whom they would like to work. Then the teacher can identify those students who are not chosen and build a group of supportive and understanding members around them.

Team or Competitive Grouping

In team learning experiences, students are placed in groups or teams to pursue a common task. In some instances, the teams compete with one another. In other cases, they strive to reach a specified criterion level of performance (see Chapter 11).

Team Accelerated Instruction or TAI (Slavin, 1987) uses a combination of individualized instruction and cooperative learning to teach elementary students math concepts. Students begin by taking a placement test and then proceed through the sequences as their respective ability levels allow. Four students who are working at the same point in the sequence are assigned to each team. Team members are required to check each other's work and assist with problems, which frees the teacher to conduct group instructional lessons (e.g., decimals, fractions, long division). Although students work for the team, individual accountability is ensured because students take individual unit tests without team assistance. Studies comparing TAI with traditional math instruction demonstrated greater achievement gains for the students participating in TAI; the effects for students with learning problems were significantly positive (Slavin, 1990).

The most recent of the team learning techniques is *Cooperative Integrated Reading and Composition* (CIRC((Slavin, 1987), a program designed to teach reading and writing to upper elementary students. Positive effects of this cooperative learning approach on achievement in reading and writing have also been documented. For example, the CIRC model has been shown to increase all students' achievement in reading, language arts, and writing, including that of mainstreamed special education and remedial students (Slavin, 1990). In CIRC, students are assigned to teams composed of pairs from two different basal reader groups. This grouping method frees the teacher to work with one reading group while the pairs of students work on higher order tasks such as predition, summarization, reading and retelling, critical analysis, and story grammar. For language arts, peers serve as an audience for the writing of their teammates. They plan and write drafts, make comments on the content and mechanics, and assist in the revision and editing process.

The CIRC program involves sequential, teacher-led instruction with team practice, team preassessments, and final quizzes. Students take quizzes when their teammates determine they are ready. They receive points, which are compiled as a team score for the various activities completed each week. The total number of points determines the type of certificate the team will be awarded.

The CIRC and TAI methods are designed to replace traditional elementary-level instruction in reading/writing and math, respectively. They would require a substantial amount of teacher inservice and curricular adaptation. Other techniques such as Student Teams—Achievement Divisions (Slavin, 1987), Teams-Games-Tournaments (DeVries & Slavin, 1978) and Jigsaw (Aronson, 1978) are more generic forms of cooperative learning that can be applied at varied grade levels and in many subject areas.

Group Communal Writing

Group communal writing is a vehicle for incorporating writing across the subject areas with minimal instruction and grading time. In traditional writing assignments, students are told to write a composition individually and turn it in to the teacher at the end of class. Consequently, before the class is concluded, many students face blank sheets of paper while others have written several pages of unfocused rhetoric. Much instructional time is taken up as the teacher tries to enlighten those students with writer's block and trim down the work of those who have overindulged on the printed word.

With group communal writing, each heterogeneous group of four composes only one written product between them. Group members contribute their strengths in areas such as experiential background, language mechanics, outlining, proofreading, and so on. In this way, everyone, regardless of ability level, can contribute something to the writing process. Additionally, good writing practices are modeled for those who are less proficient. Each group can rotate the assignment of specific roles—for example, content editor, researcher, proofreader, and recorder. After the composition is complete, group members sign the paper to indicate agreement on the final product. A group grade is given to emphasize the need for collaboration in learning.

Although it is described here in conjunction with writing assignments, the concept of a communal effort toward a single product can be applied in many areas. Groups can "put their heads together" to work through a study guide in social studies, answer chapter questions for science, study spelling words, or complete worksheets in mathematics. Such communal endeavors go a long way to promote the cooperative spirit that "we're all in this together."

Interactive Reading Guide

The interactive reading guide is a newly developed strategy (Wood, 1988) that uses cooperative learning in conjunction with the long-standing study guide. In a typical guide, students work alone, answering a series of questions based on their subject area textbook. Having the questions available as they read means that the amount of print encountered at a given time is reduced to a manageable degree. In addition, they know, while reading, what the most significant information is, rather than waiting for the end-of-chapter questions.

The interactive reading guide is similar to the typical reading guide, but, instead of always working alone, students answer questions and complete tasks in small groups, in pairs, or individually. In lieu of responding to the literal-level kinds of questions often found in the textbook, students are asked to develop associations, make predictions, analyze, read, and retell the content of a selection, or even to take the perspective of someone or something described in the text.

For the most part, the class proceeds through the guide together, with a class discussion after each segment activity or question is completed by the pairs or groups. Yet, this procedure can be varied to allow more advanced students to proceed ahead. To expedite the assignment further, time limits can be imposed on certain activities.

It would be helpful to determine the pairing or small-group assignments before implementing the strategy. Many of the cooperative learning arrangements described previously would be appropriate here, especially Fader's buddy system (1976), because it requires heterogeneous groups who have much to contribute academically to one another.

Because much student graphic and oral response is required, the interactive reading guide may take several class days to complete. However, the finished guide will be tangible evidence of the rewards of peer learning, as the class now has a written synopsis of their contributions to the lesson content.

The interactive reading guide applied to a fourth-grade social studies lesson on the Arctic region is illustrated in Figure 13-2. An illustration of it applied to an eighth-grade history lesson is presented in Figure 13-3.

How Is Grouping Used with Other Instructional Methods?

Because oral reading is most often associated with round robin reading, it has received much criticism in the professional literature. Round robin reading—the practice of calling on students individually and in sequential order to read— is prevalent not only in basal reading lessons but in subject area lessons as well.

To circumvent the boredom, apathy, and lack of educational value inherent in this form of oral reading, teachers can incorporate grouping techniques with a variety of oral reading methods. Any combination of the methods presented next is sure to help enliven the act of reading and give everyone in the class a greater chance at participation.

Paired or Assisted Reading

Two or more students can be grouped together and asked to read aloud in unison. In this way, no one has to endure the stigma of "going it alone." An entire reading group or subject area class can be divided into pairs with the directive to "take turns reading and retelling" each page to your partner.

Mumble Reading

Cunningham's (1978) mumble reading is a variation of oral reading that is especially appealing to young children. Merely being told to mumble-read (read aloud softly, but under your breath) to the bottom of the page can enliven the least interesting assignment.

Whisper Reading

Unlike mumble reading, which is somewhat unintelligible, whisper reading means carefully pronouncing the words but doing so in a low voice. This can be done individually or with an assigned partner or group member.

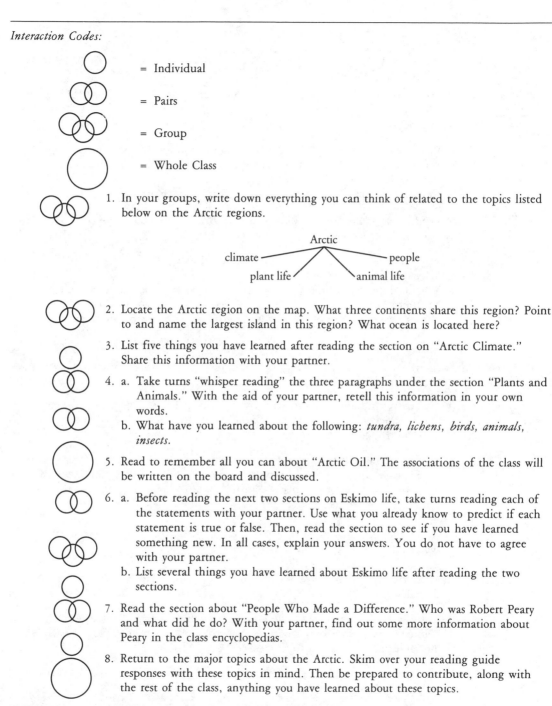

Interaction Codes:

= Individual

= Pairs

= Group

= Whole Class

1. In your groups, write down everything you can think of related to the topics listed below on the Arctic regions.

Arctic

climate ——————→ people
plant life ↗   ↘ animal life

2. Locate the Arctic region on the map. What three continents share this region? Point to and name the largest island in this region? What ocean is located here?

3. List five things you have learned after reading the section on "Arctic Climate." Share this information with your partner.

4. a. Take turns "whisper reading" the three paragraphs under the section "Plants and Animals." With the aid of your partner, retell this information in your own words.
   b. What have you learned about the following: *tundra, lichens, birds, animals, insects.*

5. Read to remember all you can about "Arctic Oil." The associations of the class will be written on the board and discussed.

6. a. Before reading the next two sections on Eskimo life, take turns reading each of the statements with your partner. Use what you already know to predict if each statement is true or false. Then, read the section to see if you have learned something new. In all cases, explain your answers. You do not have to agree with your partner.
   b. List several things you have learned about Eskimo life after reading the two sections.

7. Read the section about "People Who Made a Difference." Who was Robert Peary and what did he do? With your partner, find out some more information about Peary in the class encyclopedias.

8. Return to the major topics about the Arctic. Skim over your reading guide responses with these topics in mind. Then be prepared to contribute, along with the rest of the class, anything you have learned about these topics.

FIGURE 13-2 Interactive Reading Guide, Unit 14—Polar Regions: "The Arctic Region"

Source: K. D. Wood, "Guiding Students through the Reading of Informational Text," *The Reading Teacher,* Vol. 41, 1988, pp. 912–920. Reprinted by permission of K. D. Wood and the International Reading Association.

Interaction Code:

◯ = Individual   ◯◯ = Pairs   ◯◯◯ = Group   ◯ = Whole Group

1. In your group, write down everything you can think of that would affect people moving west out of the coastal Carolina area in the mid-1700s. We will list these on the board as a class.

2. a. Read the topics "By Land and Water" and "London Investment."
   b. Write down six (6) important characteristics of early immigrants moving into the Carolinas.
   c. In pairs, compare your list of characteristics with your partner's.

3. In your group, take turns reading orally on the topic "The Moravians." Summarize the information on the Moravians.

4. Now, individually, answer the following questions:
   a. Why did the Moravians move to North Carolina?
   b. What did these Moravians call the tract of land in which they chose to settle Northern Piedmont?
   c. List two reasons an individual could be expelled from the Moravians' community.

   In your groups, compare your answers to the questions. Discuss any differences in the groups' answers.

5. Individually, read and retell in your own words (subvocalizing) the content on the topics "Sectional Differences," "Political Representation Differences," and "Economic Differences."

6. In pairs, determine if the statements are *True* or *False*. Be sure to explain your answer and provide the information needed to make the *False* statement *True*.
   _____ a. The land in the western area of North Carolina was low, swampy, and flat, but often very fertile.
   Explain:
   _____ b. In the western area of North Carolina, the creeks and rivers were ideal for water mills.
   Explain:
   _____ c. Western farmers had large plantations and commercial enterprises.
   Explain:

7. Read the pages on the topic "Everyday Life in the Colony of North Carolina" individually. Then, with your partner, use your imagination to characterize life at this time and compare it to life today.

8. In your group, draw the way a house and family may have looked in North Carolina during the mid-1750s.

FIGURE 13-3   Interactive Reading Guide, Unit 10—"Settling the West"

Note: A special thanks to middle-level teacher David Lowe, who developed and used this guide successfully in his classroom.

Imitative Reading

Imitating the vocal patterns of the teacher can help one or more neophyte readers with pacing and fluency. The teacher begins reading a segment of the story (usually dialogue) in an exaggerated tone and then calls on one or more students to read the same segment in a similar manner.

Choral Reading

When used in moderation, and preferably in combination with some of the other oral reading methods, choral reading is an excellent way to maintain the interest of the class. Having the group or class read in unison at just the right moment in a story can heighten the suspense or emphasize an important event.

Cloze Procedure Oral Reading

In this alternative oral reading method, the teacher reads a story aloud as the students follow with their copies of the text. When the teacher stops, the students collectively respond with the missing word. This method helps keep students' attention focused on the task of reading and gives them ample opportunity to see and hear the speech-to-print match.

Four-Way Oral Reading

Four-way oral reading (Wood, 1983) involves four or more types of oral reading within a single story lesson. A combination of paired or assisted, numble, imitative, and choral reading helps students recognize the prosodic cues of language, thereby improving their comprehension. Although four types of oral reading were described originally, teachers can combine the varied approaches in any way they deem necessary. For example, students may be told to pair up and whisper-read two pages in their social studies text. After a discussion of the content, the teacher may tell them to read the next page silently and then, with the aid of their partner, to use their own words to reconstruct the content. For the remaining pages of the assignment, the teacher may elect to have them mumble-read and then get into groups of four to contribute their associations collectively.

How Can Grouping Fit into the Weekly Schedule?

An example of how grouping techniques can be incorporated into lessons in Reading, Language Arts, Social Studies, Science, and Math is presented in Figure 13-4. A sample schedule for a middle or secondary level student illustrating how grouping techniques may be engaged in throughout the day and across subject areas is presented in Figure 13-5. Notice how a combination of whole-class, small-group, and individual work has been employed with each subject area. Notice, too, how various forms of grouping have been used throughout the academic day, emphasizing the importance of cooperation and collaboration in all learning tasks.

	MONDAY	TUESDAY	WEDNESDAY	THURSDAY	FRIDAY
Reading	Introduce basal story—*paired reading,* then *group discussion.*	Continue reading basal story—use *four-way oral reading.*	Review, discuss story—*small-group.* Introduce skill lesson—*whole group.*	Students complete skills assignment—*tutorial grouping.*	Free reading.
Language Arts	Introduce descriptive paragraph writing assignment—model for *whole class.*	Students work in *buddy system groups* to compose/edit.	Students are *paired randomly* to compose a single descriptive paragraph.	Students work *individually* and then share compositions with original *buddy system group* for editing.	Students volunteer individual efforts with *whole class*—work is displayed.
Social Studies	Teacher builds background on Japan—*whole class.*	Group *retellings* of varied material.	Students begin *interactive reading guide.*	Students continue *interactive reading guide.*	Teacher poses topics for future *interest groups.*
Science	Demonstration on plants—*whole class.*	Students read relevant textbook section—*dyadic learning.*	*Whole class* discussion of textbook content.	Students choose related topics—form *research groups.*	*Research groups* continue.
Math	Teacher models long division on overhead—*whole class.*	Students practice in pairs—*tutorial grouping.*	Students practice *individually.*	Progress test given.	Students grouped according to *need.*

FIGURE 13-4   A sample weekly schedule for a fourth-grade class

Adhering to the following guidelines when using cooperative grouping methods will help avert any potential problems:

1. Set the stage for *responsible learning* at the beginning of the school year. Explain to the class that from now on they are responsible for each other's learning and that they will be asked to assist, share ideas with, and cheer on their fellow classmates. Negative comments will not be tolerated; the atmosphere is to be one of caring, interest, and positive interaction.

2. Clearly specify the *academic* objectives of the lesson. Any group or individual assignment should be preceded by one or more modeling sessions explaining the purposes of the tasks, demonstrating the skills to be learned and the assignments to be undertaken. Disorderly behavior results when students are unclear about how to proceed and what is expected of them.

3. Clearly specify the *collaborative* objectives of the lesson. Not only is an understanding of the assigned task essential, but also the students must know how they are to

Period	Class	Grouping Strategy
First	Math	Based on previous unit pretesting on equations, students work in small groups on their specific *needs*.
Second	Biology	After seeing a film and watching a demonstration on dissecting earthworms, students are assigned to *buddy system groups* to begin their own dissecting experiments.
Third	English	*Group communal writing groups* are employed to complete an assignment on persuasive writing.
Fourth	History	Students continue working through the *interactive reading guide* displayed in Figure 13-3.
Fifth	Health	An outside speaker, engaged to discuss stress, assigns students to *random groups* to work on various stress reduction techniques.
Sixth	Computer Science	Students select a programming assignment based on their *interests* and then are assigned to *research groups* to solve the problem posed.

FIGURE 13-5   A sample daily schedule for a middle- or secondary-level student

interact with one another to complete the task. For example, in the case of research grouping, students need a collaborative sequence to follow, with roles assigned to each group member. This may involve initially having each group member assigned the task of searching either the encyclopedias, magazines, or the card catalogue for information on the specific topic. Then, as the group collectively decides how to synthesize the sources, one person serves as the recorder. Next, the rough draft is read, with group members commenting on the needed revisions. A different recorder is assigned the rewriting of the next draft. Then, each group member serves in an editorial capacity, reading the paper for language, mechanical, or content modifications. After a thorough explanation of this process, it would be helpful to list these collaborative objectives on the board in an abbreviated manner. Figure 13-6 shows how such a list of tasks and roles might look for the research grouping assignment.

4. Establish *rules* to be followed when engaging in group learning. These rules may reiterate already existing classroom rules but should cover warnings such as "Speak softly," "Stay in your groups," and "Respect the opinions of others."

5. Make *decisions about placement* in groups before the lesson is started. Waiting until the lesson begins takes too much time away from instruction and communicates the notion that insufficient forethought and little advance preparation went into the lesson. Only in the case of random grouping can placement be determined at the last minute, but, again, the teacher has planned at the onset that this is the type of grouping to be used.

6. Continually *circulate* among the groups to monitor student progress, answer questions, and oversee the social interactions. When students sense that group work is a way to free the teacher to do desk work, they lose interest and do not stay on task.

Each member:	Assign research roles—encyclopedia, magazines, card catalog
Entire group:	Combine notes
Individual:	Rough draft recorder
Entire group:	Read and revise
Individual:	Second draft recorder
Each member:	Assign editorial roles: grammar, punctuation, content
Entire group:	Final copy reading and revision

FIGURE 13-6   Research group assignments

7. Use a *variety of grouping patterns* throughout the curriculum. When only one grouping technique is used, the concept becomes commonplace and monotonous. Also, employing a myriad of techniques gives students the opportunity to interact with everyone in the class.

8. Take the opportunity to *teach cooperative skills* whenever it is deemed necessary. One common pitfall encountered when employing cooperative learning strategies occurs when some students, though not disruptive, fail to join in and assume a role in the group. Sometimes one-to-one teacher counseling is effective. At other times, a discussion with group members on how to enlist the aid of a withdrawn member compassionately may be even more meaningful. Another pitfall may be the tendency of certain students or groups to dominate discussions. One solution to this problem offered by Johnson, Johnson, Holubec, and Roy (1984) is to give each student five chips (or five strips of paper) at the start of a lesson. Each time they speak while engaged in a worksheet, discussion, or other activity, they must relinquish a chip. After all the chips are used up, the students are no longer permitted to speak. More comprehensive information on teaching cooperative skills can be found in *Joining Together* (Johnson & Johnson, 1982) and *Reaching Out* (Johnson, 1981).

9. After each lesson, *have students summarize and evaluate* both the academic and collaborate objectives developed at the onset. Summarizing the content learned is a well-documented study method designed to enhance retention. Having students evaluate the group's use of effective cooperative learning skills is another valuable way to make continuous improvements and ensure lasting success.

Conclusion

Today, more than ever before, students with special learning needs are being educated in regular education classrooms with their normally achieving peers. This is how it should be. Cooperative grouping strategies, thoughtfully implemented, can play a major role in determining the success of any efforts to place exceptional students in mainstream classrooms. Structuring learning situations cooperatively enhances relations among students with disabilities and their peers who are not disabled, while maximizing the social development and achievement of all students (Johnson & Johnson, 1986). Participation in cooperative learning groups results in achievement gains for high-risk learners as well as well as their achieving peers by increasing performance in mathematics, reading, and writing (Slavin, Madden, & Leavey, 1984; Slavin, Stevens, & Madden, 1988).

The grouping techniques described in this chapter can be easily implemented in any subject area at any grade level in the resource, remedial reading, or regular classroom setting. With its many benefits, cooperative learning/grouping has the potential to be known as *the* individualized instructional method of the past, present, and future. It may well be educators' best investment for meeting the needs of diverse learners. As Mary McCracken noted in *Circle of Children,* "there is often no better teacher than another student."

References

Aronson, E. (1978). *The Jigsaw classroom.* Beverly Hills, CA: Sage Publications.

Brandt, R. (1987). On cooperation in schools: A conversation with David and Roger Johnson. *Educational Leadership, 45,* 14–19.

Carlson, H. L., Ellison, D., & Dietrich, J. E. (1984). *Servicing low achieving pupils and pupils with learning disabilities: A comparison of two approaches.* (Report No. EC 192 770). Duluth, MN: University of Minnesota. (ERIC Document Reproduction Service No. ED 283 341)

Cunningham, P. M. (1978). Mumble reading for beginning readers. *The Reading Teacher, 31,* 409–411.

DeVries, D., & Slavin, R. E. (1978). Teams-Games-Tournaments (TGT): Review of ten classroom experiments. *Journal of Research and Development in Education, 12*(1), 28–38.

Fader, D. (1976). *The new hooked on books.* New York: Berkley.

Glasser, W. (1987). The key to improving schools: An interview with William Glasser. *Phi Delta Kappan, 68,* 656–662.

Johnson, D. W. (1981). *Reaching out: Interpersonal effectiveness and self-actualization,* 2nd ed. Englewood Cliffs, NJ: Prentice-Hall.

Johnson, D. W., & Johnson, R. T. (1982). *Joining together: Group theory and group skills.* Englewood Cliffs, NJ: Prentice-Hall.

Johnson, D. W., Johnson, R. T., Holubec, A. J., & Roy, P. A. (1984). *Circles of learning; Cooperation in the classroom.* Alexander, VA: Association for Supervision and Curriculum Development.

Johnson, R. T., & Johnson, D. W. (1985). Student–student interaction: Ignored but powerful. *Journal of Teacher Education, 36,* 22–26.

Larson, C. O., & Dansereau, D. F. (1986). Cooperative learning in dyads. *Journal of Reading, 29,* 516–520.

Lehr, F. (1984). Cooperative learning. *Journal of Reading, 27,* 458–460.

McCracken, M. (1975). *Circle of Children* NYC, NY: NAL Dutton.

Masztal, N. B. (1986). Cybernetic sessions: A high involvement teaching technique. *Reading Research and Instruction, 25,* 131–138.

Putnam, J. W., & Markovchick, K. (1989). *Cooperative learning and cooperative development to promote social integration.* Report No. RC 017 284). Augusta, ME: Maine State Department of Educational and Cultural Services. (ERIC Document Reproduction Service No. ED 315 288)

Slavin, R. E. (1990). *Cooperative learning: Theory, research, and practice.* Englewood Cliffs, NJ: Prentice-Hall.

U.S. Department of Education. (1990). *Twelfth annual report to Congress on the Implementation of the Education of the Handicapped Act.* Washington, DC: Author.

Wood, K. D. (1983). A variation on an old theme: Four-way oral reading. *The Reading Teacher, 37,* 38–41.

Wood, K. D. (1984). Read first, test later: Meeting the needs of the "overskilled reader." *Reading Horizons, 24,* 133–140.

Wood, K. D. (1986). Free associational assessment: An alternative to traditional testing. *Journal of Reading, 29,* 106–111.

Wood, K. D. (1987). Fostering cooperative learning in middle and secondary level classrooms. *Journal of Reading, 31,* 10–18.

Wood, K. D. (1988). Guiding students through the reading of informational text. *The Reading Teacher, 41,* 912–920.

Ysseldyke, J. E., Algozzine, B., & Thurlow, M. (1992). *Critical issues in special education,* 2nd ed. Boston: Houghton Mifflin.

Chapter *14*

Teaching Reading to High-Risk Learners in the Twenty-first Century

KAREN D. WOOD

BOB ALGOZZINE
University of North Carolina at Charlotte

Key Concepts

- National Education Goals
- Reading progress
- Reading outcomes
- Condition of special education
- Effectiveness of special education
- Special education alternatives

Focusing Questions

- How has history recently shaped our present educational direction?
- List some proposed educational goals.
- What has been the evolution of special education and its impact on education as a whole?
- What is looked at to assess the condition of education? Who are the assessors?
- Who receives special education?
- What is the rationale for teaching special education students in regular classrooms?

Discussion Questions

- Discuss some of the education goals in this chapter. Do you feel these are realizable within the near future? If not, why?
- Why are educational goals important?
- Discuss why you think the number of students who receive special education services is increasingly annually.
- Discuss why you think more students with mild disabilities than with any other type of disability drop out of school.

As the United States entered the last decade of the twentieth century, the need for education reform once again gained momentum. In the first State of the Union address of the decade, then President George Bush outlined a set of national goals that became the driving force for education in the 1990s. The sweeping nature of the goals and the comprehensiveness of the reforms needed to achieve them will be the source of considerable research and discussion among professionals and the public alike through the remainder of the decade.

During the 1950s and 1960s, heightened interest in educational achievement and the reflection of this interest in perceptions of effective schools were very powerful forces in education. The effects of concern for achievement on the development and progress of special and remedial education are illustrated in opinions about "how the raising of reading standards, coupled with social expectations that schools help America's cold war effort and also sort students for future work roles in a stratified economy" led to the creation of the category of learning disabilities (Sleeter, 1986, p. 48). As Sleeter (1986, p. 49) noted, recommendations during the 1950s and 1960s for reforming U.S. education included (1) toughening elementary reading instruction (Trace, 1961); (2) introducing uniform standards for promotion and graduation and testing students' mastery of those standards through a regular, nationwide examination system ("Back to the 3 R's?," 1957; Bestor, 1958); (3) grouping students by ability so the bright students could move more quickly through school and then go on to college and professional careers, while slower students moved into unskilled or semiskilled labor ("Famous Educator's Plan," 1958; "Harder Work for Students," 1961; Woodring, 1957); and, (4) assigning the most intellectually capable teachers to the top group of students (Rickover, 1957) (references cited in Sleeter, 1986, p. 48). Strategies for reaching President Bush's national education goals are less well articulated at this writing, but parallels evident in those suggested to date are certainly compelling. The directives include the following:

- Strengthen the curriculum, require competency testing for students and teachers, adopt stiffer promotion guidelines and tougher licensing requirements for prospective teachers, and evaluate schools continuously (Nardini & Antes, 1991, p. 17).
- In just a few years, the federal government and key policymakers have moved from a position of entrenched opposition to any national efforts to delineate skills and

literacies that all students need to a growing sense that clear standards are needed to achieve significant national results (Catwelti, 1991, p. 2).

- It's time to develop a national achievement test, required for all students (Kean, 1991, p. 36).

Regardless of how attainment of education goals is put into practice, any measure of their national achievement can only be achieved through collaborative efforts. Partnerships among professionals currently serving students with special needs will be essential.

Education Goals

For the first time in history, clearly articulated goals, suggested and supported by the president, are driving reform and practice in education. Following a decade of extensive and significant efforts to improve education that produced mediocre changes in accepted indicators of progress (e.g., SAT scores, modal grades, dropout rates), the need for improvement was clear, and so are the boundaries for improvement:

- By the year 2000, all children in the United States will start school ready to learn (i.e., in good health, having been read to, and otherwise well prepared by parents and others).
- By the year 2000, the high school graduation rate will increase to at least 90 percent (from the current rate of 74 percent).
- By the year 2000, U.S. students will leave grades 4, 8, and 12 having demonstrated competency in challenging subject matter, including English, mathematics, science, history, or geography. In addition, every school in the United States will ensure that all students learn to use their minds in order to prepare them for responsible citizenship, further learning, and productive employment in a modern economy.
- By the year 2000, U.S. students will be first in the world in mathematics and science achievement.
- By the year 2000, every adult American will be literate and will possess the knowledge and skills necessary to compete in a global economy and to exercise the rights and responsibilities of citizenship.
- By the year 2000, every school in the United States will be free of drugs and violence and will offer a disciplined environment conducive to learning.

Professional Perspectives

As the twentieth century closes, news reports and professional journals throughout the country are featuring stories about the national goals agreed to by federal and state officials. For the first time in two hundred years of education history, the public has an education agenda with national visibility. When the nation's governors prepared a list of twenty-one objectives to supplement the goals, the commitment represented by their action was heralded as evidence of a "national crusade that put American education on the front burner" (*Education Week,* 1990). The comprehensiveness and permanence of the goals set challenges for yet another national reform agenda:

> *Making substantial progress toward achieving our national goals for education will require a* national *commitment: from business and industry, social agencies, all levels of government, parents, the general public, educators* — everybody. *(Gough, 1990, p. 259, emphasis in original)*

Further, articulation of national goals fueled issues fires among professionals that were still smoldering from other reform efforts (Ysseldyke, Algozzine, & Thurlow, 1992):

- A major concern about the national goals "movement" is whether it will produce superficial reform, by focusing primarily on setting and measuring a list of discrete objectives, or whether it will tackle the necessary structural reforms needed to achieve true educational change" (Darling-Hammond, 1990, p. 287).
- To what degree will these national goals and performance standards reverse, alleviate, or worsen the present conditions in big-city school systems? In what ways will national goals and performance standards reshape current subject matter and teaching practices? (Cuban, 1990, p. 270). What good are goals unless we can measure progress toward them? (Lewis, 1990, p. 260).
- None of our six national education goals will be attained without greatly increased support for educational research and development. . . . Unless we do the research, we will continue to fail (Gage, 1990, p. 285).

Clearly, the goals were a source of concern for professionals in varied fields (Gough, 1990). Issues reflected in the national goals are illustrated in Table 14-1.

Public Opinions

Attitudes toward the goals were obtained in public opinion polls conducted by professional organizations (Elam, Rose, & Gallup, 1991). Although the public strongly supported the goals, skepticism about attaining them was also prevalent and the pessimism was consistent across various demographic groups. In 1991, opinions about the likelihood of achieving the readiness, graduation, and challenging subject matter goals were relatively evenly divided, although more people thought attaining each was very unlikely than very likely. About two-thirds to fully three-quarters of the respondents indicated their belief that attainment of the math and science achievement, literacy, and drug-free schools goals was unlikely. A comparison of public opinions about attaining each goal is presented in Table 14-2.

Interest in education and the problems faced by those who practice it is not new. The 1970s was the decade of learning disabilities. The proliferation of programs for pupils with processing problems was unparalleled (Ysseldyke et al., 1992), and professionals and the public alike were enamored with the idea of solving educational problems evidenced by this subgroup of exceptional students. During the 1980s, members of society became more fully aware of a broader range of critical issues facing education. As noted in

TABLE 14-1   Issues Reflected in National Goals

Goal	Perspective	Concerns	Issues
Readiness	Kagan (1990)	Assessment practices to determine readiness have been challenged.	Assessment Instruction Early intervention
		School entry is individualized, and school services are homogenized.	
Graduation	Gage (1990)	Effects of dropping out are not singular.	Identification Classification Diversity School outcomes Transition
		Definitions for dropouts are varied.	
Competencies	Darling-Hammond (1990)	Curricula in U.S. schools are not challenging.	School outcomes Instruction Assessment Transition
		Testing is overused and misused in decision making.	
Math and science achievement	Rotberg (1990)	Representativeness of samples used in comparisons is questionable.	Assessment School outcomes Instruction School reform
		Test scores are not an accurate reflection of productivity.	
		Narrow definitions lead to trivial solutions.	
Literacy	Mikulecky (1990)	Success of past programs is dismal.	Transition School outcomes
		Competing perspectives exist on extent of problem.	Instruction Homes, families, community agencies School reform

Source: Data from J. E. Ysseldyke, B. Algozzine, & M. Thurlow, *Critical Issues in Special Education* (Boston: Houghton Mifflin, 1992).

A Nation at Risk, "the educational foundations of our Society are presently being eroded by a rising tide of mediocrity that threatens our very future as a Nation and a people" (U.S. Department of Education, 1983, p. 5). The litany of reasons for reform was longer and bleaker than the typical string of miseries painted in a standard country-and-western song. In this period, as in other times in history, criticism stimulated rhetoric, research, and reform regarding effective schools. Descriptions of characteristics of effective schools cropped up everywhere (cf. Good & Brophy, 1986; Purkey & Smith, 1985; Lezotte,

TABLE 14-2   Public Opinion about National Goals

	Likelihood of Goal Attainment							
	Very Unlikely		Likely		Unlikely		Very Unlikely	
Goal	1991	1990	1991	1990	1991	1990	1991	1990
Readiness	10	12	37	38	33	33	14	12
Graduation	6	10	36	35	39	37	14	12
Competencies	6	9	36	38	36	36	15	12
Math and science achievement	4	6	22	23	45	41	23	24
Literacy	6	7	25	25	41	42	23	21
Drug-free schools	4	5	14	14	38	40	39	36

Source: Data from S. M. Elam, L. C. Rose, & A. M. Gallup, "The 23rd Annual Gallup Poll of the Public's Attitudes toward the Public Schools," *Phi Delta Kappan, 73* (1991), p. 44.

1989) and "school reform" became the catch phrase of the decade. The articulation of a set of national education goals came at the end of this period of extensive education reform effort, which produced less than stellar outcomes (Ysseldyke et al., 1992).

Reflections on how well reform efforts worked and whether students were better off as a result of them was captured in a series of reports prepared by the National Center for Education Statistics (NCES) and published to provide information on the status and progress of education in the United States. This activity is mandated by law, and the "condition of education" is reflected in these public documents prepared in response to the requirements of the law (Elliott, 1990). The condition of special education is reported in "annual reports to Congress on the implementation of Public Law 94-142" (the Education for All Handicapped Children Act of 1975), recently reauthorized as the Individuals with Disabilities Education Act (IDEA). Information contained in these comprehensive analyses illustrates the state of practice in special and remedial education.

Condition of Education

How well have reform efforts worked? Are students better off today? Do students read, write, and compute better? Have any basic skill performances improved? Has public opinion about education changed? How are the schools doing in meeting broad mandates and goals related to student achievement? How effective are schools? These and other important questions are addressed in recent educational accounting compiled in the 1990 edition of *The Condition of Education* (U.S. Department of Education, 1990). The indicators provided touch on many issues related to the national goals and illustrate the state of practice in teaching key academic skills such as reading.

Reading Progress and Outcomes
Reading skills are basic to educational progress. When students lag behind in reading, they find it difficult to be successful in other academic areas as well. Most educators

agree that poor readers will also find it difficult to participate effectively in society without at least basic skill competence in reading. When reading proficiency was assessed as part of the National Assessment of Educational Progress (NAEP) in 1988, the following scale was used to evaluate student performance:

Level 150 = Rudimentary. Can carry out simple discrete reading tasks.

Level 200 = Basic. Can understand specific or sequentially related information.

Level 250 = Intermediate. Can search for specific information, interrelate ideas, and make generalizations.

Level 300 = Adept. Can find, understand, summarize, and explain relatively complicated information.

Level 350 = Advanced. Can synthesize and learn from specialized reading materials.

Overall, in recent analyses, U.S. students demonstrated continued low levels of reading performance. No group at any age level achieved an average score in either the "Adept" or "Advanced" level. Only about 42 percent of seventeen-year-olds are "Adept" readers; scores of both blacks and Hispanics are well below those of their white classmates (National Center for Education Statistics, 1990).

Condition of Special Education

In attempts to "assure that all handicapped children have available to them . . . a free appropriate public education which emphasizes special education and related services designed to meet their unique needs" (U.S. Department of Education, 1990), federal government programs provide supplementary funds for states to use in education of children and youth with disabilities. The Office of Special Education Programs (OSEP) uses many sources to evaluate the extent to which funding provided is used to achieve its purpose. Each year, personnel in the U.S. Department of Education assess progress in providing services to children and youth with disabilities and prepare a report of their findings for dissemination. These annual reports to Congress include data provided by states in compliance with requirements associated with accepting monies under these federal funding programs.

When the *Tenth Annual Report to Congress on the Implementation of the Education of the Handicapped Act* was published, it marked the end of a decade of "extraordinary change" (U.S. Department of Education, 1988, p. i). The *Tenth Annual Report* provides a "detailed description of the activities undertaken to implement the [Education of the Handicapped Act (EHA)] and an assessment of the impact and effectiveness of its requirements" (U.S. Department of Education, 1989, p. xiii). The report has historical significance, and its content is representative of the condition of special education.

Who Receives Special Education?

In recent years, more than four million students with disabilities between birth and age twenty-one received special education services (U.S. Department of Education, 1990). The number served in 1986–1987 represented an increase of 1.2 percent over the number served during the previous year and an increase of 19.2 percent over the number served ten years earlier. The most common conditions of these students were learning disabilities (43.6 percent), speech impairments (25.8 percent), mental retardation (15.0 percent), and emotional disturbance (8.7 percent); these four groups accounted for 93 percent of the students with disabilities. Growth in selected special education categories is illustrated in Figure 14-1. The number of students classified as having learning disabilities has risen consistently in recent years; the increase from 1977 to 1987 was approximately 142 percent, and it was greatest (12 percent per year) between 1977 and 1983 (U.S. Department of Education, 1988). The desire not to stigmatize students with other labels, the need to reclassify students previously called mentally retarded, and the desire to obtain funds for students who were failing in school were among the reasons provided for the large increases in numbers of students classified as learning-disabled (Ysseldyke, et al., 1992).

Numbers of students classified as disabled varies considerably at different ages. As noted in the *Tenth Annual Report,* "more 9-year-olds were served under EHA than any other age" and the "number of handicapped children counted declines substantially at age 16 and decreases rapidly for the older children" (U.S. Department of Education, 1988, pp. 12, 15). During the 1986–1987 school year, about 48 percent of the students with disabilities were between the ages of 6 and 11. Very small percentages were less than 6 years of age or older than 17 (6 percent and 5 percent, respectively). Typically, the largest group is between the ages of 6 and 11; this, of course, is the time when demands for independent academic and basic skill competencies are highest and when performance discrepancies are most likely to be first recognized. Evidence the two major groups comprising the 6- to 11-year-olds being students classified as learning-disabled and speech-impaired (U.S. Department of Education, 1988). Students classified as learning-disabled also are the largest group in the 12- to 17-year-old age group, and students classified as mentally retarded or learning-disabled were largest for the oldest age group (U.S. Department of Education, 1988).

Where Is Special Education Provided?

People in special education believe that students with special needs are more like other students than they are different from them and, therefore, that these students should be provided ample opportunities to receive all or part of their education in the same settings as their neighbors and peers. The percentage of students with different conditions served in different educational environments is presented in Table 14-3. For about 26 percent of these students, special education was provided primarily in regular classroom settings. An "additional 41 percent received special education and related services primarily in resource rooms, while another 24 percent received special education and related services in separate classes with a regular building" and "most handicapped students

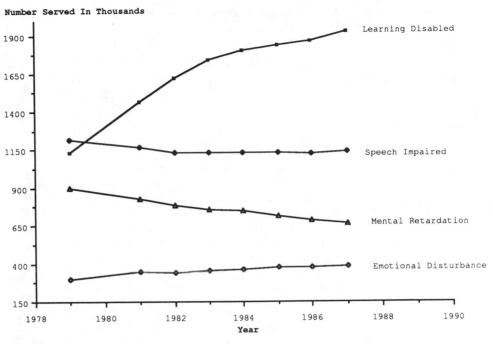

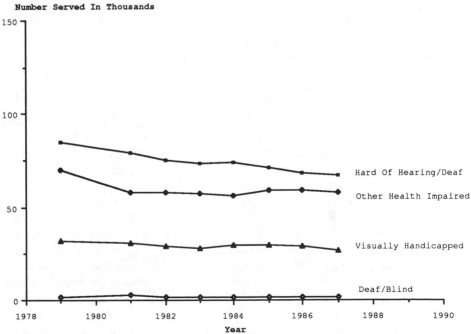

FIGURE 14-1   Trends in services provided to students with handicaps

TABLE 14-3   Percentage of Students with Handicaps Served in Different Educational Environments

Condition	Environment								
	RC	RR	SC	SF	PF	RF	RP	CF	HB
LD	15.29	61.80	21.05	0.93	0.54	0.04	0.04	0.23	0.09
SI	66.26	25.55	5.54	0.87	1.45	0.06	0.02	0.04	0.19
MR	3.06	25.29	55.81	10.12	1.90	2.78	0.35	0.27	0.41
ED	8.85	33.78	35.88	8.81	4.51	1.81	2.36	1.68	2.33
HH	12.72	21.02	34.62	9.47	3.84	10.53	1.06	0.12	0.59
MH	4.06	15.25	43.23	19.26	9.26	2.96	2.04	0.33	3.58
OI	25.62	16.14	32.03	13.06	4.12	0.61	0.44	0.09	7.70
OH	25.88	18.79	25.77	5.26	2.54	3.06	0.77	0.19	17.74
VH	31.48	24.00	19.44	10.32	2.05	10.27	0.95	0.11	1.37
DB	6.55	17.68	23.30	11.99	3.11	27.56	8.41	0.04	1.36
ALL	26.26	41.39	24.49	3.79	1.64	0.97	0.37	0.31	0.79

Source: U.S. Department of Education, *Tenth Annual Report to Congress on the Implementation of the Education of the Handicapped Act* (Washington, DC: Author, 1988), Table 10, p. 30.

Definitions: RC = Regular Class (receive special education or related services for 60 percent or less and at least 21 percent of the school day); SC = Separate Class (receive special eduction or related services for more than 60 percent of the school day); SF = Separate Public School Facilities; PF = Separate Private School Facilities; RF = Public Residential Facility; RP = Private Residential Facility; CF = Correctional Facility; HB = Homebound Environment. LD = Learning-Disabled, SI = Speech-Impaired, MR = Mentally Retarded, ED = Emotionally Disturbed, HH = Deaf or Hard of Hearing, MH = Multihandicapped; OI = Orthopedically Impaired, OH = Other Health-Impaired, VH = Visually Handicapped, DB = Deaf/Blind.

were being educated in building with nonhandicapped peers" (U.S. Department of Education, 1988, p. 29). Most (greater than 25 percent) of the students receiving special education in regular classes were classified as speech impaired (66 percent), visually handicapped (31 percent), orthopedically impaired (26 percent), or other health-impaired (26 percent). Few (less than 10 percent) of the students classified as emotionally disturbed (9 percent), deaf/blind (7 percent), multihandicapped (4 percent), or mentally retarded (3 percent) received special education services in regular classes. Most of the students classified as learning-disabled, speech-impaired, mentally retarded, or emotionally disturbed received special education at least 21 percent of the school day, but not more than 60 percent of it in resource rooms. Students in all categories except speech-impaired received special education for more than 60 percent of the school day in separate classes.

Who Fails in Special Education?

In recent years, about 43 percent of students with disabilities have graduated from high school. Approximately 60 percent of student with visual handicaps graduate with a diploma, as do 56 percent of those classified as hard of hearing or deaf and 54 percent of those with orthopedic disabilities. About half of the students with learning disabilities graduate with a diploma. An average of 312 students with handicaps drop out of high school each day (U.S. Department of Education, 1988). Interestingly, more students with mild disabilities (learning-disabled, emotionally disturbed, mentally retarded, and speech-impaired) drop out of school than students with other (e.g., physical) disabilities.

Education for the Mainstream

At least one-third of the nation's children are at risk of school failure even before they enter kindergarten, and about the same number probably will not profit from their early years of schooling (Hodgkinson, 1991; U.S. Department of Education, 1990; Ysseldyke et al., 1992). Effectively meeting the needs of these young people will require some restructuring in U.S. education.

Alternative perspectives on power are also at the base of many proposals to radically restructure the U.S. education system. For example, building on the principles postulated by W. Edwards Deming that transformed Japan into the "world's richest country" Glasser (1990, p. 3) calls for movement from boss-management to lead-masnagement as the only way to truly change the schools. Clearly much of what passes in contemporary classrooms bears strong resemblance to boss-management and little resemblance to lead-management (see Table 14-4). And although we see the principles of lead-management as truly

TABLE 14-4   Comparison of Competing Instructional Management Styles

Boss-Management	Lead-Management
Boss teacher sets the learning agenda, and students are expected to comply because it is right to do so. Students have little or no say in the process.	Lead teacher discusses content, defining critical aspects and explaining why specific topics are taught and how students can use them in their daily lives.
Boss teacher tells students to work independently and sets specific dates for assignments and tests. Students are seldom asked for input on instructional goals or methods. Preset curriculum targets control instructional time.	Lead teacher answers immediate questions and uses small cooperative groups as primary work structures. Teacher uses student input as to when test should be given. Competency and quality would be the rule. Amount of time needed to master a task would not control instruction.
Boss teacher grades students using preset standards. Students pass if they meet minimum standards (e.g., "D" or better), and plenty of students are failing.	Lead teacher involves students, as individuals and as members of groups, in evaluating the quality of their classwork, homework, and test performances.
Boss teacher gives students little authority. Control and compliance with rules for behavior are hallmarks of the management style, and plenty of time is spent "disciplining" students.	Lead teacher continually facilitates by talking to students and listening to their input on how to keep the classroom a good place to learn.

Source: Data from J. E. Ysseldyke, B. Algozzine, & M. L. Thurlow, *Critical Issues in Special Education* (Boston: Houghton Mifflin, 1992).

promising alternatives for reforming education, we believe the likelihood of significant changes happening is very small, not because people don't want to change, but more because they resign themselves to ineffective reform strategies by addressing the wrong problems and asking the wrong questions. This is evident in efforts to explain the failure of school reform to correct education's errant course (Glasser, 1990; Sarason, 1990) and in efforts to improve assessment and other important practices.

Conclusion

For the first time in history, the United States has a set of national education goals and new American schools must be responsive to these goals. All schools are places where students are exposed to curriculum content. The curriculum tht drives the new American schools must be responsive to the United States' education goals. Students who attend new American schools must leave being competent in challenging subject matter, including English, mathematics, science, history, and geography. They must leave literate and ready for the challenges of the next century. Teachers who teach in new American schools must be prepared to meet the needs of students from diverse cultural, ethnic, and educational backgrounds. They, too, must know the content of the curriculum in English, mathematics, science, history, and geography. They must be computer-literate and willing to work to keep schools, families, and communities drug-free. We believe that multidisciplinary perspectives will be required for teaching reading to high-risk learners in the next century. We hope the perspectives provided in this book will be useful in the reform, restructuring, or retraining efforts that will shape these practices.

References

Cawelti, G. (1991). Message from the executive director: Both national standards and expanded R&D needed. *Update: Association for Supervision and Curriculum Development, 33*(5), 2.

Cuban, L. (1990). Four stories about national goals for American education. *Phi Delta Kappan, 72,* 265–271.

Darling-Hammond, L. (1990). Achieving our goals: Superficial or structural reforms. *Phi Delta Kappan, 72,* 286–295.

Elam, S. M., Rose, L. C., & Gallup, A. M. (1991). The 23rd Annual Gallup Poll of the Public's Attitudes toward the Public Schools. *Phi Delta Kappan, 73,* 41–56.

Elliott, E. J. (1990). Commissioner's statement. In L. T. Ogle & N. Alsalam (Eds.), *The condition of education 1990: Volume 1. Elementary and secondary education.* Washington, DC: U.S. Department of Education, Office of Educational Research and Improvement.

Gage, N. L. Dealing with the dropout problem. *Phi Delta Kappan, 72,* 280–285.

Good, T., & Brophy, J. (1986). The social and institutional context of teaching: School effects. In M. Wittrock (Ed.), *Third handbook of research on teaching* (pp. 161–193). New York: American Educational Research Association.

Hodgkinson, H. (1991). Reform versus reality. *Phi Delta Kappan, 73*(1), 9–27.

Horn, J. L. (1924). *The education of exceptional children: A consideration of public school problems and policies in the field of differentiated education.* New York: Century.

Kean, T. H. (1991). Do we need a national achievement exam? *Education Week, 10*(31), 28, 36.

Lewis, A. C. (1990). The murky waters of monitoring

achievement of the National goals. *Phi Delta Kappan, 72,* 260–261.

Lezotte, L. W. (1989). School improvement based on the effective schools research. In D. K. Lipsky & A. Gartner (Eds.), *Beyond special education: Quality education for all* (pp. 25–37). Baltimore, MD: Brookes.

Nardini, M. L., & Antes, R. L. (1991). The right reforms. *American School Board Journal, 178*(6), 17–19.

National Center on Education Statistics. (1990). *The condition of education.* Washington, DC: Author.

Purkey, S., & Smith, M. (1985). School reform: The district policy implications of the effective schools literature. *Elementary School Journal, 85*(3), 47–83.

Sleeter, C. E. (1986). Learning disabilities: The social construction of a special education category. *Exceptional Children, 53,* 46–54.

U.S. Department of Education. (1983). *A nation at risk.* Washington, DC: Author.

U.S. Department of Education. (1990). *Twelfth annual report to Congress on the Implementation of the Education of the Handicapped Act.* Washington, DC: Author.

Vacca, R. T., & Padak, N. D. (1991). Who's at risk in reading? *Journal of Reading* (April), 486–488.

Ysseldyke, J. E., Algozzine, B., & Thurlow, M. (1992). *Critical issues in special education,* 2nd ed. Boston: Houghton Mifflin.

Index